Quilters' Travel Companion

North American Edition

Edited by: Audrey Swales
Anderson

Published By:

chalet PUBLISHING

(719) 685-5041   32 Grand Avenue
Manitou Springs, CO 80829

With all my love,
This book is dedicated to my
husband, Marlow.
Thank you for your support and
hours of
assistance.
And to Max, Min, Zeus
& Leo for putting up
with months of neglect.

"Definitions": Marlow Anderson
& John Roberts

Original Artwork: Pamela
Whiteman

Thanks for your encouragement:
Mom and Dad, John Roberts, Chris Lee,
Janet Treichler & Ruth O'Riley

How to Use this Guide

Whenever you're away from home be sure to take your *Quilters' Travel Companion* (QTC). You never know when you might have an opportunity to check out a shop. This guide includes featured listings for <u>over 1000</u> quilt shops in the United States and Canada. There is a description of each shop, including hours, featured merchandise, plus address and phone number. In addition, we provide a local map which will help you to drive right to their door. Look for the many shops who are offering discounts if you show them your QTC. Also we include the addresses of over 1000 other shops.

The shop listings are organized by state. We provide a state map which will enable you to tell at a glance where each of the featured shops is located. The number on the state map will also be found with the shop listing. In addition, for each state we include listings of area quilt guilds and other shops located in that state.

We've tried hard to include every shop in the country, but we're sure that we've missed some. If you know of one we've missed drop us a note or call us at (719) 685-5041.

There are two basic ways we see you using our guide:
1) Whenever you're traveling on business or vacation check out your route and see what shops you may be close to. The state maps should give you an idea if you'll be in the vicinity of a store. Then if you have time or can make time give yourself a break and STOP !
>   Since beginning these guides in 1992, I have certainly realized that
>   I used to drive right by shops on my travels, but not stop because
>   I didn't realize they were close.
2) Or go WILD and take a few days with family or friends and plan a whole trip going from shop to shop. Many shops are in historic / tourist places so your trip just may lead you into an unexpected adventure.
Either way, enjoy exploring all the great shops scattered across this country. We would be grateful if you'd tell them that QTC got you there.

We have made every effort for the information in this book to be up-to-date and accurate. Unfortunately shops do move, change hours, or go out of business; so if you want to be sure before you go a phone call might be prudent. All the featured shops' information was correct when published. Also note that many new telephone area codes have been added across the country and many more new ones are planned.

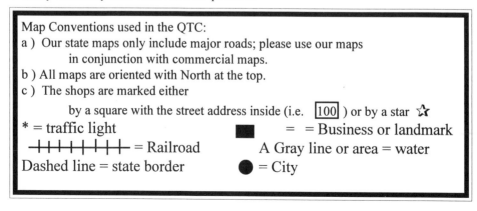

Map Conventions used in the QTC:
a) Our state maps only include major roads; please use our maps
      in conjunction with commercial maps.
b) All maps are oriented with North at the top.
c) The shops are marked either

      by a square with the street address inside (i.e. 100) or by a star ☆
* = traffic light   ■ = = Business or landmark
++++++++ = Railroad   A Gray line or area = water
Dashed line = state border   ● = City

Contents

U.S.A. Featured Shops

Have a Great Trip

Canadian Featured Shops

Ready, Set, GO !

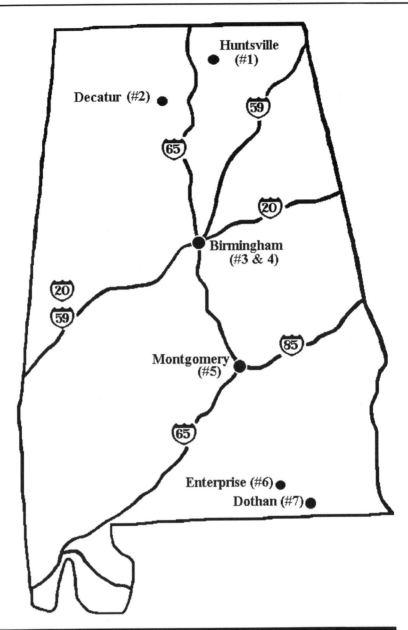

Huntsville, AL   #1

Patches & Stitches

817-A Regal Drive   35801
(205) 533-3886
Owner: Linda Worley
Est: 1978   3500 sq.ft.

**Mon - Thur
10 - 5
Thur til 6
Sat 10 - 4**

Complete line of quilt supplies, classes, books, and needlework; including cross-stitch and needlepoint. Also mail order.

Quilting Thread:
Substance used along
with love to hold
together a quilt.

Decatur, AL   #2

The Crafty Bear Shop

2208 Danville Rd. S.W.   35601
(205) 351-0420   Est: 1988
Owner: Helen DeButy   1800 sq.ft.   400 Bolts

**Mon - Fri
10 - 5
Sat 10 - 4**

Cotton Fabrics, books, patterns, supplies, and classes. The friendliest quilt shop for service, inspiration and sharing of ideas.

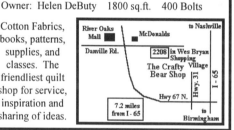

Birmingham, AL   #3

Est: 1993

Quiltmaker's Workshop

2403 1st St. NE   35215   (205) 854-4485
Owner: Annie Woods
1500 sq.ft.   2000 Bolts

**Mon - Fri 9 - 5
Sat 10 - 5
Summer
Mon - Fri
9 - 5
Sat 10 - 5**

*Everything you need for
Quilting Start to Finish.*

**Large selection of 100% cotton fabrics, books,
patterns, notions, stencils & classes.**

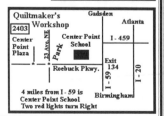

Birmingham, AL #4

Attic Antiques

Tues - Sat 9:30 - 4:30

5620 Cahaba Valley Road
(205) 991- 6887   35242
Owners: Barbara & Howard Manning
Est: 1972   3500 sq.ft.

Year around Christmas Shop. Large selection of quilts & linens. Items made with quilts. Americana & Victorian items

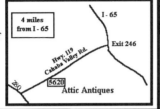

4 miles from I-65
I-65
Exit 246
Hwy. 119
Cahaba Valley Rd.
280
5620 Attic Antiques

Montgomery, AL #5

Rose of Sharon

Mon - Fri 10 - 5:30 Sat 10 - 3

3026-D Buckboard Rd.   36116
(334) 279-9945   Est: 1994
Owner: Sharon Wilson

100% cotton fabric, thread, stencils, notions & variety of classes. Quilted items for sale. Restoration work & machine quilting available.

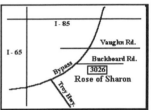

I-85
Vaughn Rd.
I-65
Buckboard Rd.
Bypass
3026 Rose of Sharon
Troy Hwy.

Enterprise, AL #6

Quilters Cottage

Mon - Fri 9:30 - 5 Sat 9:30 - 5

1304 U.S. 84 Bypass   36330
(334) 393-2443
Owner: Dee Forringer
Est: 1993   1050 sq.ft.   1000+ Bolts

A SPECIAL PLACE FOR QUILTERS

Classes, Books, Supplies and Fabrics.

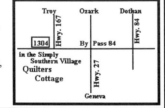

Troy   Ozark   Dothan
Hwy. 167
1304   By Pass 84   Hwy. 84
in the Simply Southern Village
Quilters Cottage
Hwy. 27
Geneva

Dothan, AL #7

The Little Quilt Shop

Mon - Fri 10 - 7 Sat 10 - 5 Sun 12 - 5

1380 Westgate Pkwy. #1
(334) 702-7822   36303
Est: 1995   1200 sq.ft.
Owners: Debbie Shelley & Linda Bigbie

We have fabric, books, supplies, quilts, classes, machine quilting, monograming & embroidery. We also have gifts & flower arrangements.

Westgate Parkway
1380   Hwy. 231N
The Little Quilt Shop
Hwy. 231S

Notes

Alabama Guilds:
Birmingham Quilters Guild, Birmingham
Enterprising Quilters, P.O. Box 30114, Enterprise, 36330
Quilter Lovers' Guild, Hartselle Library, Hartselle, 35640
Azalea City Quilters, Mobile
Kudzu Quilter's Guild, 3933 Croydon Rd., Montgomery, 36109
West Alabama Quilters Guild, 305 Caplewood Dr., Tuscaloosa, 35401

Other Shops in Alabama:

Alexander City	Midtown Fabrics & Crafts, 26 Main St.
Anniston	Cloth Patch, 2120 Noble St.
Athens	Hickory House Gift Shoppe, 23101 Hwy. 72 E
Athens	Terry's Country Craft Store, Drawbaugh Rd.
Birmingham	Calico Corners, 3663 Lorna Rd.
Fairhope	A Stitch in Time, 26 S. Section
Foley	Quilt Connection, 21188 Miflin Rd.
Jasper	Grandma's Treasures & Fabrics, Parkland Shp. Ctr.
Mobile	Fabric by the Pound, 1508 Overlook Rd.
Mobile	Fabric Works, 5441 Highway 90 W.
Montgomery	Jo's Sew & So Quilting, 7148 Woodley Rd.
Northport	The Quilted Heart, 401 20th Ave. #3
Wetumpka	Creations Galore, Inc., 105 E. Main

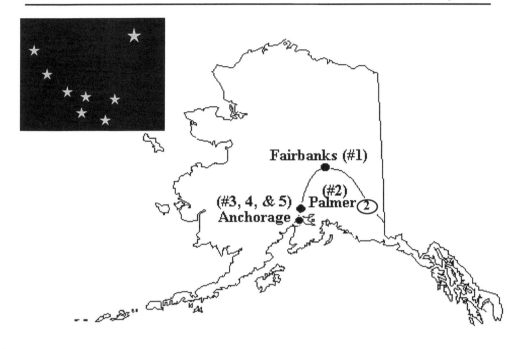

Fairbanks (#1)

(#3, 4, & 5)   (#2)
Anchorage   Palmer ②

Alaska

5 Featured Shops

Fairbanks, AK   #1

Hands All Around

927 Old Steese Hwy.   99701
(907) 452-2347
Owners: Jamie & Janet
Est: 1991   3000 sq.ft.

**Mon - Fri
9:30 - 6
Sat 9 - 5**

100% Cotton
Fabrics, Books,
Notions, Classes,
Alaskan Patterns.
Commercial
Quilting Machine.
Weaving Supplies
Quilts on display

Palmer, AK   #2

Just Sew

579 S. Alaska   99645
(907) 745-3649
Owners: Jim & Cheri Cooper
2400 sq.ft.

**Mon - Fri
10 - 6
Sat 10 - 5
Sun 1 - 5**

All your quilting
and needlework
supplies. 100%
cottons, books,
patterns, notions,
cross-stitch
supplies, yarn, and
lots more!

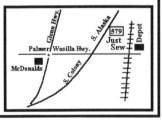

Anchorage, AK #3

The Whiffletree

Mon - Sat 11 - 6

9420 Old Seward Hwy. 99515
(907) 344-5922
Owners: Rich & Diane Melms
Est: 1983   1000 sq.ft.

Full line antique store with quality antique Quilts, tops, blocks, doilies, bedcovers, tablecloths, hankies, buttons, trims and laces.

Anchorage, AK #4

Quilt Works

**Mon - Fri 10 - 6
Thur til 8
Sat 10 - 5
Sun 12 - 5**

3030 Denali   99503
(907) 563-9773 Fax: (907) 563-9772
Owner: Sue Bergerson
Manager: Karen Tomczak

Over 2000 bolts of 100% cotton fabric. Excellent selection of books, patterns, and Alaskan patterns. Put your pin on our visitor map!

Anchorage, AK #5

Needlecrafters

**Mon - Sat 10 - 6
Sun 12 - 5**

5520 Lake Otis #105
(907) 562-9003   99507
Owner: Linda Liebeg
Est: 1988   4600 sq.ft.   3000 Bolts

Featuring a large supply of Quilting Fabric, Notions, Books & Original Alaskan Patterns. Also Silk Ribbon, Needlepoint, Cross Stitch & Tatting.

Alaska Guilds:

Cabin Fever Quilters Guild,
  Box 83608, Fairbanks, 99708
Valley Quilter's Guild, P.O.
  Box 2582, Palmer, 99645
Log Cabin Quilters
Chugach Mountain Quilters
  Guild

Other Shops in Alaska:

Anchorage	Calicos & Quilts Unlimited, 11900 Industry Way
Fairbanks	Quilts Unlimited, 1918 Jack St.
Fairbanks	Snow Goose Fibers, 3550 Airport Way #6
Haines	Seams Like Yesterday, P.O. Box 1167
Juneau	Tina's Fabrique Boutique, 8745 Glacier Hwy.
Kenai	Kenai Fabric Center, 115 N. Willow St.
Kenai	Brookie's Fabric Shop, 42680 North Rd.
Ketchikan	Silver Thimble, 2450 Tongass Ave.
Ketchikan	Alaska Country Workbasket, 619 Mission
Kodiak	The Stitchery, 202 Center Ave., Suite 310
Palmer	Simple Pleasures, P.O. Box 3250 Mile 1.4 Palmer-Wasilla
Sitka	Calico Cross Stitch, 223 Lincoln St.
Soldotna	Finer Point, 105 Shady Ln.
Wasilla	Alaska Dyeworks, 300 W. Swanson Ave. #101

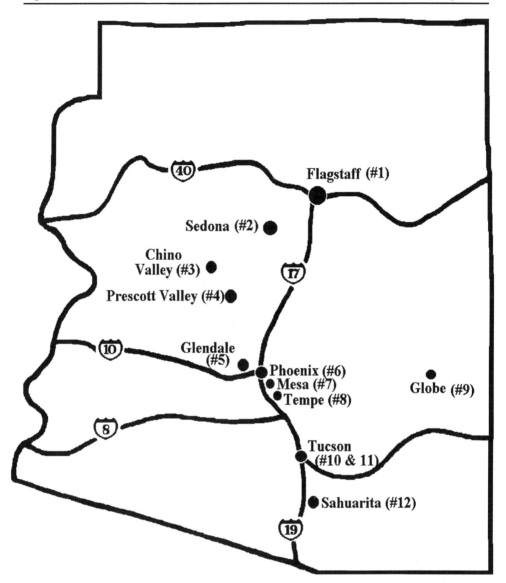

Flagstaff (#1)

Sedona (#2)

Chino
Valley (#3)

Prescott Valley (#4)

Glendale
(#5)

Phoenix (#6)
Mesa (#7)
Tempe (#8)

Globe (#9)

Tucson
(#10 & 11)

Sahuarita (#12)

ARIZONA

12 Featured Shops

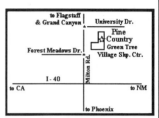

Mon - Sat   9:30 - 5

QUILTERS FRAME

Latest Quilt Books & Patterns
Over 650 Bolts of the latest 100% Cotton Fabrics.
Loads of Notions.

Chino Valley, AZ   #3

1164 S. Hwy 89   Est: 1995
P.O. Box 2170   86323
(520) 636-9492
Owners: Kerease Dunning &
Betsy Reeder

I - 40   Ashfork   to Flagstaff
to Kingman
Hwy. 89   ● Paulden
● Chino Valley
Road 2 South
Quilters
Frame   1164
to Prescott

♥ Books & Patterns
♥ Stencils
♥ Fabrics
♥ Classes
♥ Notions
♥ Quilting By
Correspondence

Prescott Valley, AZ   #4

The Quilt House

8742 E. Hwy. 69   86314
(520) 772-1230
Owners: Linda Blake &
Sandy Sligar

**Mon - Fri
9 - 6
Sat 9 - 4**

Prescott Valley
E. Hwy. 69
8742 ▲
The Quilt House
Truwood
Navaho Dr.

Glendale, AZ #5

By Jupiter!.

Mon - Sat
10 - 4

7146 N. 58th Dr.   85301
(602) 931-2658   Est: 1985   Catalog $5
Owner: Marion Sorci

Over 1100 Brass and Antique Silver Plated Charms & Findings. Fabric, Fading Kits, Pictures to Fabric Transfer gel.	Direction from I - 17 Take Glendale Ave. Exit West approx. 3 ½ miles. Turn Right on 55th Ave. Turn Left on Palmaire. Turn Right on 58th Drive. Third house on Left. In Old Home - Historic District "Catlin Court".

Phoenix, AZ #6

The Quilted Apple

Mon - Sat
9:30 - 5:30
Tues till 9

3043 North 24th St.   85016
(602) 956-0904
Owner: Laurene Sinema
Est: 1978   3600 sq.ft.   Free Catalog

1500 Bolts
100 % cotton
Fabrics, books,
patterns, notions,
classes.
Specialize in fine
hand quilting.

Rte. 51 | 24th St. | Osborn Rd. | Earll Dr. | 3043 The Quilted Apple | Thomas Rd.

Mesa, AZ #7

Common Threads

Mon - Fri
9:30 - 5:30
Thur til 8
Sat 9 - 4

142 W. Main 85201
(602) 668-0908
Est: 1995   2500 sq.ft.
Owners: Gail & Greg Biesen

1500 Bolts of
fabric
Quilting supplies,
Fabric, Books,
Patterns;
Classes. We also
have a Block of
the Month.

Country Club | Robson | 142 | Macdonald | Main St. | Common Threads | Broadway | Southern Ave. | Mesa Dr. | Superstition Frwy.

Quilter's Friends:
folks who know
better than to
schedule social
gatherings on Quilt
Guild night.

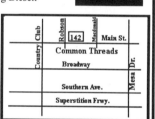

TRIANGLES ON A ROLL

Continuous Grid for Less Waste and More Control of Fabric Combinations!

Quilters' Ranch Tempe, AZ #8

A Complete Quilt Store!

107 East Baseline Road #6   85283
(In Mill Towne Center)
(602) 838-8350   Est: 1982   2700 sq.ft.
Owners: Anne Dutton & Dorothy Dodds

Mill Ave. | Southern | Superstition Fwy. | Baseline Rd. | 107 | Quilters' Ranch, Inc. | Rural Rd. | McClintock Rd | Guadalupe

Mon - Sat 9:30 - 5:30   Thurs til 9

Globe, AZ #9

Country Corner

Tues- Sat 9 - 5:30

383 South Hill Street   85501
(602) 425-8208
Owners: Johnny & Janice McInturff
Est: 1986   6000 sq.ft.

Quilts, Fabric, Notions-- Antiques Hardware, Tack, Boots, Vet Supplies, Chain saws--parts and service.

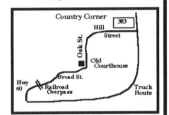

Tucson, AZ #10

Quilt Basket, Inc.

Mon - Sat 9:30 - 5

6538 C E. Tanque Verde Rd.
(602) 722-8810   85715
Owner: Peggy Peck
          Est: 1990   1500 sq.ft.

Lots & Lots of beautiful fabrics . . . .

Everything for today's busy quilter . . . .
Come see us !

Tucson, AZ #11

Precious Hands Needleworks

Mon - Sat 9 - 6:30 Tues & Thur til 9 Sun 12 - 4

2917 E. Grant Rd.   85716
(520) 325-8010   Est: 1994
Owner: Jean Firestine   2000 sq.ft.

Bright Beautiful Cotton Fabrics, Quilting Supplies, Classes, & Notions. We also offer machine quilting. Come see our quilting machine!

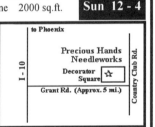

QUILTERS DESERT

16121 S. Country Club Rd.   85629

Sahuarita, AZ #12

Owner: Phyllis Sirrine   (520) 648-1533
Est: 1985   1050 sq.ft.
Stuffed with Bolts & Flat Folds.
Friendly, helpful service. We're happy to open by appointment for travelers in the summer.
Great selection of cottons.

Mon - Fri 9 - 5   Sat 9 - 12
Summer Hours (June, July, August)
Fri & Mon 9 - 5 or by Appt.

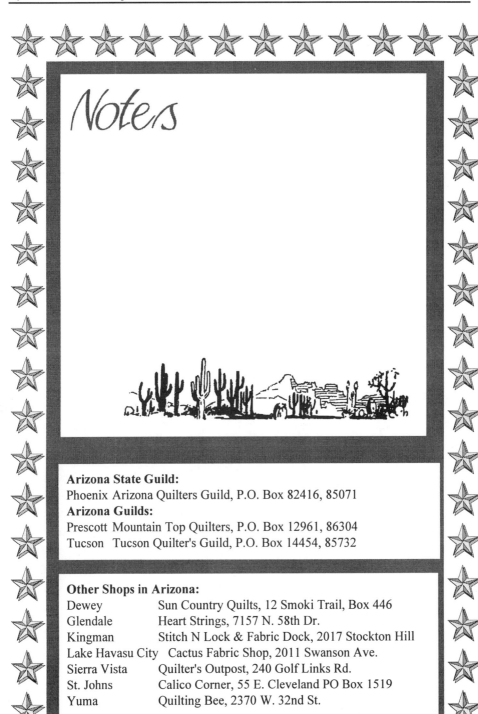

Notes

Arizona State Guild:
Phoenix Arizona Quilters Guild, P.O. Box 82416, 85071
Arizona Guilds:
Prescott Mountain Top Quilters, P.O. Box 12961, 86304
Tucson Tucson Quilter's Guild, P.O. Box 14454, 85732

Other Shops in Arizona:
Dewey   Sun Country Quilts, 12 Smoki Trail, Box 446
Glendale   Heart Strings, 7157 N. 58th Dr.
Kingman   Stitch N Lock & Fabric Dock, 2017 Stockton Hill
Lake Havasu City Cactus Fabric Shop, 2011 Swanson Ave.
Sierra Vista   Quilter's Outpost, 240 Golf Links Rd.
St. Johns   Calico Corner, 55 E. Cleveland PO Box 1519
Yuma   Quilting Bee, 2370 W. 32nd St.

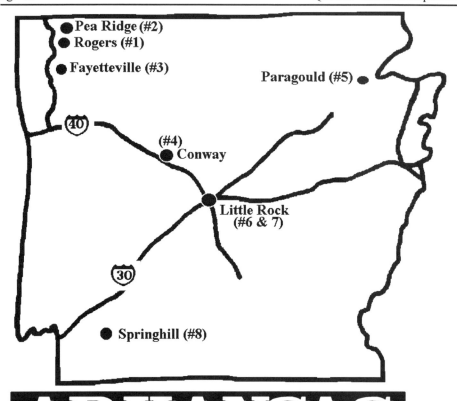

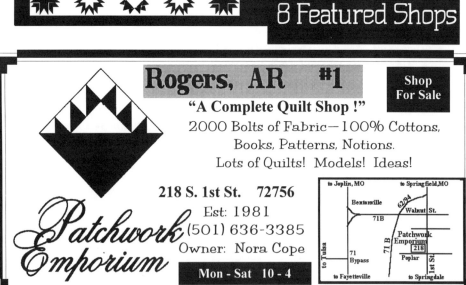

Pea Ridge, AR   #2

Country House Quilting

Mon - Fri
8:30 - 5
Thur til 7

16324 N. Hwy 94   72751
(501) 451-8978   Est: 1982
Owners: Charlotte & Ronald Foster   1600 sq.ft.

Fabrics, Notions
Quilts
Machine Quilted.
Supplies, Books,
Patterns,
Q-snap frames,
Classes.

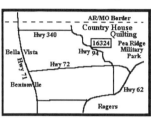

Fayetteville, AR   #3

Quilt Your Heart Out

Mon - Sat
10 - 5

125 E. Township #11   72703
(501) 587-0307
Owner: Lila Rostenberg
Est: 1993   1000 sq.ft.

800 Bolts of
100% cotton
fabric. Lots of
patterns, books &
notions.
Homespuns,
1930's & 1800's
reproduction
pieces.

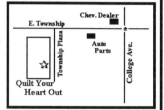

Idle-Hour Quilts & Design

Tue - Sat
10 - 5

2216 Washington Ave.   72032

(501) 329-3323 Owner: Jaynette Huff   Est: 1992 1400 sq.ft.

Your Complete, Full-Service Quilt Store.

Offering superior quality supplies,
fabrics (Over 1500 Bolts)
notions, books, frames, and classes.

Free Newsletter

Whether you are a new quilter who needs
help with the basics, an intermediate quilter
taking steps to stretch and develop your
skills, or an accomplished quilter-
extraordinaire! IDLE-HOUR QUILTS
AND DESIGN can deliver the quilting
service and supplies you need, promptly
and professionally.

Conway, AR   #4

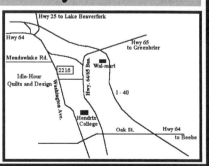

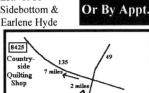

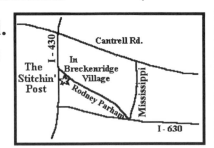

Springhill, AR #8

Massey's Hog Heaven

589 Hwy. 65 N   72058
(501) 679-6400
Owners: Bud & Barbara Massey
Est: 1994   3200 sq.ft.   *We ♥ Quilters!*

Quilt Fabrics,
Patterns, Lessons,
Quilt Supplies.
Pfaff & Elna
Dealership.
Nolting Quilt
Machines.
Parsons Cabinets
Come On By!

Tues - Fri
10 - 5
Sat 10 - 4

[Map: 589 Massey's Hog Heaven, to Harrison & Branson, MO, Hwy. 65 N, 6 miles from Conway, I-40, Exit 125]

Arkansas State Guild:
Arkansas Quilters Guild, 4219 Sugar Maple Ln., Little Rock, 72212

Arkansas Guilds:
Saline County Quilters Guild 224 W. South St., Benton, 72015
Q.U.I.L.T., 823 Lakeside Dr., Fayetteville, 72701
Belle Point Quilters' Guild, P.O. Box 3853, Fort Smith, 72913
Hill 'n Hollow Quilters Guild, P.O. Box 140, Mountain Home, 72653
Hope Quilter's Guild, 624 Cale Rd., Prescott, 71857

Other Shops in Arkansas:

Batesville	Marshall Wholesale Fabrics, P.O. Box 2313
Booneville	Cheryl's General Store, 200 W. Main St.
Conway	The Quilt Patch, 273 Hwy. 36
Elm Springs	Reetex Fabrics, 106 Water St.
Eureka Springs	The Gingham Goose, 7 N. Main
Eureka Springs	Sharon's Quilts, 2 Center
Eureka Springs	Cameo & Country Craft Shoppe, Hwy 62 East
Eureka Springs	Honeysuckle Rose Quilts & Gifts, 89 S. Main St.
Eureka Springs	The Cotton Patch, 1 Center
Glencoe	Quilt Palace, PO Box 75
Gurdon	Judy's Fabric Outlet, 109 E. Joslyn
Hot Springs	Log Cabin Crafts, 450 S. Rogers Rd.
Huntington	Mama's Log House, 3715 E. Clarks Chapel Rd.
Jonesboro	Dianna's Quilt and Craft Shop, 711 W. Washington Ave.
Little Rock	Sew Smart, 9700 N. Rodney Parham Rd.
Lowell	Makin Memories Fabric Shop, 5731 Primrose Rd.
Mena	Quilts, Inc., 607 N. Mena St.
Mountain View	Remember Me Quilt Shop, P.O. Box 1618, 220 W. Main
Omaha	Quilting Bee, U.S. Hwy. 65 N
Paragould	Hillcrest Quilt Shop, 8802 Hwy 412 W
Pelsor	Country Palace Ozark Crafts, HC 30 Box 108
Pelsor	Nellie's Craft Shop, HC 30 Box 102
Russellville	Sue's Fabrics, 57 Old Baptist Cemetary Rd.
Russellville	Ozark Heritage Craft Village, I-40 & Hwy 7

Yreka (#1)
Mt. Shasta (#2)
McCloud (#3)
Trinidad (#4)
Arcata (#5)
Sacramento (#9)
Davis (#13)
Colusa (#7)
Roseville (#10)
(#6) Albion
Vacaville (#14)
Loyalton (#8)
Santa Rosa (#15)
Sebastopol (#16)
Orangeville (#11)
Elk Grove (#20)
Sonoma (#17 & 18)
(#12) Galt
Petuluma (#19)
Altaville (#21)
San Francisco Area Shops #34 thru #51 See Page 32
Pacific Grove (#25)
Modesto (#22)
Turlock (#23)
Bishop (#24)
(#26) Oakhurst
Carmel (#27)
Clovis (#33)
Reedley (#28)
Bakersfield (#31 & #32)
Tehachapi (#29 & #30)

For Southern California
See Page 37
Shops #52 thru #82

CALIFORNIA

82 Featured Shops

Yreka, CA　#1

Crafty Collectibles Fabric Country

333 W. Miner　96097　Est: 1987
(916) 842-5550　2200 sq.ft.
Owners: Wes & Marian Hamilton

**Mon - Fri
9 - 5:30
Sat 9 - 5**

A most unusual store. Full service fabric store specializing in quilting and wedding fabrics. Pfaff sewing machines too.

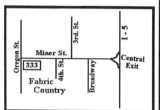

Mt. Shasta, CA　#2

Sew Unique

412 S. Mt. Shasta Blvd.　96067
(916) 967-0768
Owner: Tina Seres
Est: 1989　1400 sq.ft.　Large Inventory

**Tues - Sat
10 - 5**

Designer fabric, quilting supplies, books and gifts. Classes and Quilting Retreats. Call for newsletter. Fun, Friendly Store. New Home Dealer.

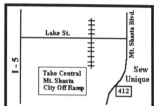

"The Oldest & Largest Quilt Shop in Northern California"

Mail Order Welcome

McCloud, CA　#3

**207 Quincy Ave.
P.O. Box 347
96057
(916)
964-2500**

Mon - Sat　10 - 5

Custom Quilts & Crafts

Home of McCloud Quilt Weekends. Enjoy 2 full days of undisturbed quilting in historic McCloud. Call for a brochure!

**Books, Patterns, Supplies Friendly Service.
Over 1000 Bolts of FABULOUS FABRICS**

Trinidad, CA #4

Ocean Wave Quilts

**Open 6 days
9:30 - 5:30
Closed Tues**

529 Trinity St.   95570
(707) 677-3770
Owner: Sandi Globus   Est: 1994
800 sq.ft.   1000 Bolts

A unique shop containing fabulous fabrics, books and notions located in a historic fishing village nestled between redwoods and beaches.

Arcata, CA #5

Fabric Temptations

**Mon - Sat
10 - 5:30
Sun 11 - 4
Summer
Sats 9 - 5:30**

942 'G' Street   95521
(707) 822-7782
Owner: Lennie   Est: 1984
Swatch Set $4

Natural Fiber Fabrics. Liberty of London. Battings: Cotton, Silk, Wool & Polyester. Quilting & Sewing Supplies. Mail order.

Albion, CA #6

Rainbow Resource Co.

Phone for Appointment

P.O. Box 222   95410
(707) 937-0431
Owner: Charlene Younker
Est: 1969   Send LSASE for Catalog

My own line of hand silk-screened fabric for quilters, along with related fabrics from various companies. Unusual Buttons, & Fun Stuff.

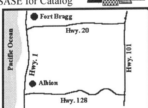

Colusa, CA #7

The Fabric Fair

**Mon - Fri
9:30 - 5:30
Sat 9:30 - 3**

221 - 5th St.   95932
(916) 458-5484
Owner: Marty Zeleny
Est: 1973   2000 sq.ft.   1400 Bolts

A fun shop full of Models. Quilting Fabric, Notions, Books & Patterns Viking - White Dealer Friendly Service.

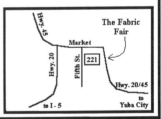

Loyalton, CA #8

Garden Gate Fabrics

**Mon - Sat
10 - 5**

600 Main St. (Hwy. #49) 96118
(916) 993-0224
Owner: Joan Carroll   1300+ Bolts

100% Cotton Fabric, Classes, Books, Patterns, Notions, Quilts on Display. Also mail order. Call for info.

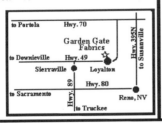

Sacramento, CA #9

Quilters' Corner

**Mon - Fri
10 - 6
Sat 10 - 4
Sun 12 - 4**

3020 'H' St. 95816
(916) 442-5768
Owner: Lindy Munday
Est: 1981

100% cottons, books, patterns & notions. Classes Seminar, retreats. Ask about Quilt Camp

Orangevale, CA #11

A Quilters Inn

Tues - Fri
10 - 5
Sat 10 - 4

6210 Hazel Ave.   95662
(916) 988-7103
Owner: Annie Beard
Est: 1983   900 sq.ft.   1000+ Bolts

Cotton Fabrics,
Quilting Books,
Craft / Quilt &
Wearable Art
Patterns. Notions
Gifts, Antiques.
Professional
Machine Quilting
Quilt Classes

to Reno
6210
A Quilters Inn
Greenback Lane
I - 80
Hazel Ave.
to Sacramento   Hwy. 50   to Lake Tahoe

Galt, CA #12

Quilted Treasures

Mon - Fri
9:30 - 5:30
Sat 10 - 5

1067 C St. #112   95632
(209) 745-1605
Owner: Kim Puleo
Est: 1992   1200 sq.ft.

Fabric, Notions,
Classes, Cross-
Stitch, Handmade
Gifts & Crafts.
Quilt in a Day,
Debbie Mumm,
Patchwork Place
and Much More!

We have recently
moved to "C" Street.
Please call
for Directions

Davis, CA #13

Pincushion Boutique

Mon - Fri
10 - 6
T, W, Th til 8
Sat 10 - 5
Sun 11 - 5

825 Russell Blvd.   95616
(916) 758-3488   Est: 1977
Owner: Beth Murphy
1000 sq.ft.   3000 Bolts

Home of Sweet
Treat Medleys.
2000 Hoffmans
1000 other.
Helpful quilters on
Staff. Mail Order &
Sweet Treat
Subscription.

Sycamore
University Mall ☆
Anderson
Hwy. 113 Woodland
Russell Blvd. / 5th St.
Pincushion Boutique
I - 80
to San Francisco   to Sacramento

Vacaville, CA #14

The Unique Spool

Hours by Appt.

407 Corte Majorca   95688
(707) 448-1538
Owner: Roberta Whitworth
Catalog—$1.00

African and
Australian
Fabrics plus
domestic prints,
ethnic quilt
patterns, notions
& quilt frames.

Corte Majorca
407
Crestview Dr.
Alamo
Orchard
The Unique Spool
Merchant St.
Hwy. 80

Santa Rosa, CA #15

TREADLEART

1965 Mendocino 95401
(707) 523-2122
Owner: Janet Stocker
Est: 1994 2300 sq.ft.

Mon - Sat
10 - 6
Sun 12 - 5

Supplies for all your quilting and sewing needs.
5000 bolts of fabric, patterns, books, stencils, decorative thread, machine accessories notions.

Steele
1965 TreadleArt
Hwy. 101
Mendocino

Sebastopol, CA #16

EASTWIND ART

P.O. Box 811 95473
(707) 829-3536 Est: 1973
Owner: Joanne Newcomb
Catalog $2

Phone
for Appt.

We specialize in Japanese-style items. We carry sashiko supplies, charms, cotton print yardage. We manufacture patterns, buttons, crafts and other interesting stuff.

Healdsburg Ave.
Covert Ln.
Ragle Rd.
Main St.
Petaluma Ave.
Hwy. 12
Valley View Bodega Ave.
May Cl.
Hwy. 116

Sonoma, CA #17

Quilts of The Past

P.O. Box 2279 95476
(707) 938-9535
Owner: Gaby Burkert Est: 1981

By Appt.
Only

Send $20 for 12 Heirloom Quilt Greeting Cards
Museum Quality
Incl. Shipping
A Great Saving!

Antique & Old
Quilts
Plan a trip to the
Wine Country.

Sonoma, CA #18

Kay's Fabrics

201 W. Mapa St. #14
Sonoma Mkt.Pl. 95476
(707) 996-3515
Est: 1963 2600 sq.ft.
4000 Bolts
We do Mail Orders &
Invite Fabric Requests.

Mon - Fri
9:30 - 6
Sat 10 - 5:30
Sun 12 - 4

Complete line of quilting fabrics, books, patterns and notions. Hoffman, RJR, VIP, Kona & Many Unusual Fabrics.

Hwy. 12
Santa Rosa
Sonoma
Kay's Fabrics
Second St.
U.S. 101
San Francisco

Petaluma, CA #19

Quilted Angel

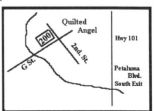

200 G St. 94952
(707) 763-0945
Owner: Susie Ernst
Est: 1991 2200 sq.ft. 2850 Bolts

Mon - Sat
10 - 5:30
Thur til 7:30
Sun 12 - 4

A "destination" Quilt Store Fabrics from all major suppliers, books (600 titles) notions, patterns, doll supplies & classes.

Quilted Angel
200
2nd. St.
G St.
Hwy 101
Petaluma Blvd. South Exit

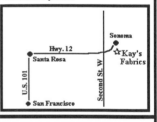

Elk Grove, CA   #20

Country Sewing Center

**Mon - Fri 10 - 6
Sat 10 - 5**

9639 E. Stockton Blvd.   95624
(916) 685-8500
Owners: Susan & Bill Zimlich
Est: 1993   2400 sq.ft.   800+ Bolts

Conveniently located off Hiway 99. Great selection of 100% fabrics, books & notions. Friendly, small-town service.

Altaville, CA   #21

Country Cloth Shop

457 S. Main St. (Angels Camp)
(209) 736-4998   Est: 1980
Owners: Chuck & Ginger Duffy
1600 sq.ft.   1000+ Bolts

Mon - Sat 10-5

Quilting: Large selection of Books & Fabrics. Cross Stitch: Brazilian Emb. Bernina Sales and Service. Classes. General Craft and Sewing Supplies.

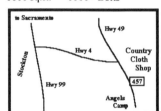

Modesto, CA   #22

R. Lily Stem Quilts

**Mon - Fri 9:30 - 5:30
Sat 10 - 5
Sun 12 - 4**

815 W. Roseburg Avenue   95350
(209) 577-1919
Owner: Marilyn Nelson
Est: 1986   1400 sq.ft.

Fabulous fabrics, books, patterns, cross-stitch, custom comforters, classes and great service !

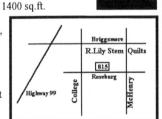

Turlock, CA   #23

California QuiltMakers

**Mon - Fri 10 - 5:30
Sat 10 - 5
Sun 12 - 4**

134 West Main Street   95380
(209) 632-0899
Est: 1991   3000 sq.ft.
Owners: Pat Fryer & Pam Howland

Fabric, Books, Patterns, Quilts for sale, Machine Quilting. Quilting Machines. In - store quilt show.

Bishop, CA   #24

The Fabric Store

Mon - Sat 10 - 5

1343 Rocking W. Dr.   93514
(619) 873-6808
Est: 1982   1280 sq.ft.
Owners: Marti & Randy Witters

New Owners
A Quilter's Haven
Classes in Quilting

Pacific Grove, CA   #25

The Hand Maden

**Mon - Sat 10 - 5:30
Sun 12 - 4**

620 Lighthouse Ave.
(408) 373-5353
Owners: Olivia & Don Shaffer
Est: 1983   3000 sq.ft.

3000 bolts of quilters cotton. All supplies & patterns needed. Extensive Needlework selections. Viking Machines.

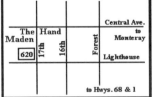

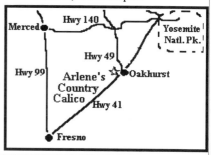

Carmel, CA #27

California QuiltMakers

Ocean Ave. at Monte Verde
P.O. Box 7237　93921
(408) 625-2815
Owners: Pat Fryer & Pam Howland
Est: 1995
500 sq.ft.

7 Days a Week 11 - 5

Quilts for Sale.
Quilted Clothing.
Books, Patterns
Fabric Pieces.

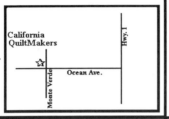

Reedley, CA #28

Mennonite Quilt Center

1012 "G" St.　93654
(209) 638-3560　2500 sq.ft.
Mgrs: Jeanne Heyerly & Kathleen Heinrichs
450 Bolts

Mon - Fri 9:30 - 4:30 Sat 10 - 2

100% Cotton
Fabrics, notions,
Books, Patterns, &
Battings. Quilters
on site Monday
mornings. Quilt
show year around.
Tours Avail.

Tehachapi, CA #29

♥ 5 Heart Quilts & Fabric ♥

122 E. Tehachapi Blvd. #C
(805) 822-8709　93561
Owner: Claudia Blodget Priddy
Est: 1993　900 sq.ft.　1000 Bolts

Tues - Fri 9:30 - 3:30 Sat 10 - 2

A Quilters Heaven
With all of the
Colors - 100%
Cotton, Hoffman,
Alex. Henry,
Mumms, Books,
Notions and
Classes. To Your
Needs.

Tehachapi, CA #30

Clear Creek Homeworks

"The Quilting & Fabric Shoppe"
20608 South St.　93561
(805) 823-9108　Owner: Ann Webster

Tue - Fri 10 - 5 Sat 10 - 4

A shoppe of
distinction for the
most discriminating
quilter.
A palette of
extraordinary
colors and patterns
to stimulate your
imagination.

Bakersfield, CA #31

Strawberry Patches

6439 Ming Ave. #C　93309
(805) 835-1738　Est: 1985
Owner: Suzanne Zingg
2500 sq.ft.

Mon - Fri 10 - 5:30 Sat 10 - 5

Our store is
brimming with an
extensive selection
of the finest 100%
cotton fabric
available
anywhere. We
also offer the
newest patterns,
books & notions
for todays quilter.

The Bobbin Spinner

(805) 325-5244
3401 Chester Ave. Suite J   93301
Owners: Sharon & Ray Payne
Est: 1994   1500 sq.ft.

Bakersfield, CA   #32

✤ **FABRICS** (100% Cotton)
✤ **BOOKS**
✤ **NOTIONS**
✤ **CLASSES**

Chester Ave.
34th St.
3401
The Bobbin
Spinner

Mon - Thur
9 - 6
Fri & Sat
9 - 5

Unique Country Fabrics

Clovis, CA   #33

QUILTERS' PARADISE

- helpful, friendly service
- great selection of newest
  fabrics, books, patterns
  and notions
- silk ribbon, doll and bear
  making supplies
- new merchandise arriving
  daily
- mail orders & special orders
  welcome
- Visa, Mastercard, Discover

339 Pollasky   93612
(209) 297-7817
Est: 1978   5000 sq.ft.
Owners: Jennifer Wheeler

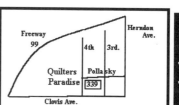

Freeway 99
Herndon Ave.
4th 3rd.
Quilters Paradise Pollasky
339
Clovis Ave.

Mon & Fri
10 - 8
Tues, Wed,
Thur 10 - 6
Sat 10 - 5

 **Just What the
Shop Name Says!!**

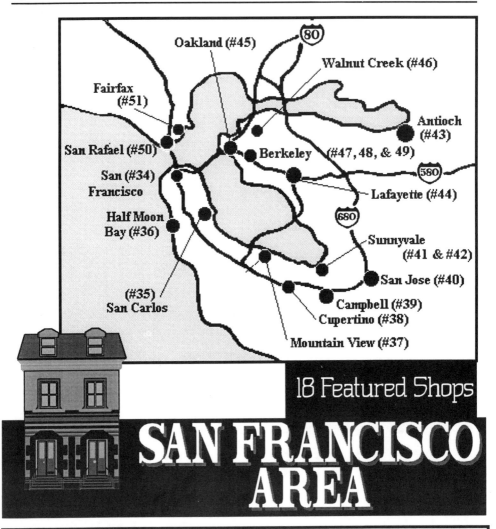

Oakland (#45)

Walnut Creek (#46)

Fairfax (#51)

Antioch (#43)

San Rafael (#50)

Berkeley (#47, 48, & 49)

San (#34) Francisco

Lafayette (#44)

Half Moon Bay (#36)

Sunnyvale (#41 & #42)

San Jose (#40)

(#35) San Carlos

Campbell (#39)

Cupertino (#38)

Mountain View (#37)

18 Featured Shops

SAN FRANCISCO AREA

San Francisco, CA #34

Mendels
Far-Out Fabrics

1556 Haight St.   94117
(415) 621-1287
Owner: Bette Mosias   3900 sq.ft.

**Mon - Fri
10 - 6
Sat 10 - 5:30
Sun 12 - 5**

Lots of wonderful cotton fabrics, unusual ethnic - large selection textile dyes, paints, great buttons, trims and an art supply store.

Clayton St. | Mendels Far-Out Fabrics | Ashbury St.
1556
Haight St.

San Carlos, CA #35

The Laurel Leaf

648 Laurel Street   94070
(415) 591-6790
Owner: Julie Murphy
          Est: 1983   2200 sq.ft.

**Mon - Sat
10 - 5**

100% Cotton Fabric, Books, Patterns, Quilting Supplies, Classes. Authorized Bernina Dealer. 10 Min. South of San Francisco Airport

the Laurel Leaf
San Carlos
Cherry
648
Laurel
El Camino
Holly
Hwy 101

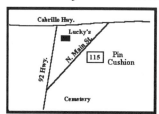

20 mi. South of San Francisco

Pin Cushion

115 N. Main St.   94019

(415) 726-4247

Owner: Vee Raeside   Est: 1976

150 sq.ft.   300 Bolts

Half Moon Bay, CA   #36

Quilt Books

Threads — Cotton DMC Embroidery — DMC Pearle

Located on the beautiful Coast Highway.

Mon - Sat
10 - 5
Sun 12 - 4

Mountain View, CA   #37

The **Quilting Bee**

357 Castro Street 94041

(415) 969-1714 ★ 800-492-6397

Web Site:http://www.quiltingbee.com

Owner: Diana Leone

Est: 1976 5,000 sq. ft.

M-F 9-8:30
Sat 9-5
Sun 11-5

4,000 Bolts of Cotton

750 Books

Classes, Notions

Appraisals

Quilts Bought & Sold

Special Orders Our Specialty

BERNINA **WHITE** **VIKING**

Cupertino, CA   #38

Whiffle Tree Quilts

Mon - Sat
10 - 6
Thurs til 8

10261 S. DeAnza Blvd.   95014

(408) 255-5270   Est: 1982

Newsletter On-Line: http://www.danish.com/wtq

Owners: Marsha Burdick & Louise Horkey 1280 sq.ft.

A terrific store
full of fabric,
patterns, &
notions & books.
A place to share
ideas and get
inspired.

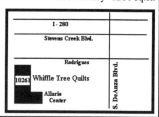

Campbell, CA   #39

Golden State
Sewing Center

Mon - Fri
10 - 6
Thur til 8
Sat 10 - 5
Sun 12 - 4

2435 South Winchester Blvd.

(408) 866-1181   95008

Owners: Margrit Schwanck

Est: 1951

1600 sq.ft.

A great place for
those addicted to
Quilting and
Cross Stitch !
Oldest Elna
Dealership in the
Valley.

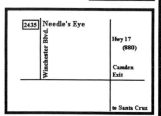

San Jose, CA   #40

American Museum of
Quilts and Textiles

Tues - Sat
10 - 4

60 S. Market St.,

P.O. Box 1058   95108

(408) 971-0323   Est: 1977

Non-profit Public Benefit Museum

Regularly changing exhibits of Quilts and
Textiles. Museum Store has extensive
assortment of books on quilting.
Call for Directions.

Sunnyvale, CA #41

The Granary

1326 S. Mary Ave.   94087
(408) 973-0591
Owner: Karen Yancey
                    Est: 1973

Mon - Sat
10 - 6
Last Sunday of
Month 10 - 4

1200 bolts of
100% cotton
fabric.
Quilting
Supplies,
Patterns,
Classes.

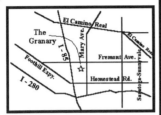

Sunnyvale, CA #42

Carolea's Knitche

586 South Murphy Ave.   94086
(408) 736-2800
Owner: Carolea Peterson
Est: 1973   1400 sq.ft.

Mon - Fri
10 - 6
Sat 10 - 5

The very latest in
Hoffman, Alex
Henry, Jinny
Beyer, Kaufman,
Tony Wentzel,
Gutcheon . . .
Mail orders
welcome.

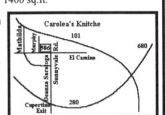

Antioch, CA #43

Cotton Patch

3341 Deer Valley Road   94509
(510) 757-7240
Est: 1991   1700 sq.ft.
Owner: Carolie Hensley   Mgr: Shari Vancil

Mon - Fri
9:30 - 5:30
Sat 10 - 5
Sun 12 - 4

Bernina Dealer.
Repair all makes &
models of
machines. Cotton
fabrics, books,
patterns, classes.
Visit our sister
shop in Lafayette.

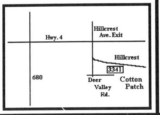

Lafayette, CA #44

Cotton Patch

1025 Brown Avenue   94549
(510) 284-1177
Owner: Carolie Hensley
Est: 1978   1400 sq.ft.

Mon - Fri
9:30 - 5:30
Sat 10 - 5
Sun 12 - 4

Bernina Dealer.
Repair all makes
& models of
machines. Cotton
prints & one
room full of solid
cottons. Patterns,
books, gifts, &
notions etc.

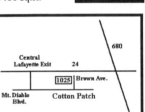

Berkeley, CA #47

New Pieces
Fabric & Chamber Music

1597 Solano Ave.   94707
(510) 527-6779
Owner: Sally Davie

Mon - Sat 10 - 6
Sun 12 - 5

Est: 1984

Stimulating,
Colorful, Helpful,
Knowledgeable,
Convenient,
Variety, Friendly,
Quilt Oriented,
Contemporary
Fabrics, Books
Exhibits

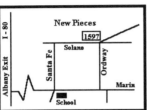

Berkeley, CA #48

The Ames Gallery

2661 Cedar Street   94708
(510) 845-4949   Est: 1970
Owner: Bonnie Grossman

Open During Exhibitions Call for Schedule

An Extensive
collection of
antique utilitarian
items as well as
primitive, naive
and outsider art.

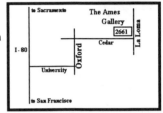

Berkeley, CA #49

Stonemountain & Daughter Fabrics

2518 Shattuck Ave.   94704
(510) 845-6106   Est: 1981
Owners: Suzan & Bob Steinberg
6000 sq.ft.   Thousands of Bolts

Mon - Fri 9:30 - 6:30
Sat 10 - 6
Sun 11 - 5:30

Huge Selection of
Quality, Unique
Cottons at
affordable prices!
Ethnic, Quilting &
Basic Cottons.
Wools, Silks,
Rayons, & Linens
also Available.

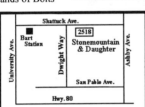

San Rafael, CA #50

Sawtooth Quilts

1560 Fourth St.   94901
(415) 453-1711   Est: 1981
Owner: Susan Bradford

By Appointment Only

Please call Susan Bradford for quilt
restoration, wet cleaning, private
consultations, appraisals, workshops,
lectures, judging and hand or machine
quilting.

Fairfax, CA #51

Rainbow Fabrics

50 Bolinas Rd.   94930
(415) 459-5100
Owner: Rose Taber

Mon - Sat 10 - 6
Sun 12 - 4

Unique country
store. Cotton,
Rayons, Books,
Beads, Notions.
Open daily.
Helpful staff
Classes for Adults
and Children

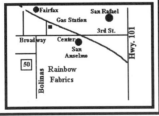

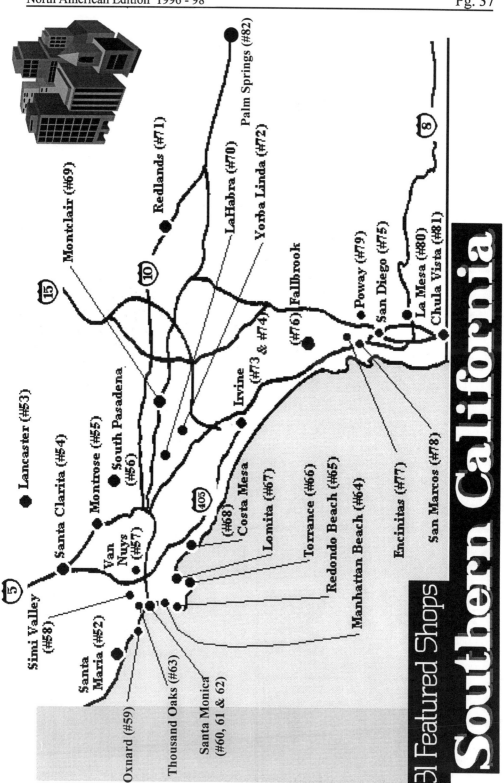

Southern California

3l Featured Shops

- Palm Springs (#82)
- Redlands (#71)
- LaHabra (#70)
- Yorba Linda (#72)
- Montclair (#69)
- Fallbrook (#76)
- Poway (#79)
- San Diego (#75)
- La Mesa (#80)
- Chula Vista (#81)
- Irvine (#73 & #74)
- Lancaster (#53)
- Montrose (#55)
- South Pasadena (#56)
- Santa Clarita (#54)
- Costa Mesa (#68)
- Lomita (#67)
- Torrance (#66)
- Redondo Beach (#65)
- Manhattan Beach (#64)
- Encinitas (#77)
- San Marcos (#78)
- Van Nuys (#57)
- Simi Valley (#58)
- Santa Maria (#52)
- Oxnard (#59)
- Thousand Oaks (#63)
- Santa Monica (#60, 61 & 62)

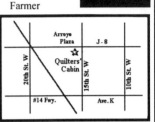

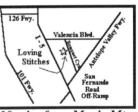

Van Nuys, CA #57

Sandy White Antique Quilts

14936 Gault St.   91405
(818) 988-0575
Est: 1985

By Appointment Only

Lovely Selection of Appealing Antique Quilts for both Home and Office, For the Collector and Decorator.

Please Call for Directions

Simi Valley, CA #58

WHISTLE STOP

Quilt Station

Tues - Sat 10 - 6

4385 Valley Fair St.   93063
(805) 584-6915
Owner: Judy Ragan   Est: 1984

Full line Quilting and related crafts. Classes for kids and adults.
1600 Bolts

Oxnard, CA #59

Fabric Well

**Mon - Fri 9:30 - 8
Sat 9:30 - 6
Sun 11 - 5**

3075 Saviers Road   93033
(805) 486-7826
Owners: Ray & Bev Hicks
Est: 1975   13,200 sq.ft.   1000+ Bolts

One of the Largest Selections of Quilting Fabrics and Supplies you will find anywhere.

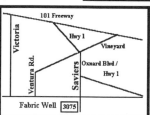

Santa Monica #60

McGuire's Quilt & Needlework

Mon - Sat 10 - 6

521 Santa Monica Blvd.   90401
(310) 395-7753   Est: 1982
Owner: Gerry McGuire   900 sq.ft.

100% Cotton fabrics, books, patterns, and notions. We have Computer Software to design your quilts for sale.

Santa Monica, CA #61

Crazy Ladies & Friends

Mon - Sat 10:30 - 5:30

1604 Santa Monica Blvd. 90404
(310) 828-3122   Est: 1977   1800 sq.ft.
Owner: Mary Ellen Hopkins   Free Catalog

The Quilt Shop that offers words of encouragement. 3000 Bolts of Cotton Fabric chosen with the Quilter in mind.

Santa Monica, CA #62

Santa Monica Antique Market

**Mon - Sat 10 - 6
Sun 12 - 5**

1607 Lincoln Blvd.   90404
(310) 314-4899   20,000 sq.ft.
Featured Dealer: Sandy White Antique Quilts

Recognized as one of the Top 10 Collectives in America. Large Inventory of Antique Quilts in a Beautiful Surrounding.

Thousand Oaks, CA #63

Mary's Quilt Inn

1772 Avenida de los Arboles #E
(805) 241-0061   91362
Owner: Mary Freeman   1575 sq.ft.   900+ Bolts
Est: 1978

Mon - Thur
10 - 6
Fri & Sat
10 - 5

We offer a large variety of fabrics, classes, quilting supplies, books & patterns.

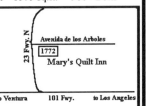

Manhattan Beach, CA #64

Luella's Quilt Basket

1840 N. Sepulveda Blvd.
(310) 545-3436   90266
Est: 1988   1400 sq.ft.
Owners: Luella Fournell

Mon - Sat
10 - 6
Sun 11 - 4

We offer a wide variety of Fabrics, Classes and quilting supplies: 3 miles south of L.A.X.

Redondo Beach, CA #65

THE COTTON SHOP
FINE FABRICS

(310) 376-3518
1922 Artesia Blvd.   90278
Est: 1959 8400 sq.ft. 2000+ Bolts

Mon - Thur
10 - 7
Fri & Sat
10 - 6
Sun 11 - 5

Full Line Fabric Store with Large Quilting Dept. Probably the Largest Selection of Hoffman Prints in Southern California

Torrance, CA #66

Quilts Unlimited

2202-F West Artesia Blvd.
(310) 532-9203   90504
Owner: Judy Wood
Est: 1978   2000 sq.ft.

Mon - Fri
10 - 5:30
Sat 10 - 4

Fabric (all major brands) Books, Patterns, Notions, Classes. Lots of Samples to inspire you !

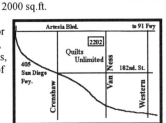

Lomita, CA #67

TREADLEART

25834 Narbonne Ave.   90717
(310) 534-5122
Owner: Janet Stocker
Est: 1978   7000 sq.ft.
Catalog $3

Mon - Sat
10 - 6
Tues til 9
Sun 12 - 5

Supplies for all your quilting and sewing needs. 5000 bolts of fabric, patterns, books, stencils, decorative thread, machine accessories notions.

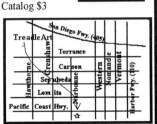

Costa Mesa, CA #68

Piecemakers Country Store

1720 Adams Avenue   92626
(714) 641-3112   Est: 1978
Owners: 35 Piecemakers !
Catalog $2.00   12,000 sq.ft.   2000 Bolts
Mail @ piecemakers. com   http://piecemakers. com

Mon - Fri
10 - 9
Sat 10 - 5:30
Sun 10 - 5:30

Complete line of quilting supplies, fabrics, books, notions, dolls, handmade quilts, unique gifts & hundreds of classes every month. Four Craft Fairs per year call for information.

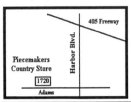

Montclair, CA   #69

**Mon - Sat
9:30 - 5
Sun 12 - 3**

5436 D Arrow Highway 91763
909-985-9000
Fax: 909-985-9163

Marie White
Carolyn Reese
Since 1981

So. California's Largest, Most Complete Quilt Shop
3000 bolts of 100% cotton
300 book titles
More than 1000 craft and quilt patterns
Large selection of notions
Gift items for Quilters and their friends
We do mail order
Use the Central Ave. exit on I - 10

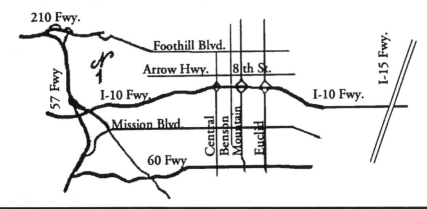

Redlands, CA #71

The Calico Horse
Mon - Fri 10 - 6
Sat 10 - 5

461 Tennessee St. Suite J 92373
(909) 793-1868 or 824-6198
Owners: Debra & Doug Grantz
Beverly & Bill Dean Est: 1986 1580 sq.ft.

Large selection of 100% cotton fabrics and supplies. Patterns & Books. Orange crate labels on muslin. Friendly, expert advice. Mail Order Avail.

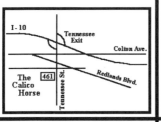

Yorba Linda, CA #72

The Calico House
Mon - Fri 9:30 - 5
Sat 9:30 - 4
Sun 12 - 3

4801 Park Ave. 92686
(714) 993-3091
Owners: Jane, Janice, Cari
Est: 1981 1500+ Bolts

Complete Quilt Shop.
Books, Fabrics, Notions, Classes. Helpful Staff Friendly.

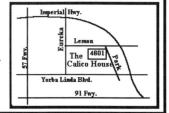

Irvine, CA #73

FLYING GEESE FABRICS
Mon - Fri 9:30 - 8
Sat 10 - 6
Sun 12 - 5

14210 Culver Dr. Suite D 92714
(714) 552-3809
Owner: Bonnie Boyd Est: 1986

Newest Quilt Fabrics, Books, And Patterns. Great Selection of Buttons for Clothing and Quilt Embellishment. Classes

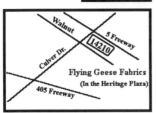

Irvine, CA #74

Fabric Emporium
Mon - Fri 9:30 - 8
Sat 10 - 6
Sun 12 - 5

4720 Barranca Pkwy. 92714
(714) 552-5151
Owner: Pat Cramer
Est: 1981 1800 sq.ft. 1000+ Bolts

Located in Woodbridge Village Center, next to Pavilions. Large selection of cotton fabrics, fat quarters, books, craft patterns & classes.

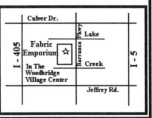

San Diego, CA #75 *Rosie's Calico Cupboard*

7151 El Cajon Blvd. Suite 'F' 92115 (619)697-5758 FAX:(619)465-8298

Catering to Quilters and Crafters Since 1983

Offering over 2700 Square Feet (stocked to the brim) with over
6000 Bolts of '**First Quality**' 100% Cotton Prints,
Plus Books, Batting, Notions, Patterns, Thread, Silk Ribbon,
and a 'Trunk Full' of over 500 lbs of Buttons,
Plus Much, Much More and ALL at Everyday **DISCOUNT** Prices

•Well Stocked Sale Rack, values from 50% OFF Sugg. Retail Price
•New Stock arriving daily
•Mail Orders and Special Orders Welcome
•Visa, Master Card, Discover and American Express Accepted
•On Going Mystery Quilts by Mail
•Once a year '**24 Hr. Fall Quilters Madness**' (call for date)
•Be a part of our '1997' Quilters Cook Book (call for information)

Open Seven Days a Week

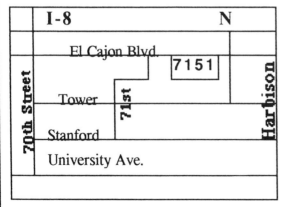

Mon/, Tues., Thurs.,Fri.	9am - 5pm
Wednesday	9am - 8pm
Saturday	8am - 5pm
Sunday	11am - 5pm

Closed New Years Day, Easter, Thanksgiving and Christmas

Hwy **8** to 70th St., exit.
Travel So. on 70th St. for
1/2 mile to El Cajon Bl.,
Turn left (east) onto
El Cajon Blvd., travel for a
block-and-a-half. We will be on
your right hand side, in the
College Plaza Center, east of
the Boll Weevil.
From Hwy. 94, take the
Mass. Exit,travel north to
University Ave., turn left,
follow to 70th St., turn right,
follow to El Cajon Blvd.,turn
right, travel for 1 1/2 blocks.

Poway, CA #79

Zook's Warehouse for Quilters

Mon, Fri
Sat 9 - 5
Tues, Wed
Thur 9 - 8

12625 Danielson Ct. #111
(619) 486-0696 92064
Fax: (619) 486-1618 Est: 1994
Owner: Kristin Zook 3800 sq.ft. 1700 Bolts

A full service quilt
shop carrying
fabrics, books,
patterns, notions
and gifts.
Mail Order Avail.
Free Catalog

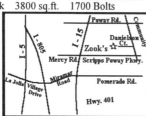

La Mesa, CA #80

Stitch in Time Quilt Shoppe

Mon - Fri
9:30 - 6
Wed til 8
Sat 9:30 - 5

6119 Lake Murray Blvd. 91942
(619) 466-0977
Owner: Kathleen Wendling
  1800 bolts of   2400 sq.ft.
  100% cotton.
Great selection of
solids. Over 400
quilting books
plus soft fabric
craft patterns too.
  Notions and
classes of course.

Chula Vista, CA #81

Quilters' Choice

Mon - Sat
9:30 - 5:30
Sun 1 - 5

423 Third Ave. 91910
(619) 425-2545
Owner: Nancy Letchworth
Est: 1992   1000+ sq.ft.

100% Cotton
Fabric, Books,
Patterns, Notions,
Classes and
Always Friendly
Service.

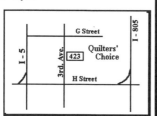

Creative Expressions OF PALM SPRINGS

MONDAY - SATURDAY
9:00 AM TO 5:00 PM

1111 South Palm Canyon Drive
Palm Springs, CA • 92264
619/327-2587   **#82**

A FULL-SERVICE QUILT SHOP

100% COTTON FABRICS in every shade
and color, prints and solids, and the latest
in holiday designs. **NOTIONS AND BOOKS**
for any project!

BEADS FROM AROUND THE WORLD
Crystals, Precious and Semi-precious
stones, Glass, Ethnic Pieces and more!

CLASSES IN QUILTING AND BEADING
are available for beginners on to the more
advanced! Call today for your
COMPLIMENTARY schedule of classes!

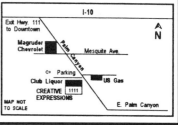

Easy Access
from I-10 and
Hwy 111.
Parking in the
Rear, enter
from North
side of Club
Liqour and you
will find us on
the South side
of the building!

California Guilds:
East Bay Heritage Quilters, Box 6223, Albany, 94706
Delta Quilters, P.O. Box 154, Antioch, 94509
Pajaro Valley Quilt Assoc., Box 1412, Aptos, 95003
Independence Hall Quilters, Box 842, Arnold
South County Quilt Guild, Box 656, Arroyo Grande, 93421
Foothill Quilters Guild, P.O. Box 5653, Auburn, 95604
Cotton Patch Quilters, Box 9944, Bakersfield
Carquinez Strait Quilters, Box 1101, Benicia, 94510
Busy Bear Quilt Guild, Box 6513, Big Bear Lake, 92315
Desert Quilters Guild, 410 W. C St., Brawley, 92227
Citrus Belt Quilters, Box 626, Bryn Mawr 92318
Camarillo Quilters Assoc., P.O. Box 347, Camarillo, 93011
Santa Clara Vly Quilt Assoc. Box 792, Campbell, 95009
Valley Quiltmakers Guild, P.O. Box 589, Canoga Park, 91305
Chester Piece Makers, P.O. Box 1702, Chester, 96020
Anne's Star Quilt Guild, P.O. Box 4318, Chico, 95927
LA Quiltmakers Guild, 16167 Augusta Dr., Chino Hills, 91709
Clear Lake Quilters Guild, P.O. Box 5323, Clear Lake, 95422
Pacific Flyway Quilters, 1974 Wescott Rd, Colusa, 95932
Inland Empire Quilt Guild, P.O. Box 2232, Corona, 91718
Diablo Valley Quilt Guild, Box 1884, Danville, 94526
Gold Bug Qujlters, P.O. Box 516, Diamond Springs, 95619
Mountain Star Quilters, Box 647, Downieville, 95936
Sunshine Quilters, P.O. Box 20483, El Cajon, 92022
Redwood Empire Quilters Guild, Box 5071, Eureka, 95501
North Wind Quilters, P.O. Box 2891, Fairfield, 94533
Fallbrook Quilters Guild, P.O. Box 1704, Fallbrook, 92028
Folsom Quilt & Fiber Guild, P.O. Box 626, Folsom, 95630
Piecemakers Quilt Guild, Box 2051, Fremont, 94536
San Jaquin Vly Quilt Guild, P.O. Box 5532, Fresno, 93755
Orange Grove Quilters Guild, Box 453, Garden Grove, 92642
Glendale Quilt Guild, P.O. Box 5366, Glendale, 91201
Pine Tree Quilt Guild, P.O. Box 3133, Grass Valley, 95945
Log Cabin Quilters, P.O. Box 1359, Hayfork, 96041
Valley Quilters, P.O. Box 2534, Hemet, 92545
Mountain Quilters, P.O. Box 603, Idyllwild, 92349
Coachella Valley Q. G., 43-761 Towne St., Indio, 92201
Flying Geese Quilters, P.O. Box 19608-154, Irvine, 92713
Friendship Square Q. G., P.O. Box 681, La Habra, 90633
Antelope Valley Quilt Ass., P.O. Box 4107, Lancaster, 93534
Tokay Stitch-N-Quilt Guild, Box 1838, Lodi, 95241
ADA Quilt Guild, 3460 Wilshire Blvd, Los Angeles, 90010
Westside Quilters, 1019 Walnut Wood Ct., Los Banos, 93635
Sierra Valley Guild, Loyalton, 96118

Quilters Etc., P.O. Box 2507, Lumpock, 93438
Heart of California Q. G., 415 Camden Way, Madera, 93637
Manteca Quilters, P.O. Box 1558, Manteca, 95336
Gateway Quilters, P.O. Box 3793, Merced, 95344
Country Crossroads, P.O. Box 577063, Modesto, 95355
Piece by Piece Quilters, 114 Cochrane Rd, Morgan Hill, 95037
Continued on the next page

California Guilds continued from Previous Page:
Napa Valley Quilters, P.O. Box 405, Napa, 94558
Los Angeles County Quilt Guild, Box 252, Norwalk, 90651
Mountain Quilters Guild, Oakhurst Library, Oakhurst
Sierra Mountain Quilters Guild, Box 1359, Oakhurst, 93644
El Camino Quilt Guild, Box 1952, Oceanside, 92051
Orange County Quilters Guild, Box 3108, Orange, 92665
Oroville Piecemakers, P.O. Box 1604, Oroville, 95965
Monterey Pen. Quilters Guild, Box 1025, Pacific Grove, 93950
Southern CA Council of Quilt Guilds, 2342 W. Avenue N., Palmdale
Ridge Quilters Guild, P.O. Box 1668, Paradise, 95969
Northern CA Quilt Council, 3935 Sloat Rd, Pebble Beach, 93953
Petaluma Quilt Guild, Box 5334, Petaluma, 94955
Sierra Gold Quilt Guild, P.O. Box 1078, Pine Grove, 95665
Cactus Sew-Ables, P.O. Box 317, Pioneertown, 92268
Guild of Quilters of Contra Costa County, Box 23871, Pleasant Hill, 94523
Amador Valley Quilters, P.O. Box 955, Pleasanton, 94566
Porterville Quilters, P.O. Box 1881, Porterville, 93257
Friendship Quilters, P.O. Box 1174, Poway, 92074
Redding Quilters Sew-ciety, Box 492581, Redding, 96409
Peninsula Quilters, P.O. Box 2423, Redwood City, 94064
San Fernando Valley Quilt Assoc., Box 1042, Reseda, 91337
Rocklin Pioneer Quilt Guild, Box 126, Rocklin, 95677
Schoolhouse Quilt Guild, PO Box 356, Rosemead, 91770
River City Quilters Guild, Box 15816, Sacramento, 95852
S. CA Council of Quilt Guilds, 3299 Villanova Avenue, San Diego, 92122
Seaside Quilt Guild, P.O. Box 9964, San Diego, 92109
Canyon Quilters, P.O. Box 22465, San Diego, 92192
San Francisco Q. G., P.O. Box 27002, San Francisco, 94127
Peninsula Stitchery , 15780 E. Alta Vista Way, San Jose, 95127
North County Quilting Assoc., Box 982, San Marcos
Marin Quilt Lovers, P.O.Box 6015, San Rafael, 94903
Mt. Tam Quilt Guild, P.O. Box 6192, San Rafael, 94903
Coastal Quilters Guild, P.O. Box 6341, Santa Barbara, 93106
Santa Clarita Vly Q. G. Box 802863, Santa Clarita, 91380
Santa Maria Vly QG, P.O. Box 2933, Santa Maria, 93457
Moonlighters, P.O. Box 6882, Santa Rosa, 65406
Santa Rosa Quilt Guild, P.O. Box 9251, Santa Rosa, 95405
Legacy Quilters, 9320 Lake Country Dr., Santee, 92071
Wandering Foot QG, P.O. Box 9431, Sierra Madre, 91025
Simi Valley Quilt Guild, Box 3689, Simi Valley, 93093
Sonoma Vly Quilters, 1463 Mission Dr., Sonoma, 95476
Sierra Quilt Guild of T.C., P.O. Box 43, Standard, 95373
Tuleburg Quilt Guild, P.O. Box 692151, Stockton, 95269
Tehachapi Mt. Quilters, 30300 Lower Vly Rd., Tehachapi, 93561
Valley of the Mist QG, 27475 Ynez Rd., Temecula, 92391
Almond Ctry Quilters, P.O. Box 914, Templeton, 93465
South Bay Q. G., P.O. Box 6115, Torrance, 90504
Valley Oak Quilters, P.O. Box 1093, Tulare, 93275
Turlock Quilt Guild, P.O. Box 66, Turlock, 95381
Night Owl Quilters Guild, P.O. Box 5019, Upland, 91786
Vallejo Piecemakers, P.O. Box 5515, Vallejo, 95381
Desert Winds Quilt Guild, P.O. Box 1989, Victorville, 92392
Afro-American Quilters, 22544 Califa, Woodland Hills, 91367
Valley Quilt Guild, P.O. Box 1463, Yuba City, 95992

Other Shops in California:

Atascadero	Quilts & Other Pleasures, 7575 El Camino Rd.
Atascadero	The Yardstick, 8310 C El Camino Real
Auburn	Feathered Nest, 157 Sacramento
Berkeley	Ninepatch, 2001 Hopkins
Berkeley	Kasuri Dyeworks, 1959 Shattuck Ave.
Big Bear Lake	Mountain Country Merc, 40671 Village Dr.
Biggs	Honan's, 491 B St.
Burbank	Q is for Quilts, 401 S. Glenoaks Blvd
Cambria	Sew & So, 1602 Main
Carmichael	Design Studio, 4034 Wayside Lane #E
Chico	Honey Run Quilters, 1230 Esplanade
Dublin	Home Lovin Quilting, 8544 Valencia St.
El Cajon	Calico Junction, 753 Jamacha Rd.
Fair Oaks	Tayo's Fair Oaks Fabrics, 10127 Fair Oaks Blvd.
Grass Valley	Quilt Loft, 762-C Freeman Ln.
Grass Valley	Heidi's Fashion Fabrics, 11671 Maltman Dr.
Gualala	Loose Goose Conspiracy, 39150 S. Hwy 1
Half Moon Bay	Calico Barn, 604 Main St.
Heldsburg	Fabrications, 118 Matheson
La Mesa	The Country Loft, 8166 LaMesa Blvd.
Lakeport	Kerrie's Sewing & Quilting, 2695 Hartley St.
Lawndale	YCFC, P.O. Box 426
Lodi	My Favorite Pastime, 1355 Lakewood Mall
Los Gatos	The Makings, 798 Blossom Hill Rd. #12
Lower Lake	Magoon's General Store, 16195 Main
Madera	Calico Bunny, 1705 Howard Rd.
Manhattan Beach	Once Upon a Quilt, 312 Manhattan Beach Blvd.
Marysville	Remember When, 417 7th St.
Marysville	The Cinnamon Heart, 511 "D" St.
Mendocino	Crossblends, 45156 Main
Modesto	Helens Yardage, 1331 Crows Landing Rd.
Morro Bay	The Cotton Ball, 475 Morro Bay Blvd.
Mountain View	Buttons & Bolts Factory Outlet, 264 Castro
Newhall	Aunt Ida's Attic, 24251 San Fernando Rd.
Norco	Quilt n Cross, 2395 Hamner Ave. #I
Oceanside	Cotton Patch, 307 N. Hill St.
Oxnard	Me & Thee Quilts, 200 Iowa Pl.
Pasadena	Bearly Stitching Fabric Center, 2245 East Colorado Blvd.
Petaluma	Chanticleer Antiques, 145 Petaluma Blvd. N
Pico Rivera	S & J Quilts, 7860 Paramount Blvd.
Pleasanton	Going to Pieces, 1989 F Santa Rita Rd.
Quincy	Quincy Emporium, P.O. Box 450

Other Shop Continued on Next Page

Other Shops in California Continued from Previous Page

R.S. Margarita	De'cor Aum Enterprises, 22431-B 160 Antonion Pkwy, #485
Redding	Sew Simple, 3001 Bechelli Ln.
Redwood City	Adams Notion & Yardage, 2090 Broadway
Rocklin	Quilt Connection, 5050 Rockland Rd. #4A
Sacramento	Seams Like Old Times, 5484 Carlson Dr.
San Anselmo	Greenfield Antiques, 10 Greenfield Ave.
San Bernardino	Crafts, Quilts & Etc., 390 E. 6th St.
San Diego	Fabriholics, 3205 Midway Dr.
San Francisco	Sonya Lee Barrington, 837 47th Ave.
San Francisco	San Francisco Fabrics, 1715 Polk St.
San Marcos	Calico Station, 727 Center Dr. #117
San Mateo	Calico Barn, 138 2nd. Ave.
Santa Ana	Quilting Possibilities, 2207 S. Grand Ave.
Santa Barbara	B's Country Store, 512 Brinkerhoff Ave.
Santa Rosa	Richman Cotton Co., 529 5th St.
Sky Forest	Sew Fun, 28589 Hwy 18
Summerland	Sally's Alley, PO Box 876
Sunnyvale	Celtic Design Company, 834 W. Remington Dr.
Sutter Creek	Anelie's Sewing Basket, 21 B Eureka
Torrance	Sew Fun, 16908 Prairie Ave.
Truckee	Donna's Stitchery, 10098 Donner Pass Rd.
Truckee	Truckee Fabrics, Crafts, & Quilts, 11429 Donner Pass Rd.
Valencia	Quilted Heart, 24201 Valencia Blvd. #1371
Woodland Hills	The Quilt Emporium, 4918 Topanga Canyon Blvd.
Yucca Valley	Stitchin & Quilting, 57365 29 Palms Highway

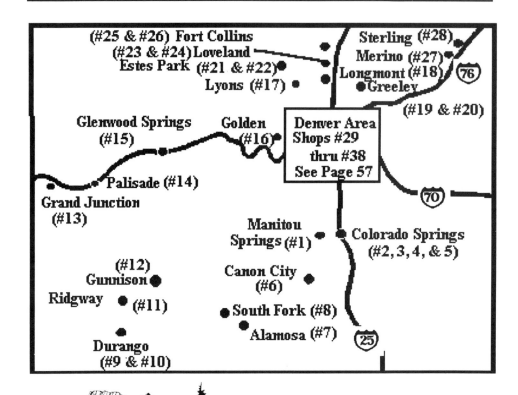

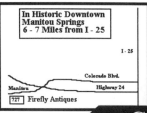

Colorado Springs, CO #4

High Country Quilts

4771 N. Academy Blvd.
(719) 598-1312   80918
Owner: Barbara L. Blutt   Est: 1983

QUILTING SUPPLIES & INSTRUCTIONS
Large assortment of cotton Fabrics, Books, Patterns, and Notions.

Mon - Fri 10 - 5:30
Saturday   10 - 5
Sunday   1 - 4

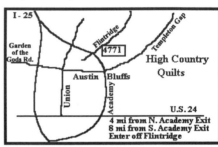

Colorado Springs, CO #5

Crazy For Quilts

Mon - Sat
10 - 6
Sun 12 - 5

2 S. 25th St.   80904
(719) 475-7963
Owners: Pat Joy & Liz Jensen
Est: 1996

WE'RE SELLING FUN!

Brand new in '96
Come in and
join the fun.
Look for us in the
old Victorian
House.
Fabric, Supplies
& Gifts.

Canon City, CO #6

Rocky Mountain Quilt Emporium

Summer
7 days a
week

840 S. 1st St.   81212
(719) 269-1577   1500 sq.ft.
Owner: Susan Ulrich

Fabric, Books,
Notions, Patterns,
& Supplies.
Creative Quilting
Classes.

Alamosa, CO #7

Gray Goose Fashion Fabric

Mon - Sat
9:30 - 5:30

614 Main St.   81101
(719) 589-6982
Owner: Janet Davis   Est: 1985   2000+ Bolts

100% Cottons &
Fashion Fabrics,
notions, quilting
supplies, books,
and patterns.
Daytime, evening
and Saturday
Classes.

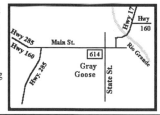

South Fork, CO #8

Fabric Trunk

Tues - Sat
10 - 5

31070 Hwy. 160
P.O. Box 451   81154
(719) 873-0211   Est: 1993
Owner: LaWanna Pair   700 sq.ft

Fabrics, Patterns,
Notions, Classes.
One Day Classes
for those Visiting.
Quilts, Books,
and Gifts.

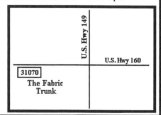

Durango, CO #9

Forget-Me-Not Fabrics

Mon - Sat
9:30 - 5:30
Sun 1 - 5

144 E. 8th St.   81301
(970) 247-0080
Est: 1982   2250 sq.ft.   1500 Bolts
Owners: Carolyn Norton & Keira Linterman

We are a full
fabric store with
heavy emphasis
on quilting,
Stitchery and
speciality yarns.

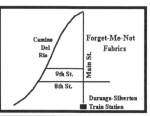

Durango, CO #10

Animas Quilts

Summer
10 - 5:30
Winter
10 - 5
Sun 12 - 4

600 Main Avenue   81301
(970) 247-2582   Est: 1988
Owner: Jackie Robinson 2600 sq.ft.
    "A quilter's   Free Catalog
paradise" on the
western slope of
Colorado. 1000
Bolts of wonderful
cottons! Publisher
of books by Jackie
Robinson & other
great authors.
Plus more

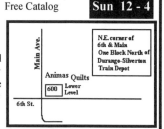

Ridgway, CO #11

Piecemakers Country Store

Winter:
Daily 10 - 5
Summer:
Daily 10 - 6
Wed & Fri til 9

550 Hunter Pkwy.   81432
(970) 626-4348   600 Bolts
  NOW OPEN IN COLORADO !
http://piecemakers.com
Catalog $2
    Classes, fabrics,
handmade quilts and
dolls, original books
and patterns. Times
and Seasons Quilt
Calendars and
Cards. Gifts and
clothing.

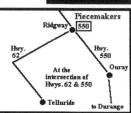

Gunnison, CO #12

E & P Sewing Emporium

135 N. Main St.   81230
(970) 641-0474   (800) 736-4281
Owners: Ellen Harriman & Pat
2000 sq.ft.   Est: 1985   Venturo

Mon - Sat
9 - 5:30
Sun 12 - 4

We are a full-service
sewing store offering
New Home Sewing
Machines, quilting
and sewing classes.
Home of the Rainbow
Quilt Festival in mid-
August.

Grand Junction, CO #13

Hi Fashion **Fabrics, Inc.**

2586 Patterson Rd.   81505
(970) 242-1890   Est: 1965
Owners: Arlene & Jeff Vogel
11,500 sq.ft.   3000 Bolts Cottons
8000 Bolts Overall

**Mon - Sat
9:30 - 5:30**

Huge Selection of
Quilting Cottons,
Books, and Supplies.
Complete Line of
Other Fabrics:
Bridal, Fashion,
Outer Wear, Drapery
& Upholstery.

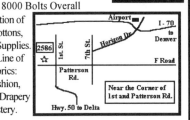

Near the Corner of
1st and Patterson Rd.

Palisade, CO #14

Rocky Mountain Quilts

By Chance or Appointment

3877 Alt. 6 & 24
(970) 464-7294 or (800) 762-5942
Owner: Betsey Telford   Est: 1986

Over 200 antique quilts for sale. We also have
quilt tops, blocks, antique fabric & feed sacks.
Reconstruction of antique quilts, coverlets, and
hooked rugs using vintage fabrics. Special order
anything to do with quilts. All work guaranteed
and insured. Dealers and decorators welcome.
Open by chance or appointment 7 days a week.
Catalog $7 refundable with purchase.

Glenwood Springs, CO #15

Glenwood Sewing Center

822 Grand Avenue   81601
(970) 945-5900
Owners: Bob &
        Sandy Boyd
Est: 1977
5000 sq.ft.

**Mon - Sat
9:30 - 5:30
Sun 12:30 - 4**

1500 Bolts
Treasures for
creative people -
for quilting - for
home decor - for
fashion and active
wear.

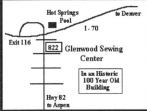

In an Historic
100 Year Old
Building

Golden, CO #16

Rocky Mountain Quilt Museum

**Tues - Sat
10 - 4**

1111 Washington Ave.   80401
(303) 277-0377
Non-Profit Self Supporting Museum
Adm: James J. Prochaska   Est: 1990

The only Quilt
Museum in the Rocky
Mountains. Exhibits
change every two
months. Send
S.A.S.E. for schedule.
Admission $1.

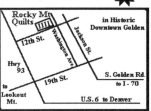

Lyons, CO #17

Berry Patch

**7 days a week
11- 6**

304 1/2 Main   P.O. Box 581
(303) 823-9443   80540
Owner: Terry Goetz
Est: 1994   525 sq.ft.

Area's Finest
Selection of
Ribbons, Trims,
Charms—for Silk
Ribbon
Embroidery,
Ribbon Jewelry,
Crazy Quilt
Embellishment.
Bears & Dolls Too!

Longmont, CO #18

The Patch Works

**Mon- Sat
10 - 5:30
Mon &
Thur til 7
Sun 12 - 4**

700 Ken Pratt Blvd. #101   80501
(303) 772-3002
Owner: Terri Miller   Est: 1988
2000 sq.ft.   800+ Bolts

Friendly
atmosphere, clean
bathroom, lots of
fabric, books,
patterns, notions.
Some 1 day
classes available.

Greeley, CO #19

Country Crafts & Supplies

Mon - Fri 9 - 5:30
Sat 9 - 4:30

903 E. 18th St.   80631
(970) 353-1774
Owners: Jean Baker & Sherry Monteith
Est: 1983   1200 sq.ft.   1000 Bolts

Quilters' Heaven
Wide selection of 100% cotton fabrics, notions, and lots of critter and doll patterns. Mail Orders Welcome.

Map: 8th Ave. | U.S. 85 Bypass | 1st. Ave. | Balsam Ave. | Country Crafts & Supplies | East 18th St. | (U.S. 34 Bus) | 903 | RR

Greeley, CO #20

wild n woolly

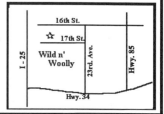

Mon - Fri 9:30 - 5:30
Sat 10 - 5

2308 17th St.   80631
(970) 356-0335
Owner: Ruth Dixon
Est: 1978   1800 Bolts

Needlework Shop Quilting Supplies, Hand Knitting Yarns. Needlepoint Hardanger and Cross Stitch

Map: 16th St. | 17th St. | I-25 | Wild n' Woolly | 23rd. Ave. | Hwy. 85 | Hwy. 34

Estes Park, CO #21

Maggie Mae's Quilts 'N

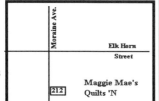

Year 'round 10 - 5
Closed Wed.

212 Moraine Ave. P.O. Box 4857
(970) 586-4257   80517
Owner: Margaret McCormick
Est: 1990   900 sq.ft.

Featuring Patterns by Colorado Designers. Kits - Handmade Wooden Quilt Racks - Fabrics - Christmas Projects & Unique Wearables.

Map: Moraine Ave. | Elk Horn Street | 212 | Maggie Mae's Quilts 'N

Estes Park, CO #22

Mountain Lady Quilt Shop

205 Park Ln., P.O. Box 436
(970) 586-5330   80517
Owners: Connie Westley & Joanne Olson

Open Daily Except Mondays

Everything for Quilters. Classes & Half Day Workshops. American Made Quilts, Custom Quilts, Mail Order. Pfaff Machines.

Map: Rocky Mountain Nat. Park | Estes Park | to Fort Collins | U.S. 34 | Grand Lake | Hwy. 7 | U.S. 36 | Lyons | Fall River Hwy. 66 | Hwy. 7 | U.S. 40 | Longmont

Loveland, CO #23

Gifts from the Heart

Mon - Fri 9 - 6
Sat 9 - 3

1479 West Eisenhower   80538
(970) 669-6820   Est: 1989
Owners: Suzanne Thayne, Carol McKenna & Mae Lewis

We have quilting fabrics and supplies, books, and patterns. Plus great handmade gifts and crafts.

Map: I-25 | 1479 | Gifts from the Heart | West Eisenhower / Hwy 35 | Taft | Approx. 5 miles from I-25

Loveland, CO #24

Treadle Quilts

Tues - Sat 10 - 5

205 E. Eisenhower Blvd.
#7 Valley Center   80538
(970) 635-9064   Est: 1993
Owner: Kim D. Garber   1040 sq.ft.

Machine Quilting Lessons, Fabrics Books, Notions Patterns

Map: Cleveland Ave. | Lincoln Ave. | I-25 | E.15th. | Treadle Quilts (Shop Faces Cleveland) | 205 | E. Eisenhower Blvd. | Hwy 34

The Fig Leaf — Ft. Collins, CO #25

Located in two shops inside "The Square"

The Fig Leaf — 3000 sq.ft. with fabrics, books, patterns, notions and gifts.
The Fig Leaf, Too — Country Furnishings & accessories in 5400 sq.ft.

3500 S. College   80525
(970) 226-3267
Owners: Rob & Laura Shotwell
Est: 1982   8500 sq.ft.

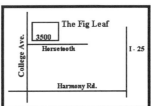

Mon - Fri
10 - 7
Sat 10 - 6
Sun 12 - 5

Ft. Collins, CO #26

Calico "Cat"

Tues - Sat
10 - 5

148 W. Oak   80521
(970) 493-0203
Owner: Lorraine Williams
Est: 1985   2000 sq.ft.   1000 Bolts
'All' the Books
Patterns Galore !
1000 Bolts
(100 Solids)
Beautiful Yarns
Wearable Arts
Quilts, Dolls,
Animals

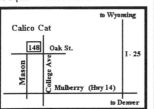

Merino, CO #27

D & J Country Antiques

By Chance
or By
Appointment
Please Call

R.R. #2   P.O. Box 29   80741
(970) 842-5813   Est: 1967
Owners: Dorothy & Jake Leis & Family

Vintage Quilts -
tops - blocks -
Fabric - 30's Feed
sacks - Notions -
Lace - Antique
sewing tools &
machines.

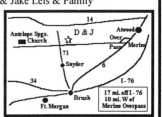

Sterling, CO #28

(970) 522-0146

Quilts-N-Creations   Est: 1987

Mon - Sat 9 - 5:30

201 Ash   P.O. Box 991   80751
Owners: Everett & Dorothy Duncan
Mgr: Leta Propst   Asst. Mgr: Shauna Houser

1000 Bolts of Printed & Solid Cottons
Bridal Headquarters for N.E. Colorado including
Bridal Fabric & Trims. Tuxedo Rentals with over 70
varieties to choose from. Authorized Bernina Dealer.
Custom sewing including crafts, quilts, garments or
Bridal. Custom, Traditional & Heirloom Quilting.

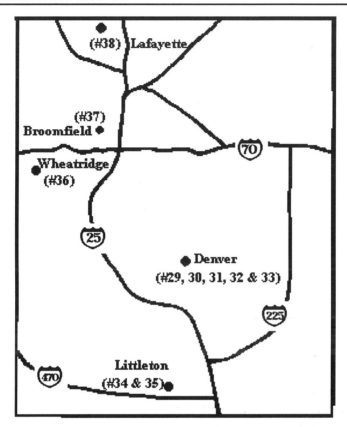

(#38) Lafayette

(#37)
Broomfield

Wheatridge
(#36)

70

25

Denver
(#29, 30, 31, 32 & 33)

225

Littleton
(#34 & 35)

470

DENVER AREA

10 Featured Shops

Denver, CO #29

Quilts in the Attic

Mon - Fri
9:30 - 5:30
Sat.
9:30 - 4:30

1025 South Gaylord St.   80209
(303) 744-8796
Est: 1972   1200 sq.ft.
Owners: Joyce Luff, Marge Hedges,
       Margaret Hill & Brenda Klinowski

Fabric - all 100%
cotton - Books,
Patterns, Batting,
Notions. Ideas
and Friendly
Service.
Classes.

	Gaylord	Vine	University
			Tennessee
1025	Quilts in the Attic		
			Mississippi

Denver, CO #30

The Country Line Antiques & Quilts

Tues - Sat
11 - 5

1067 S. Gaylord St.   80209
(303) 733-1143
Owner: Genna Morrow Est: 1988

Antique Quilts
from $20 to $2000
Also—quilt scraps,
pieces, & "cutters"
Gifts made from
Antique quilts our
specialty.

			Tennessee
The Country Line			
1067			
Gaylord	Vine	University	Mississippi

Denver, CO #31

Denver Fabrics

Mon - Fri
9:30 - 8
Sat 9:30 - 6
Sun 12 - 5

2309 S. Federal   80219
(303) 934-7415

Denver's Largest
Selection of
Fabrics, Buttons,
Notions, and
Patterns.
Also Quilting Books,
Patterns &
Supplies

Map: Evans, 2309 Denver Fabrics, Federal Blvd., Santa Fe, Broadway, I-25, Hampden, Hwy 285

Denver, CO #32

The Creative Needle

Mon - Thur
10 - 6
Fri & Sat
10 - 5

2553 South Colorado Blvd.   80222
(303) 692-8115
Owner: Marge Serck
Est: 1992   2400 sq.ft.

One stop for
quilting, cross-
stitch heirloom
and smocking.
Elna machine
sales and service.
Sister shop in
Littleton.

Map: I-25, Colorado Blvd., Evans, The Creative Needle, In University Hills West 2553, Colorado National Bank, Yale, Hampden

Denver, CO #33

Great American Quilt Factory

Mon - Fri
9:30 - 6
Wed til 8:30
Sat 9:30 - 5
Sun 12 - 5

8970 East Hampden Ave.   80231
(303) 740-6206   Est: 1981
Owners: Nancy Smith & Lynda
2000 sq.ft.   Milligan

Welcome !
Fabric, 2000 Bolts +
Books, Patterns, Notions.
Home of Possibilities—
Publishers of Dream
Spinners, I'll Teach
Myself and Possibilities
Books. Free Catalog

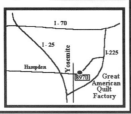
Map: I-70, I-25, Yosemite, I-225, Hampden, 8970 Great American Quilt Factory

Littleton, CO #34

The Creative Needle

Mon - Thur
10 - 6
Fri & Sat
10 - 5
Sun 12 - 4

6905 South Broadway #113
(303) 794-7312   80122
Owner: Marge Serck
Est: 1978 3500 sq.ft. 700 Bolts

One stop for
quilting, cross-
stitch, heirloom
and smocking.
Elna machine
sales and service.
Sister shop in
Denver

Map: Arapahoe Rd., Broadridge Plaza 6905, The Creative Needle, Ridge Rd., Mineral, S. Broadway, I-470

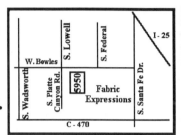
Machine Quilting:
makes that magic
word 'finished'
much more
attainable.

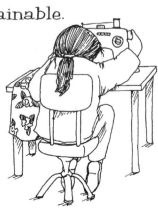

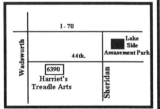

Quilter's Block:

NOT

a condition that keeps one from quilting.

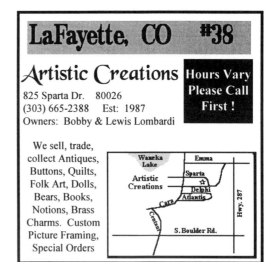

Colorado State Guild:
Colorado Quilting Council, P.O. Box 2056, Arvada, 80001

Colorado Guilds:
Piecemaker Quilt Group, Aurora
Royal Gorge Quilt Con., 1402 1/2 Sherman Ave., Canon City, 81212
Piecing Partners, 1111 Martin Dr., Colorado Springs 80925
Colorado Sprgs Quilt Guild, P.O. Box 8069, Colorado Sprgs, 80907
African American Quilters and Collectors Guild, Denver
La Plata Quilter's Guild, P.O. Box 2355, Durango, 81302
Arapahoe County Quilters, P.O. Box 5357, Englewood, 80155
Estes Valley Quilt Guild, P.O. Box 3931, Estes Park, 80517
Alpine Quilters, Genesee
Colorado West Quilt Guild, 1320 Houston Ave., Grand Junction
Rocky Mt. Wa Shonaji, Littleton
Front Range Cont. Quilters, 7133 Gold Nugget Dr., Longmont, 80503
San Luis Valley Quilt Guild, Monte Vista Coop, Monte Vista, 81144
Pride City Quilt Guild, 60 Portero Dr., Pueblo, 81005
Columbine Quilters, Wheat Ridge

Other Shops in Colorado:

Aspen	Katie Ingham Antique Quilts, Box 706
Aurora	Evans Crafts, 2353 S. Sahavana
Boulder	Elfriede's Fine Fabrics, Arapahoe Village Shp. Ctr.
Buena Vista	Bev's Stitchery, 202 Tabor St. Box 1773
Colorado Springs	Mill Outlet Fabric Shop, 2906 N. Prospect
Estes Park	Traditions Remembered, 800 B Moraine Ave.
Fort Collins	Calico Country, 4604 Terry Lake Rd.
Fort Morgan	Inspirations, 724 W. Railroad
Fort Morgan	Quilting Corner, 328 Main
Glenwood Springs	Tivo Rivers Textiles, 0136 County Rd. 130
Golden	Leman Publications Quilt Gallery, 741 Corporate
Grand Junction	Quilt Junction & Gallery 412, 412 Main
Leadville	Mountain Top Quilts, 129 E. Seventh St.
Longmont	Bernina Sewing Center, 510 4th Ave.
Monte Vista	Quilting Hoop, 206 Adams
Monte Vista	Shades, Quilts, & Etc, 129 Adams
Ouray	The Quilt Cellar, P.O. Box 1834
Parker	Chameleons Three, 8916 Mad River Rd.
Sedalia	Weedpatch Loveables, 3567 N. Winnebago Dr.
Steamboat Springs	Sew What, 437 Oak
Sterling	Sew Together, 320 N. 4th
Wheat Ridge	B & R's Keepers Cove, 7230 W. 38th Ave.

9 Featured Shops

CONNECTICUT

Darien, CT #1

Appalachian House

**Mon - Sat
10 - 5**

1010 Boston Post Rd.   06820
(203) 655-7885   Est: 1973
6 Rooms in a picturesque House

A non-profit Craft Shop. We provide a Market Place for Mountain Crafts People Dependent on their skill and Talent for their Livelihood.

Directions from I-95 North--
Take exit 11--Turn Left--
Store is on the Right 1/4th mile on Rt.1
Directions from I-95 South--
Take Exit 11--Turn Right--
Store is on the right after 1st Traffic Light.

Fairfield, CT #2

Contemporary Quilting

**Mon - Sat
10 - 5**

173 Post Road   06430
(203) 259-3564   Est: 1984
Owner: Florence Osborne   900 sq.ft.   2400 Bolts

Over 2000 bolts 100% cotton and all quilting supplies. Inquire about mail order fabric club. "Fabrics of the Month"

Please Call for directions.

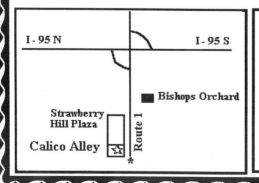

Portland, CT #4

Patches & Patchwork

Tues - Fri
10 - 5
Sat 10 - 3

216 Main   06480
(860) 342-4567   Est: 1980
Owner: Jane Wilk Sterry   1200 sq.ft.

We carry the unusual in fabrics. Latest books, patterns and notions. Classes. Antique quilt repair! Commission quilts

Portland, CT #5

Carolyn's Quilting Bee

73 Ames Hollow Rd.   06480
(860) 342-1949
Owner: Carolyn Johnson
Est: 1980

By Appointment

Located in the Blacksmith Shop of an 18th Century Farm. Visitors are always welcome.

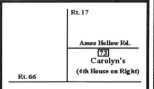

Colchester Mill Fabrics

(800) 253-1937   Est: 1973   10,000 sq.ft.   (860) 537-2004
51 Broadway (Rt. 85)   06415
Owner: Carolyn Chyinski   Mgr. Cheryl Marchenkoff

Colchester, CT #6

Full line textile outlet specializing in home dec. & quilting. Over 3000 cotton prints & solids in stock. Battings, Books, Notions & Needlework.

Mon - Fri
9:30 - 5:30
Thur til 8
Sat & Sun
10 - 5

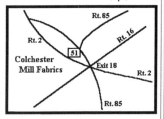

Morris, CT #7

The Fabric Barn

Wed - Sun
10 - 5

11 Watertown Rd.   (Rt. 63)
(860) 567-5823   06763
Owner: Marjorie Munson
Est: 1978   800 sq.ft.

Full stock of calicos and quilting supplies. Specializing in remnants and closeouts. Call for info on classes. Open all year.

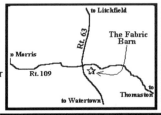

Southbury, CT #8

Dagmar's Fabrics

Mon - Sat
9:30 - 6
Thur til 8

1481-6 Southford Rd.   (Route 67)
(203) 262-1206   06488
Owner: Dagmar Ferguson

Area's largest selection of quilting books, patterns, & supplies. Knowledgeable, Friendly Staff, Quality Fabrics - over 3000 bolts. Classes. Gift Cert.

Est: 1989
2500+ sq.ft.

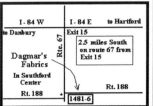

⊤HE QUILT SHOP

Danbury, CT   #9

16 Padanaram Rd.
Rt. 37   06811
(203) 743-0543
Fax #: (203) 797-0936
Owner: Ginny Murphy
Est: 1994   1500 sq.ft.

Over 1000 Bolts of Fabulous 100% Cotton Fabric.
Area's Authorized Bernina Dealer
Featuring Complete Line of Machines & Accessories.
Plus a Tremendous Selection of Books & Classes.

FOR ALL YOUR QUILTING SUPPLIES

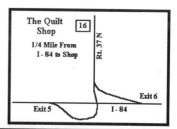

The Quilt Shop
1/4 Mile From I - 84 to Shop
Rt. 37 N
Exit 6
Exit 5   I - 84

Mon - Sat   9 - 5
Thur til 8

Connecticut Guilds:
Clamshell Quilt Guild, P.O. Box 3, Hartford, 06385
The Greater Hartford Quilt Guild, P.O. Box 310213, Newington, 06131
Thames River Quilters, New London, 06320
Trumbull Piecemakers, 34 St. Mary's Lane, Norwalk, 06851
Heart of the Valley, Portland, 06480

Other Shops in Connecticut:
Avon	Country at Heart, P.O. Box 992, 35 Old Avon Village
Bethel	J. H. Homestead, 79 Putnam Park Rd.
Cheshire	Calico Etc., 116 Elm
Clinton	J & N Fabrics, 55 W. Main St.
Danielson	P/R Fabrics - Quilt Shop, Rt. 6
Glastonbury	Close to Home, 2717 Main
Old Saybrook	Quilters Edge, 455 Boston Post Rd.
Stamford	Gingham Dog & Calico Cat, 219 Bedford St.
Torrington	Gingham Rocker, 84 Main
Torrington	Eleanor's Fabrics, 29 Water St.
Woodbury	Country Repeats, Box 869, 107 Main St. N.

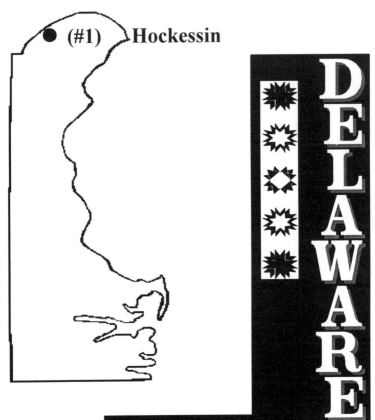

● (#1) Hockessin

DELAWARE

1 Featured Shop

Other Shop in Delaware:
Middletown   Needles & Hoops, Hwy 71 & 301, Summitville Rd.

Traditions Past .... Future Heirlooms

Notions Patterns

Quilt Essentials

Books Classes

Fabric

Hockessin, DE   #1

1304 Old Lancaster Pike #D   19707
(302) 234-9926   Owner: Bonita Kirchart
Opened: 1992   1800 sq.ft.

A complete Quilt Shop with over 3000 bolts of
quilting fabric including calicos, homespuns,
flannels, denims, and wools. We specialize in
the unusual from such makers as Hoffman, RJR,
South Sea and Momen House to name just a few.
Our subspecialty is Sewn Dolls including a
complete selection of Bear making supplies:
Synthetic Furs and Mohairs, joint kits and
other hard to find items.

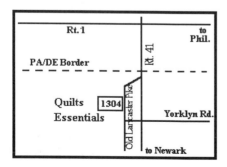

**Mon - Sat
10 - 4:30
Wed & Thur til 8**

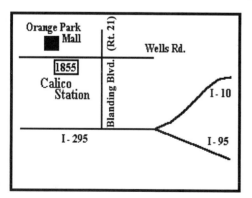

Saint Augustine, FL #2

Material Things

Mon 10 -8
Tues - Fri
10 - 5
Sat 10 - 4

77 Saragossa St.   32084
(904) 829-3778   Est: 1991
Owner: Joyce Snyder
1575 sq.ft.

Most beautiful selection of 100% cottons in the area. Over 1,000 bolts. Wide variety of books, patterns, notions and classes.

Cordova St.
Orange St.
Sevilla St.
Saragossa St.
Riberia St.
Herbie
Wiles Ins.
Material Things
77 Quilt Shop
Rt. 16
U.S.1
Rick's Muffler
Rt. 207
I - 95

Ormond Beach, FL #3

Grammy's Quilt Shoppe

Mon - Sat
9:30 - 4

489 S. Yonge Street U.S. # 1
(904) 673-5484   32174
Owner: Mary K. Tate
Est: 1981   1800 sq.ft.

Fabrics -- Notions
Books -- Patterns
Gifts -- Classes
Everything for
the Quilter !

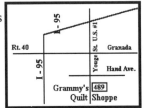

I - 95
Rt. 40
Yonge St. U.S. #1
Granada
Hand Ave.
Grammy's 489 Quilt Shoppe

South Daytona, FL #4

Mon - Fri 9:30 - 4:30
Thurs til 7:30
Sat 9:30 - 3

Pelican Needlework Shoppe

One stop for quilting, needlepoint & silk ribbon embroidery. 1500 Bolts of 100% Cotton.   Classes.   Notions & Books!
Home of the original "Grannie Suzannie".
Paper foundation patterns.
Catalogue of patterns - $1.00
Complete Kits available. Send S.A.S.E. for current list.
Mail Orders Welcome on All our Stock ! !

905 Big Tree Road 32119
(Palm Grove Plaza)
(904) 761-8879
Owner: Suzy Komara
Est: 1979   1600 sq.ft.

S. Daytona Exit
Beville
Clyde
Morris
Nova
U.S. #1
I - 95
Big Tree Rd.
905
Pelican Needlework

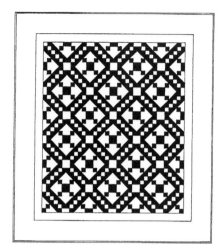

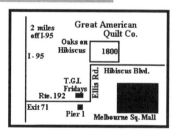

Ft. Pierce, FL #7

Tomorrow's Heirlooms

Mon & Wed - Sat 9 - 5

1840 S. King's Hwy.   34945
(407) 461-9510
Owners: Theresa & Earle Field
500 Bolts

100% Cottons
Quilting Patterns
Quilting Supplies
Instruction Books
Pine Furniture
Sculptured Crafts
Wooden Crafts
& Much More

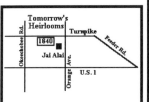

Jupiter, FL #8

Quilters' Choice

Mon - Fri 10 - 5 Sat 10 - 4

1695 West Indiantown Rd.
(407) 747-0525   33458
Owner: Vivian Irwin   1500 sq.ft.
1000 bolts of   Est: 1992
100% cotton.
Complete
selection of
Notions, Books &
Patterns.
Authorized
Bernina Dealer.
Great classes and
friendly service.

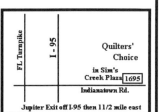

Quilters Marketplace

Est: 1987
950 sq.ft
Owner: Marilyn Dorwart

524 E. Atlantic Avenue 33483

(407) 243-3820

Delray Beach, FL #9

Mon - Sat 10 - 5

1200 bolts of 100% cotton including a beautiful
array of tropical and Bali fabrics. Complete Notion
Dept. Many patterns and a large selection of books.
Gifts and a Friendly Staff.

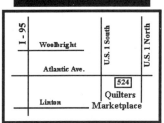

Key Largo, FL #10

The Cotton Shoppe

Wed - Fri 10 - 2 Or By Appt.

P.O. Box 3168 MM99 U.S. # 1
(800) 856-4923   33037
(305) 453-0789   Est: 1992

Hoffman, RJR,
ME Hopkins and
more! WE DO
MAIL-ORDER !
Send $6 for
swatches or $20
to join our
Fabric Club.

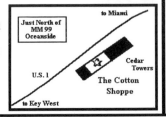

Coral Springs, FL #11

Country Stitches

Mon - Sat 10 - 5 Sun 12 - 4

11471 W. Sample Road   33065
(305) 755-2411
Owner: Gayle Boshek
Est: 1982   3200 sq.ft.

**Your one
stop quilting
shoppe.**
Over 4000 bolts
of fabric and
patterns !
You'll be glad
you came !

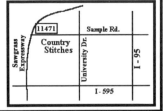

Royal Palm Beach, FL #12

Suzanne's
QUILT SHOP Inc.

Est: 1988

1112 Royal Palm Beach Blvd. 33411
(407) 798-0934
Owner: Suzanne Leimer

Monday - Saturday
10 - 5:30
Evenings During Classes

2,000 Bolts of 100% Cotton Fabrics
Books and Patterns for Quilts,
Clothing, and Dolls
Notions, Batting, Stencils
Crazy Quilt Embellishments
Silk Ribbon Embroidery
Mohair Bear Kits
Classes and Private Lessons,
Quilt Planning

Map: Okechobee Blvd. / 1112 / Royal Palm Beach Blvd. / S.R. 7 / 441 / Suzanne's Quilt Shop / Turnpike / Military Trail / I - 95 / Southern Blvd. / Lake Worth Rd.

Sebring, FL #13

Crafty Quilters

Tues - Fri
10 - 5
Sat 10 - 4

4920 U.S. 27 South   33870
(941) 382-4422
Owners: Dee Dee Bedard &
Est: 1990   Lois Ucciferri

For all your
Quilting Needs.
Only Brazilian
Dealer in Area.
Gift items &
Classes Available.

Map: Avon Park / Sebring / Lake Shore Mall / U.S.27 / 4920 Crafty Quilters / Lake Placid

Kissimmee, FL #14

Queen Ann's Lace

Mon - Fri
10 - 6
Tues til 9
Sat 10 - 5

715 East Vine Street   34744
(407) 846-7998
Owners: Ginny & Tom King
Est: 1991   1400 sq.ft.

3500 Bolts of
100% Cotton plus
supplies, notions,
& patterns--
Everything
you'll need.
Also many other
craft supplies.

Map: to Orlando / Hwy 107 - 92/441 / Queen Ann's Lace in Rainbow Plaza / 715 / to Disney / Hwy.192 / Vine St. / to St.Cloud / Downtown Kissimmee

YESTERDAY'S QUILTS INC.
ORLANDO, FLORIDA

Fabric ❤ *Books*
Patterns ❤ *Notions*
Supplies

Half & Full Day Quilt Classes
for the Vacationing Quilter

For information send SASE to:

Yesterday's Quilts Inc.
7036 International Drive
Orlando, Florida 32819

Telephone (407) 354-0107

#15

Orlando, FL   #16

Patchwork Cottage Quilt Shop

2413 Edgewater Dr.   32804
(407) 872-3170
Owner: Rae Harper

**Mon - Fri
9:30 - 5
Sat 9:30 - 3**

100% Cottons,
Quilting
Supplies,
Books, &
Patterns.
**Good Times to
be had here!**

Scissors:
cutting tool,
which never seems
to be where
        you left it.

Lakeland, FL   #17

Fabric Warehouse

3032 North Florida Ave.   33805
(941) 680-1325
Owner: Becky Garland & Doty
Est: 1977   Gumtow

**Mon - Sat
10 - 5:30**

Hoffman
Alex. Henry
Concord
Peter Pan, etc.
90" Sheeting
in several
colors

Lakeland, FL   #18

Granny's Trunk

4644 Cleveland Heights Blvd.
(941) 646-0074   33813
Owner: Jean Keene
Est: 1981   700 sq.ft.

**Mon & Tues
10 - 6
Wed - Sat
10 - 5**

Over 2,000 bolts
of quilting fabrics,
classes, gifts.
Better dress and
wearable art
fabrics and trims.
Many models on
display.

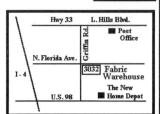

AK Sew & Serge
1602 6th Street SE
Winter Haven FL
(941) 299-3080
1-800-299-8096

call for directions
just 25 minutes off I-4
near Cypress Gardens
Mon-Fri 9am to 8pm
Sat 9am to 5:30pm
Family Owned and Operated

Florida's Premier Sewing Center

Over 4000 bolts, 100% cottons, heirloom fabrics, fashion and designer fabrics under one roof. Books, notions, patterns and supplies. Call or stop in for our schedule of classes and special events. Authorized dealer for Viking, White, Elna, New Home, Babylock, and Esante. Your one stop source for all of your sewing needs.

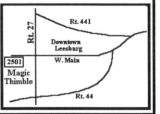

Dade City, FL   #23

Pioneer Florida Museum Association

Tues - Sat
1 - 5
Sun 2 - 5

15602 Pioneer Museum Rd.
(904) 567-0262   33526
Owned: Pioneer Florida Museum Assoc.
Est: 1975

Handmade items on consignment. Wooden toys & games, T-shirts, cups, cookbooks, books, jelly, candy, postcards, etc.

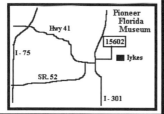

Dade City, FL   #24

Quilts Etc.

Mon - Sat
10 - 5

13230 South Hwy. 301   33525
(904) 567-0444
Owners: Suzanne & Bill Stewart
Est: 1988   4000 sq.ft.   1500 Bolts

Fabric, Quilting Supplies, Books, Patterns. Custom Machine Quilting & Quilts for Sale.

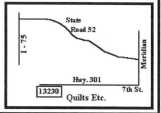

Tampa, FL   #25

Julia's Sewing Center

Tues - Sat
9 - 5

14930 N. Florida Ave.   33613
(813) 961-7543   (800) 403-5674
Owner: Julia Hughes
Est: 1978   2800 sq.ft.   1500 Bolts

Complete line of classes & supplies for quilting, heirloom sewing, and English smocking. Mail order available.

Dunedin, FL   #26

941 Broadway (Alt 19) 34698
(813) 733-8572   Est: 1982
Owner: M. Facsina   6900 sq.ft.

Rainbow's End

Over 5000 Bolts of Cotton Fabric.
Complete line of Notions. Over 1000
Books and Patterns. Crazy Quilting,
Beadwork & Silk Ribbon Embroidery.

Mon - Sat 10 - 5
Mon & Wed til 8

St. Petersburg FL #27

Sewing Circle Fabrics

408 33rd. Avenue N.
(813) 823-7391   33704
Owner: Family Owned &
        Operated
Est: 1961   4500 sq.ft.

**Mon & Tues
9 - 8
Wed - Sat
9 - 5**

200 Quilts on display, both new and antique.

*Home of the
Continuous Quilt Show*

Quilting Supplies

*New Home
Sewing
Machines*

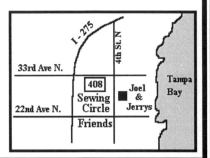

Country Quilts "N" Bears, Inc

1810 Drew Street   34625

(813) 461-4171   Est: 1986   600 sq.ft.

Owne   rs:

Clearwater, FL   #28

Country Store with a Christian Heart

Mon - Fri 9 - 5
Tues til 9
Sat 9 - 4

Country Quilts "N" Bears
1810 Front Porch Shopping Center
Drew
◄ 3/4 mile west
Hercules
Belcher
U.S. 19
Rt. 60 (Gulf to Bay)

A fully stocked quilt shop —
1400 bolts of cotton fabrics.
Large selection of
homespuns.
Friendly Service.
Classes in quilting, country clothing, soft
sculptured dolls & miniature bears.
Beginner bears, advanced and limited
edition Teddy Bear classes
taught by Francy Gordon.
Mohair, luxury plush acrylic fur, glass eyes,
joints and Bear accessories available.

Gainesville, Fl #29

My Favorite Quilt Shop

M, T, W, F 10 - 5:30
Th 12 - 8:30
Sat 10 - 4

4113 NW 13th St.   32609
(352) 372-4720 Fax: (352) 372-1222
Owner: Mary E. Derry Est: 1995
2500 sq.ft.   E:Mail MaryEDerry@msn.com

North Central Florida's Newest and finest Quilt Shop.
E-Z on-off I - 75 Take Exit #77.
WE LOVE QUILTERS

Tallahassee, FL #30

A Stitch in Time, Inc.

Mon - Sat 10 - 6

3425 Thomasville Rd.   32308
(904) 894-3030   Carriage Shp. Ctr.
Owners: Shirley & Ken Roux
Est: 1992   2000 sq.ft.

We offer a wide selection of fabrics including Hoffman, RJR, & Debbie Mumm. Silk Ribbon embroidery supplies, smocking, needlepoint & Cross Stitch.

Florida Guilds:
West Pasco Quilt Guild, 12232 Magnolia Grove Lane, 34667
Gold Coast Quilter's Guild, P.O. Box 710, Boca Raton, 33429
Manatee Patchworkers, P.O. Box 356, Bradenton, 34206
Central Florida Quilter's Guild, Inc., P.O. Box 180116, Casselberry, 32718
Creative Quilters of Citrus County, 7165 W. Riverbend Rd., Dunellen, 34433
Palm Patches Quilt Guild, P.O. Box 07345, Ft. Myers, 33919
Tree City Quilters Guild, Inc., PO Box 140-698, Gainesville, 32614
Citrus Friendship Quilters, 3384 S. Diamond Ave., Inverness, 34452
Florida Keys Quilters, PO Box 1251, Key Largo, 33037
Ocean Waves Quilters, 6421 S. Mitchell Manor Cir., Miama, 33156
Pelican Piecemakers, 2636 Sunset Dr., New Smyrna Beach, 32168
Flying Needles, Niceville
Country Road Quilters, P.O. Box 2042, Ocala, 32670
Stitch Witches, 9020 2-C S.W. 93rd. Lane, Ocala, 34481
Honeybee Quilters Guild, P.O. Box 0003, Orange Park, 32067
First Coast Quilters Guild, Orange Park
Cabin Fever Quilter's Guild, 1318 Sweet Briar Rd., Orlando, 32802
Country Stitchers, 2043 Sue Harbor Cove, Orlando, 32750
Racing Fingers Quilt Guild, P.O. Box 730544, Ormond Beach, 32173
Largo Cracker Quilters, Palm Harbor
Saint Andrews Bay Quilters Guild, P.O. Box 16225, Panama City, 32406
Pensacola Quilter's Guild, P.O. Box 16098, Pensacola, 32507
Pine Needles Quilters, P.O. Box 535, Silver Springs, 32688
Ocean Waves Quilt Guild, P.O. Box 43-1673, South Miami, 33243
Possum Creek Quilters, P.O. Box 430, Sparr, 32091
St. Augustine Piecemakers, St. Augustine
Quilters Unlimited of Tallahassee, P.O. Box 4324, Tallahassee, 32315
Quilters' Workshop of Tampa Bay, 12717 Trowbridge Ln, Tampa, 33624

Other Shops in Florida:

Auburndale	Quilting Etc., 1113 U.S. Hwy 92W
Cocoa	Dawn's Fabric Cottage, 959 N. Cocoa Blvd. #2
Crestview	Granny's Attic, 396 S. Main St.
Ellenton	Country Charm Quilts, 2418 Hwy. 301
Gulf Breeze	Fabric Yarn & Sew Much More, 2823 Gulf Breeze
Hollywood	Ben Raymond Fabrics, 2050 Hollywood Blvd.
Jacksonville	Calico Corners, 4725 San Jose Blvd.
Key West	Key West Hand Print Fabrics, 201 Simonton St.
Lakeland	The Yarn Place, 612 N. Ingraham Ave.
Miami	Craft World, 9003 S.W. 107th Ave.
Miami	Quilt Scene, 9505 S. Dixie Highway
Mossy Head	Calico Country Fabrics, P.O. Box 1280
New Smyrna Beach	Brian's, 1421 S. Dixie Freeway
Ocala	Fabric Plus, 2391 S.W. College Rd.
Orange Park	Country Crossroads, 799-3 Blanding Blvd.
Orlando	Gingersnap Station Limited, 2401 Edgewater Dr.
Palm City	Mary Jo's Needles & Pins, 3063 S.W. Martin Downs
Palm Harbor	Classic Cloth, 34930 U.S. Highway 19 N.
Pembroke Pines	The Quilt Shop, 7161 Pembroke Rd.
Pensacola	The Thread & Needle Crossing, 1805 Creighton
Port Charlotte	Charlotte County Sewing Ctr, 3280 Tamiami Trail
Rockledge	Marilyn's Fabrics & Bernina, 1715 Golfview Dr.
Sanford	Country Courtyard, 222 E. First St.
Sarasota	Classic Cloth II, 3985 Cattleman
Tampa	Grand Ole Country Store, 8709 40th St. N.
Tampa	Cracker House, 4121 Macdill Ave. S.
Tampa	Quilted Sampler, 4109 S. MacDill Ave.
Tampa	Necchi Singer Sewing Centers, 104 Fletcher Ave. E.
Venice	Deborah's Quilt Basket, 327 W. Venice Ave.

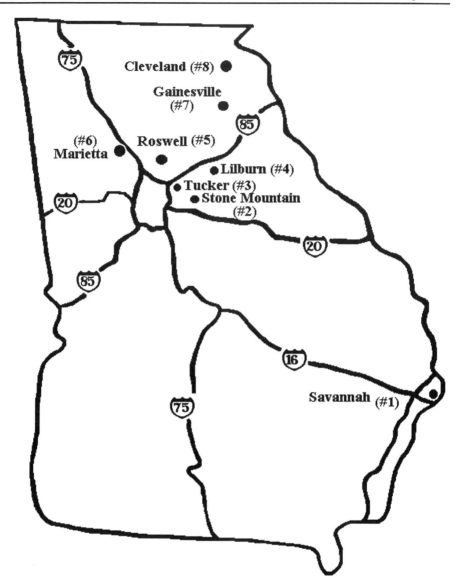

Cleveland (#8)

Gainesville (#7)

(#6) Marietta

Roswell (#5)

Lilburn (#4)

Tucker (#3)

Stone Mountain (#2)

Savannah (#1)

GEORGIA

8 Featured Shops

Savannah, GA #1

Colonial Quilts
"The Quilt Store"

11710 A Largo Dr.
(912) 925-0055   1000 Bolts

Located in historic
Savannah, we offer
a wide array of
fabric, notions,
classes, books and
patterns for quilting,
cross-stitch, French
sewing, smocking,
etc. Complete Jinny
Beyer palette.

Owner: Marcia
Hammond   2500 sq.ft.

**Mon - Fri
10 - 6
Sat 10 - 4**

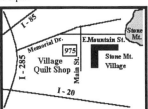

Stone Mountain, GA #2

Village Quilt Shop

975 Main St.   30083
(770) 469-9883
Owner: Joyce P. Selin
Est: 1981   1200 sq.ft.

**Mon - Sat
9 - 5
Thur til 8**

**A "One-stop
Quilt Shop"**
Quilts -- Quilting
Supplies -- Books
Fabrics -- Notions
Class schedule
Available.

Tucker, GA #3

Dream Quilters

2343-A Main Street   30084
(770) 939-8034   Est: 1991
Owners: Pam Cardone & Libby
1988 sq.ft.   1500 Bolts   Carter

**Mon - Fri
10 - 5:30
Thur 12 - 7
Sat 10 - 4**

The latest in
cotton fabrics,
books, patterns &
notions.
**A nice place
to visit.**

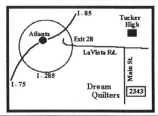

Quilting Adventures, Inc.

Est: 1994   **Lilburn, GA #4**

700 Beaver Ruin Rd.   30247   (770) 931-2727
Owners:
Gail Reed & Bonnie Kivett

**Tons of Fabric, Classes, Notions,
Books & Patterns. Senior
Discounts! In store Machine Use.
We Love Beginners!
15% discount with this book.**

**Mon - Thur
10 - 6
Fri & Sat
10 - 5
Sun 1:30 - 5**

**1500 sq.ft.
800 Bolts**

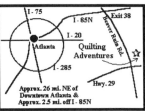

Calico Quilter

14 Elizabeth Way   30075
(770) 998-2446   Est: 1983   2000 sq.ft.
Owners: Ellen Jennings
**   and Elizabeth van den Heuvel**

Roswell, GA   #5

In addition to the fabrics & notions you would
expect to find in a traditional quilt store, we also
carry a wide selection of high quality & specialty
threads. We have ribbons including silk ribbon
& French wire edged ribbon; buttons, patterns &
notions for quilted clothing; patterns & supplies
for dollmakers; and an assortment of unusual and
beautiful books.

Mon
9:30 - 9
Tues - Sat
9:30 - 5

Marietta, GA   #6

Tiny STITCHES

Mon - Sat
9:30 - 5:30

2520 E. Piedmont Rd.
(770) 565-1113   30062
                                    Est: 1992

Just off I - 75,
Tiny Stitches is a
convenient stop
for traveling
quilters. Over
2000 bolts of
fabric and
hundreds of
books and
patterns.

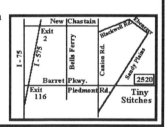

Gainesville, GA   #7

Quilted Hearts Ltd.

Mon - Sat
10 - 5

2415 G Old Cornelia Hwy.   30507
(770) 536-3959   Est: 1991   2500 sq.ft.
                        Owners: Leslie Peck &
Located North of   Sally Babcock
Atlanta, we offer
over 2000 Bolts
of 100% cotton
fabrics, books,
patterns, notions,
classes &
INSPIRATION

BERNINA

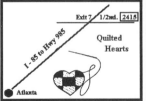

Cleveland, GA   #8

The Calico Barn

Everyday
10 - 6

Rte. 384, 3599 Duncan Bridge Rd.
(706) 865-9029   30528
Owners: Grace Giebert &
               Jacqueline Stoner   Est. 1992

Over 1500 Bolts
of Designer
Fabrics, Patterns,
Books, Stencils,
and Quilting
Supplies.

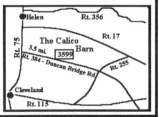

Notes

Georgia Guilds:

Gala Quilters Guild, 1816 St. Elmo Dr., Columbus, 31901
Hall County Guild, 5845 Hidden Cove Rd., Gainesville, 30504
N. Georgia Quilt Council, 7292 Cardif Place, Jonesboro, 30236
East Cobb Quilter's Guild, P.O. Box 71561, Marietta, 30007
Calico Stitchers, P.O. Box 13414, Savannah, 31416
Ogeechee Quilters, Savannah
Yellow Daisy Quilters, Box 1772, Stone Mountain, 30086

Other Shops in Georgia:

Atlanta	Lewis Textile Co., 912 Huff Rd. NW
Augusta	Sewing Gallery, 362 Fury's Ferry Rd. #D
Blue Ridge	The Cotton Patch, Inc., 965 Main St.
Columbus	Southern Sewing Center, 2507 Manchester Expy.
Evans	Strictly Country Inc., 4313 Washington Rd.
Fort Oglethorpe	Bentley's Fabrics, 1943 Old Lafayette Rd.
Lumpkin	Westville Historical Handicrafts, PO Box 1850
Macon	Calico & Lace, 7440 Thomaston Rd.
Savannah	Stitch 'N Originals, 305 W. St. Julian
St. Simons Island	Stepping Stones Quilts, 301 Skylane Rd.
St. Simons Island	Stitch N. Originals, 132 Retreat Village

Kailua (#4)

Hawaiian Guild: Hawaii Quilt Guild, 172 Kaopua Loop, Mililani, 96789

(#2) (#3)
Honolulu Lahaina

(#1)
Lihue

HAWAII

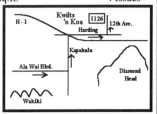

4 Featured Shops

Lihue, Kauai, HI #1

Kapaia Stitchery

Mon - Sat 9 - 5

P.O. Box 1327   96766
3-3561 Kuhio Hwy.

(808) 245-2281
Est: 1973   Visa, MC, Discover

We Love Quilting !
Send $24 (postage included) for our original "pineapple" Hawaiian Quilting Pillow Kit—Dk. Green/Natural Hand Applique 18" x 18"

5 minutes from the Airport
Airport Hwy. 51
Hwy. 51
570
Wilcox Hospital
Hwy 56   Hwy. 56
Kuhio Hwy.
3-3561 Kapaia Stitchery

Honolulu, HI #2

Kwilts 'n Koa

**Mon - Fri 10 - 6
Sat 10 - 4**

1126 12th Avenue   96816
(808) 735-2300 Fax: (808) 737-2300
Orders (800) 787-1855
Owners: Kathy Tsark & Tsarkie Catalog $10yr.
Est: 1991   650 sq.ft.   4 Issues
100+ bolts

Hawaiian quilting classes, patterns, kits / supplies; Hawaiian gifts & Koa wood.

Kwilts   1126
H-1   'n Koa   12th Ave.
Harding
Kapahulu
Ala Wai Blvd.   Diamond Head
Wakiki

Lahaina, Maui, HI #3

Quilter's Corner

Mon - Fri 10 - 5

283 Wili Ko Place   P.O. Box 1562
(808) 661-0944   96767   Est: 1992
Owners: Kathy & Larry Dunlap   Catalog $3

Hawaii's Largest selection of Hawaiian Quilt Patterns and Finished Gift Items. Over 150 Tropical Print Fabrics. Maui's largest selection of Needlepoint & Counted Cross-stitch.

Other Shops in Hawaii:
Hilo	Helen's Fabric Shoppe, 199 Kilauea Ave.
Hilo	Dragon Mama, 266 Kamehameha Ave.
Honolulu	Quilts Hawaii, 2338 S. King
Honolulu	Creative Fibers, 3022 Hinano St.
Honolulu	The Calico Cat, 1223 Koko Head Ave.
Honolulu	Kona Bay Fabrics, 3043 Lopeka Pl.
Honolulu	Needlepoint Etc., 2863 Kihei Place
Honolulu	Kaimuki Dry Goods, 1144 10th Ave.
Honolulu	Musashiya1, 450 Ala Moana Blvd.
Honolulu	Mynah Bird Fabrics, 4715 B Kahala Ave.
Kailua	Hawaiian Quilt Connection, PO Box 158
Kailua-Kona	Kona Kapa, PO Box 391121
Kamuela	Upcountry Quilters, P.O. Box 2631
Kihei	The Island, 1178 Uluniu Rd.
Lahaina	Ka Honu Gift Gallery, 277 Wili Ko Pl.
Lahaina	Rhonda's Quilts, 210 Nohea Kai #111

Elizabeth's Fancy
HAWAIIAN QUILT & GIFT GALLERY

Elizabeth's Fancy is one of those one-of-a-kind Oahu shops on the "visitors must see" list of local residents and a vacation destination of first time and repeat visitors. Oahu born owner, Elizabeth Root, is a well known designer - her Hawaiian quilt designs are in private collections around the world. She is a popular author of Hawaiian quilt pattern and Hawaiian counted cross stitch chart books as well as the designer/creator of hundreds of hand quilted items, kits and gift items - all are made to her requirements of uncompromising quality.

Each quilted item portrays the finest, competition quality, needlework offered in Hawaii. Hundreds of items are in stock and custom orders are welcomed with workmanship guaranteed.

Elizabeth's Fancy is a mixture of Elizabeth's own 300+ private label products which bear her original Hawaiian quilt designs as well as selected gifts from island artists, small manufacturer's and a delightful array of things she, quite simply, fancies.

On your next trip to Hawaii, we hope you'll put us on your "must see" list......we even have a comfortable chair for you know who...

♥ CHRISTMAS STOCKINGS ♥ 18" PILLOW COVERS ♥ 26" EURO SHAMS ♥ BABY QUILTS ♥ WALL HANGINGS ♥ BED QUILTS ♥ PILLOW, WALL HANGING & BED QUILT KITS ♥ PATTERN BOOKS ♥ COUNTED CROSS STITCH BOOKS ♥ EMBOSSED CARDS ♥ GIFT WRAP ♥ BEVERAGE NAPKINS ♥ JEWELRY ♥ BOOKMARKS ♥ CHRISTMAS ORNAMENTS ♥ MUGS ♥ PRESERVES ♥ SAUCES ♥ TEA ♥ COFFEE ♥ TEE SHIRTS & TEE NIGHT SHIRTS ♥ APRONS ♥ TRIVETS ♥ HOT PADS ♥ WINE BAGS ♥ MOUSEPADS ♥ AND NEW ITEMS ALWAYS IN THE WORKS... ♥

767B Kailua Road, Kailua, Oahu, HI 96734
OPEN Tuesday - Saturday 10am - 4pm
♥ (808) 262-7513 ♥

For more information, (wholesale inquiries welcome) please send $3 to: PO Box 1167, Kailua, HI 96734

From Honolulu take Pali Hwy (61) which becomes Kailua Rd at Castle Hospital (Junction 61/72). Continue to first stop light of Kailua town - cross street Hamakua - continue on Kailua Rd to end of two story white building on right side, turn into their parking lot - you'll be facing Elizabeth's Fancy.
Bus 56 & 57 from Ala Moana Shopping Center stops at "Bus"

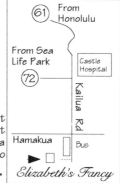

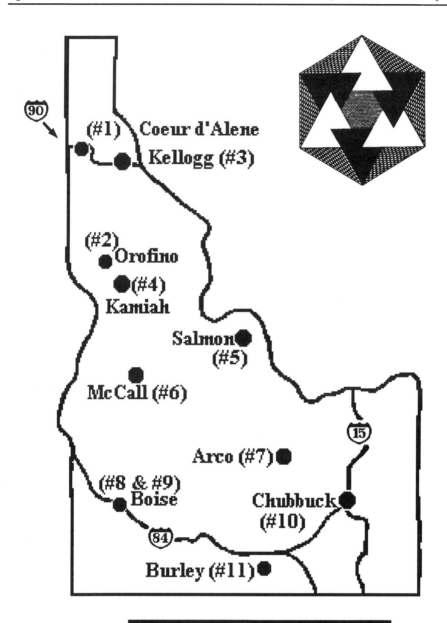

Coeur d'Alene, ID   #1

A Stitch In Time
Quilt Shop

7352 N. Government Way #H
(208) 772-0560   83814 Est: 1994
Owner: Stephanie Muehlhausen

Tue - Fri
9:30 - 5:30
Sat
10 - 4:30

Quilt Shop & Smocking
& French handsewing
Supplies.
Bernina Sewing
Machines—sales and
service. Wide Selection
of Quilting Fabrics,
Supplies, Books &
Patterns.
Many classes available.

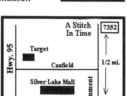

Orofino, ID   #2

LURA'S
FABRIC
SHOP

10494 Hwy. 12
83544
(208) 476-7781
Est: 1981
Owner:
Lura Mullikin

Tue 10 - 8
Wed - Fri
10 - 6
Sat 10 - 4

"We cater to quilters!"

Great Selection of
100% Cottons. The
latest Quilting Books
& Patterns. Pfaff
Sewing Machines &
Sergers. Quilting
Notions & Gadgets.
Complete line of
Kwik Sew Patterns.
Classes.

Silver Needle Textile

Mon - Sat
9:30 - 5:30

100% Cottons — Notions — Patterns
Quilting Supplies — Friendly Service
T-shirts — Sweat Shirts — Souvenirs

205 Main St.   83837   (208) 783-8901
Owner: Brenda Stinson
Mgr: Sherrill Christensen   1800 sq.ft.

Kellogg, ID   #3

Kamiah, ID   #4

KAMIAH KWILT & KRAFTS

417 Main St.   83536
(208) 935-2431
Owner: Joyce Anderson
Est: 1992

Mon - Fri
9:30 - 5
Sat 9 - 4

Cotton Fabrics,
Quilting & Sewing
Notions & Tools,
Books, (complete
line of "Quilt In A
Day®") Yarns,
DMC, Machine
Quilting, Classes &
Lots More.

Salmon, ID   #5

McPherson's

Mon - Sat
9 - 5:30

301 Main St.   83467
(208) 756-3232
Fax: (208) 756-4279
Est: 1902   2000 sq.ft.   1500+ Bolts

Our fabric
Department features
quilt fabric,
patterns, batting,
notions and
instruction books.
We also stock
fashion fabrics &
patterns.

McCall, ID   #6

Granny's Attic

Mon - Sat 10 - 5

104 N 3rd,
Village Square
(208) 634-5313   83638
Est: 1980

Quality cotton
fabric · patterns
classes · notions
books · kits
needlework
florals
mail order

Arco, ID   #7

Sew-A-Lot FABRICS

Mon - Sat 10 - 6

2555 U.S. 93 North
Rt. 1, Box 475   83213   (208) 527-3586
Owner: Roxana Lewis   Est: 1994

High Mountain
Hospitality is our
specialty. Lots of
fabrics, books,
notions & quilting
supplies. Quilts &
Crafts from the
Lost River Valley.

Boise, ID   #8

The Quilt Shop

**Mon - Sat 10 - 6
Sun 12 - 4**

618 E. Boise Ave.   83706
(208) 387-2616
Owner: Kathy Sterndahl
Est: 1994   2300 sq.ft.   1200 Bolts

We specialize in
100% cotton
fabrics, books,
notions, classes,
friendly service
and all the help
you need.

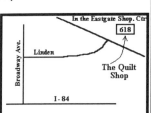

Boise, ID   #9

The Quilt Crossing

**Mon - Sat 10 - 6
Sun 12 - 5**

6431 Fairview Avenue   83704
(208) 376-0087
Owner: Patty Hinkel
Est: 1987   3000 sq.ft.   1200 Bolts

Specializing in
distinctive 100%
cotton fabrics,
classes, books,
gifts & quilt / soft
sculpture
patterns.

Chubbuck, ID   #10

Sherry's Sewing

**Tue - Fri 10 - 6
Sat 12 - 4**

4876 Yellowstone #3   83202
(208) 237-5315
Owner: Sherry Barnett
Est: 1992

100% Cotton
Fabrics, Notions,
Classes.
Hand Guided
Machine Quilting.
Quilts pieced
and printed.

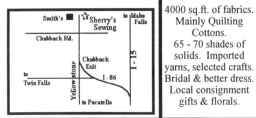

Burley, ID   #11

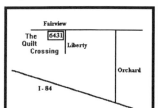
Carleen's fabrics & crafts. etc.

Snake River
Plaza 83318
(208) 677-3573
Est: 1995
Mgr: Carleen
Clayville

**Mon - Fri 10 - 8
Sat 9:30 - 6
Sun 1 - 5**

12-1500 Bolts

4000 sq.ft. of fabrics.
Mainly Quilting
Cottons.
65 - 70 shades of
solids. Imported
yarns, selected crafts.
Bridal & better dress.
Local consignment
gifts & florals.

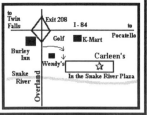

Idaho Guilds:

Lost River Hospital Auxillary, P.O. Box 145, Arco, 83213
Piecemakers, 9 W. River Rd., Blackfoot, 83221
Boise Basin Quilters Guild, P.O. Box 2206, Boise, 83701
Mt. Harrison Quilt Guild, Burley
Syringa Quilters Group, 405 Denver, Caldwell, 83605
Bits and Pieces, P.O. Box 1082, Challis, 83226
Council Mountain Quilters, P.O. Box 829, Council, 83612
Sew-Ciety, 207 W. Main, Grangeville, 83530
North Idaho Quilters, P.O. Box 777, Hayden Lake, 83835
Mt. Harrison Quilters, Rt. 2, Box 2150, Heyburn, 83336
Snake River Valley Quilt Guild, 1450 Paul St., Idaho Falls, 83401
Central Idaho Quilters, P.O. Box 278, Kamiah, 83536
Panhandle Piecemakers, P.O. Box 39, Kootenai, 83840
Seaport Quilter's Guild, P.O. Box 491, Lewiston, 83501
Pine Needle Quilters, P.O. Box 567, McCall, 83638
Palouse Patchers, P.O. Box 9795, Moscow, 83843
El-Y-Hee Quilters, Mt. Home, 83647
Clearwater Quilters, P.O. Box 2748, Orofino, 83544
Happy Hands Quilt Club, 40 Davis Dr., Pocatello, 83201
Lemhi Piecemakers, 517 River St., Salmon, 83467
Valley Piecemakers, 905 Main, St. Maries, 83861
Desert Sage Quilters, P.O. Box 812, Twin Falls, 83301
Thread Bears, 690 Adobe Dr., Weiser, 83672

Other Shops in Idaho:

Bayview	Empty Spool, 16805 Limekiln Rd., P.O. Box 790
Blackfoot	Country Calicos & Quilts, 617 W. Hwy. 26
Boise	Fabric Frolics Sewing Machines Plus, 1208 Vista
Bonners Ferry	Gini Knits, 7225 Main St.
Challis	Craft Lady, 415 Main St., HC 63, Box 1788
Challis	Patchwork Pig Pen, 600 Main St.
Coeur d'Alene	Lyle's, 600 E. Best Ave.
Eagle	Seams Etc., 124 E. State St.
Grace	Fabulous Fabrics, P.O. Box E
Grangeville	Melinda's Fabrics, 207 W. Main
Idaho Falls	Quilts 'N' Things, 1375 E. 49th N
McCall	Mountan Fabrics, 123 E. Lake, P.O. Box 468
Mountain Home	The Gift Box, P.O. Box 1356
Nampa	Alice's Fabrics, 511 12th Ave. Rd.
Oakley	Liz's Fabrics, 495 N. Lincoln
Pocatello	Mill End Fabrics, 4415 E. Brunside Ave.
Pocatello	The Fabric Center, 251 N. Main St.
Post Falls	Joanne & Bucks Clothing & Fabric, E. 511 Seltice Way
Post Falls	Florence's Fabrics, 103 E. 10th Ave.
Sandpoint	The Cotton Mill, 402 Cedar St.
Soda Springs	Nifty Needle, 120 S. Main
Weiser	Calico Corner, 455 State St.

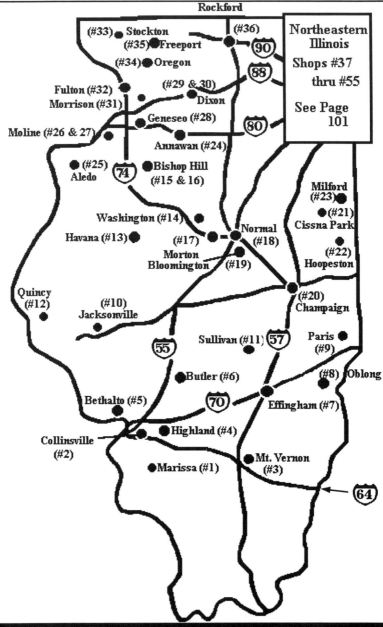

Rockford

(#33) Stockton
(#35) Freeport
(#34) Oregon

(#36)
90
88

Northeastern
Illinois
Shops #37
thru #55

See Page
101

Fulton (#32)
Morrison (#31)

(#29 & 30)
Dixon

Geneseo (#28)

Moline (#26 & 27)

80

Annawan (#24)

(#25)
Aledo

74

Bishop Hill
(#15 & 16)

Milford
(#23)
(#21)
Cissna Park

Washington (#14)

Normal
(#18)

Havana (#13)

(#17)
Morton
Bloomington

(#22)
Hoopeston

(#19)

(#20)
Champaign

Quincy
(#12)

(#10)
Jacksonville

55

Sullivan (#11)

57

Paris
(#9)

Butler (#6)

(#8) Oblong

Bethalto (#5)

70

Effingham (#7)

Collinsville
(#2)

Highland (#4)

Marissa (#1)

Mt. Vernon
(#3)

64

ILLINOIS

55 Featured Shops

Marissa, IL #1

Fancyworks

106 N. Main   62257
(618) 295-2909
Owner: Cindy Galle
Est: 1991

Mon, Tue,
Thur, Fri
9 - 5
Sat 9 - 2

RJR Fabrics,
South Seas
Imports & more.
Full line of quilt
supplies, notions
and books.
Classes
Available.

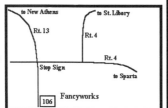

Mt. Vernon, IL #3

4112 Broadway   62864
(618) 244-5856
Owner: Dana Tabor   2000 sq.ft.

Mon - Fri
9:30 - 6
Sat 10 - 5

Fabrics, Quilting
Supplies.
Viking Sewing
Machines &
Sergers. Patterns,
Books, Smocking
Heirloom.
Come & Browse.

Highland, IL #4

Rosemary's Fabric & Quilts

812 Ninth St.   62249
(618) 654-5045   Est: 1988
Owner: Rosemary Seifried

Mon - Fri
9 - 5
Sat 9 - 4

Over 3000
Bolts of
Fabric.
Everything a
Quilter Needs!

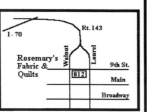

Collinsville, IL #2

110 W. Main St. 62234
(618) 345-3661
Owner: Mary Solomon
Est: 1990   2000 sq.ft.

Mon - Sat
9 - 3
Tues & Thur
til 7:30

Over 1500
Bolts of
100%
Cottons
Designer
Fabrics too
Books, 1000+ Patterns
Threads, Silk Ribbons
& Heirloom Sewing
Supplies.
Bernina Sewing
Machines and Sergers

Cross Patches

Only 12 min. from downtown St. Louis

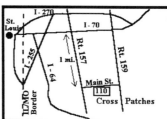

Show us this AD and we will
give you a 10% (one time)
discount on Fabric purchases.

Bethalto, IL #5

Martha's Quilt Shoppe

Wed - Sat 10 - 4 or by Appt.

3511 Seiler Rd.   62010
(618) 259-1759
Owners: Martha & Clarence Gerdt
Est: 1989   500 sq.ft.

Fabric
Notions
Books
Patterns
Classes

Martha's Quilt Shoppe
← 1 mi. → 3511
Seiler Rd.
Fosterburg Rd.
5 mi.
Rte. 140
Alton, IL

Butler, IL #6

Calico Quilt Frames

Mail Order: 14323 Il. Rt. 127
(217) 532-2676   62015
Owner: Judy Tucker

By Appt. Only

Quilting Frames:
Klaus Rau, Hinterberg
Q-Snap
Plans Only: Snap
Tension
Speed Cutting tools
Stamped embroidery
blocks & tops
Limited quantities of
frames in stock.

Please phone for
showroom
appointment to
compare frames.

Effingham, IL #7

Dusts' Quilt & Craft Shop

Mon - Sat 9 - 5

R.R. #1   Box 310   62401
3 1/2 miles from Rt. 33 turn off
(217) 536-6756   2000 Bolts

Large selection of
fabrics, books,
patterns and
stamped textiles for
embroidery.
Notions, laces,
embroidery flosses,
crochet thread
Low Prices.

Keller Rd.   Rt.45
I-57/70   I-70
Exit 160
Exit 162
Fayette Ave.   Rt. 40
Willow St.   1300/
1700   Rt.33
I-70
Dusts'
I-57
1650/1025

Oblong, IL #8

The VILLAGE Stitchery

Mon - Sat 9 - 5 Evenings by Appt.

110 E. Main   62449
(618) 592-4134   1500 sq.ft.
Owner: Lisa Pinkston   Est: 1982

Visit our unique
shop which
carries a complete
line of fabrics and
supplies for the
beginning to
expert quilter.

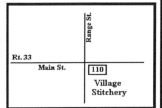

Range St.
Rt. 33
Main St.   110
Village
Stitchery

Paris, IL #9

Lori's Pins 'N Needles

Mon - Sat 9 - 5 Fri til 8

109 N. Central Ave., P.O. Box 815
(217) 465-5541   61944
Owner: Lori Bridwell   Est: 1980   2000 sq.ft.

Over 1000 Bolts
of 100% Cotton.
Quilt Backings,
Battings, and
Large Selection
of Books &
Patterns.
Authorized
Viking Dealer.

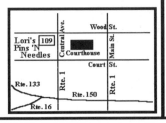

Wood St.
Lori's 109
Pins 'N
Needles   Courthouse
Court St.
Central Ave.
Main St.
Rte. 133
Rte. 1
Rte. 150
Rte. 16

Jacksonville, IL #10

Joy's Vogue Fabrics

Mon - Sat 9 - 5

68 Central Park Plaza   62650
(217) 245-5510
Owner: Joy Tuggle

We Specialize In:
Fine Fabrics - Silk,
Wool, Cottons
Trims - Lace,
Ribbon, Appliques.
Buttons
Complete selection
of sewing notions.
Patterns
Machine Quilting

Central
Park
Plaza   68   Joy's
W. State   E. State
Morgan
College   to
Springfield
to Quincy   Morton
Rt. 67
I-55
Mauvaisterre
Sandy
Main

Sullivan, IL   #11

(217) 728-4511

Mon - Fri
8 - 4:30
Sat 10 - 3

P.O. Box 376   61951   916 W. Jackson St.
Owners: Carol & Howard Risley   Est: 1992

Quilts By Carol

Near Lake
Shelbyville & Illinois
Amish Country

A Unique Quilt Gallery of machine quilted, 100% cotton quilts & other quilted items for sale. Custom piecing & Quilting Dealers Welcome

---

Quincy, IL   #12

The Quilt Connection

Rt. #1, Box 228   Mail: Mendon,IL
(217) 434-8428   62351
Owner: Laurie Vance   Est: 1989
Family quilt shop,   250+ Fabrics
children   Friendly Service

I'm Open When
I'm Home
Mon 10 - 4
Last Sat of
Month 10 - 4
Or by Appt.

WELCOME!
Original line of foundations in miniature & 6". Books, notions, classes. Finished quilts, custom orders. Mail Order Newsletter $6 yr.

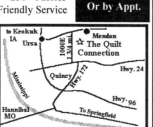

Havana, IL   #13

Grannie Annie's Antique, Stitchery & What-Not Shoppe

128 N. Plum   62644
(309) 543-6827
Est. 1981   2,000 sq.ft.

Mon - Sat
9 - 5

7 Rooms
Quilting Supplies
Lace Curtains
Counted
Cross Stitch
Stenciling
Country &
Victorian Gifts
Antiques

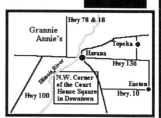

Washington, IL   #14

127 Peddlers Way   61571   1400 sq.ft.
(309) 444-7667   Est: 1985
Owners: Peggy Hessling & Lillian Cagle
Authorized Pfaff Dealer

Peg & Lil's Needle Patch

"The friendly place for happy Stitchers"

FABRICS - 1000 bolts 100% cottons
QUILTING - Large selection of Fabrics, Books, Patterns, Rotary tools, Stencils and Classes.
CRAFTERS - Patterns & Homespuns
Lots of Samples on display.

Mon 10 - 7
Tues - Fri
10 - 5
Sat 10 - 4

Bishop Hill, IL #15

The Prairie Workshop

April - Dec
Daily
10 - 5

Box 23   61419
(In the Historic Village)
(309) 927-3367   Est: 1983
Owner: Betty Robertson

Fabric,
Quilting Supplies,
Books,
Handmade Items

In the Historic
Village of Bishop
Hill, Illinois

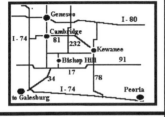

Bishop Hill, IL #16

Village Smithy

Closed
Jan - April
Daily
10 - 4

309 N. Bishop Hill St. 61419
(309) 927-3851
Owner: Marilyn Nelson
Est: 1984   3200 sq.ft.

Vintage Quilts,
Fabrics, Patterns,
& Books for the
Quilter.
Also old Linens,
Glassware,
Collectibles &
Antiques.

We are Located in
The Historic
Village of Bishop Hill,
Henry County, Illinois

Morton, IL #17

The Quilt Corner

Mon - Thur
9:30 - 8
Fri - Sat
9:30-4:30

2037 S. Main Street   61550
(309) 263-7114
Owner: Karen Ehrhardt
Est: 1988   2000 sq.ft.   1500 Bolts

Complete line of
Quilting Fabrics,
Books, Patterns &
Notions.
Complete line of
Silk Ribbon

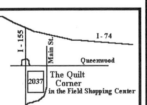

Normal, IL #18

Sewing Studio

Mon - Fri
9:30 - 6
Sat 9:30 - 5
Sun 12 - 4

1503 E. College, Suite C   61761
(309) 452-7313   Est: 1983
Owners: Margaret Couch
2600 sq.ft.

Quality quilting and
fashion fabrics.
Quilting & sewing
classes, books.
Quilting & heirloom
supplies & notions.
Bernina / Viking /
White Dealer

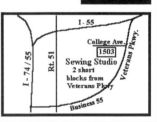

Bloomington, IL #19

The Treadle

Mon - Sat
10 - 5
Sun 12 - 4

2101 Eastland   61704
(309) 662-1733

Over 5000 Bolts
of Calico Prints.
Largest selection
of quilt books,
quilt patterns,
craft patterns in
the state of
Illinois.

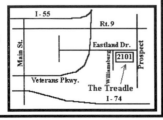

Champaign, IL #20

The Treadle

Mon - Sat
10 - 5
Sun 12 - 4

53 Marketview   61820
(217) 359-8636

Over 5000 Bolts
of Calico Prints.
Largest selection
of quilt books,
quilt patterns,
craft patterns in
the state of
Illinois.

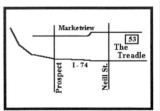

Annawan, IL #24

Memory Lane

303 W. Front St.   61234
(309) 935-6366   Est: 1994
Owner: Mary Moon
                    2800 sq.ft.

Mon - Fri 10 - 5
Sun 1 - 5

1000 bolts 100% cotton. Newest books, patterns, notions. Friendly service with a smile. Antiques & collectibles for the family to explore.

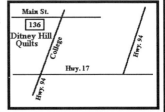

Aledo, IL #25

Ditney Hill Quilts

136 W. Main St.   61231
(309) 582-3625
Owner: Dee Wayne
Est: 1994

Tues - Fri 10 - 5
Sat 10 - 2

Cotton Fabrics & Batting. Patterns, Books, Notions, Quilts & Gift Items.

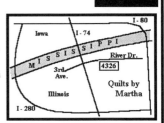

Moline, IL #26

Quilts By the Oz

3201 - 23rd. Ave.   61265
(309) 762-9673 or (800) 735-9673
Owner: Harlene Rivelli

2000+ bolts 100% cotton. Large

Mon - Fri 10 - 5
Sat 10 - 2

Est: 1987
2400 sq.ft.

assortment of Books, Patterns, Notions, Bulk Buttons, Machine Quilting--White Sewing Machines Tri-Chem Paints Quilts & Quillos

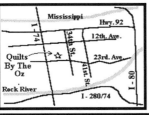

Moline, IL #27

Quilts by Martha

4326 River Drive   61265
(309) 762-8503
Owner: Martha Thorpe
Est: 1988

Open by Appt. or by Chance

Quilts, old and new, Bought and sold. Tops, pieces and old fabric too. Over 100 Quilts in a B&B--River Drive Guest House.

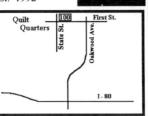

Geneseo, IL #28

Quilt Quarters

100 N. State St.   61254
(309) 944-2693
Owners: Roger & Dianne Peterson
                    Est: 1992

Mon 10 - 4
Tue - Fri 10 - 5
Sat 10 - 3

Satisfying Quilters and their needs. Fabrics, books, patterns, notions, and "how to" classes. Hand made gifts by local artists.

Meals: Something the rest of a quilter's family seems to think they need regularly.

Dixon, IL   #29

The Quilt Cellar

Tues - Sat 10 - 5

541 Penrose Road
61021
(815) 288-5594
Est: 1992
Owner: Sue
      Ramage

Over 600 Bolts of
P&B, Benartex,
Marcus, and other
quality fabrics.
Quilting supplies
and classes.

Dixon, IL   #30

Viking Sewing Shop

**Mon - Fri 9 - 5:30
Sat 9 - 5**

302 W. 1st St.   61021
(815) 288-3219
Est: 1971   1200 sq.ft.

500+ Bolts of
quilt fabric.
Batting & quilt
supplies.
Machine quilting.
Sewing
Machines.

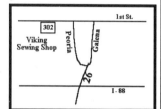

Morrison, IL   #31

CONstantly Stitching N' More

**Mon 12 - 9
Tues - Fri 10 - 6
Sat 10 - 5
Sun 12 - 4**

13690 Lincoln Road   61270
(815) 772-2833   Est: 1992
Owner: Connie Barr
           5000 sq.ft.

Machine Quilting,
Fabric, Notions,
Books, Patterns,
Quilt Classes.
Basket Weaving
Classes. Gift
Items. Ready
Made Crafts.
Antiques.

Fulton, IL   #32

Calico Creations

**Tues - Sat 10 - 5
Sun 12 - 5**

1108 Fourth Street   61252
(800) 676-2284 or (815) 589-2221
Owner: Jane Huisingh

Quilting, Crafts,   Est: 1986   8,000 sq.ft.
Patterns, Fabric,
Books, Stencils &
Tools.
Professional
Machine Quilting
and Instructors.
Large Class area
and 3 floors of
Antiques.

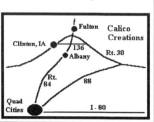

Stockton, IL   #33

Patty's Patchwork

**Mon, Thur, Fri, & Sat 10 - 5
Sun 12 - 5
Tues & Wed By Appt.**

8040 U.S. Rt. 20   61085
(815) 947-2862
Owner: Pat Kluckhohn
          Est: 1992
Located in a white
frame country
farm home.
Fabric, notions,
books and
patterns. Largest
fabric shop in Jo
Daviess Cty.
Classes.

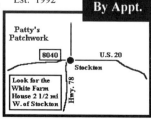

Oregon, IL #34

Holly's Homespun

109 S. 3rd. St.   **61061**   **(815) 732-4204**
Owners: Don & Holly Woodyatt   **Est: 1991**

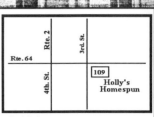

Rte. 64 | Rte. 2 | 3rd. St.
4th. St. | 109 Holly's Homespun

Charming shop filled with everything you need for all your quilting and cross stitch projects as well as lots of gift items including greeting cards, note cards & stationery, pottery, t-shirts, primitive folk art and more. We have over 700 bolts of fabric including lots of homespun as well as all the new prints from your favorite companies like Marcus Bros, P&B, RJR, Moda, Benartex & Red Wagon. In addition, we carry all the newest books and patterns.

Mon - Sat 10 - 5
Sun 12 - 4

Freeport, IL #35

The Quilter's Thimble

Mon - Sat 10:30 - 5

17 South Van Buren   61032
(815) 235-1892
Owner: Carol Jacobs
Classes, Fabrics,   Est: 1986   1200 sq.ft.
Supplies for
Quilting. Custom
Quilting and
designing.
Silk Ribbon
Embroidery classes
& Supplies.
Send SASE for
Newsletter.

The Quilter's Thimble
17   Van Buren
Rt. 20   Galena Ave.
One Way   Main St.

Rockford, IL #36

Quilter's Haven

Mon - Sat 10 - 4 Wed til 7

4616 E. State St.   61108
(815) 227-1659
Est: 1995   1200 sq.ft.
Owners: Stephanie Gauerke & Cathy Johnson

We carry 100% cotton fabrics, quilting supplies. Classes. Doll Supplies and Basket Classes. Located in the Lower Level

to Wisconsin
4616   Quilters' Haven in the Lower Level
Ridgeview
East State St. Business 20
Apline Rd.   I - 90
I - 39   to Chicago

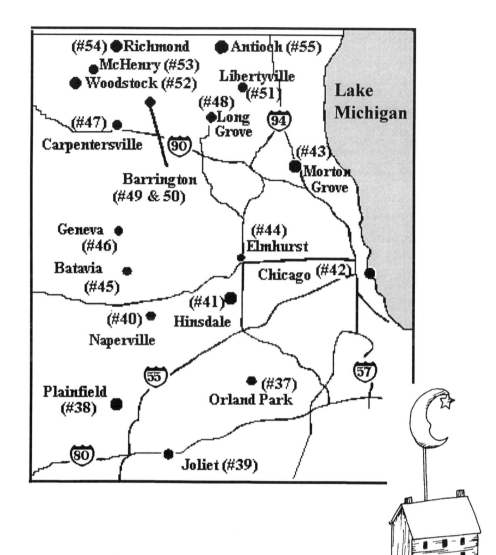

Joliet, IL   #39

Roberts Sewing Center

255 North Chicago St.   60431
(815) 723-4210   Est: 1930
Owner: Ken Roberts   2500 sq.ft.

"A Quilter's Paradise"

4000 Bolts Cotton Fabric
The Lowest Prices in Illinois
Pfaff - - Singer - - Brother
Home & Industrial Machines

Bus Tours
Please Call Ahead
800-273-9111

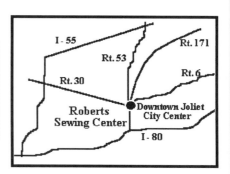

Mon - Sat   9 - 5

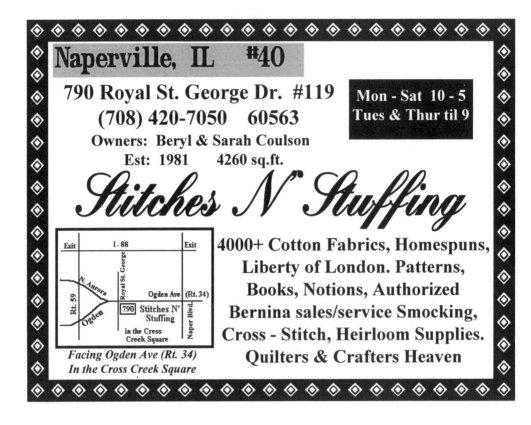

Naperville, IL   #40

790 Royal St. George Dr. #119
(708) 420-7050   60563

Owners: Beryl & Sarah Coulson
Est: 1981   4260 sq.ft.

Mon - Sat 10 - 5
Tues & Thur til 9

Stitches N' Stuffing

Exit   I - 88   Exit
N. Aurora   Royal St. George
Rt. 59   Ogden   Ogden Ave   (Rt. 34)
790   Stitches N' Stuffing
Naper Blvd.
in the Cress Creek Square

Facing Ogden Ave (Rt. 34)
In the Cross Creek Square

4000+ Cotton Fabrics, Homespuns, Liberty of London. Patterns, Books, Notions, Authorized Bernina sales/service Smocking, Cross - Stitch, Heirloom Supplies. Quilters & Crafters Heaven

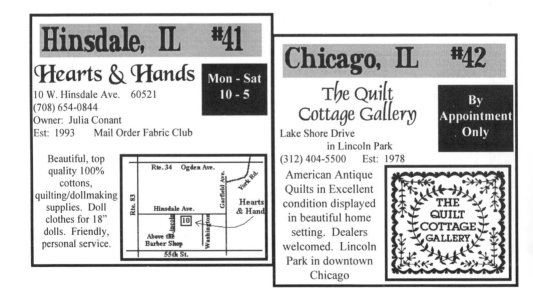

Hinsdale, IL   #41

Hearts & Hands

10 W. Hinsdale Ave.   60521
(708) 654-0844
Owner: Julia Conant
Est: 1993   Mail Order Fabric Club

Mon - Sat 10 - 5

Beautiful, top quality 100% cottons, quilting/dollmaking supplies. Doll clothes for 18" dolls. Friendly, personal service.

Rte. 34   Ogden Ave.
Rte. 83   York Rd.   Garfield Ave.
Hinsdale Ave.   Hearts & Hand
Lincoln   10   Washington
Above the Barber Shop
55th St.

Chicago, IL   #42

The Quilt Cottage Gallery

Lake Shore Drive
in Lincoln Park
(312) 404-5500   Est: 1978

By Appointment Only

American Antique Quilts in Excellent condition displayed in beautiful home setting. Dealers welcomed. Lincoln Park in downtown Chicago

THE QUILT COTTAGE GALLERY

(847) 966-1882

Morton Grove, IL #43

Just North of Chicago

Cotton Pickers' Fabrics

5926 Dempster St.
60053

Mon - Sat
10 - 5
Sun 12 - 4

5000 sq.ft.

The Midwest's Largest Quilt Supply Shop

We carry 4000+ different calicos

400 Books — Stencils — Patterns

Over 100 Quilts Displayed

Elmhurst, IL #44

Fabrics Etc. II

Mon - Sat
9:30 - 5

446 N. York Rd.   60126
(708) 279-1482

Est: 1995   2000 sq.ft.

We have 800+ bolts
of Fabric for
Quilting,
Smocking,
Heirloom,
Stretch n' Sew
Patterns Plus
Classes
Baby Lock & Euro
Pro Machines

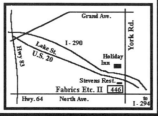

Batavia, IL #45

Quilting Books Unlimited

Mon - Fri
10 - 5
Thurs til 8
Sat 10 - 4
Sun 12 - 4

1911 W. Wilson   60510
(708) 406-0237   Est: 1983
Owner: Rob Roberts   3000 sq.ft.

Boasting a collection
of over 1000 quilting
books, we are the
only resource you'll
ever need for hand-
made quilts, quilting
supplies, 100%
cottons, and classes.
Country Gifts too.

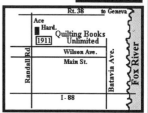

Geneva, IL #46

Quilted Fox

Tues - Fri
10 - 5
Sat 10 - 4

322 West Hamilton St.   60134
(708) 232-4888   Est: 1978
Owner: Sara Buchholz
1400 sq.ft.

Large selection of
unusual & better
fabrics: including
Liberty—Hoffman
Japanese, etc.
Pfaff & Viking
sewing machines.
Custom Quilts &
Art Clothing.

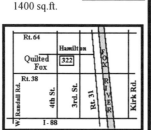

Carpentersville, IL #47

Grist Mill Ends & Things

Mon - Fri
10 - 4:30
Sat 10 - 2

39 E. Main St.   60110
(847) 426-MILL

Located in   Est: 1976   1500 sq.ft.
Historic Grist
Mill.
Decorator Fabrics
& Calicos.
Quilting Supplies
including bonded
Polyester Fill,
Linings, Threads
& Notions.

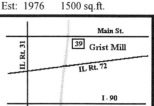

Long Grove, IL #48

Prints Charming, Ltd.

Mon - Sat
10 - 5
Sun
Noon - 5

221 R.P. Coffin Road   60047
(847) 634-1330   Est: 1978
Owners: Joan & Steve Attenberg
3000 sq.ft.

Oldest quilt shop
in northwest
Suburban
Chicago. 100%
Cottons, Quilting
Notions, Classes.
Hundreds of
unique craft
patterns and
supplies.

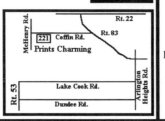

Barrington, IL #49

Barrington Sewing Center, Inc.

Mon - Sat
10 - 5
Mon &
Thur til 8
Sun 12 - 4

762 W. Northwest Hwy.   60010
(847) 304-4500   Est: 1994
Owner: Sharon Turskey   2400 sq.ft.

Unusual 100%
cotton fabrics.
Sueded Look
Hand-dyed Fabric.
Books, Patterns,
Notions, Classes.
Viking Sewing
Machines.

Barrington, IL #50

A Touch of Amish

Tues - Sat 10 - 4

130 Applebee
60010
(847) 381-0900
Est: 1986   1000 sq.ft.
Owner: Lynn Rice

Wonderful fabrics, Viking sewing machines, books, patterns, custom quilting, free weekly demonstrations, and always great service.

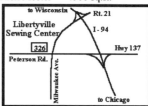

Libertyville, IL #51

Libertyville Sewing Center

**Mon - Thur 9 - 9
Fri & Sat 9 - 5**

326 Peterson Rd.   60048
(Brookside Shopping Center)
(847) 367-0820 Est: 1982
Owners: Linda & Rick Mosier   4500 sq.ft.

Large selection of calicos featuring Hoffman.
Quilting Supplies.
Sales & Service —
Bernina, Viking, Pfaff & Babylock

Woodstock, IL #52

The Quilt Studio, Inc.

**Mon - Fri 10 - 6
Thur til 8
Sat 10 - 5
Sun 12 - 4**

114 W. Calhoun St.   60098
(815) 338-1212
Est: 1994   2000 sq.ft
Owners: Diane Webster

Fabric, Quilting Supplies. Ready-Made and Custom-Made Quilted Items. Sewing Collectibles & Antique Quilts. Quilt Racks & Handcrafts.

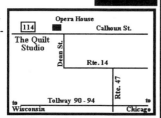

McHenry, IL #53

Granny's Quilts

**Mon - Fri 10 - 6
Sat 10 - 4**

4509 W. Elm St.   60050
(815) 385-5107
Owner: Lois Shea

Est: 1976   2500 sq.ft.

2500 Bolts Cotton Fabric. Books, Patterns, Notions, Specialty Threads, Authorized Pfaff and Viking Sewing Machine Sales, service, accessories and classes.

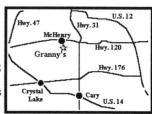

Richmond, IL #54

Sunshine and Shadow Quilt Shoppe

**Mon - Sat 10 - 5
Sun 12 - 5**

10307 Main St.   60071
(815) 678-2603   2000 + Bolts
Owner: Linda Rullman Est: 1991
In Historic Richmond among Antique & Unique Shops

Purveyor of fine fabrics, books, patterns, quilting notions, doll making items, sundry gifts & Collectibles.
Classes Offered.

Antioch, IL #55

Quilter's Dream, Inc.

**Mon - Thur 11 - 6
Fri & Sat 10 - 4**

388 Lake St.   60002
(847) 395-1459
Est: 1994   900 sq.ft.
Owners: Wendy Maston
         & Robin Kessell

A complete line of Quilting Supplies & 100% cotton fabrics. A very unique town.
We love visitors.
Stop in & chat!

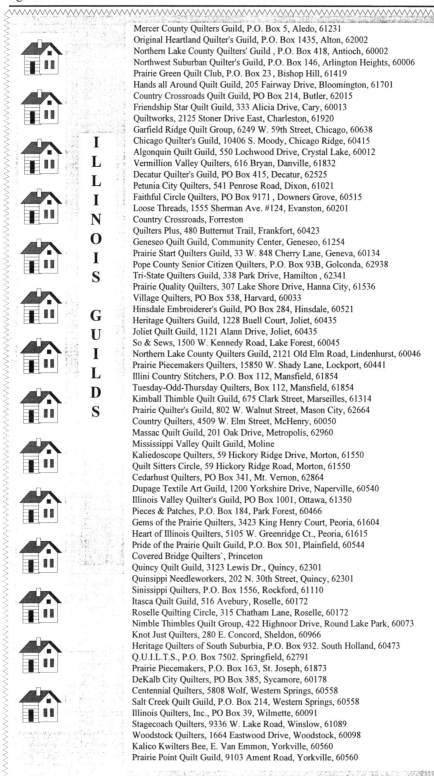

Mercer County Quilters Guild, P.O. Box 5, Aledo, 61231
Original Heartland Quilter's Guild, P.O. Box 1435, Alton, 62002
Northern Lake County Quilters' Guild , P.O. Box 418, Antioch, 60002
Northwest Suburban Quilter's Guild, P.O. Box 146, Arlington Heights, 60006
Prairie Green Quilt Club, P.O. Box 23 , Bishop Hill, 61419
Hands all Around Quilt Guild, 205 Fairway Drive, Bloomington, 61701
Country Crossroads Quilt Guild, PO Box 214, Butler, 62015
Friendship Star Quilt Guild, 333 Alicia Drive, Cary, 60013
Quiltworks, 2125 Stoner Drive East, Charleston, 61920
Garfield Ridge Quilt Group, 6249 W. 59th Street, Chicago, 60638
Chicago Quilter's Guild, 10406 S. Moody, Chicago Ridge, 60415
Algonquin Quilt Guild, 550 Lochwood Drive, Crystal Lake, 60012
Vermillion Valley Quilters, 616 Bryan, Danville, 61832
Decatur Quilter's Guild, PO Box 415, Decatur, 62525
Petunia City Quilters, 541 Penrose Road, Dixon, 61021
Faithful Circle Quilters, PO Box 9171 , Downers Grove, 60515
Loose Threads, 1555 Sherman Ave. #124, Evanston, 60201
Country Crossroads, Forreston
Quilters Plus, 480 Butternut Trail, Frankfort, 60423
Geneseo Quilt Guild, Community Center, Geneseo, 61254
Prairie Start Quilters Guild, 33 W. 848 Cherry Lane, Geneva, 60134
Pope County Senior Citizen Quilters, P.O. Box 93B, Golconda, 62938
Tri-State Quilters Guild, 338 Park Drive, Hamilton , 62341
Prairie Quality Quilters, 307 Lake Shore Drive, Hanna City, 61536
Village Quilters, PO Box 538, Harvard, 60033
Hinsdale Embroiderer's Guild, PO Box 284, Hinsdale, 60521
Heritage Quilters Guild, 1228 Buell Court, Joliet, 60435
Joliet Quilt Guild, 1121 Alann Drive, Joliet, 60435
So & Sews, 1500 W. Kennedy Road, Lake Forest, 60045
Northern Lake County Quilters Guild, 2121 Old Elm Road, Lindenhurst, 60046
Prairie Piecemakers Quilters, 15850 W. Shady Lane, Lockport, 60441
Illini Country Stitchers, P.O. Box 112, Mansfield, 61854
Tuesday-Odd-Thursday Quilters, Box 112, Mansfield, 61854
Kimball Thimble Quilt Guild, 675 Clark Street, Marseilles, 61314
Prairie Quilter's Guild, 802 W. Walnut Street, Mason City, 62664
Country Quilters, 4509 W. Elm Street, McHenry, 60050
Massac Quilt Guild, 201 Oak Drive, Metropolis, 62960
Mississippi Valley Quilt Guild, Moline
Kaliedoscope Quilters, 59 Hickory Ridge Drive, Morton, 61550
Quilt Sitters Circle, 59 Hickory Ridge Road, Morton, 61550
Cedarhust Quilters, PO Box 341, Mt. Vernon, 62864
Dupage Textile Art Guild, 1200 Yorkshire Drive, Naperville, 60540
Illinois Valley Quilter's Guild, PO Box 1001, Ottawa, 61350
Pieces & Patches, P.O. Box 184, Park Forest, 60466
Gems of the Prairie Quilters, 3423 King Henry Court, Peoria, 61604
Heart of Illinois Quilters, 5105 W. Greenridge Ct., Peoria, 61615
Pride of the Prairie Quilt Guild, P.O. Box 501, Plainfield, 60544
Covered Bridge Quilters`, Princeton
Quincy Quilt Guild, 3123 Lewis Dr., Quincy, 62301
Quinsippi Needleworkers, 202 N. 30th Street, Quincy, 62301
Sinissippi Quilters, P.O. Box 1556, Rockford, 61110
Itasca Quilt Guild, 516 Avebury, Roselle, 60172
Roselle Quilting Circle, 315 Chatham Lane, Roselle, 60172
Nimble Thimbles Quilt Group, 422 Highnoor Drive, Round Lake Park, 60073
Knot Just Quilters, 280 E. Concord, Sheldon, 60966
Heritage Quilters of South Suburbia, P.O. Box 932. South Holland, 60473
Q.U.I.L.T.S., P.O. Box 7502. Springfield, 62791
Prairie Piecemakers, P.O. Box 163, St. Joseph, 61873
DeKalb City Quilters, PO Box 385, Sycamore, 60178
Centennial Quilters, 5808 Wolf, Western Springs, 60558
Salt Creek Quilt Guild, P.O. Box 214, Western Springs, 60558
Illinois Quilters, Inc., PO Box 39, Wilmette, 60091
Stagecoach Quilters, 9336 W. Lake Road, Winslow, 61089
Woodstock Quilters, 1664 Eastwood Drive, Woodstock, 60098
Kalico Kwilters Bee, E. Van Emmon, Yorkville, 60560
Prairie Point Quilt Guild, 9103 Ament Road, Yorkville, 60560

Other Shops in Illinois:

Arthur	The Calico Workshop, 228 South Vine
Avon	The Clothesline, 102 N. Main PO Box 122
Barrington	High Point Farm, 404 High Point Dr.
Barrington	Finn's Fabrics, 113 North Cook
Carthage	Country Pastimes Craft Shop, 541 Main St.
Charleston	Needle Nook, Rt. 4, Box 182
Charleston	Golden Thimble, 940 18th St.
Dunlap	Quilt Crossing, 1719 W. Woodside Dr. Suite B
Edwardsville	Edwardsville Sewing Center, 110 N. Main St.
Effingham	Calico Shoppe, 1108 N. Merchant St.
Elmhurst	Granny's Goodies Attic Shops, 116 N. York St.
Evanston	Wide Goose Chase Quilt Gallery, 1511 Chicago Ave.
Glen Ellyn	Village Fabrics, 430 N. Main
Herrin	Quilt & Cottage Crafts, 1221 S. Sixteenth St.
Hutsonville	Apple Blossom Quilt Shop, St. Route 1
Lebonon	Patsy's Place & Grandma's Things, 222 W. St. Louis St.
Long Grove	The Patchworks, 223 Robert Parker Coffin Rd.
Mascoutah	Patchwork Corner Crafts, 200 N. Jefferson St.
Nashville	Lee's Fabric and Craft, 212 E. St. Louis St.
New Lennox	Sew What, 410 E. Joliet
Oak Park	Choices, 1000 Lake
Odin	Mary's Vogue Shop, 105 Green US Hwy 50
Oneida	Country Needle Arts, P.O. Box 322
Pittsfield	The Pin Cushion, 510 N. Jackson St.
Princeton	Old Times--Quilter Heaven, 954 North Main
Rockford	Gingerbread & Calico, 4125 Charles St.
Springfield	A-1 Quilters, 1052 E. Stanford
Virdon	The Sewing Basket, 183 E. Jackson St.
Woodstock	Prairie Patchworks Mercantile, 106 Cass

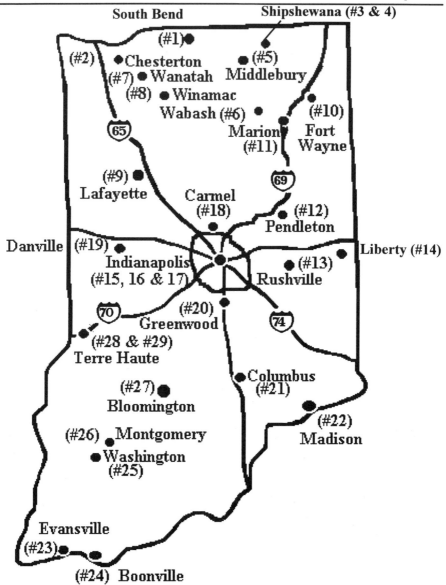

South Bend
Shipshewana (#3 & 4)

(#1)●

(#2)   ● Chesterton   (#5)●
(#7) ● Wanatah   Middlebury
(#8) ● Winamac
      Wabash (#6) ●   (#10)
                        Marion●   Fort
                        (#11)   Wayne

65

(#9) ●
Lafayette   Carmel
                 (#18)   (#12)
                                    Pendleton

69

Danville (#19)●   Liberty (#14)
       Indianapolis   (#13)●
       (#15, 16 & 17)   Rushville

70   (#20)●
       Greenwood   74
(#28 & #29)
Terre Haute

                        ● Columbus
             (#27)●   (#21)
           Bloomington
                                   ●
(#26) ● Montgomery   (#22)
    ● Washington   Madison
      (#25)

Evansville
(#23)● ●
(#24) Boonville

INDIANA

29 Featured Shops

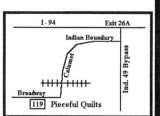

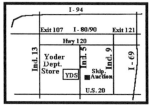
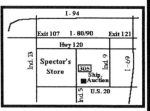

Middlebury, IN   #5

Mon - Sat 10a.m. - Evening Hrs. April - Dec.

Quilts by Esther

240 U.S. 20   (219) 825-9471

- ♥ Quilts
- ♥ Wall Hangings
- ♥ Cotton Fabrics
- ♥ Largest selection of Quilt Stencils in area
- ♥ Books
- ♥ Free Inspiration

Owner: Esther A. Hershberger
Est: 1986
1200 sq.ft.
AT ESSENHAUS RESTAURANT

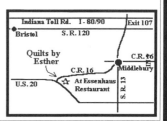

Wabash, IN   #6

Nancy J's Fabrics

Mon - Fri 10 - 5:30
Sat 10 - 5

1604 South Wabash   46992
(219) 563-3505
Owners: Nancy Jacoby &
Est: 1980   Miriam Peebles

The latest & greatest Fabrics. Books and Patterns for quilts, dollmaking & clothing. Plan to spend a day in Historic Wabash!

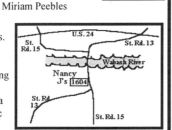

Wanatah, IN   #7

Prairie Point Quilt Shoppe

Tues- Fri 10 - 5
Sat 9 - 2

213 North Main   P.O. Box 383
(219) 733-2821   46390
Owner: Susie Mack   Est: 1989   1000 sq.ft.

Our shop is in an old Victorian House, stocked with over 650 bolts of fabric and a large variety of patterns, books, notions and models. Classes.

Winamac, IN   #8

The Country Patch

Mon - Fri 9 - 5
Sat 9 - 2

102 N. Monticello St.   46996
(219) 946-7799   Est: 1992
Owners: Eddie Ploss & Gladys Knebel

New and Unique Quilt Shop featuring 100% cotton 650+ bolts. Springmaid, RJR, Etc.

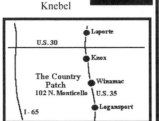

Lafayette, IN   #9

Sally's Sewing Basket

Mon - Wed 9 - 6
Thur 9 - 8
Fri & Sat 9 - 5

533 Main St. 47901
(317) 423-4744 Est: 1994
Owner: Sally Carter 1200 sq.ft.
400 bolts & growing

Sally's carries quality quilting fabrics, books, and notions. Also cross-stitch supplies. Adult and children classes, too.

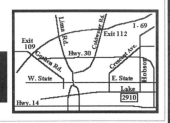

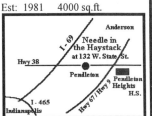

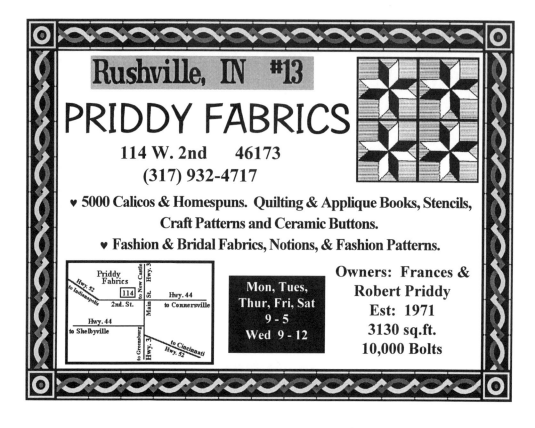

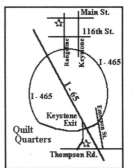

Danville, IN #19

Ventura's Quilting Center

Mon - Fri 9 - 4
Sat 10 - 2

35 Lawton Ave. 46122
(317) 745-2989
Owner: Patricia A. Montgomery
Est: 1987   3300 sq.ft.

Danville | Washington St. | Lawton Ave. 35 Ventura's | I - 465 | Indianapolis
U.S. 36
Rockville Rd. | Exit 13B

Over 700 bolts of 100% cotton Fabrics. (Hoffmans, Jinny Beyers, VIP's, Etc.) Books, Notions, Batting, Backings, Classes and Samples Galore.

Greenwood, IN #20

The Back Door, Inc.

2503 Fairview Place #W   46142
(317) 882-2120
Owners: Linda Hale &
Est: 1973   Teri Dougherty
4000 sq.ft.

Mon - Thur 9:30 - 9
Fri 9:30-6
Sat 9:30 - 5

Full line of quilt supplies, bear and dollmaking, tolepainting, counted cross stitch and many many samples. Great place to shop

Indianapolis | I - 465 | Hwy. 135 Meridian | U.S. 31 | Southport Rd. | I - 74
County Line Rd.
Greenwood Mall | Main St.
Fry Rd.
Marsh
2503 The Back Door | In Fairview Place - Turn at "Flowers by Steve"
Meijer

Columbus, IN #21

Craig's Vac & Sew

419 7th St. 47201
(812) 378-5211
Owners: David & Kate Craig
Est: 1988
450+ Bolts & Growing

Quality 100% cottons, quilt supplies, books & patterns, sewing machine repair.

M, T, Th, F, Sat 10 - 3
Mon - Thur Eves 6 - 9

In Downtown Columbus
Washington | 7th St. | 419 Craig's Vac & Sew | Franklin St.

Madison, IN #22

Margie's Country Store

721 W. Main St.   47250
(812) 265-4429
Owner: Marjorie Webb   Est. 1970   900 Bolts

Mon - Fri 10 - 5
Sun 1 - 5

For Quality fabrics, books, patterns, country clothing come visit us. Many made-up samples to inspire you. Also gifts and home decorations

Margie's Country Store
(State Hwy 56) Main St.
721
Cragmont | Vernon | Plum | Mill | Vine

Evansville, IN #23

Quilter's Barn

7915 Marx Rd.   47720
(812) 963-6336
Owner: Bettye J. Sheppard
Est: 1988

Tues, Thurs, & Sat 10 - 4

Full service shop. Fabrics, Classes, Books, Patterns, Wooden Frames. Quilt til the cows come home in a warm country atmosphere.

Harmony Way
Quilter's Barn | Diamond
7915
Korressel Rd. | Marx Rd. | Red Bank | St. Joe
Hwy 62 | Lloyd Expry.

Boonville, IN #24

MERCANTILE

123 S. 2nd. St.   47601
(812) 897-5687
Owners: Betty & Steve Cummings
Est: 1992   3000 sq.ft.   2500+ bolts
Mon - Sat 10 - 5   Thurs til 8
20 min. east of Evansville; 10 min. south of I - 64, exit 39
West side of the Historic Town Square

Turn of the century charm boasting a fantastic collection of 100% quilting cottons & homespuns. Hundreds of quilting books; patterns for quilts, critters & clothes; kits; silk ribbon supplies. Large selection of ceramic buttons; notions, stencils plus unique gifts for the quilt enthusiast. Quality crafts & antique consignment an added bonus. Be inspired by our many samples of wall hangings, clothing & critters. Kits available or to order on any project.

Coming Spring '96
—Join us for lunch at **Victoria's Tea Room**—
gourmet coffees, teas, salads, and decadent desserts.
Old fashioned candy store.

	I - 64	Exit 39
to Evansville		at Lynnville
	BOONVILLE	Main St.
The Village Mercantile 123		Courthouse Square
Hwy 62		Locust St.

12 miles · 2nd. St. · 3rd. St.

Plan to spend the day with us - You won't be disappointed!

Washington, IN #25

The Stitching Post

Mon - Sat 9 - 5   Fri 9 - 6

400 East Main Street   47501
(812) 254-6063   Est: 1986
Owner: Mary Dell Memering 1200 sq.ft.

Southwest Indiana's largest selection of quality quilting fabrics--1800 bolts 100% cottons including Plaids&Hoffmans. Quilting supplies, notions, books, & patterns.

Montgomery, IN #26

David V. Wagler's Quilts

Mon - Sat Daylight Hours

R.R. 1 Box 73   450 E. 200 N.
(812) 486-3836   47558
Owners: David & Anna Wagler   Est: 1980
1900 sq.ft.   1500+ Bolts

Hand Made Quilts on display. Quilts made to order, applique, pieced, & wholecloth tops. 100% Cotton Fabrics, Stencils, Books, Patterns, Kits

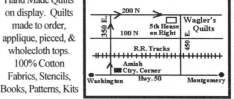

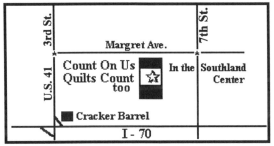

Indiana State Quilt Guild, 14 Briar Patch Rd., Bargersville, 46106
Indiana Guilds:
Anderson Evening Guild, 1112 North Drive, Anderson, 46011
Redbud Quilter's Guild, 111 E. 12th Street, Anderson, 46016
Americus Quilting Club, PO Box 312, Battleground, 47920
Quarry Quilters, PO Box 975, Bedford, 47421
Bloomington Quilter's Guild, PO Box 812, Bloomington, 47402
Raintree Quilters Guild, Chandler
Clay City Calico Quilters, Box 107, Clay City, 47841
Columbus Star Quilter's Guild, PO Box 121, Columbus, 47202
Conner Quilters Guild, 704 W. Third Street, Connersville, 47331
Quilt Patch Quilt Club, 210 Elm Street, Corydon, 47112
Heritage Quilters, PO Box 8, Crown Point, 46307
Love 'N Stitches, 116 S. Muessing, Cumberland, 46229
Hendricks County Quilters Guild, Senior Center, Danville, 46122
Heartland Quilters, 55922 Channelview Dri., Elkhart, 46516
Calico Cut-ups Quilt Club, 10013 Teton Court, Fort Wayne, 46804
Crossroads Quilt Club, 3625 Amulet Drive, Fort Wayne, 46815
Qu-Bees Quilt Club, 1512 Irene Avenue, Fort Wayne, 46808
Spring Valley Quilt Guild, 7164 W. Reformatory Rd., Fortville, 46040
Greenfield Guild, 3842 E. 200 S., Greenfield, 46140
Quilt Connection Guild, 2321 Willow Circle, Greenwood, 46143
Hill Valley Quilting, 607 W. Ralston, Indianapolis, 46217
IQ's, 3370 N. Highwoods Dr., Indianapolis, 46222
Quilter's Guild of Indianapolis, PO Box 68853, Indianapolis, 46268
Dune Country Quilters, PO Box 8526, Michigan City, 46360
Hands All Around Quilt Club, 10729 CR 46, Millersburg, 46453
New Paris Puzzle Quilters, 10729 CR 46, Millersburg, 46543
Carolina Quilters, 413 Conduit Road, Mooresville, 46158
Evening Quilter's Guild, 4001 W. State Road 28, Muncie, 47303
Muncie Quilters Guild, 812 W. Cromer, Muncie, 47303
Pioneer Women of Brown County, PO Box 668, Nashville, 47448
Hoosier Favorite Quilters, 1715 Duart Court, New Haven, 46774
Common Threads Quilt Guild, 5811 S. 500 W., New Palestine, 46163
Indiana Puzzle Quilt Club, 68535 CR 23, New Paris, 46553
Raintree Quilters Guild, PO Box 118, Newberg, 47630
Spring Valley Quilt Guild, Pendleton
Stitch & Chatter Quilt Guild, 221 W. Seventh Street, Portland, 47371
Piecemaker's Quilt Guild, 211 N. Main Street, Salem, 47167
Sew-n-Sew Quilt Club, 19887 Alou Lane, South Bend, 46637
Vigo County Quilters Guild, 1907 S. 3rd Street, Terre Haute, 47802
Randolph County Art Assoc., PO Box 284, Union City, 47390
String-along Quilt Guild, PO Box 2363, Valparaiso, 46384
The Old Tippecanoe Quilt Guild, 3059 Sullivan, W. Lafayette, 47906
Spinning Spools Quilt Guild, 4111 CR 16, Waterloo, 46793

Other Shops in Indiana:

Corydon	Follow Your Heart, 210 N. Elm
Frankfort	Mary's Crafts and Quilts, 52 W. Armstrong St.
Goshen	Calico Point, 24810 County Rd. 40
Goshen	Meredith's Sewing Corner, 712 W. Lincoln Ave.
Grabill	Country Shops of Grabill, 13756 State
Huntington	Patchwork Acres, 5279 W. River Rd.
Kokomo	Pastime Quilts & Country Furniture, 1268 E. 400 S.
Loogootee	The Fabric Shop, 219 1/2 N. JFK
Lynnville	Betty's Quilts and Fabrics, 244 West Third St.
Madison	Joan's Quilts & Crafts, 115 E. Main
Middlebury	Country Quilt Shoppe, 200 W. Warren
Monticello	Needles in the Haystack, 116 North Illinois
Morrisville	Colonial Outlet, 490 E. St. Clair
Nashville	The Quilt Parlor, 173 N. Van Buren
Nashville	Browntown Embroidery, 175 S. Jefferson St.,
Nashville	Fabric Addict, P.O. Box 620
Noblesville	Arbuckle's Railroad Place, 1151 Vine
Odon	Hopes and Seams, 105 W. Main St.
Paoli	Carriage House Quilts, 210 W. Main St.
Rochester	Thread Shed, 806 Main St.
Salem	Craft Town, North Side of Public Square
Shipshewana	Quiltmakers, P.O. Box 640
Shipshewana	Rebecca Haarer Arts & Antiques, 165 Morton St.
Shipshewana	Lolly's Fabrics & Quilt Shop, 228 W. Main
Shipshewana	Fabric Outlet, 440 S. Van Buren PO Box 487
South Bend	Erica's Craft & Sewing Center, 1320 N. Ironwood
Valparaiso	Needle & Thread, 60 Jefferson
West Lafayette	The Country Girl, 1185 Sagamore Pkwy W.
Zionsville	Liberty Farmhouse, 25 Cedar St.
Zionsville	Country Corner, 70 E. Hawthorne

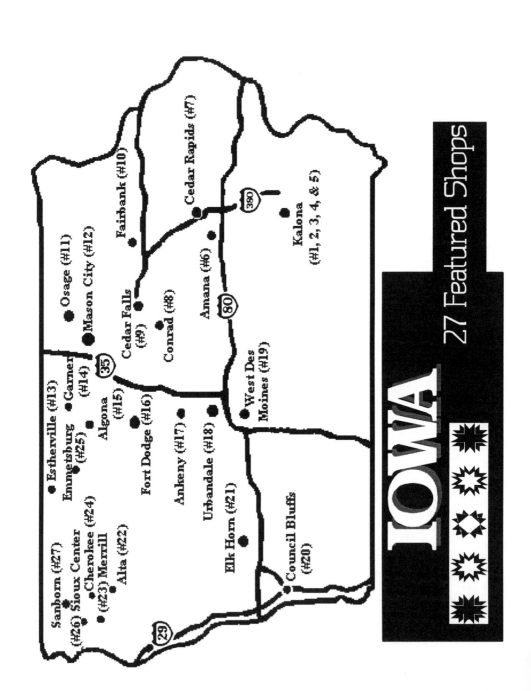

Kalona, IA #1

Woodin Wheel

**Mon - Sat
10 - 5**

515 "B" Ave.   52247
(319) 656-2240
Owner: Marilyn Woodin
Est: 1973

Over 250 New &
Antique Quilts
for Sale
plus a Private Quilt
Museum.

Downtown
Kalona
5 Blocks off
Highway 1

Kalona, IA #2

Stitch 'n Sew Cottage

**Mon - Fri
9 - 5
Sat 9 - 3**

207 4th St.   P.O. Box 351
(319) 656-2923   52247
Owners: Dorothy, Paul & Cande
Est: 1981   Schumann & Niva Burkholder

"Where Ma Saves
Pa's Dough"
Fabrics, Notions,
Quilting Supplies
Pillow Forms,
Embroidery
Supplies, batting.
1000+ Bolts

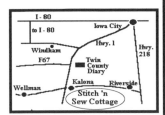

Kalona, IA #3

Kalona Kountry Kreations

2134— 560th St. S.W.   52247
(319) 656-5366
Owner: Sara M. Miller
Est: 1977   2500 sq.ft.

**Mon - Sat
9 - 5**

We have 5000 -
6000 bolts of
fabric, both
domestic &
imported. Plus
quilts, new &
antique.

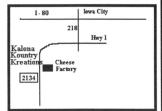

Kalona, IA #4

Ellen's Sewing Center

**Mon - Sat
8:30 - 5**

405 "B" Ave.   52247
(319) 656-3303
Est: 1975

Large selection of
Quilt Books,
Quilt Supplies,
Fashion Fabrics.
Bernina Machines
& Supplies.

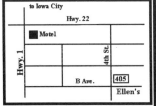

Kalona, IA #5

Stitches Galore

**Mon - Sat
9 - 5
Evenings
by Appt.**

109 1st. St. Hwy 1   52247
(800) 233-4189   Est: 1982
Owner: Linda Hiatt

Free Bi-Monthly Newsletter

Elna & Pfaff
Dealer. Sewing
instructors &
supplies they
use—includes
quilting,
smocking, tatting,
Brazilian Emb &
more.

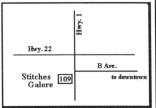

Amana, IA #6

Heritage Designs

Mon - Sat 10 - 5
Sun 12 - 4

4517 220 Trail   52203
(319) 622-3887
Est: 1978   1200 sq.ft.   1000 Bolts

An exclusive shop featuring unique quilting & needlework supplies & accessories. Exclusive fabrics, books, craft patterns, buttons, cross stitch and more.

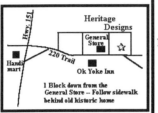

1 Block down from the General Store -- Follow sidewalk behind old historic home

Cedar Rapids, IA #7

The Quilting B

Mon - Fri 10 - 5
Thurs til 7
Sat 10 - 4

232 Second St. SE   52401
(319) 363-1643
Owner: Beverly Thornton
Est: 1986   750 sq.ft.

Complete Line of Supplies & Notions. Doll and Santa Patterns Yarns for Santa Beards & Doll Hair. Finished items for sale.

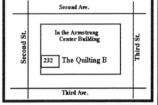

Conrad, IA #8

Conrad General Store

Mon - Sat 9 - 5

101 N. Main St. 50621
(515) 366-2043   Est: 1983
Owners: Brenda Shine, Jeannie Zehr, Janice Juchems

Large selection of Quilting Fabrics & Supplies. Country Gift Ware. Heritage Lace, & Nan's Cornhusk dolls in an original store since 1894

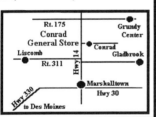

Cedar Falls, IA #9

Tues - Sat 10 - 5

The Quilt Emporium

322 Main St.   50613   (319) 277-8303   Est: 1993
Owners: Marlys Kauten & Barbara Newcomer

Full Service Shop.
Featuring—1000 Bolts of 100% Cotton Fabric
Large Supply of Notions, Books, & Patterns
Mail Order Available

A Great Quilting Experience !

Fairbank, IA #10

Jo's Thread & Thimble

Mon - Sat 9 - 5

105 Grove St. 50629
(319) 635-2119   Est: 1974
Owner: Jo Haberkamp   2500 sq.ft.

N.E. Iowa's finest quilt shop. Very large selection of fabrics, notions, patterns, books, and quilting supplies. Quilted Gift Items Also.

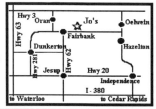

Osage, IA #11

The Fabric Shoppe

Mon - Sat 9 - 5
Thur til 7
Fri til 6

705 Main St.   50461
(515) 732-3669
Owner: Pam Schaefer - Smith
Est: 1988   1900 sq.ft.

Over 3000 bolts quality 100% cotton fabrics. Large selection of books, patterns, & notions. Classes. Well worth the trip!

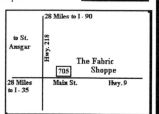

Mason City, IA #12

Joyful Stitches Quilt Shop

Mon - Sat 10 - 3
Wed Eve. 6 - 9
Or By Appt. 423-5572

14 - 5th St. NE 50401
(515) 421-7725
Owner: Vicky Davis   Est: 1995

Over 3000 bolts quality 100% cotton fabrics. Large selection of books, patterns, & notions. Classes. Well worth the trip!

Heartland Americana

Shop Estherville's original 1910 City Hall & Fire Station building where you find three "open levels" housing a wonderful *Quilt Shop, Gift Shop,* and *Gallery* with custom framing.

Our full service Quilt Shop has over 2000 bolts of 100% cotton fabrics by Hoffman, Benartex, South Seas, Marcus Brothers, Mission Valley, P&B, Red Wagon, Dan River, RJR, Monarch and many others. A great place to buy your next quilt book (250+ titles) along with patterns, books and notions.

Bernina Sales & Service

Come in and sew on one of our Berninas, *(you can't beat our prices)* Many classes offered throughout the year.

"Fabric Express"

Join *"Fabric Express"* (our fabric club), and swatches of our newest fabrics will be delivered to you each month. Also receive:
* 20% birthday discount & other discounts!
* a free pattern of your choice in December
* complimentary yard card with subscription
* monthly freebies and other perks!!
Annual membership is $17.85, (Includes tax).

We accept Visa, Mastercard, & Discover!!
Open 9-5:30 M-F,
Thur. until 8 pm, Sat until 5 pm

Heartland Americana **# 13**
24 S 6, Estherville, IA 51334
(712) 362-2787
(located 1 block South of library square, across from the Dairy Queen!)

We welcome tour busses and mail orders!!

Garner, IA #14

2345 Palm Ave.
(800) 544-6852

Mon - Sat 10 - 5

Owners: Mary Tendall & Connie Tesene
Est: 1984   2500 sq.ft.   2500 Bolts

Full service quilt shop in a chicken coop. Features 100% cotton fabric, patterns, books, notions, classes and machine quilting. Bus tours welcome. Catalog $1.50

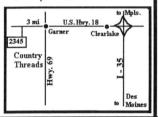

Algona, IA #15

Seams to Me

**Mon - Fri 9 - 5
Thur til 8
Sat 9 - 4**

17 E. State   50511
(515) 295-5841
Owner: Karen Boyken

Quality 100% cotton fabrics. Full line of notions & crafts. Walls filled with models & displays. Custom machine quilting. Home of "Stitchin' Friends" patterns. Mail Order Avail.   Est: 1987

IOWA

Fort Dodge, IA #16

Grandma's Quilts, Crafts & Needlework

**Mon - Sat 10 - 5
Tues &
Thur til 7**

1422—1st. Ave. North   50501
(515) 955-1521   Est: 1987
Owner: Mary Consier
                2000 sq.ft.   4-500 Bolts

In a House built in 1896 with a black wrought iron fence. We carry crafts, fabric, and lots of books and patterns. We also carry yarn.

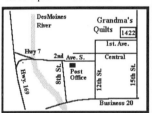

Ankeny, IA #17

Country Clutter

**Tues - Fri 10 - 5:30
Sat 10 - 4
Sun 1 - 4**

305 S.W. Walnut St.   50021
(515) 964-2747
Owner: Sue Ites   Est: 1985
Group Appts. Available

Cozy Quilt Shop featuring 500+ bolts of fabric, quilt books, counted cross-stitch, & 100's of doll patterns.
A Quilter's Dream!

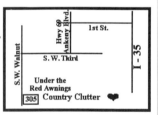

Urbandale, IA #18

Living History Farms

**Mon - Sat 9 - 5
Sun 11 - 6**

2600 N.W. 111th   50322
(515) 278-2400   24 Hr. Info. Line
                Non-Profit

Our farm is a 600 acre, open-air farming museum. We display a portion of our collection of 300 quilts Oct. 3 - 6. Other gifts and crafts may be purchased in The Gallery

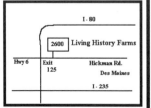

West Des Moines, IA #19

The Quilt Block

**M -S 10 - 5
Thur 10 - 7
Sun 1 - 4**

325 5th Street   50265
(515) 255-1010   Est: 1987
3000 sq.ft.   2000 Bolts
Owners: Marilyn Parks & Mary Miller

Full line quilt supply store-- fabrics, notions, books, patterns. Authorized Bernina dealer.

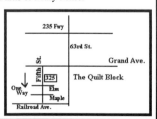

Council Bluffs, IA   #20

Kanesville Quilting
Gingham Goose

19851 Virginia Hills Rd.
(712) 366-6003   51503
Est: 1990   3000 sq.ft.
Owners: Mavis Hauser & Karen Krause

**Mon - Fri
10 - 5:30
Sat 10 - 4**

100% Cottons,
Books, Patterns,
Notions, and
Classes.
We do machine
quilting on your
tops.

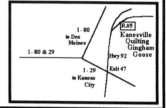

Elk Horn, IA   #21

Prairie Star Quilts

**Mon - Sat
10 - 5**

4132 Main St.   51531
(712) 764-7012
Owner: Julie Larsen
Est: 1986   1500 sq.ft.

We Love Mail Order

Over 1000 bolts of 100% cotton fabric.
ALEXANDER HENRY, JINNY BEYER,
MOMEN HOUSE, HOFFMAN, GUTCHEON
The latest in quilting notions, books and patterns.
Largest selection of fabric craft patterns in Western Iowa

Custom Machine Quilting

Alta, IA   #22

The Quilt Shoppe

206 S. Main   51002
(712) 284-2724
Owner: Pat Patten
Est: 1987   1200 sq.ft.

**Mon, Tue,
Thur, Fri
9:30 - 5:30
Thur til 8
Sat 9:30 - 3**

All cotton fabrics,
books, patterns,
notions, classes.
Consignments
welcome.
Personalized
helpful service
for all your
quilting needs.

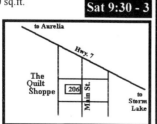

Merrill, IA   #23

The Quiltworks

518 Webster Street
(712) 938-2059   51038
Owner: Mary K. Roder
Est: 1991

**Mon - Fri
9 - 5
Sat 9 - 12**

Custom Machine
Quilting.
Approximately 10
quilts on hand.
Wood quilt racks
and shelves.

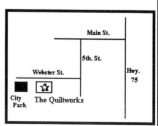

Cherokee, IA #24

Hi Fashion Fabrics & Quilts

102 E. Main   51012
(712) 225-2746   Est: 1970
Owner: Mary Kehrwald
1800 sq.ft.   1200 Bolts

| Mon - Fri |
| 9 - 5 |
| Thur til 8 |
| Sat 9 - 4 |

We Carry a Complete Line of 100% Cotton Fabrics along with all the supplies. Books, batting, patterns and notions.

Quilter's Husband: a man who's bought one quarter yard of fabric at every store in town and doesn't complain about it.

Emmetsburg, IA #25

Calico Cupboard

2201 Main St.   50536
(712) 852-2098
Owner: Deborah Hite
Est: 1981   2500 sq.ft.   700 Bolts

| Mon - Sat |
| 9 - 5 |
| Thur til 8 |

Large selection of quilting fabrics, notions, books, quilt & craft patterns and stencils. Great classes and friendly service !

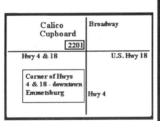

Sioux Center, IA #26

Roelofs

24 3rd St. NW   51250
(712) 722-2611   Est: 1976
Owner: Dixie Roelofs   2000 sq.ft.

| Mon - Sat |
| 9 - 5:30 |
| Thur til 9 |

Quilting Fabrics & supplies; Fabric craft patterns and supplies; wall hanging kits; hemstitched flannel receiving blankets ready for crochet edge.

Quilter's Children: well-educated young people, who know better than to jump on the bed or use mom's scissors to cut construction paper.

Sanborn, IA #27

Quilter's Coop

6063 - 280th St.   51248
(712) 736-2204
Owner: Judy Flanagan
Est: 1992   1280 sq.ft.   800 Bolts

| Tues - Sat |
| 10 - 5:30 |

Cotton Fabrics, Notions, Patterns & Books, Original Patterns, Country feel in an old Chicken Coop.

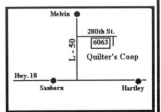

Iowa Guilds:

East Iowa Heirloom Quilters, P.O. Box 1382, Cedar Rapids, 52406
Mississippi Valley Quilters Guild, P.O. Box 2636, Davenport, 52809
Des Moines Area Quilt Guild, 6222 University Ave., Des Moines
Iowa Quilter's Guild, Box 65, 31446 Prairie St., Garden City, 50102
Old Capitol Quilters Guild, Iowa City
Quilting for Fun, 1305 Yewell St., Iowa City, 52240
North Iowa Quilters Guild, Mason City, 50401
Northeast Iowa Quilter's Guild, P.O. Box 43, Monona, 52159
Sioux Prairie Quilters, 116 Colorado NW, Orange City, 51041
Four Seasons Quilt Guild, P.O. Box 178, Sloan, 51055

Other Shops in Iowa:

Altoona	Back Door Fabrics, 106 2nd St. S.E.
Boone	Memory Lane, 715 Carroll St.
Cedar Rapids	West Side Sewing Machine Shop, 418 First St. S.W.
Cedar Rapids	Crazy Lady Quilt Shoppe, 710 J Ave. NE
Chariton	The Sampler, 102 S. Grand
Chariton	Ben Franklin Quilt Shop, 907 Braden Ave.
Clarinda	Seam-A-Dream, 105 E. Main
Corydon	J's Nook, 105 S. Franklin
Creston	Knits & Other Notions, 209 W. Montgomery
Decorah	The Sewing Basket, 519 W. Water
Denison	Memory Lane Fabrics, 28 N. Main St.
Des Moines	Bartlett's Quilts, 820 35th St.
Estherville	Wooden Thimble, 9 N. 5th St.
Fairfield	The Sewing Room, 59 W. Broadway
Fayette	Country House Cottons, P.O. Box 375
Indianola	Stitching Place, 110 W. Ashland Ave.
Iowa Falls	Iowa Falls Sewing Machine Co., 520 Washington Ave.
Kalona	Log Cabin Creations, 615 3rd. St.
Kalona	Country Livin', 1369 Hwy. 1
Kalona	Yoders Antiques, Gifts & Quilts, 432 B Ave.
Kalona	Willow Creek Collectibles, 417 B Ave.
Keokuk	Stitch N Crafts, 1000 Main St.
Lamoni	The Fabric Patch, 140 N. Linden
Le Mars	Crafters Delite, 25 Plymouth St. NE
Marion	Connie's Quilt Shop, 785 Eighth Ave.
Marion	Sanctuary Antiques Center, 801 Tenth St.
Monona	Suhdrons's The Mall, 120 W. Center
Muscatine	Neal's Sewing Center, 309 E. 2nd. St.
New Hampton	Material Magic, 22 E. Main St.
Newton	Nina's Quilt Patch, 213 W. 2nd St. N
Oelwein	Louann's Fabrics, 21 E. Charles
Ottumwa	Country Accents, 101 N. Court
Ottumwa	Homespun Traditions, 1111 N. Quincy #120
Ottumwa	Calico Connection, P.O. Box 215 Rural Route 6
Parkersburg	The Stitchery, 903 Muller
Postville	Sudron's Fabrics, 138 W. Greene, Box 225
Red Oak	Quilting on the Square, 503 3rd. St.
Red Oak	The Country Heart, 210 Coolbaugh
Sheldon	Sheldon Fabric & Custom Quilting, 301 9th St.
South Amana	Fern Hill, Highway 6 & 220
St. Olaf	Country Calico, R.R. #1, Gunder Rd.
Strawberry Point	Keppler Krafts, 35536 Hwy. 13 N
Waukon	Joyce's Quilt Lodge, 920 2nd St. NW
Webster City	Gingerbread House, 309 Bank St.
West Des Moines	Donna's Dolls & Country Collections, 234 5th St.

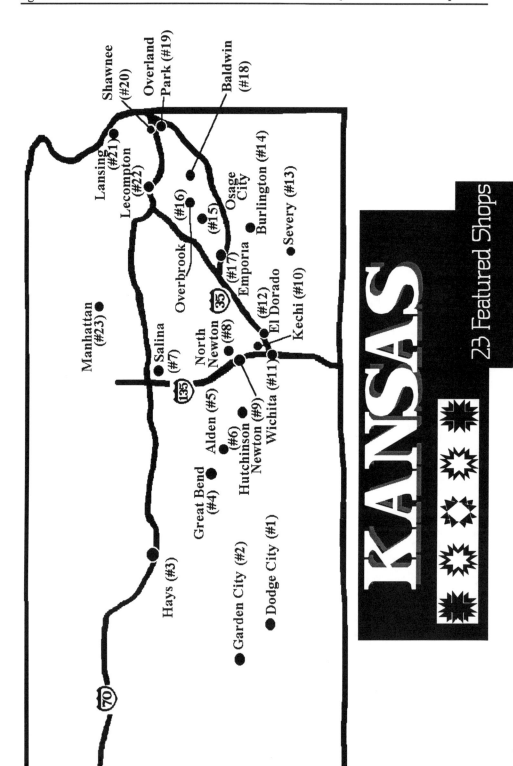

Dodge City, KS #1

Roselle's Fabrics

Mon - Sat
9:30 - 6

618 Second   67801
(316) 225-0004
Owner: Roselle Calihan
Est: 1981   1800 sq.ft.

Lots of quilt books, patterns, and quilting aids, 100% cottons and other fabrics.

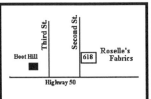

Garden City, KS #2

The Quilt Rack

605 Kansas Plaza   67846
(316) 275-8786
Owner: Jeaninne McCarthy
                    Est: 1987

Mon - Fri
9:30 - 5:30
Sat 10 - 5

Quilting and all the Extras!
Threads! Threads! Threads!
Cross-Stitch
Hardanger
Needlepoint
Silk Ribbon
Embroidery

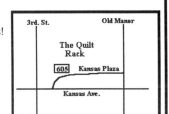

Hays, KS #3

Quilt Cottage Co.

"The Place for Ideas"

Mon - Fri
9 - 5:30
Sat 10 - 3

202 Centennial Center (corner of Centennial and Vine)   67601
Est: 1994   3000 sq.ft.   1200 Bolts
Owners: Debbie Huebner, Mary Krob & Kari Schultz

(913) 625-0080

Top quality quilting fabrics.
The area's finest selection of books,
patterns and notions.
Gift lines including candles, baskets,
whimsical jewelry and more.

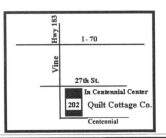

Great Bend, KS #4

The Calico Shoppe

Mon - Sat 9:30 - 5:30

1415 Main St.   67530
(316) 793-8900   Est: 1987
Owner: Kaye Damm   3750 sq.ft.

2000+ bolts.
Country Craft
Patterns.
Classes.
Finished
Quilts for Sale.

Alden, KS #5

Prairie Flower Crafts

205 Pioneer St.   67512-0158
(800) 527-3997
Owner: Sara Fair Sleeper
Est: 1970   5370 sq.ft.

Mon - Sat 10 - 4:30

25 years collecting
cotton fabric for
quilts. Over 20
fabric companies
represented:
extensive designer
fabric selection.
Notions, Books, &
Patterns.

Hutchinson, KS #6

COUNTRY FABRICS

Mon - Sat 9 - 5:30

R. R. #1   6411 W. Morgan Road
(316) 662-3681   67501
Est: 1977
Owners: Janet, Randy, & Leland Headings

100% Cotton
Solids and
calicos. Quilting
Notions, Books,
& Batting.
Fashion Fabrics,
Sewing Notions
& Patterns.

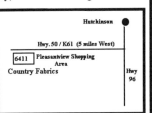

Gadgets: something a
quilter can never have
enough of; you must
have the right tool for
the job.

IS FOR QUILTING!

Salina, KS   #7

Quilting Bee

120 S. Santa Fe   67401
(913) 823-9376
Owner: Shirley Wolf
Est: 1979   4000 sq.ft.

Mon - Sat
9:30 - 5:30
Thur til 6:30
Sat 9:30 - 5

4000 Square Feet devoted to cotton quilting fabrics, notions, books, and classes. All major fabrics, lots of plaids. 3500 bolts.

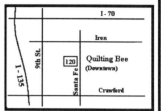

The Quilt Shop, Ltd.

2511 N. MAIN · N. NEWTON, KS 67117

Mon - Fri
9 - 5
Sat 9 - 1

Owners: Laura Flaming & Wilma Schmidt

Est: 1988   1120 sq.ft.   3000 Bolts

(316) 283-2332

Wide choice of fabrics, books, patterns & notions.
Experienced, friendly shop.
Personnel offer help and extend a warm welcome.

North Newton, KS   #8

Newton, KS   #9

Charlotte's Natural Fabrics

612 N. Main St.   67114
(316) 284-2547
Est: 1985

Mon - Fri
9:30 - 5:30
Thur til 8
Sat 9:30 - 5
Sun 1 - 5

Specializing in beautiful fashion fabrics: lots of cotton, rayon, silk, linen & wool. Unique trims, buttons & wearable art ideas!

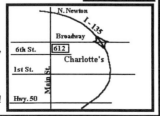

Kechi, KS   #10

Kechi Quilt Shop

134 E. Kechi Rd., P.O. Box 357
(316) 744-8500   67067
Est: 1996   500 Bolts
Owners: Janet Robinson & Shirley Padding

Mon - Sat
10 - 5

A cozy little shop situated in the "Antique Capital of Kansas" Cottons, stencils, books, patterns, notions.

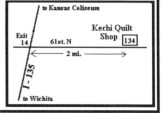

Wichita, KS   #11

Gramma's Calico Cupboard

Mon - Sat
9:30 - 5

1945 S. Hydraulic   67211
(316) 264-0274   Est: 1982
Owner: Betty Webb   3500 sq.ft.   3000 Bolts

Quilting & Craft fabric & supplies. Christmas room open all year. Antiques, gifts including Muffy Vanderbear.

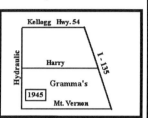

El Dorado, KS   #12

Sew N Sew

Mon - Fri
10 - 5:30
Sat 9 - 5:30

105 S. Main   67042
(316) 321-7600
Est: 1992
Owner: Karen Hayes

Featuring Hoffman, P&B, Concord House, RJR, & other fine quilt fabrics. Books, notions, classes, fun. Come see us!

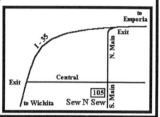

Severy, KS   #13

Needle In A Haystack

Mon &
Wed - Sat
9 - 5
Sun 1 - 5

R.R. #1, Box 174   67137
(316) 736-2942
Owner: Lois Klepper   Est: 1991
1500 Bolts

Fabric - Books
Notions
Machine Quilting
Cross Stitch
Supplies
Handcrafted items for sale.
Summer Hours 7 day a week.

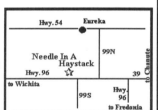

Burlington, KS   #14

Silver Threads & Golden Needles

Mon - Sat
9:30 - 5:30
Sun 12 - 5

321 Neosho   66839
(316) 364-8233
Est: 1985
2000 sq.ft.

Owners: Whitey & Jerry Anne Hoyt

Top Quality Fabric $1.99 yd. & up. Patterns, Notions, Crafts, Books, Quilting Supplies, Craft Patterns & More Wholesale/Retail

Osage City, KS   #15

Calico Cupboard

Tues - Fri
9 - 5
Sat 9 - 3

513 Market   66523
(913) 528-4861
Owners: Lewis & Lora Lee Meek
Est: 1983

We specialize in machine made quilts ! Usually 100 or more in stock ! **OR** choose from our 1000 bolt inventory for a custom order. Fabric also sold by the yard.

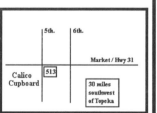

Overbrook, KS   #16

Overbrook Quilt Connection

Tue - Sat
10 - 5

500 Maple P.O. Box 50   66524
(913) 665-7841
Est: 1994   4300 sq.ft.
Owners: Roxane Fawl & Carolyn Meerian

1000 bolt inventory, books, patterns, notions. Classes for Quilting & Dollmaking Free Flier

Fabric Corner

Est: 1992

1800 sq.ft.   1500+ bolts

(316) 342-3040

416 W. Sixth Ave.   66801

Owners: Colleen Janssen
& Joan Kloppenberg

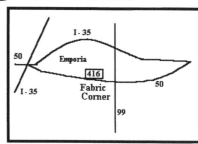

Emporia, KS   #17

Quilting classes, supplies and fabrics - Hoffman, RJR, Jinny
Beyer, Springmaid, P&B & South Seas.
We also carry a wide selection of craft and applique patterns.
We carry over 250 book titles from publishers such as:
That Patchwork Place, Quilt in a Day, C&T Publishing, and
many others.

Mon - Fri 9 - 6   Sat 9 - 5

Emporia is located in the heart of the Kansas Flint Hills on two major
highways, which makes Fabric Corner easily accessible on your next trip through
Kansas. With an abundance of service and lots of good conversation, we're sure
this is one quilt shop you'll be glad you stopped in.

Baldwin City, KS   #18

Quilters' Paradise

Mon - Sat
9:30 - 5

713 8th St. 66006
(913) 594-3477   Est: 1986
Owner: Sharon A. Vesecky

Quilting supplies, books, patterns,
fabric—Hoffman,
Jinny Beyer,
Debbie Mumm,
Nancy Crow,
Springs, Concord.
Needlework
supplies. Gifts
Machine Quilting.
Kansas Products.

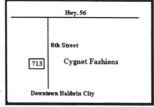

Overland Park, KS   #19

The Saltbox Sampler

Mon - Fri
9:30 - 5:30
Tue & Thur
til 8:30
Sat 10 - 4

106th & Roe   66207
(913) 642-0180   Est: 1983
Owners: Gloria Case & Karen
Overstedt
1300 Bolts

Cottons for
quilting &
sewing, notions,
books, loads of
homespun
fabrics.
Cross stitch
supplies.
Wonderful
samples. Classes.

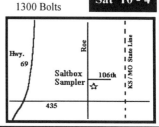

Shawnee, KS #20

Prairie Point

7341 Quivira Rd.   66216
in Westbrooke Village Shp. Ctr.
(913) 268-3333   Est: 1995
Owner: Vonda K. Sinha   2720 sq.ft.

Mon - Thur
10 - 8:30
Fri & Sat
10 - 5:30
Sun 1 - 5

1500 Bolts
Finest quality
fabrics for quilting
and cross stitch.
Wide variety of
notions, books and
patterns.
Friendly Service.

Lansing, KS #21

Fabric Mart

On the Corner of Eisenhower
and 73 Highway at Lansing, KS
(913) 727-1639   Est: 1986
Owners: Ron & Mildred Gerdes
3200 sq.ft.   Catalog $5.50 - 6 books

Mon - Fri
9:30 - 6
Sat 9:30 - 5
Sun 1 - 5

Midwest's Largest
Quilt Shop with
over 5000 Bolts and
Growing! Large
Selection of Books,
Notions/Laces.
Don't Miss This
One !

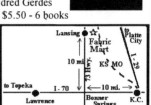

Kansas Quilters Organization, 1721 Weile, Winfield, 67156
Kansas Guilds:
Silver Needles Quilt Guild, 5500 S. Ohio Rd., Assaria, 67416
Central Kansas Thread-Benders, 1400 Truman, Great Bend, 67530
Big Creek Quilt Guild, 1061 Catherine Road, Hays, 67601
Heart of Kansas Quilt Guild, P.O. Box 271, Hutchinson, 67504
Sunflower Quilter's Guild, P.O. Box 69, Iola, 66749
Kaw Valley Quilters Guild, 924 Vermont, Lawrence, 66044
Olathe Quilters Guild, 151st Street & Blackbob Rd. Olathe, 66061
Little Balkans Quilt Guild, P.O. Box 1608, Pittsburg, 66762
Quilters Guild of Greater K.C., 1617 W. 42nd Street, Kansas City
Miama County Quilters Guild, P.O. Box 453, Paola, 66071
Silver Needles Quilt Guild, Box 1132, Salina, 67402
Walnut Valley Quilters Guild, 1615 East 20th Ave., Winfield, 67156

Lecompton, KS #22

Country Quilting

**Tue - Thur
10 - 6
Or By
Appt.**

1719 E. 150 Rd.   66050
(913) 887-6554
Owners: Dennis & Ava McCarthy
1500 sq.ft.

Fabrics, Books,
Patterns &
Classes in a
country setting.
Large selection
of quilts for sale.
Machine
Quilting.

to Topeka   Hwy. 40   to Lawrence
050 Rd.
Country Quilting
☆
1700 N
1023 Rd.
45th St.

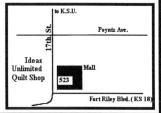

Manhattan, KS #23

Ideas Unlimited Quilt Shop

**Mon - Fri
11 - 5:30
Thur til 7
Sat 10 - 3**

523 South 17th   66502
(913) 539-6759   Est: 1987
Owners: Dorine & Stan Elsea
1000 sq.ft.
2500 Bolts

Unique fabrics for
quilts & fashions.
Large selection of
books & patterns
for quilts and
pieced garments.

to K.S.U.
17th St.
Poyntz Ave.
Ideas
Unlimited
Quilt Shop
523
Mall
Fort Riley Blvd. (KS 18)

Other Shops in Kansas:

Anthony	Pride of the Prairie Quilt Shoppe, 131 West Main
Clay Center	Clione's Collections, 709 5th St.
Derby	Prairie Quilts, Inc., 836 Nelson Dr.
Emporia	Quilts & Yardage Plus, 7 E. 6th Ave.
La Crosse	Patchwork Parlor, 812 Main St.
Lawrence	Stitch on Needlwork Shop, 926 Massachusetts St.
Lincoln	Calico Country
Marysville	Fabric Center, 818 Broadway
Norton	The Sewing Box, 128 S. State PO Box 125
Ottawa	Chris' Corner, 229 S. Main St.
Phillipsburg	The Pin Cushion, 747 3rd.
Topeka	Wallace's Stitchin Post II, 4004 S.W. Huntoon St.
Topeka	Bennett's Sewing Center, 2044 N. W. Topeka Blvd.
Wichita	The Sewing Center, 2255 N. Amidon St.
Wichita	Prairie Quilts, Inc., 5614 E. Lincoln
Winfield	The Sewing Basket, 211 E. 9th Ave. #A

Quilt Show Ahead !

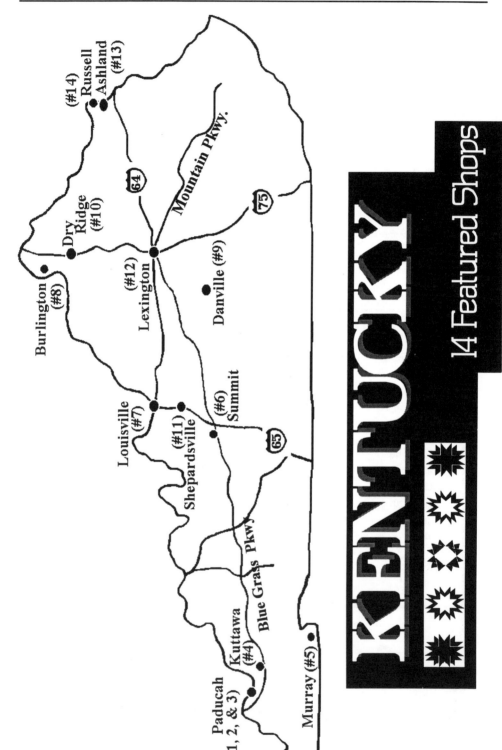

KENTUCKY

14 Featured Shops

Russell (#14)
Ashland (#13)
Mountain Pkwy.
64
75
Dry Ridge (#10)
Burlington (#8)
Lexington (#12)
Danville (#9)
Louisville (#7)
Summit (#6)
Shepardsville (#11)
65
Blue Grass Pkwy.
Kuttawa (#4)
Paducah (#1, 2, & 3)
Murray (#5)

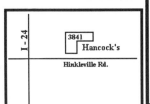

Paducah: "Quilt City U.S.A."

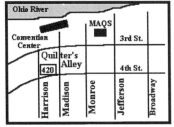

Kuttawa, KY #4

Harbor House Bed & Breakfast

1730 Lake Barkley Dr.
(502) 388-4012
Owners: Lee & Betty Bird

Specializing in Sewing or Quilting Retreats

From Paducah, KY:
—Go on I - 24 to Exit 40
  (Kuttawa/Eddyville Exit)
—Go west 1/2 mile to exit #295
—Turn left and follow road
  around to 1730 Lake
  Barkley Dr.

Murray, KY #5

The Magic Thimble

Tues - Sat 10 - 5

813 Coldwater Road   42071
(502) 759-4769
Owner: Peggy Smith   Est: 1986
1000 sq.ft.   300 Bolts

100% Cotton Fabrics, Patterns. Friendly Atmosphere & knowledgeable staff

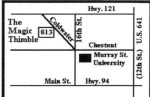

Summit, KY #6

Quaint Quilts

Mon, Tues, Wed, Fri, & Sat 10 - 5

16117 Leitchfield Rd.   42783
(502) 862-9708   Est: 1985
Owner: Kathryn Richardson
672 sq.ft.

Quilts, Curtains, Machine & Hand Quilting, Oil Paintings, Prints, Basketry, Rugs & Rug Weaving. Approx. 100 printed quilt top fabrics.

Louisville, KY #7

Happy Heart Quilt Shop

Mon - Fri 10 - 5 Sat 10 - 4

7913 3rd. St. Rd.   40214
(502) 363-1171   Est: 1985
Owner: Yvonne Fritze   1200 sq.ft.

Large selection of fabrics including Hoffman, RJR, Jinny Beyer, P&B, Liberty/London. Quilt Kits Extensive line of books, patterns and notions.

Burlington, KY #8

Cabin Arts

Mon - Sat 10 - 6 Some Evenings During Classes

5878 N. Jefferson St.   41005
(606) 586-8021
Est: 1992   1300 sq.ft.
Owners: Linda Whittenburg & Sarah O'Neil

Quality Quilt Fabrics plus notions, books & more. Local Handcrafted Treasures. Classes Available. Located in historic district in 1850's Log Cabin

Danville, KY #9

World Wide Fabrics

Mon - Sat 10 - 6

104 Man O'War Blvd.   40422
(606) 236-1175   Est: 1976
Owners: Earl & Jean Steinhauer
4000 sq.ft.

Authorized Bernina Dealer Calico Cottons Quilting Books and Supplies Bridal Fabrics and accessories Complete line of Notions, Drapery & Upholstery

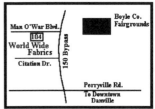

Dry Ridge,   KY   #10

The Quilt Box

The Quilt Box is one of Kentucky's nicest Quilt Shops. Its special charm begins on the tree shaded gravel road leading to Walnut Springs Farm where the shop is located - only 3 miles from Exit #159 on I-75 in the scenic bluegrass country - half way between Cincinnati and Lexington.

The Quilt Box opened 13 years ago in a restored 150 year old log cabin - on the farm - and has since been expanded to an adjoining two-story structure.

 Chosen by Better Homes & Gardens "Quilt Sampler" magazine as one of the top 10 quilt shops in North America, this is truly a one stop Quilting Shop for all of your quilting needs, and a fun place to shop! - staffed by knowledgeable, friendly and helpful people anxious to fulfill all of your quilting needs.

In addition to our broad assortment of quilting related items we are proud of our 2,000+ bolts including the latest designer fabrics at reasonable prices.

We welcome all visitors and always enjoy taking the time to make you feel at home and unhurried. You'll be glad you came and weather permitting, are welcome to enjoy our large patio and deck. Bring and enjoy a picnic lunch, look over the farm animals, and enjoy the scenery.

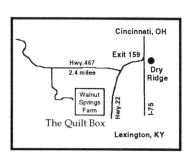

Mon - Sat 9:30 - 5:00 Closed on Sunday
The Quilt Box At Walnut Springs Farm Hwy. 467 N.
Dry Ridge, KY. 41035 (606) 824-4007

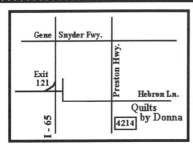

Shepherdsville, KY #11

(502) 955-8673

4214 N. Preston Highway   40165

Mon 9 - 8
Tues - Fri 9 - 6
Sat 9 - 5

Owner: Donna Sharp
Est: 1982   1800 sq.ft.

Quilts by Donna

100's of bolts of fabric.
Books & Patterns
Tops, Etc.
Up to 100 +Finished Quilts.

Home of the original
Quilts by Donna Calendar.

Lexington, KY #12

Quilter's Square

Mon - Sat
9:30 - 5:30

2416 Regency Road   40503
(606) 278-5010

**BERNINA
DEALER.**
All Quilting
Supplies, Kits,
Repairs, old quilts
restoration.
Smocking &
Heirloom sewing
supplies. Large
selection of books
& patterns.

Owner: Mary Charles
Est: 1982   2400 sq.ft.

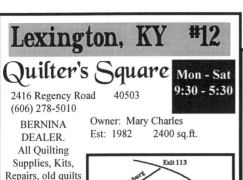

Ashland, KY #13

Craft Attic
Quilt Shop

Mon - Sat
10 - 5
Wed 2 - 5

2027 Hoods Creek Pike 41102
(606) 325-1212
Owner: Donnie Maggard
Est: 1982   1500 sq.ft.   1000 Bolts

100% Cotton
Fabrics.
Full Line of
Quilting Supplies.
Books
Stencils
Classes

Bernina Center **Historic Russell, KY #14**

The Quilting Connection

406 Belfonte St.   41169
(606) 836-9920
Owner: Melvina Blair
Finest Fabrics & supplies for
   the quilter and sewing enthusiast. Plus
   Bernina sewing machines and supplies.
You'll find everything you need right here.

Mon - Thur
10 - 7
Fri & Sat
10 - 4

Est: 1995

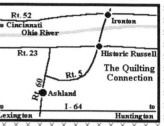

Rt. 52
to Cincinnati
Ohio River
Ironton
Rt. 23
Historic Russell
Rt. 5
The Quilting Connection
Rt. 60
Ashland
to Lexington
I - 64
to Huntington

Kentucky Guilds:
Gone to Pieces Q.G., 2027 Hoods Creek Pike, Ashland, 41102
Stringtown Quilters Guild, 4706 Limaburg Rd., Hebron, 41048
Louisville Nimble Thimbles, P.O. Box 6234, Louisville, 40206
Graves County Piecemakers, Rt. 3, Box 236-2, Mayfield, 42066
Murray Quilt Lovers, P.O. Box 265, Murrary, 42071
Owensboro Quilters Guild, Owensboro, 42301
Murray Quilt Lovers, P.O. Box 975, Paintsville
Licking Valley Quilters, 907 Mary St., Villa Hills, 41017

Other Shops in Kentucky:

Barbourville	Know Discount Fabric, Hwy. 229 & 25 E
Benton	Needle & Thread, P.O. Box 78
Bowling Green	Kwik N Ezy Fabric, 1751 Scottsville Rd.
Corbin	The Kentucky Quilt Co., 1878 Cumberland Falls Hwy.
Flatwoods	Monogram & Quilt Cottage, 1402 Brentwood Ct.
Frankfort	Treadleworks, 235 W. Broadway St.
Golden Pond	Home Place - 1850, Land between the Lakes
Louisville	Baer Fabrics, 515 E. Market St.
Magnolia	The Jewel Box, 10075 N. Jackson Hwy.
Mt. Vernon	Heritage Crafts, Hwy. 461
Murray	Murray Sewing Center, 700 N. 12th St.
Owensboro	Donna's Stitchery Nook, 2845 Parrish Ave.
Paducah	Quilt City Fabric Inc., 428 Broadway
Philpot	The Quilting Place, 5996 Old Kentucky 54
Pineville	Kathy's Needle & Thread, P.O. Box 118 Route #2
Salyersville	Quilting Shop, East Mountain Parkway, PO Box 998
Somerset	Mill Outlet, 4502 S. Highway 27
Whitesburg	Cozy Corner, 210 E. Main St.

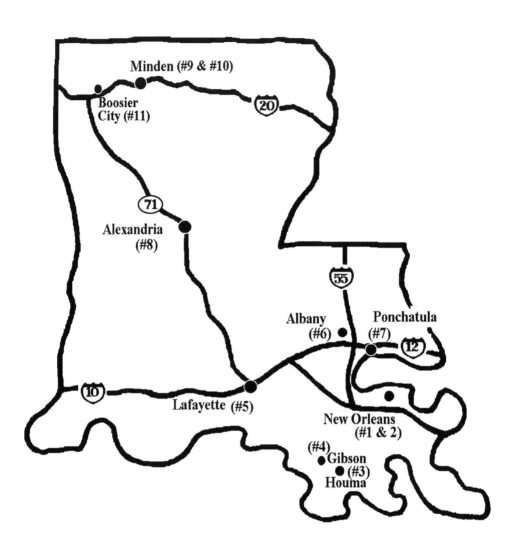

Minden (#9 & #10)

Boosier
City (#11)

71

Alexandria
(#8)

55

Albany   Ponchatula
(#6)   (#7)   12

10

Lafayette (#5)

New Orleans
(#1 & 2)

(#4)
Gibson
(#3)
Houma

LOUISIANA

ll Featured Shops

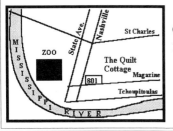
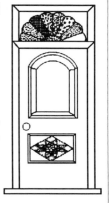

Gibson, LA #4

Alice & Lee's Quilts & Crafts

Tue - Fri 10 - 5

6233 Bayou Black Dr.   Hwy. 90
(504) 575-2389   P.O. Box 858   70356
Est: 1992

Friendly shop. Mother/Daughter operation. Quilts for sale, fat quarters, notions. Craftwork, hand embroidery & crochet. Cajun items Etc.

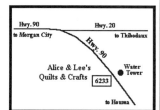

Lafayette, LA #5

Ginger's Needleworks

Usually Open
Tues - Thurs 10 - 5   Sat 11 - 3
Closed to work Quilt Shows:
See our Booths at Paducah, Houston, Dallas,
the Embellishment show in Houston and
many other smaller Quilt Shows.

905 East Gloria Switch Road
(318) 232-7847   70507
Owner: Ginger Moore   Est:1984
450 sq.ft. Quilting   200 sq.ft. Yarns

Quilting fabrics, notions, supplies and quilts for sale. Yarns.

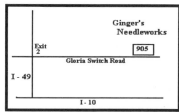

CATALOG $1
Send us your name & address,
ATTN: Dept QTC

Albany, LA #6

Patchwork Plus by Vera

Tues - Fri 9 - 5
Sat 9 - 3

29937 S. Montpelier Ave.   70711
(504) 567-5269   Est: 1989
Owner: Vera Honea   1100 sq.ft.   1500 Bolts

Great selection of 100% cotton fabrics, quilter's fat quarters, books, quilting supplies, patterns, notions, silk ribbon. Classes Friendly & Helpful

Ponchatoula, LA #7

Yesteryear Antiques & Quilts

Mon - Sat 10 - 5
Sun 12 - 5

165 East Pine   70454
(504) 386-2741   Est: 1982
Owners: Pat Zieske & Lee Barends

We do Custom Made Quilts !
We have samples and fabrics at the shop for you to look at - you choose your own pattern and colors.

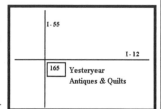

Alexandria, LA #8

Quilting Quarters

Mon - Fri 9 - 5
Sat 9 - 12

6524 Masonic Drive   71301
(318) 473-9104
Owner: Geraldine Gerami
Est: 1985   1200 sq.ft.

We have 1000 Bolts of 100% Cottons ! Also Patterns, books, and notions. ANYTHING FOR QUILTING ! !

Minden, LA #9

The Little Country Quilt Shop

Tues - Fri
9 - 5
Sat 10 - 2

534 Old Arcadia Rd.   71055
(318) 377-2462
Owner: Nona Sale   ` Est: 1983

We have approx. 1000 bolts. All the latest books, patterns, & supplies. Also a variety of classes. Plus we have old and new quilts for sale.

From I - 20 take Exit 49. Go North 3&1/2 miles to the 2nd blinking light. At the light turn right for 1/4 mile to Parish 131. Shop is 1 mile on the left. Watch for Signs ! !

Minden, LA #10

Fabric Boutique

Mon -Sat
9:30 - 5:30

1134 Homer Rd. 71055
(318) 377-1549
Owner: Shirley C. Warren
Est: 1972

Unique combination of classes, quilting supplies & fabrics. Authorized Bernina, Brother & Viking Sewing Machine dealer.

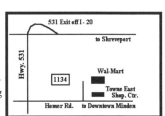

Louisiana Guilds:
Strawberry Patch Quilters
       Albany LA
Red River Quilters, P.O. Box 4811,
       Shreveport, 71134
Jefferson Parish Quilting Guild,
       711 Ridgelake Dr, Metairie
Gulf States Quilting Assoc.,
       P.O. Box 8391, Metairie,
       70011
North Louisiana Quilters, Monroe
Southern Samplers, 165 E. Pine Street
       Ponchatoula, 70454

Bossier City, LA #11

Fabric Boutique

Mon - Sat
10 - 6

1701 Old Minden Rd. 71111
(318) 742-0047
Owner: Shirley C. Warren
Est: 1986

Unique combination of classes, quilting supplies & fabrics. Authorized Bernina, Brother & Viking Sewing Machine dealer.

Other Shops in Louisiana:

Baton Rouge	Peaceful Quilter, 12318 Jefferson Hwy
Bossier City	Fabric Boutique, 1701 Old Minden Rd.
Leesville	JC's Fabric Shop, 3091 Lake Charles Hwy.
Metairie	The Quilting Bee, 3537 18th St. #15
New Orleans	Alder Sewing & Vacuum Center, 8217 Oak St.
New Orleans	Krauss Dept. Store, 1201 Canal St.
New Orleans	Old Craft Cottage, 816 Decatur St.
New Orleans	Partners Pillow Talk, 541 Chartres
West Monroe	Creatively Sew, 2400 Cypress Ste 22

Madison (#9)

95

Litchfield (#7)   Belfast (#8)
Auburn (#6)
Dixfield
(#5)
(#4)
Windham
Waterboro
(#3)
Berwick   South Portland
(#1)

9 Featured Shops

MAINE

Waterboro, ME   #3

Route 202
04087
(207) 247-4665
Est: 1988
Owner: Betty Ann Hammond

**Mon - Fri
9:30 - 5
Sat 9:30 - 3**

Fine Cotton Fabrics, Quilting supplies, Books, Quality Yarns, Pattern Books for Knitting & Crocheting, Floss and more!
Classes Available.

Windham, ME   #4

Calico Basket Quilt Shop

40 Page Road   04062
(207) 892-5606
Owner: JoAnne Hill
Est: 1982   1300 sq.ft.

**Mon - Fri
9:30-4:30
Tues til
8:30
Sat 9:30-4**

Over 3000 Top Quality Fabrics. The Latest -- Books, Notions, Craft Patterns, and Quilting Supplies.

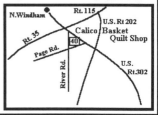

Dixfield, ME   #5

Log Cabin Craftworks

31 Main   04224   Est: 1981
(207) 562-8816   350 Bolts
Owner: Norine Clarke· 2500 sq.ft.

**Tues 9:30-8
Wed - Fri
9:30 - 5
Sat 9:30 - 1**

Located in the foothills of Western Maine we offer a variety of Fabrics, Current Books, Tools and Notions.

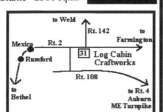

Auburn, ME   #6

Quiltessentials

1146 Minot Ave.   04210
(207) 784-4486
Est: 1994

**Mon - Fri
10 - 6
Sat 10 - 4**

Full line of Quilt and Basket Making supplies & classes. Unique selection of 100% cotton fabrics, books & notions.
Handmade Baskets

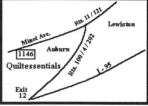

Litchfield, ME   #7

The Busy Thimble

Rt. #1 Box 1040   04350
(207) 268-4581
Owner: Cynthia Black
Est: 1990   1000 sq.ft.

**Mon - Sat
10 - 5
or by Appt.**

A Quilter's Paradise
More than 700 bolts of 100% cotton fabric. Complete Library & Notions galore!

Belfast, ME #8

Nancy's Sewing Center

HCR #80 (Rte. 3)   04915
(207) 338-1205
Owner: Nancy E. Black
Est: 1984   1200 sq.ft.

7 Days a Week
9 - 5

1000 Bolts of Fabric. Notions, quilt Supplies, Classes. Bernina Sewing Machines.

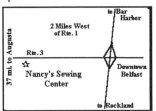

Madison, ME #9

The Fabric Garden

Rt. 201 North   04950
(207) 474-9628
Owner: Michaela Murphy
Est: 1978
2400 sq.ft.

Inspiring Collection of Fine Quilting Cottons. Wonderful Silk Ribbon Emb. Supplies. Quilts for Sale. "A Fabric Lover's Home Away From Home."

Mon - Fri
9 - 6
Sat 9 - 5
Sun 12 - 5

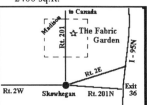

Maine Guilds:
Nimble Thimbles, Community Center, Windham, 04062
Pine Tree Quilter's Guild, RD Box 252, Turner, 04282

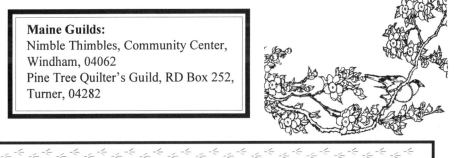

Other Shops in Maine:

Bar Harbor	Sewing by the Sea, RFD #1
Brewer	Viking Sewing Center, 46 Betton St.
Columbia Falls	The Calico Cupboard, Inc., Rural Route 1
Farmingdale	The Busy Thimble, Litchfield Rd.
Freeport	Quilt & Needlecrafts, 22 Main St. R.R. #1
Jefferson	Country Creations, Route 32, P.O. Box 949
Kennebunk	Mainely Quilts, 108 Summer St.
Lisbon Falls	Mill Fabric Center, 2 Ridge
Milo	Roses & Old Lace, 27 W. Main St.
Newcastle	Alewives Fabrics, R.R. #1, Box 480
Newport	Robyn's Nest Fabrics, Rt. 7
North Edgecomb	On Board, Route 27 Booth Bay Rd.
Pittsfield	Quilter's Dream, 9 Easy St.
Portland	Design Cotton Fabrics, 399 Fore
Rumford	The Pin Cushion, 94 River St.
Saco	Patchwork Boutique Quilt Shop, 304 Beach
Searsport	Cat's Meow, Rural Route 1
Wiscasset	The Marston House, P.O. Box 517

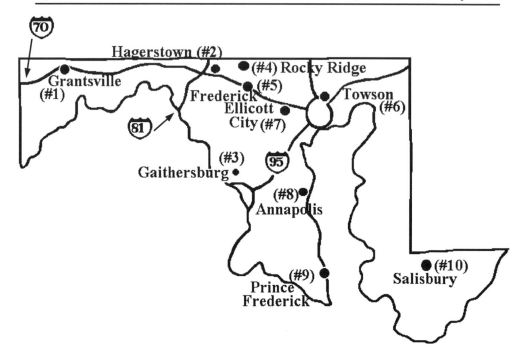

Maryland

10 Featured Shops

Grantsville, MD   #1

Four Seasons Stitchery

**Mon - Sat
9 - 5**

P.O. Box 218   Main St.   21536
(301) 895-5958
Owner: Jane Benson   Est: 1985

Most Complete
Quilting Shop in
the Tri-State area.
Over 1000 bolts
all cotton fabrics.
Books & Notions
Cross Stitch
Supplies.

Grantsville   Alt. 40
☆ Four
Seasons
Stitchery
(In the old
school bldg.)
Rt. 495
to
Morgantown   I - 68
Exit   to
19   Cumberland

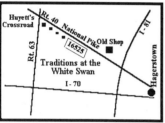

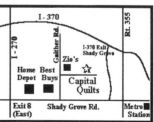

Rocky Ridge, MD #4

Dolls & Quilts Barn

9459 Longs Mill Rd.   21778
(301) 898-0091
Owner: Yvonne Khin
Est: 1990   3500 sq.ft.

**Tues - Sat
10 - 3**

Revolving exhibits of
Dolls and Quilts with
changing seasons.
Special consultations
for Dolls or Quilts by
Appt. Only
Admission: $2.50
Seniors $2.00

Frederick, MD #5

Needles ✄ Pins

310 E. Church St.   21701
(301) 695-7199

**Mon - Sat
9 - 9
Sun 12 - 5**

Located in historic
Everedy Square.
Downtown
Shopping,
Antiques, and More
Dollmaking,
quilting and
clothing patterns.
Fabric & Supplies.

Towson, MD #6

**Mon - Fri
9:30 - 8
Sat 9:30 - 4
Sun 12 - 4**

BEAR'S PAW

8812 Orchard Tree Lane
21204
(410) 321-6730
(800) 761-2202
Owner: Judy Munro
Est: 1996   5400 sq.ft.

An assortment of over 2000
bolts of the finest cottons,
knits, flannels, etc. "In-house"
talent to help with all your
sewing questions. Stop in and
share our excitement!

PATTERNS, BOOKS, NOTIONS & TOOLS

Ellicott City, MD #7

**Winter
Sun.&Tue 12-5
Wed - Sat 10 - 5
Summer
Sun&Mon 12 - 5
Tues - Sat 10 - 5**

8167 Main St.   21043   ·(410) 465-7202
Owner: Inge Stocklin Est: 1989   (800) 734-3581

Quilts, Pillows, Wall-
hangings: Quilt Racks,
Hangers, & Frames:
Clothing, Jewelry,
Cards: Restoration,
Appraisals,Lectures.
Fabric, Supplies &
Classes. Gifts too.

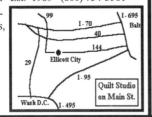

Annapolis, MD #8

Cottonseed Glory

4 Annapolis St.   21401
(410) 263-3897
Owner: Pat Steiner
Est: 1978

**Mon - Sat 10 - 5
Sunday
Fall & Winter Only
1 - 4**

3500 bolts
from over 40
manufacturers.
Books,
Gourmet Notions,
PATTERNS,
PATTERNS,
PATTERNS !

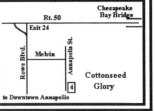

Prince Frederick, MD #9

Calvert Quilting Shop

MD Rt. 4 at Industry Lane   20678
(410) 535-0576   Fax: (410) 535-1197
                        Est: 1966
                        2000 sq.ft.
                        2000+ Bolts

Mon - Thur 9 - 6
Fri 9 - 7
Sat 9 - 4

We carry major manufacturers of Quilting Products 100% Cotton, Name Brand Fabrics, Notions, Cutting Equip., Classes. New Home Sewing Machine Sales and Service.

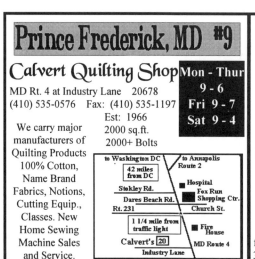

Salisbury, MD #10

Jenny's Sewing Studio

311 Civic Avenue   21804
(410) 543-1212
Owner: Jennifer Friedel
Est: 1982   3200 sq.ft.

Mon, Wed, & Fri 10-8
Tue, Thur, & Sat 10 - 6

Full service quilt shop & sewing machine dealer. (Bernina, New Home, Pfaff, Singer) Over 1000 bolts of fabric and approx. 30 classes offered.

Maryland Guilds:
Annapolis Quilt Guild, 98 Spring Valley Dr., Annapolis, 21403
Baltimore Heritage Quilters' Guild, P.O. Box 66537, Baltimore, 21239
Faithful Circle Quilters, 5012 Lake Circle West, Columbia, 21044
Friendship Star Quilters, P.O. Box 8051, Gaithersburg, 20898
Eternal Quilter, 346 Chalet Dr., Millersville, 21108

Other Shops in Maryland:

Boonsboro	Old School Fabrics, 230 Potomac
Catonsville	Seminole Sampler, 71 Mellor Ave.
Chestertown	The Yardstick, 111 S. Cross St.
Clinton	Quilters Haven, Old Branch Ave.
Edgewater	Quiet Comforts Inc., 224 Mayo Rd.
Ocean City	Marie's Fabric Shop, 9935 Stephen Decatur Hwy.
Rockville	Anna Marie's Fashion Fabrics, 2011 Veirs Mill Rd.
Rockville	G Street Fabrics--Jake Kupiec, 11854 Rockville Pike
Sykesville	Main Street Dry Goods, 7548 Main St.
Upper Marlboro	Stitches & Sew On, 9020 Trumps Hill Rd.

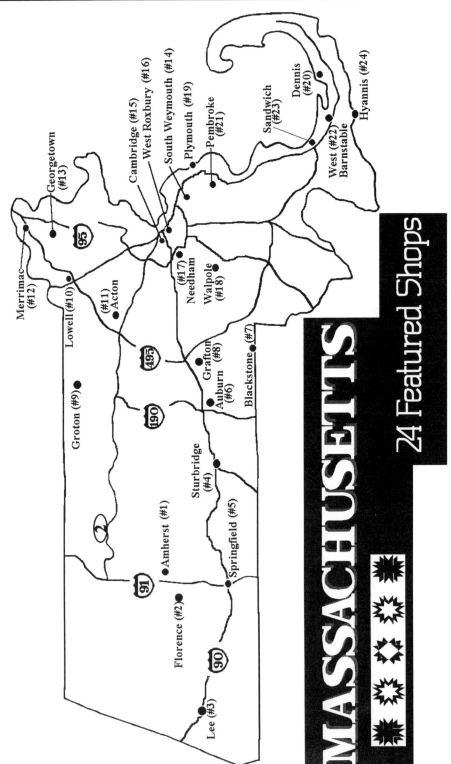

MASSACHUSETTS

24 Featured Shops

Georgetown (#13)

Cambridge (#15)
West Roxbury (#16)
South Weymouth (#14)
Plymouth (#19)
Pembroke (#21)

Sandwich (#23)
Dennis (#20)
Hyannis (#24)
West (#22)
Barnstable

Merrimac (#12)
Lowell (#10)
(#11) Acton
(#17) Needham
Walpole (#18)

Grafton (#8)
Auburn (#6)
Blackstone (#7)

Groton (#9)

Sturbridge (#4)

Springfield (#5)

Amherst (#1)

Florence (#2)

Lee (#3)

Amherst, MA   #1

My Favorite Quilt Shop Inc.

Tues., Wed., Fri. 10-5:30
Thurs. 12-8
Sat. 10-4

Owner: Marion Newell   1000 sq.ft.

65 University Drive
Amherst, MA 01002
(413) 549-6009

Everything for quilters—batting, books, classes, cutters, hoops, mats, needles, patterns, rulers, over 500 bolts of fabric plus friendly service.

Florence, MA   #2

Calico Fabrics

Mon - Fri 10 - 5
Sat 10 - 3
Winter Suns 12 - 3

52 Main St.   01060-3165   (413) 585-8665

Owner: Joan Trecartin
Est: 1980   1000 sq.ft.

Choose from 1000+ bolts of top name fabrics. Hoffman, RJR, South Seas, Northcott Silk, Country Style Plaids. Books, Quilt Supplies. Classes.

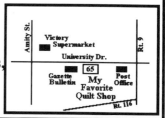

Lee, MA   #3

Pumpkin Patch

58 W. Center St.   (Rt. 20)
(413) 243-1635   01238
Est: 1985   800 sq.ft.
Owners: Susan & Dan Sullivan

Mon - Sat 10 - 6
Sun 12 - 6

Located in the beautiful Berkshires! Cotton fabrics, books, patterns, etc. . . . Classes, machine quilting . . . .

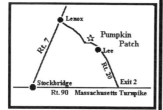

Sturbridge, MA   #4

The Quilt and Cabbage

P.O. Box 534   01566
538 Main St.
(508) 347-3023

Mon & Wed - Sat 9:30 - 4:30
Sun 11 - 4
Closed Tues

Quality fabrics with an extensive variety of quilting stencils, books, & supplies. Custom quilts & pillows. Woolen throws, capes, caps & Scarves. Gift Items.

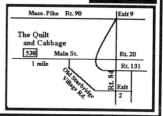

Springfield, MA #5

Double T Quilt Shop

Mon - Sat 10 - 4

219 Berkshire Ave.
(413) 737-9605   01109
Owner: Jean Thibodeau   Est: 1983   700+ Bolts
Samples $4

We carry a wide stock of fabrics from Hoffman, A.Henry, RJR, Libas, MEH, P&B, Bali and Guatemalan types. Plus Books and Notions.

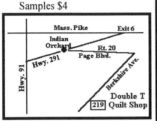

Auburn, MA #6

Appletree Fabrics

**Mon - Wed 10 - 8
Thur - Sat 10 - 5**

59 Auburn St.   01501
(508) 832-5562
Owner: Lois Therrien
Est: 1991

Hundreds of beautiful cotton prints, solids & homespuns. Large selection of books & patterns. Handcrafts for sale. Classes.

Blackstone, MA #7

Quilter's Quarters

**Tues - Sat 10 - 5
Thur til 8**

157 Main St., Rt. 122   01504
(508) 883-4140
Owner: Kathy Lemay
Est: 1995   1000 sq.ft.

Gorgeous selection of the best quality cottons along with supplies, books & patterns. Classes. Come browse in our relaxed atmosphere.

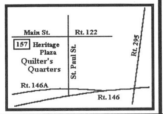

Grafton, MA #8

Calico & Co.

**Tues - Sat 10 - 5
Sun 12 - 5**

10 Grafton Common   01519
(508) 839-5990
Owner: Joanne & Richard Erenius
Est: 1984   1000 sq.ft.   500 Bolts

Helpful & Friendly Service & Supplies for your every Quilting & Cross Stitch need. Classes to inspire your creativity.

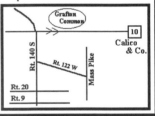

Groton, MA #9

The Quilt Loft

Daily 10 - 5

In Kilbridge Antiques
134 Main St.
(Rt. 119) 01450
1000 sq.ft.

Antique Quilts, fabrics, quilt blocks, tops, feedsacks. All pre 1945! Located on the second floor of Kilbridge Antiques.

Lowell, MA #10

The New England Quilt Museum

**Mon - Sat 10 - 5
Sun 12 - 5
Call ahead for Mon and early closing info Nov to May**

18 Shattack St.   01852
(508) 452-4207 Free to Members
Adm: $4, $3 Seniors & Students

Directly across from the National Park Visitor Center. From Boston's North Station trains are served by a bus every 15 minutes.

Ralph Jordan's
... your Quilt Destination

**Everything for your Special Quilting
Projects from
beginning to end . . . and More.**

Over Two Thousand 100% Cotton Prints and Solids by
Hoffman, RJR, South Seas, Concord,
Moda, VIP, Springmaid, P&B, Peter Pan, Marcus,
John Kaldor, Northcott, Mission Valley, Kona Bay,
Alexander Henry, Spiegel, and Momen House

A complete selection of quilting books,
patterns, templates, stencils, scissors, rotary cutters,
mats, hoops and much, much more.

We also offer over 80 classes in quilting and
crafts for beginner to advanced students.

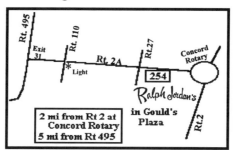

We honor All Quilt Guild Membership cards for 10% off quilt fabric,
books and notions. (AQS, NEQG, and EQA included!)

**254 Great Rd.   Rt. 2A   Goulds' Plaza   01720
(508) 263-0606**
**Tues, Wed, Thur 9:30 - 9:00   Mon, Fri, Sat 9:30 - 5:30
Sunday 12:00 - 5:00**

Acton, MA   #11

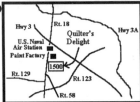

Cambridge, MA #15

Cambridge Quilt Co.

**Mon - Sat
10 - 6
Sun 12 - 5**

14 A Eliot St.   02138
Diagonal to the Charles Hotel
(617) 492-3279   Est: 1975
Owner: Cathy Berry
1000 sq.ft.

Our shop maintains 1200 bolts of fabric and over 400 current quilt books, plus the latest in quilting supplies and classes!

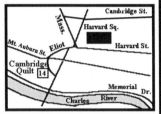

West Roxbury, MA #16

Quilter's Nook

**Tue - Sat
10 - 4
Thur til 8**

1766 Centre   02132
(617) 325-5633
Owner: Fran Monahan
Est: 1988   800 sq.ft.

Quilter's Nook is a very warm and friendly shop. We have over a thousand bolts of fabric, lots of books and classes too!

The Button Box
Needham, MA #17

**1081 Great Plain Ave.   02192
(617) 449-1810   Est: 1995
Owner: Catherine Gentile
1500 sq.ft.   1000 Bolts**

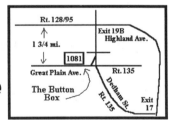

We are a hardware store for needlewomen !

**Mon - Sat 9:30 - 5:30
Wed & Thur til 8
Sundays 12 - 5
Sept. thru June**

*10% discount when you show
a guide membership card.*

Comtemporary Designer Cottons
our specialty.
Needlepoint Supplies.
The best Button Shop in Massachusetts,
1000's to choose from.

Walpole, MA #18

Quilts Ltd.

958 Main St.   02081
(508) 668-0145   Est: 1983
Owners: Margaret Ransom
                & Lynn DiRusso

**Mon - Sat
10 - 6
Wed & Thur
til 8:30
Sun by Chance**

We carry all your
quilting needs.
Over 1000 bolts of
quality cotton
fabric.

Plymouth, MA #19

Sew Crazy

5 Main St. Extension   Rt. 3A
(508) 747-3019   02360
Owner: Dottie Krueger
Est: 1977

**Mon - Fri
9 - 5:30
Sat 9 - 5**

Elna, & New
Home Sewing
Machines. Over
900 bolts
of fabric
and more coming.
Notions & Lots
of Patterns.

Dennis, MA #20

612 Route 6A Main Street   02638
(508) 385-2662   Est: 1982
Owner: Barbara Prue   1050 sq.ft.

**Fabric!
(100% Cottons)
Quilts!
Supplies - Books -
Lessons
Yarn - Needlepoint
We do mail order,
give us a call.**

**Mon - Sat   10 - 5
Year Round
Sundays in the summer 12 - 5**

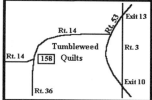

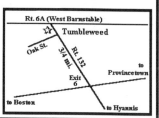

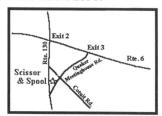

Largest Quilt Shop on Cape Cod

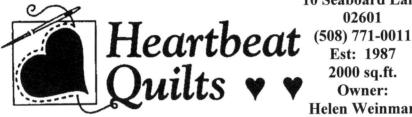

Heartbeat Quilts ♥ ♥

10 Seaboard Lane
02601
(508) 771-0011
Est: 1987
2000 sq.ft.
Owner:
Helen Weinman

Hyannis, MA   #24   Bus Tours Welcome

Fabrics: (Hoffman, RJR, Benartex,

Hi-Fashion, Liberty of London, & John Kaldor)

Fantastic Book Selection

Embellishments, Fancy Threads,
Silk Ribbon, Buttons, Fancy
Velvets, Tapestry.
Workshops
Free Newsletter
Available (3x year)

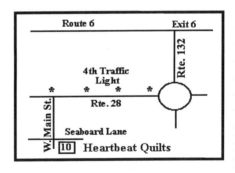

Mon - Sat 10 - 6
Sun 12 - 5

Over 3500+ Bolts of Fabric

Massachusetts Guilds:
Hands Across the Valley, P.O. Box 831, Amherst, 01002
Pioneer Valley Quilters, P.O. Box 202, Aqawam, 01001
Quilter's Connection, 12 Monadnock, Arlington, 02174
Plymouth Country Cranberry Quilters, P.O. Box 149, Carver, 02330
Chelmsford Quilters Guild, P.O. Box 422, Chelmsford, 01824
Merrimack Valley Quilters, P.O. Box 1435, Haverhill, 01831
New England Quilters Guild, P.O. Box 7136, Lowell, 01852
Barberry Quilters of Cape Cod, P.O. Box 1253, Orleans, 02653
Yankee Pride Quilt Guild, P.O. Box 833, Pittsfield, 01202
East Coast Quilters Alliance, P.O. Box 711, Westford, 01886

Other Shops in Massachusetts:

Arlington	Fabric Corner, 783 Massachusetts Ave.
Boston	North End Fabrics, 31 Harrison Ave.
Brewster	The Yankee Craftsman, 230 Route 6A West
East Brookfield	Calico Crib, 108 Howe St.
East Longmeadow	Thimbleworks, 56 Shaker Rd.
Falmouth	Fabric Corner, 12 Spring Bars Rd.
Greenfield	The Textile Co., Inc., Power Square
Greenfield	Bear's Paw Quilts & Crafts, 1182 Bernardston Rd.
Holden	Betsey's Sewing Connection, 1085A Main St.
Ipswich	Loom N' Shuttle, 190 High St.
Lawrence	Malden Mills, 46 Stafford St.
Medford	Quilter's Hideaway, 84 High St.
Medway	Sisters, 97 Summer
Pocasset	Quilts & Things, 674-B MacArthur Blvd.
South Hadley	The Calico Shop, Village Commons
South Hamilton	Cranberry Quilters, 161 Bay Rd.
Southampton	South Hampton Quilts, P.O. Box 364
Springfield	Osgood Textile Co., 30 Magaziner Pl.
Tyngsboro	The Quilters Corner, 130 Middlesex Rd
Vineyard Haven	The Heath Hen Yarn & Quilt Shop, Tisbury Market Place
Wakefield	Susie Kate's Quilt Shop, 1117 Main
Wales	Ilona's Whim, Stafford Rd.
Woburn	Fabric Place, 300 Mishawun Rd.
Worcester	Shirley's Sewing Center Inc., 452 W. Boylston St.

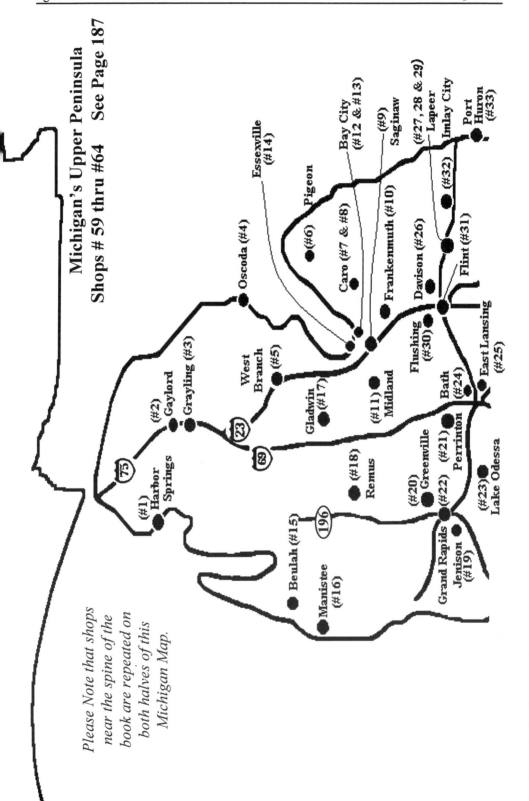

Michigan's Upper Peninsula   See Page 187
Shops # 59 thru #64

Please Note that shops near the spine of the book are repeated on both halves of this Michigan Map.

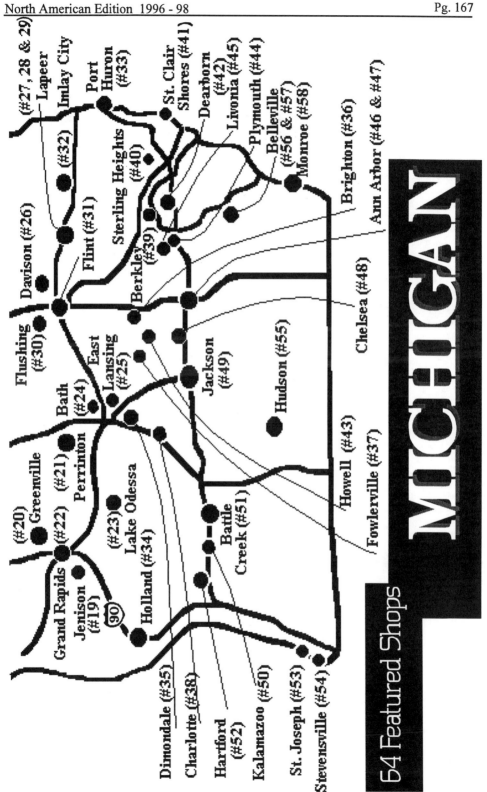

MICHIGAN

64 Featured Shops

(#27, 28 & 29) Lapeer
Imlay City
Port Huron (#33)
St. Clair Shores (#41)
Dearborn (#42)
Livonia (#45)
Plymouth (#44)
Belleville (#56 & #57)
Monroe (#58)
Brighton (#36)
Ann Arbor (#46 & #47)
(#32)
Sterling Heights (#40)
Davison (#26)
Flint (#31)
Berkley (#39)
Chelsea (#48)
Flushing (#30)
East Lansing (#25)
Jackson (#49)
Hudson (#55)
Bath (#24)
Greenville (#22) (#21) Perrinton
Howell (#43)
Fowlerville (#37)
(#20)
(#23) Lake Odessa
Battle Creek (#51)
Holland (#34)
Grand Rapids
Jenison (#19)
90
Dimondale (#35)
Charlotte (#38)
Hartford (#52)
Kalamazoo (#50)
St. Joseph (#53)
Stevensville (#54)

Harbor Springs, MI #1

Quilting Barn

**Mon - Sat
10 - 5
Year -
round**

1221-A West Conway Road
(616) 347-1116   49740
Owners: Dolores P. Boese &
            Karen Boese Schaller
Est: 1978   850 sq.ft.

Emmet County's
Complete Prof.
Quilting Store.
We have over
2000 bolts of
100% cotton fabric
and 19 years of
experience.

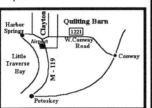

Gaylord, MI #2

Robin's Nest

**Mon - Sat
9- 5**

400 W. Main St.   49735
(517) 732-0732
Owner: Robin Ely
Est: 1994   1200 sq.ft.   500 Bolts

100% cotton
fabrics, books,
patterns, quilting
supplies, cotton
thread, Hobbs
batting, classes
and help anytime.

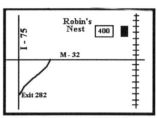

Grayling, MI #3

The Ice House Quilt Shop

**Mon - Sat
10 - 5**

509 Norway Street   49738
(517) 348-4821
Owner: Jill Wyman   Est: 1980

A unique shop for
the person
seeking quality in
all quilting
supplies.
Bernina Dealer.
Gifts--Gourmet
Foods.

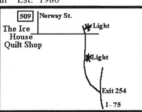

Oscoda, MI #4

Loose Threads Quilt Shop

**Mon - Sat
10 - 5
Summer
Sundays
12 - 4**

208 S. State St.   48750
(517) 739-7115   3500 sq.ft.
We Accept Visa, MC & Discover

Over 3500 sq.ft. of
Quilters Heaven !
More than 1200
Bolts of Fabric by
Benartex,
Hoffman, Spiegel,
Jinney Beyer,
P&B, & More
250 Quilt Books.

West Branch, MI #5

Button Hole

**Mon - Fri
9 - 6
Sat 9 - 5**

208 West Houghton   48661
(517) 345-0431
Owner: Darlene Jones
            Est: 1981   2000 sq.ft.

We have
Everything for
the Quilter ! !
Located in a
Victorian,
downtown
West Branch on
Business
Loop I - 75

Fabriholic: an affliction. symptoms = wandering glassy eyed through the bolts at the quilt shop; purchasing enough fabric for this lifetime and the next; cold sweats when discussing the latest patterns.

Pigeon, MI #6

Pigeon River Mercantile & Wool Co.

40 S. Main 48755
(517) 453-2311 Est: 1992
Owners: Ed & Wanda Eichler

**Mon - Fri
9 - 5:30
Fri til 8
Sat 9 - 5**

Over 1000 bolts 100% cottons, wool batts, custom comforters, cross stitch & knitting supplies. Country Gifts and Toys.

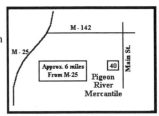

Caro, MI #7

Quilt Talk Antiques

209 N. State St. 48723
(517) 673-7997 Res. 673-6115
Owner: Marilyn Van Allen
Est: 1990 1700 sq.ft.

**Tues - Thur
10 - 5:30
Fri 10 - 8
Sat 9 - 2**

Quilts and Tops 1890-1970. Some new Quilted Items. Antique furniture pieces, Attic Treasures — old and enjoyable. Quilt Classes

Caro, MI #8

Ruby's Yarn & Fabric

124 N. State 48723
(517) 673-3062
Owner: Ruby Reid Est: 1966

**Mon- Wed & Sat 9-5:30
Thur & Fri 9 - 7**

Complete line of Quilting Fabrics & Supplies. Classes in Machine Quilting, Crazy Quilting, Applique, Wearable Art, Designing, and Silk Embroidery.

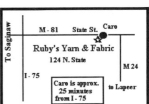

Saginaw Quilted Apple

Apple of the Quilter's Eye

7402 Gratiot Rd. 48609
(517) 781-1202
Est: 1993 2000 sq.ft.
Owner:
Pam Mikkola

**Mon - Sat 9:30 - 5:30
Tues til 8 Sun 1 - 5**

EVERYTHING FOR THE QUILTER & SEWING ENTHUSIAST
Quality Fabrics, Books, Patterns, Notions and many classes. BERNINA

Saginaw, MI #9

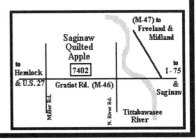

Bay City, MI   #12

The Fabric Fair

**Mon - Fri
10 - 7
Sat 10 - 4**

206 Fifth St.   48708   (517) 893-8971
Owner: Bunny Rosenbrock
Est: 1955   7000 sq.ft.   2500+ Bolts

**We have everything you need. We are a complete fabric store.
Wool, Flannel, Children's Prints, Silks, Ultrasuede
Bridal Appliques & Beaded Fabric, Headpieces & Veils
Laces & Trims, Unique Fashion Fabrics.**

I - 75   One Way   Saginaw   Fifth St.
206
Fabric Fair
Exit 162A   Over Bridge First Light
Downtown Bay City

Bay City, MI   #13

Snail's Trail
Quilt Shop

**Mon - Fri
10 - 5:30
Wed til 7
Sat 10 - 3**

3461 E. North Union Rd.
(517) 684-0190   48706
Owners: Pat LaRoche & Kathy
Baker

Fabrics including
Hoffman & South
Seas. Crafters,
you'll love our
Button Crock!
Large Selection of
Patterns featuring
wearable art.
Classes.

Snail's
Trail   3461   Burger King
Long John Silvers
I - 75   Union
Wood Bridge   Total
Midland   Euclid
U.S. 10

Essexville, MI   #14

Marjorie's

**Mon - Sat
9:30 - 5:30
Closed First two
Weeks of July &
Sat in July & Aug**

1602 Woodside   48732
(517) 893-8611
400+ Bolts of Calico

My three
specialties are
Calicos, Bathing
Suit Fabrics, &
Lingerie Fabrics.
Notions.
We also teach
many classes.

Woodside
1602
Marjorie's   Pine   1 1/2 mi.
McDonalds
M - 25 East   (Center Ave.)
About 3 miles from Downtown Bay City

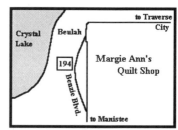

Manistee, MI #16

The Quilted Heart

Mon - Sat 10 - 5

607 Parkdale   49660
(616) 723-7069
Owner: Judy Dunlap
Complete Line of   Est: 1989   700 sq.ft.
Quilting Supplies.
Fabrics, Books,
Notions, Craft
Patterns,
Handmade Quilts
Dolls, Unique
Gifts, Classes in an
old Farm House

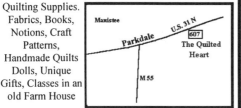

Gladwin, MI #17

The Log Cabin Fabric Shoppe

Tues - Sat By Appt.

1901 Lakeshore Dr.   48624
(517) 426-1422
Owner: Cherie Thornton

We are now located in a beautiful shop in the country. Come visit our brand new barn full of quilting delights.

Remus, MI #18

Towne Fabrics, Gifts, & Crafts

Mon - Fri 9 - 5:30
Sat 9 - 4

135 W. Wheatland Ave.   49340
(517) 967-8250
Owners: Ann Jensen and Jann Parks
Est: 1989   2300 sq.ft.

Quilts supplies from fabrics to frames. Also reed and cane supplies. Our staff is knowledgeable & caring.

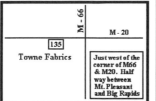

Jenison, MI #19

Country Needleworks

Mon - Sat 9:30 - 9

584 Chicago Dr.   49428
(616) 457-9410   Est: 1981
Owners: Cheryl Van Haitsma & Barb Langerak

Your complete needlework shop carrying: quilt fabric & accessories, cross-stitch supplies, knitting yarns, largest stamping center in West Michigan. Giftware.

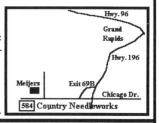

Greenville, MI #20

Janie's Button Box

Mon - Fri 9 - 8
Sat 9 - 6

218 S. Lafayette St.   48838
(616) 754-5544
Owner: Gail L. Besemer
Est: 1994   4000 sq.ft.
Janie's Button Box is a quaint retail fabric and craft supply shop. We have a large quilting department with over 1800 bolts of quality fabric and hundreds of quilting notions.

Perrinton, MI #21

Calico Cupboard

Tue & Thur 9 - 5:30
Sat 9 - 12
Other Days by Appt.

4625 MacArthur Rd.   48871
(517) 236-7728 or (800) 594-7728
Owners: Denise Rossman, Nancy Davis, & Doreen Slavik
200 sq.ft. 340 Bolts

Family owned quilt fabric shop since 1986. We carry brand name fabrics, notions and some crafts. Classes and alterations offered.

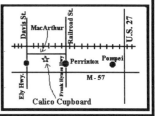

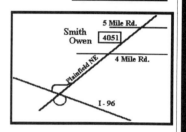
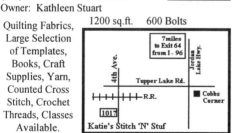

Davison, MI #26

Davison Fabrics

Mon - Sat
9 - 5:30
Mon til 8

231 N. Main Street   48423
(810) 653-2641
Owner: Donna Fritts
Est: 1975   1850 sq.ft.

We specialize in 2,800 bolts of calico prints, which are top of the line companies. Thousands of Craft Patterns!

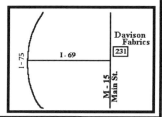

Lapeer, MI #27

Jill's Fabrics & Craft Supply

Mon - Fri
9 - 6
Sat 10 - 5

2268 N Lapeer Rd.   48446
(810) 667-4025
Owner: Jill Hurd   Est: 1988

100% cotton Fabrics, Quilting Supplies, Books, Templates, Stencils, Classes. New Home Sewing Machine Sales & Service. Helpful & Friendly.

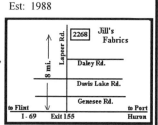

Needle: a metal tool meant to pierce the quilt layers not your fingers.

Lapeer, MI #28

Pine Ridge Quilting

Wed - Sat
1 - 6

3167 Roods Lake Rd.   48446
(810) 667-4247
Owner: Brenda Armstrong

Machine Quilting Specializing in Homespun Plaids by Red Wagon & Mission Valley 100% cotton Prints Quilting Supplies Quilts for Sale.

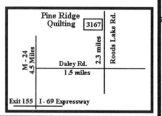

Lapeer, MI #29

Bernina– Lapeer Fabrics

Mon 9:30 - 7
Tues - Fri
9:30 - 5:30
Sat 9:30 - 3

110 W. Park St.   48446
(810) 667-9098
Owner: Linda White   Est: 1981

We carry Bernina and Bernette Sewing Machines and Sergers. Calicos, Knits, Ribbing, Lingerie, Notions, Specialty Threads, Bridal, Books, Patterns & more!

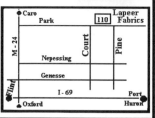

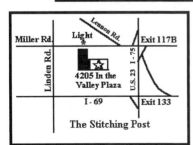

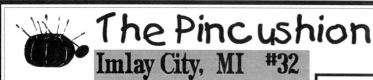

The Pincushion
Imlay City, MI #32

113 East Third Street   48444
(313) 724-7065
Est: 1971   Owner: Joyce Schihl   1800 sq.ft.

Quality Quilting Supplies & Fabrics. Extensive
Books & Pattern Selection. Buttons by the cup or
each. Cotton, Wool & Polyester Batting.
Small Town Friendly Service.
Our Customers are our Friends.

M 21 (Imlay City Rd.)
The Pincushon
Almont Ave. | 113 | M - 53
3rd. St.
I- 69

Mon - Thur   9:30 - 5:15
Fri   9:30 - 6   Sat 9:30 - 5

Port Huron, MI #33

Sew Elegant

3909 Pine Grove Rd.
(810) 982-6556   48059
Est:1986   4880 sq.ft.
Owner: Linda Anderson

Krafft Rd.
Rt. 25
Pine Grove Rd.
Sew Elegant | 3909 | China Lite | 24th Ave.
Rt. 136
Stop Light
Pine Grove Rd.

Our Shop is full of
100% cotton Fabrics--
over 4,000 bolts
FINE LACES,
BOOKS FOR QUILTERS,
SMOCKING PATTERNS & PLATES
QUALITY PFAFF SEWING MACHINES

Mon - Sat 10 - 5:30   Sun 12 - 4:30

Holland, MI   #34

Field's World of Fabrics

Mon - Sat 9 - 9

281 East 8th   49423
(616) 392-4806
Owner: Jack Veldman
Est: 1953   9000 sq.ft.

Packed with Fabrics !
5000+ Bolts
Many Unique Prints.

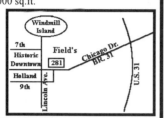

Dimondale, MI   #35

The Quilt Barn

**Tues - Fri 10 - 8
Sat 8 - 4**

127 N. Bridge, P.O. Box 189
(517) 646-7059   48821
Owners: Nola Haines &   Virginia
Machine quilting.   Kitchen   Feedsack Club
OVER ALL restorations.
Vintage Material
Individual Classes
Feedsacks
Consignments.
Members of AQS
& Island City
Piecemakers.

The Quilt Barn

Brighton, MI   #36

The Quilter's Shoppe

**Mon - Fri 11 - 6
Sat 11 - 4**

213 W. Main, Suite #4
(810) 220-0434   48116
Owner: Christine Laginess

A cozy quilt shop carrying a large selection of 100% cotton fabric, books, patterns, hand dyed fabric and notions.

Fowlerville, MI   #37

Forgotten Arts

**Mon - Fri 10 - 5
Sat 10 - 3**

Friendliest Little Quilt Shop in Livingston County
124 E. Grand River   (517) 223-7992
P.O. Box 938   48836

Owner: Marsha West   Est: 1993   1700 sq.ft.

Silk & Brazilian Embroidery. Quilting & Crazy Quilting. Large selection of 100% cottons. Full line of P&B Solids, Books, Notions, Classes.

Charlotte, MI   #38

Hen House of Charlotte

211 S. Cochran 48813
(517) 543-6454
Owner: Nancy Conn
Est: 1974

Mon - Sat 10 - 5:30

A craft shop specializing in quality materials including 100% cotton and homespun fabrics, Stenciling, X-Stitch, Tole Painting and Basket Supplies

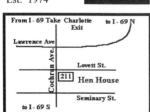

Berkley, MI   #39

Guildcrafters Quilt Shop

**Mon - Fri 10 - 6:30
Sat 10 - 5
Sun 12 - 3**

2790 West 12 Mile Rd.   48072
(810) 541-8545   Est: 1982
Owner: Jo Merecki   2500 sq.ft.

3500 Bolts
Largest Quilting Fabric, Notion, Stencil & Book supply in the area.
Classes, Gifts.
Friendly Service.

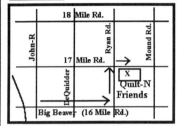

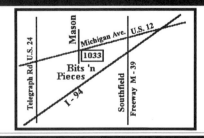

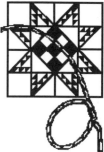
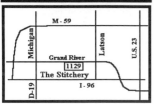
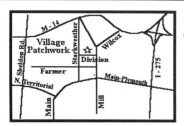

Creative Quilting

Jean Coleman
Designer

HOURS BY APPOINTMENT

Please call or write for a flier

A CUSTOM MACHINE QUILTING SERVICE

(313) 425-6385

36749 Angeline Circle
Livonia, MI 48150

Livonia, MI #45

Viking *Sewing Center*

5235 Jackson Rd.   48103
(313) 761-3094
Owner: Dale Houghtaling
Est: 1968   4000 sq.ft.

Over 3000 Bolts 100% of Cotton Fabrics
Battings, Q-Snap frames, Classes, Books,
Patterns, Notions, Heirloom Supplies,
Unique threads.

Viking,
White, &
Bernina
Machines

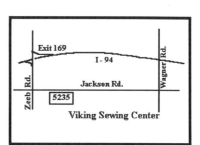

Exit 169

I - 94

Zeeb Rd.

Jackson Rd.

Wagner Rd.

5235

Viking Sewing Center

Ann Arbor, MI   #46

Mon - Fri
10 - 6
Sat 10 - 4

Ann Arbor, MI #47

THE
LOOKING
GLASS
QUILT SHOP
1715 Plymouth
48105

Mon - Thur
10 - 6
Fri & Sat
Winter 10 - 5
Summer 10 - 4

(313) 662-2228
Carla Aderente

A full line quilt shop
with wonderful
fabrics, books,
patterns, and notions.
Come Say Hi !

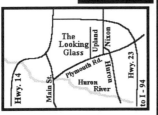

Chelsea, MI #48

The Quilter's
Quarters Ltd.

Mon - Fri
10 - 5
Thur til 7
Sat 10 - 4

118 S. Main St.   48118
(313) 475-5848   Est: 1994
Owner: Lynn VanNest   1200 Bolts

International
fabrics, 100%
cottons, Books,
Notions, Classes,
Mail Order,
Special Orders.
MC & visa

Jackson, MI #49

Hearts All Around

Mon - Fri
10 - 5:30
Sat 10 - 4

2614 Kibby Road   49203
(517) 789-8228   Est: 1983
Owner: Barbara Markowski
                    2,000 sq.ft.   1000 Bolts

Fabrics, books,
patterns,
quilt "gadgets",
classes!
Machine quilting
services.
Authorized Pfaff
sewing machine
dealer.

Kalamazoo, MI #50

Viking Sewing Center

Mon - Fri
9 - 5:30
Wed til 7
Sat 9 - 4

5401 Portage Rd.   49002
(616) 342-5808
Owners: Phil & Julie Rotzien
                    2500 sq.ft.

1000+ bolts of
100% cotton fabric.
Quilting, heirloom,
garment and
specialty sewing
classes. Viking &
White sewing
machine sales &
service.

1540 East Columbia Ave. 49017
(616) 965-2116   Est: 1981   2500 sq.ft.
Owners: Patty Pastor & Lynne Evans

The Quiltery

HUGE selection of quality 100% cottons by
Hoffman, RJR, Jinny Beyer, P&B, Benartex,
Red Wagon, Gutcheon, Roberta Horton,
and others; Complete line of
notions, books, patterns; Bernina
Sewing Machines. Call for a free
newsletter listing classes and sales.

Tues - Fri
10 - 5
Wed til 7
Sat 10 - 1

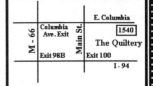

Battle Creek, MI #51

Hartford, MI #52

Sue Ellen's Quilt Shop

Sun - Wed 10 - 5

59591 Jerrdean Dr.　49057
(616) 463-5622　Est: 1980
Owner: Ruth Howader

100% Cotton Fabrics
Books, Patterns,
Notions, Custom
Hand Quilting, Quilt
Making, and other
Quilting services.
Cloth doll patterns
and findings.

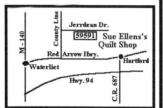

St. Joseph, MI #53

Elsie's Exquisiques

**Mon - Fri 9:30 - 5:30
Sat 10 - 5
Sun 12 - 5**

208 State St.　49085
(616) 982-0557　ext. 16
Est: 1993

Distinctive
Fabrics and
Supplies for the
Sophisticated
Quilter. Open 7
days a week in a
historic shopping
district.

Stevensville, MI #54

Loving Stitches QUILT SHOP

7291 Red Arrow Hwy. 49127

**Mon, Tues, Wed, Fri 10 - 3
Thur 2 - 5
Sat 10 - 2**

(616) 465-3795
Owner: Holly Martin　Est: 1996

A cozy shop with
100% cotton
fabrics, patterns,
books and supplies.
Stroll through our
perennial flower
and herb garden.

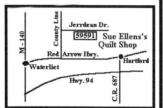

Hudson, MI #55

Needles & Threads Quilt Shop

**Mon - Fri 9 - 5
Sat 9 - 4**

227 W. Main St.　49247
(517) 448-5901　Est: 1989
Owners: Bob & Maridell McKnight　1500 sq.ft.

A large
assortment of
100% cotton
fabrics. Quilting
books, patterns,
notions, classes &
Custom Machine
Quilting.

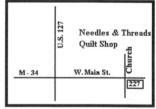

Belleville, MI #56

Threads 'n Treasures Quilt Shop

**Mon - Sat 10 - 6
Sun 12 - 5
Other Hours by Chance Or Appt.**

129 South St.　48111
(313) 697-9376
Owner: Kay Atkins　Est: 1996

Mail Order
Batting, Books,
Notions, Lessons.
Quilts for Sale.
Hand Quilting a
Specialty.
Fabric, Lace,
Ribbon and
Boutique Items.

Belleville, MI #57

Sue's Quilt Shop

**Mon - Fri 10 - 5
Sat 10 - 4**

48120 Harris　48111
(313) 461-6540
Owner: Sue Crain
Est: 1989　504 sq.ft.

Fabrics, supplies,
books and classes
available. Quilts
for Sale. Hand
quilting service
and custom orders
taken.
Reasonable prices

Monroe, MI #58

GERWECK'S

HOMESPUN FABRICS

15221 S. DIXIE HWY.   48161
SOUTH MONROE PLAZA
(313) 242-9528

One of Michigan's largest quilt shops.
with 4,000 sq. feet of quilting!

Over 3,000 bolts of fabrics
1,500 plus of books and patterns
Complete supply of notions
100's of samples to inspire you
Gift items for quilters & Sewers
Complete line of PFAFF sewing
machines
Classes
Personal, helpful, and friendly
service
Quality machine quilting service
7 years experience
Backings & battings available

Hours: Mon-Sat   10:00-5:00
(fall & winter) Tues 10:00-9:00
Closed Sundays
Bus Tours
Welcome

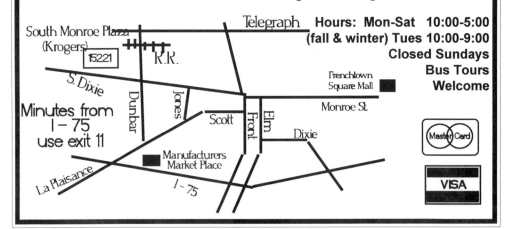

South Monroe Plaza
(Krogers)
15221
Telegraph
R.R.
S. Dixie
Dunbar
Jones
Scott
Front
Elm
Frenchtown
Square Mall
Monroe St.
Dixie
Minutes from
I-75
use exit 11
Manufacturers
Market Place
La Plaisance
I-75

MasterCard

VISA

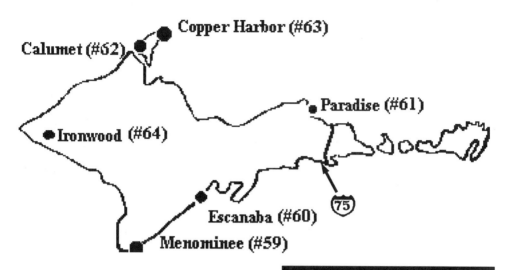

6 Featured Shops

MICHIGAN'S UPPER PENINSULA

Menominee, MI #59

Country Treasures

W 6607 2.5 Lane   49858
(906) 863-6368
Owner: Nancy Zeratsky
Est: 1993   5500 sq.ft.
750+ Bolts

Mon - Fri
10 - 5
Sat 10 - 4
Nov & Dec
Sun 12 - 4

100% Cotton Fabric
for Quilting and
Crafts. Notions,
Books, Patterns,
Craft Supplies,
Wood, Cross Stitch,
Beads, Flowers &
much more. Classes

Escanaba, MI #60

The Sewing Room

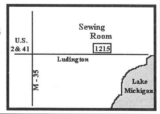

1215 Ludington Street   49829
(906) 789-9595
Owner: Carmel Edgar
Est: 1988

Mon - Fri
10 - 5
Sat 10 - 3

Specializing
in quilt classes
and supplies.
Also Cross-
Stitch and
special orders.

Paradise, MI   #61

Village Fabrics & Crafts

Summer
Daily 10-7
Winter
10 - 5
Closed Tue
Sun 12 - 5

Hwy M-123 W.   P.O. Box 254
(906) 492-3803   49768
Owner: Vicki Hallaxs   Est: 1986

Quilting, Counted
Cross Stitch,
Plastic Canvas,
Silk Ribbon Emb.
Unique Crafts.
Hundreds of Books
and Patterns—
Many of Area
Attractions. Gifts.

Village Fabrics & Crafts
Whitefish Point Rd.
M 123
Paradise
1/2 Mile West of Intersection
M 123
Whitefish Bay
Lake Superior

Calumet, MI   #62

Traditions

Mon - Sat
9:30 - 5:30
May 1 - Jan 1

U.S. 41, Rt. #1, Box 86   49913
(906) 482-8674   Est: 1993
Owners: Barb Heinonen,
Carole Ryynanen & Sue Pietila

Books, Fabrics &
Supplies for
Quilting,
Smocking, French
Hand Sewing &
Silk Ribbon Emb.
Also unique Hand
Made Gifts.

CALUMET
HANCOCK HOUGHTON
Lake Superior
U.S. 41
to MARQUETTE

Half-way Between Hancock & Calumet

Copper Harbor, MI   #63

North Station

Daily
9 - 9

420 Gratiot St.   49918
(906) 289-4653
Owner: Jody Wheeless
Est: 1990

100% cotton quilt
fabrics, books,
patterns, classes
& quilted gift
items.

Lake Superior
M - 26
420
North Station
U.S. 41

Quilter's
Relatives:
often the
lucky
recipients of
something
wonderful.

Ironwood, MI　#64

The Fabric Patch

Owners: Arlene Wanink, Ruth Potter,
& Joanne Kuula

121 N. Lowell St. 49938　　　(906) 932-5260
Opened: 1981　　　1000 sq.ft.

Mon - Thur
9:30 - 5
Fri 9:30 - 6:30
Sat 9:30 - 4

Quilting, Rubber Stamping,
and Craft Headquarters
of the North
Largest Selection in The U.P.
and Northern Wisconsin

Choose from over
3500 Bolts of Quilting Fabrics
Huge Selection of
Quilting Books and Craft Patterns

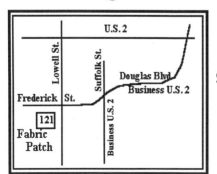

Authorized Dealer for
Viking and White
Sewing Machines & Sergers

Mail Order
Available

Michigan Guilds:
Trinity Piecemakers, 9077 Allen Road, Allen Park, 48101
U of M Faculty Women's Quilters, 2481 Trenton Court, Ann Arbor, 48105
Michigan Quilt Network, PO Box 339, Atlanta, 49709
Thunder Bay Quilters, Box 960, Atlanta, 49709
McKay Library Quilters, 105 S. Webster Street, Augusta, 49012
Berrien Towne & Country Quilters, 4218 E. Tudor Rd, Barrien Springs, 49103
Cal-Co Quilters' Guild, PO Box 867, Battle Creek, 49016
Bay Heritage Quilters Guild, 321 Washington Ave., Bay City, 48708
Western Wayne County Quilting Guild, 129 South St., Belleville, 48111
Pieceable Friends, 1991 E. Lincoln, Birmingham, 48009
Needlework & Textile Guild, 3219 Woodside Court, Bloomfield Hills, 48013
Brighton Heritage Quilters, 10281 Carriage Drive, Brighton, 48116
Casual Quilter's, 5418 Ethel, Brighton, 48116
North Star Quilters, 8436 E. 48th Road, Cadillac, 49601
Keweenaw Heritage Quilters, Calumet, 49913
Rivertown Patchworkers, 1849 Richmond, Cheboygan, 49721
Thumb Thimbles Quilt Guild, 5140 English Road, Clifford, 48727
West Michigan Quilters Guild, 13646 48th Avenue, Coopersville, 49404
General Dearborn Quilting Society, 915 Brady Road S., Dearborn, 48124
The Monday Night Quilters, 79939 40th Street, Decatur, 49045
St. Raymond's Quilters, 20212 Fairport , Detroit, 48205
The Crazy Quilters, 51106 Glenwood Rd., Dowagiac, 49047
Island City Piecemakers, P.O. Box 14, Eaton Rapids, 48827
Victorian Quilters Guild, PO 149, Empire, 49630
Bay deNoc Quilt Guild, P.O. Box 567, Escanaba, 49829
Care & Share Quilters, 4052 Fairgrove Rd., Fairgrove, 48733
Greater Ann Arbor Quilt Guild, 36437 Saxony, Farmington, 48335
Crazy Quilters, 7870 Peninsula, Farwell, 48622
Evening Star Quilters, 5327 Hopkins, Flint, 48506
Genesee Star Quilters, 614 S. McKinley Road, Flushing, 48433

Rumpled Quilts Kin, PO Box 587, Frankfort, 49635
Tall Pine Quilters, 2073 Baldwin, Fremont, 49412
North Country Piecemakers, PO Box 10, Glennie, 48737
Au Sable Quilt Guild, PO Box 198, Grayling, 49738
Claire County Crazy Quilters, 5189 Hamilton, Harrison, 48625
Tulip Patch Quilting Organization, 600 Woodland Dr., Holland, 49424
Composing Threaders, 144 N. Trybom Drive, Iron River, 49935
Pieces & Patches Quilt Guild, Box 6294, Jackson, 49202
Log Cabin Quilters, 6632 Woodlea , Kalamazoo, 49004
West Michigan Quilter's Guild, PO Box 8001, Kentwood, 49518
Capitol City Quilt Guild, 7131 Willow Woods Cr., Lansing, 48917
Lansing Area Patchers, 3305 Sunnylane, Lansing, 48906
Thimble Buddies Quilt Guild, 3167 Roods Lake Rd., Lapeer, 48446
Continued on Next Page

Michigan Guilds Continued from Previous Page:
Anchor Bay Quilters, 5757 N. River Road, Marine City, 48039
Marquette County Quilters Assoc., PO Box 411, Marquette, 49855
Midland Mennonites, 364 E. Gordonville, Midland, 48640
Quilters Squared Quilt Guild, 2715 Whitewood Dr., Midland, 48640
Patchers at the Lake Shore, 926 Wellington Court, Muskegon, 49441
Niles Piecemakers, 1347 Louis Street, Niles, 49120
Greater Ann Arbor Quilt Guild, 22452 Meadow Brook, Novi, 48375
Calico Patch Quilters, 1550 W. Drahner Rd., Oxford, 48371
Little Traverse Bay Quilters Guild, PO Box 2022, Petoskey, 49770
Pinckney Quilting Sisters, 11383 Cedar Bend Dr., Pinckney, 48169
Island City Quilters, 180 S. Sherwood, Plainwell, 49080
Plymouth Piecemakers, 11768 Turkey Run, Plymouth, 48170
Portage Quilt Guild, 6278 Redfern Circle, Portage, 49002
Loose Threads, 37550 Hebel Road, Richmond, 48062
Oakland County Quilt Guild, 282 Rose Briar Drive, Rochester Hills, 48309
Piece to Peace Quilting Club, 3914 Mission, Rosebush, 48878
Keeping the Piece Quilt Guild, Sault Ste. Marie, 49783
Friendship Ring Quilt Guild, 305 E. Harrison St., Shelby, 49455
Wyandotte Museum Quilters, 13407 Pullman, Southgate, 48195
Piecemakers Quilt Guild, 202 Jay Street, St. Charles, 48655
Tri County Quilt Guild, 4619 Hatherly Place, Sterling Heights, 48310
Sunrise Quilters, 318 N. McArdle Road, Tawas City, 48763
Eton Center Quilters, 7946 McKinley, Taylor, 48180
Trenton Quilters, 3398 Norwood Dr., Trenton, 48183
Cass River Quilters' Guild, 6977 Sohn Road, Vassar, 48768
Northern Lights Quilt Guild, 1315 Dewey, Wakefield, 49968
Greater Ann Arbor Quilt Guild, 29807 Autumn Lane, Warrren, 48093
Metro Detroit Quilt Guild,
6148 28 Mile Road,
Washington, 48094
Barrien County Coverlet
Guild, PO Box 529,
Watervliet, 49098
Quilt-N-Friends,
6332 Aspen Ridge Blvd.,
West Bloomfield, 48332
OTLB Quilters, 2831
Highland Drive, West
Branch, 48661

Other Shops in Michigan:

Allegan	Material World, 258 Lincoln Rd.
Au Gres	Bayview Calicoes & Ceramics, 3631 E. Huron Rd. #2
Bad Axe	The Country Goose, 163 E. Huron
Beaverton	Lelia's Place, 1333 McKimmy Dr.
Brethren	Studio North, 5630 Farnsworth Rd.
Cadillac	Julie Ann Fabrics, 111 S. Mitchell
Caledonia	Rainbow's End, 9343 Cherry Valley Ave.
Commerce	Quilt Corner, 8275 Cooley Lake Rd.
E. Tawas	The Cotton Patch, 616 Newman St.
Fenton	Sandy's Stitchin' Coop, 619 N. Leroy
Grand Haven	The Stitching Post Plus, 106 Washington Ave.
Grand Rapids	The Daisy Den Stitchery, 2290 44th S.E.
Ishpeming	Nancy's, 322 S. Lake
Lambertville	Village Fabrics & Crafts, 8019 Summerfield Rd.
Mason	Keans Hallmark & Variety, 406 S. Jefferson
Mason	Yards of Fabric, 116 E. Ash
Mio	The Fabric Shoppe, 432 E. Kittle Rd.
Norway	Jerri's Quilt Patch, Kimberly Rd.
Novi	Banks Vacuum Corp., 43039 Grand River
Omer	Quilt Patch Antiques, 429 E. Center St.
Petosky	Calico Crafts, 1691 Spring P.O. Box 2390
Plymouth	Quiltworks, 580 Forest Ave. #4
Port Huron	Mary Maxim, Inc., 2001 Holland Ave.
Port Sanilac	Country Magic II, 56 S. Ridge
Portland	Quilters Gallery, 1419 E. Grand River
Prudenville	Chris' Frabrics, 3088 W. Houghton Lake Dr.
Reading	Kathryn's Country Fabrics, 7911 S. Edon Rd. M-49
Richmond	Sew Together, 69295 Main St.
Riverdale	Sheila's Fabrics, 11995 W. Monroe Rd.
Royal Oak	Sew Quick, 510 S. Washington (moving)
Saline	Cross Roads Fabric & Quilt Shop, 12620 Jordan Rd.
South Haven	Calico Creations, 70325 16th Ave.
Traverse City	BJ's Cozy Quilts, Etc., 2772 Garfield Rd. N.
Traverse City	Boyd's and Sew Much More, 1723 S. Garfield Ave.
Yale	Sew 'N Sew, 1 N. Main St.
Zeeland	It's Stitching Time, 150 E. Main St.

Philosophy of the Guides

I enjoy and appreciate my local quilt shops. I love quilting and find that it helps me get through much of every-day life.

I also love finding a quilt shop when I'm traveling. Traveling is stressful and a visit to a quilt shop can get things back into perspective. While traveling I have at times even gone out of my way to visit a shop.

Often this departure from the most direct route has led to other adventures and very enjoyable days (even for my husband).

My hope is that publishing this directory will make finding shops easier. Then we can all visit new shops, see what other people are up to, make new friends, and ensure a strong future for quilting.

SPICED WITH LOVE

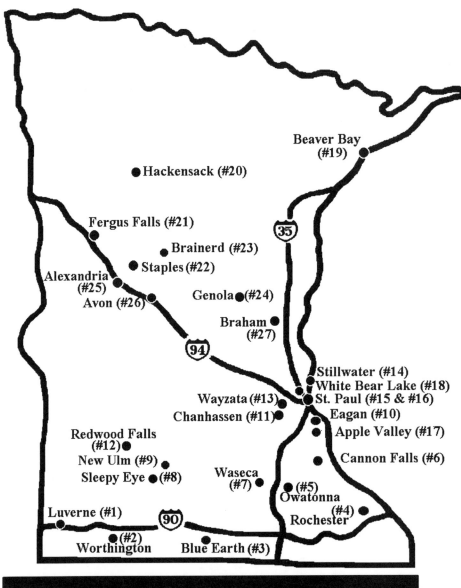

Beaver Bay (#19)

Hackensack (#20)

Fergus Falls (#21)

35

Brainerd (#23)

Staples (#22)

Alexandria (#25)

Genola (#24)

Avon (#26)

Braham (#27)

94

Stillwater (#14)
White Bear Lake (#18)

Wayzata (#13)   St. Paul (#15 & #16)

Chanhassen (#11)   Eagan (#10)

Apple Valley (#17)

Redwood Falls (#12)

New Ulm (#9)   Cannon Falls (#6)

Sleepy Eye (#8)   Waseca (#7)

(#5)

Owatonna (#4)

Luverne (#1)   90

Rochester

(#2)

Worthington   Blue Earth (#3)

MINNESOTA

27 Featured Shops

Luverne, MN   #1

The Sewing Basket

204 E. Main   56156
(507) 283-9769
Est: 1979   1200 sq.ft.

Mon - Sat
9 - 5
Thur til 9

A nice selection of better quilting fabrics. Also books, patterns & supplies. Lots of samples on display.

Main Street Luverne, Minnesota just north off Interstate 90

Worthington, MN   #2

CRAFTY CORNER
Quilt & Sewing Shoppe

1820 Oxford St.   56187
(507) 372-2707
Owner: Zuby Jansen
Est. 1982   2600 sq.ft.

Mon - Thur
9 - 5:30
Fri 9 - 9
Sat 9 - 4

We sell 100% cotton fabrics. 1500 bolts in stock. Many Patterns Bernina Sewing Machine sales & Service Quilting Supplies!

Blue Earth, MN   #3

Quilt Company

120 S. Main   56013
(507) 526-2647
Est: 1988   1300 sq.ft.
Owners: Lola Hendrickson, Jolyn Olson, & Tracy Peterson

Mon - Sat
9 - 5
Thur til 8

Complete line of Quilting Needs. Fabric, Patterns, Notions, Classes, Service. Also Custom Quilting.

Rochester, MN   #4

Patchwork & Pinafores

324 Elton Hills Drive N.W.
(507) 288-2040   55901
Owner: Susan Dillinger   Est: 1990
2375 sq.ft.

Mon - Sat
9 - 5
Tues & Thur til 8

2000 + Bolts of fabric, books, patterns. notions, gifts, classes.

Owatonna, MN   #5

The Cotton Patch

110 W. Broadway   55060
(507) 451-5979   Est: 1993
1800 sq.ft.   1000+ Bolts
Owners: Cathy Torrey, LeAnn Werner & Jeralene Staska

Mon - Fri
9 - 6
Sat 9 - 4:30

Quality 100% cotton fabrics; large selection of homespuns; patterns; books; notions; silk ribbon embroidery. Located on downtown's charming Central Park.

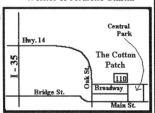

Cannon Falls, MN   #6

Quilts by the Falls

402 W. Mill St.   55009
(507) 26302528
Owners: Marilou & Larry Welt   3000 sq.ft.

Mon - Sat
9 - 5
Thur 9 - 8

Complete quilt shop featuring 100% cottons & homespuns. Notions, patterns, books, backings, battings, classes. Unique gift bags & cards. Quilts for sale. Needlework Supplies. Inspiration always avail.

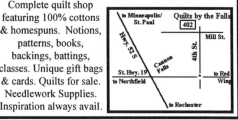

Waseca, MN #7

The Happy Hands Shoppe

107 2nd St. NW   56093
(507) 835-5081   Est: 1983
Owners: Darcy Barnes & Martha Waddell

M, Th 10 - 6
T, W, F 10 - 5
Sat 10 - 4

Supplies for:
Quilting,
Hardanger,
Stenciling, Counted
Cross-stitch,
Painting, Crafts.
Lots of Patterns,
Books, Classes.
Consignment Gifts.

Sleepy Eye, MN #8

Prairieville Quilting

R.R. #3, Box 115   56085
(507) 794-2466
Owner: Joycy Neyers Est: 1993

Evenings &
Weekends By
Appointment

A unique custom
machine quilting
service.
Specializing in
custom designing
your quilts.
Large variety of
block & border
designs available.

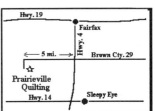

New Ulm, MN #9

Muggs Fabric & Bridal

101 N. German   Marktplatz Mall
(507) 359-1515   56073
Owner: Margaret Meyer
3000 sq.ft.

Mon - Fri
9:30 - 9
Sat
9:30 - 5:30
Sun 12 - 5

Friendly quilt shop
with over 2000
bolts of quality
100% cottons
including
Hoffman, RJR,
Debbie Mumm.

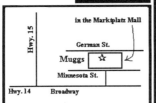

Eagan, MN #10

Country Needleworks

3924 Cedarvale Blvd.
(612) 452-8891   55122
Owner: Sandy Quam   Est: 1989
1600 sq.ft.   1000 Bolts

Mon - Thur
9:30 - 8
Fri & Sat
9:30 - 5

A Country Shop
offering the finest
in cotton fabrics,
books, patterns
and quilting
supplies.
Classes & Gifts
available.

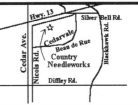

The Sampler

535 W. 78th St.   55331
(612) 934-5307
Owner: Karol Plocher
Est: 1977   2650 Sq.ft.

1600 Bolts
Cotton Fabric
Quilting,
Wall Stencils,
Cross-Stitch.
Lots of Patterns
& Gifts.

Mon - Fri
9:30 - 6:30
Saturday
9:30 - 5:30
Sunday
12 - 4:30

Chanhassen, MN #11

Directions:

Take Highway 494 to Highway 5 West -
go to Great Plains Blvd (Chanhassen
exit) — turn Rt. — Follow street around
Chanhassen Dinner Theater to first left.

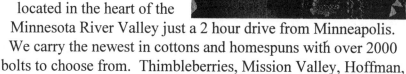

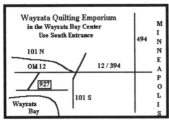

THE
COUNTRY PEDDLER QUILT SHOP

St. Paul, MN   #16

2230 CARTER AVENUE   55108   (612) 646-1756

Est: 1973   Owner: Jean Humenansky

Mon & Thur 9:30 - 8:30
Tues, Wed, Fri, & Sat 9:30 - 5:00
Sun 12 - 4:00

The latest in Fabric, Notions, Patterns, and Books for all your quilting needs.
3500+ bolts of cotton fabric.
Quarterly class newsletter.
Peddlers Pieces Fabric Club
Experienced & Friendly Staff

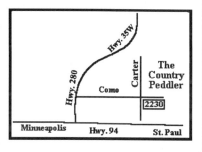

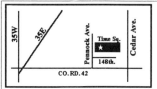

Fabric Town

Mon. - Fri.
10 - 8:30
Sat. 10 - 5
Sun. 12 - 5

7655 W. 148th St., Apple Valley, MN 55124
Phone: 612 / 432-1827 • 1-800-475-2137

Owner: Barbara Sherman — Est. 1981

Apple Valley, MN   #17

• Our <u>3,000 sq.ft.</u> store features:
3,000 BOLTS OF 100% COTTON,
BOOKS, PATTERNS, KITS, HUNDREDS OF SAMPLES

"Fabriholics Club" - Receive fat quarters of newest fabrics each month. Call for more information.

LOOKING FOR SOMETHING? WE SHIP!

Our friendly, knowledgeable staff is look forward to meeting you!

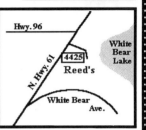
Beaver Bay, MN #19

Quilt Corner

Mon - Sat
10 - 4
Sun 12 - 4

Beaver Bay Mini Mall, P.O. Box 304
(218) 226-3517
Owner: Roxanne Johnson
Est: 1990   800 sq.ft.

Over 500 Bolts of
Cotton Fabric.
Books, Notions,
Patterns, &
Stencils. Many
Quilts for sale.
Gifts too.

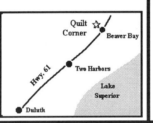

Hackensack, MN #20

Piecemakers Quilt Shop

Mon - Thur
10 - 5
Fri til 7
(May - Dec)
Suns 12 - 5

Hwy. 371 North   56452
(218) 675-6271   Est: 1984
Owners: Mary & Pam Curo

Unique shop
nestled in the
"Land of Lakes
and Majestic
Pines".
Fine 100%
cottons.
Extensive line of
books & patterns.

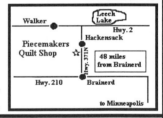

Fergus Falls, MN #21

Quilters Cottage

Tues - Fri
10 - 5
Sat 10 - 3
Closed
July Sats

316 N. Tower Rd.   56537
(218) 739-9652
Owner: Cheri Steenbock
Est: 1988   1500 sq.ft.

Everything
you need for
quilting
including help
and a friendly
smile.

Staples, MN #22

Quilting Memories

Tues - Fri
10 - 5:30
Sat 10 - 3

216 2nd. Ave.   56479   (218) 894-1776
Owners: Sue Caquelin & Linda Melby

Pfaff Sewing
Machines,
Yarn & Knitting,
Cross Stitch
Custom Machine
Quilting,
Fabric,
Quilting Supplies,
Patterns, Classes

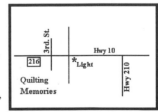

Brainerd, MN   #23

909 S. 6th St.   56401   (218) 829-7273
Owner: Lou Rademacher   Est: 1971

Country Fabrics, Quilts, & Collectibles

Show us this coupon and receive
10% off your purchase.
1 time only.

Mon - Sat
9:30 - 5:30
Fri til 7:30

Our 1800 Mercantile is filled with over 2000 calicoes by the leading designers:
Thimbleberries, Country Threads, P&B, Marcus, Hoffman, Roberta Horton,
Debbie Mumm and more. We have a large selection of craft and wearable art
patterns. We are your authorized Viking, Elna & Brother sewing
machine/serger dealer. If you are not into quilting, visit our 'quaint' 2nd floor
gift shop. We offer a wide variety of classes throughout the year. Drop us a
note or give a call and we will mail you our newsletter.

Gruber's Market Genola, MN   #24

#1 Main Street   56364   (320) 468-6435
Est: 1934   8000 sq.ft.   Free Catalog
Owners: Sue Poser & Paul Gruber

Mon - Sat
5a.m. - 10p.m.
Sun 7a.m. - 10p.m.

The most unique Quilt Shop you'll ever enter.
8000 Bolts of Cotton. Home of the "Lap Hoop"
All the latest patterns & books—100's of Titles
A true General Store with German sausages,
meats and more!

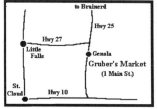

Alexandria, MN #25

B's Fabric & Sewing Center

1321 Broadway   56308
(612) 762-8892
Owner: Bonnie Walker
Est: 1990   8500 sq.ft.   2000+ Bolts

Mon - Fri 10 - 6
Sat 9 - 5

We have a whole lot of Cotton Fabrics, Books, Patterns & Notions. Along with Pfaff, Singer, Viking & White Sewing Machines.

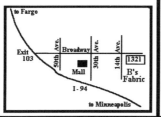

Avon, MN #26

Aunt Annie's Quilts & Silks

P.O. Box 359   109 Avon Ave. S
(320) 356-1061   56310
Owners: Lucy Senstad & Helen Frie
Full service shop   1000 Bolts

Mon - Thur 9 - 6
Fri 9 - 8
Sat 9 - 4

Fine Cottons: Traditional, Liberty of London, Owner Hand-Painted, Balis. Silks, Classes. Assistance with Color Selection.

Braham, MN #27

Rosemary's Quilts & Baskets

103 W. Central Dr.   55006
(612) 396-3818   Est. 1988
Owner: Rosemary Brabec
1500 sq.ft.

Mon - Thur 9 - 5
Fri 9 - 6
Sat 9 - 4
Closed July Sats

Quilting Fabrics, patterns, notions and large selection of books. Classes year 'round. Friendly, expert service. Also basketry supplies and classes.

Minnesota State Guild:
Minnesota Quilter, Inc., 8616 Darnel Rd., Eden Prairie, 55344
Minnesota Guilds:
Lakes Area Quilting Guild, 1219 S. Nokomis, Alexandria, 56308
Hands all around Quilters, P.O. Box 329 Braham, 55006
Pine Tree Patchworkers, P.O. Box 935, Brainerd, 56401
Quilters along the Yellowstone Trail, P.O. Box 261, Buffalo Lake, 55314
Common Threads, 500 E. Minnesota St. Cannon Falls, 55009
Chaska Area Quilt Guild, P.O. Box 44, Chaska, 55318
Minnesota Quilter Inc., 8616 Darnel Rd., Eden Prairie, 55344

Piecemakers Quilt Guild, R.R. #1, Box 150, Gibbon
Loon Country Quilters, 4646 Hwy. 2 E., Grand Rapids, 55744
Heartland Quilters, Hackensack
Prairie Piecemakers, 101 N. German, New Ulm, 56073
Rochester Quilters' Sew-Ciety, P.O. Box 6245, Rochester, 55903
Thief River Falls Quilter's Guild, P.O. Box 121, Thief River Falls, 56701

Other Shops in Minnesota:
Crookston	Z Place, 101 N. Main
Hayward	Calico Hutch, P. O. Box 51
Marshall	Fabrics Plus, 237 W. Main St.
Minneapolis	Glad Creations Inc., 3400 Bloomington Ave. S.
Minneapolis	Eydie's Country Quilting, 2822 West 43rd St.
Northfield	Jacobsen's, 419 Division St.
Pelican Rapids	Calico Cupboard, 25 1st Ave. NW, P.O. Box 336
St. Charles	Amish Market Sq., I - 90 & Hwy 74
Waconia	The Sew & Vac, 115 S. Olive St.
Walnut Grove	Plum Creek Patchwork, Rt. 2, Box 95
Wells	The Creative Needle, 135 S. Broadway

MISSISSIPPI

1 Featured Shop

Jackson, MS   #1

Ann's Quilt Shop

| Mon - Sat |
| 9:30 - 5:30 |

5738 Hwy. 80 W   Suite A
(601) 922-6228   39209
Owner: Ann Root
Est: 1979   1100 sq.ft.   800 Bolts

Complete Line of
Quilting Fabrics,
Books, Notions.
Personal assistance
and friendly
service.

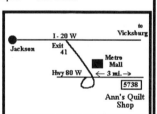

Jackson (#1)

Mississippi State Guild:
             Mississippi Quilt Association, 909 N. 31st Ave., Hattiesburg, 39401
Shops in Mississippi:

Hattiesburg	The Quilted Heart, 1901 Hardy St.
Jackson	Joy's Busy Hands, 2565 Mcfadden Rd.
Laurel	Magnolia Blossom Fabrics, North Laurel Shopping Center
Lucedale	The Fabric Barn, 125 E. Main
Maben	Springer's Dry Goods, 124 Highway 15
Meridian	The Craft Cottage, 2928 N. Hills St.
Summit	Wards Linen Outlet, 814 Robb St.
Tupelo	Heirlooms Forever, 1413 W. Main St.
Vicksburg	Stitch - N - Frame Shop, 2222 S. Frontage Rd.

30 Featured Shops

MISSOURI

Springfield, MO #1

The Quilt Shoppe

**Tues - Fri
9:30 - 5:30
Sat 10 - 4**

2762 South Campbell   65807
(417) 883-1355
Owners: Rosalie Carey & Gilda
Est: 1978   2100 sq.ft.   Young

1500 Bolts of
100% cotton,
books, patterns,
stencils, notions,
Q-snap frames,
Hinterberg
Frames, Classes

Springfield, MO #2

The Quilt Sampler

**Mon - Fri
10 - 5
Thur til 8
Sat 10 - 4**

1936 B. South Glenstone 65804
(417) 886-5750 "On the Plaza"
Owner: Cristen Powell   Est: 1994
"Where friends and   2000 sq.ft.
fabric meet."
Over 1750 Bolts,
books, patterns, and
classes.
Professional
Machine Quilting
Friendly staff offers
service, instruction
and inspiration.

Mt. Vernon, MO #3

Turner's Calico Country
& Ben Franklin

**Mon - Sat
8:30 - 5:30
Sun 1 - 5**

207 E. Dallas   65712
(417) 466-3401

Quilt Show Everyday, Lace, 1000's of Calicos, Quilting Supplies, 100's of Sewing & Craft Patterns, Old Time Candy Case, Ozark-Made Oak Baskets.

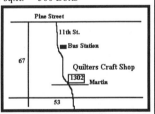

Branson

Quilts & Q

1137 West Hwy. 76   6
in Branson Heights Shoppin
(417) 334-3243
Owner: Marlys Michaelson
Est: 1981   8,000 sq.ft.

Largest and most complete quilting shop in the 4 state area. Handmade Quilts. Over 4000 bolts of Calico and Gifts !

Pg. 206

Wentzvill

9 - 6 Daily

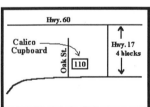

Poplar Bluff, MO #5

Quilters Craft Shop

**8:30 - 5:30
Except Fri.
close @ 5**

1302 South 11th   63901
(573) 785-6514
Owner: Mary L. Hoeinghaus
Est: 1984   800 sq.ft.   500 Bolts

100% cottons, books & Patterns specialize in Quilts, quilt racks and many other crafts.

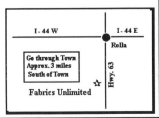

Mountain View, MO #6

Calico Cupboard

**Mon - Fri
10 - 5
Sat 10 - 3**

110 Oak St.   65548
(417) 934-6330   Est: 1981
Owner: Darlene Godsy
1500 sq.ft.   Catalog $2.00

600 bolts of cotton fabrics, lots of patterns, books, notions, counted cross stitch books and supplies plus friendly Ozarks service.

Rolla, MO #7

Fabrics Unlimited

**Mon - Sat
9:30 - 5:30
Sun 1 - 5**

13795 U.S. 63 S   65401
(573) 364-5245
Owner: Betty I. Lewis
1600 sq.ft.   2500 total bolts, 1100+ quilt fabric

Quilting Fabrics, Notions, Batting, Quilt Books. Machine Quilting Machine Binding. Our main business is quilt supplies.

Chesterfield, MO #8

Dotty's Quilt Shop

**Mon - Fri
9 - 4
Sat 10 - 2**

769 Spirit of St. Louis Blvd.
(314) 532-7300   63005
Est: 1968   1500+ Bolts
Owners: Jim & Judy DeVries

Machine & Hand Quilting, Calico Fabrics, Craft Patterns and Items.

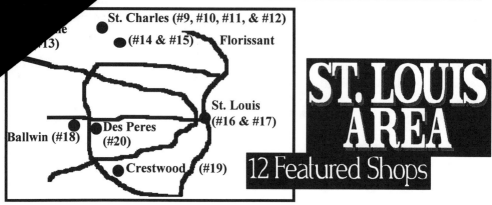

St. Charles (#9, #10, #11, & #12)

(#14 & #15)   Florissant

(#13)

ST. LOUIS AREA
12 Featured Shops

St. Louis (#16 & #17)

Ballwin (#18)   Des Peres (#20)

Crestwood   (#19)

St. Charles, MO   #9

Patches Etc. Quilt Shop

337 South Main   63301
(314) 946-6004
Owner: Ann Watkins
Est: 1979   850 Sq.ft.
1000 Bolts   Catalog $1

Mon - Sat
9:30 - 5
Sun 11 - 5

Quilts, Fabric and Patterns -- Certified appraisals by Ann Watkins. Also visit out Craft Center and Button Shoppe

First Capitol Dr.
Fifth St.
Patches Etc. 337
Boonslick Rd.
South Main
Frontier Park
Missouri River
I-70

Historic Saint Charles

St. Charles, MO   #10

Huning's Quilt Fair

334 North Main Street   63301
(314) 946-5480   Est: 1860
Owner: Monica Vandeven   2700 sq.ft.

huning's   quilt fair

"THE STORE FOR QUILTERS"
Handmade Quilts
Stamped Embroidery Goods
Pillow Cases
Pillow Case Doll Kits
Quilt Tops (Bucilla & Tobin)
Quilt Blocks
Flosses (DMC & J & P Coats)
Quilting Stencils & Frames
Quilt Backing, Books & Patterns
Large Selection of Cotton Calico
   Fabrics and Solid Fabrics
Nancy Frock Dresses
Nursing Home Dresses
Hospital Gowns
   VISA MASTER DISCOVER

Huning's   334
Washington
Jefferson
1st Capitol
94
Boonslick Rd.
I-70
Sixth
Fifth
Second
Main
MISSOURI RIVER

Mon - Sat
9 - 5:30
Sun
11 - 5

St. Charles, MO #11

Kalico Patch

Mon - Sat
10 - 5
Sun 12 - 5

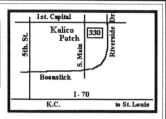

330 S. Main St.   63301
(314) 946-9520 Owner: Karel Owens
Est: 1976   1000 sq.ft.

"Out of the scraps of my life God has made a beautiful quilt."

1500+ Bolts of Fabric

Quilts—Hand & Machine.   Classes. Baby Quilts & Bibs, Quilted Bags, Pillows, Bears, Dolls, Pictures and Quilted Clothing, Quilt Shelves & Racks. Custom Orders are Welcomed. Machine Quilting Available.

St. Charles, MO #12

Quilt 'n Craft Corner

1522 Caulks Hill Rd.
63303
(314) 939-0000
Est: 1995
Owner: Doris Jinkerson

Mon - Fri
10 - 7
Sat 10 - 2

Come browse through my 'garden' of 100% cotton fabrics, homespuns, and flannels. Books, patterns & notions available. 1200+ Bolts & growing. Smiles Free!

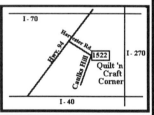

Wentzville, MO #13

Prairie Way
Antique/Quilt Shop

Sun - Fri
9 - 3

110-B E. Pearce   63385
(314) 327-5609
Owners: Tom & Judy Love
Est: 1984   4000 sq.ft.

Large Selection of Antique Quilts & Tops, Quilting Templates, Cotton Feed Sacks, Kansas City Star Quilt Patterns, Hand Quilting Done.

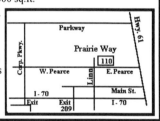

Florissant, MO #14

Helen's
Hen House

Mon - Sat
10 - 4
Tues &
Wed til 8

180 Dunn Rd.   63031
(314) 837-7661
Est: 1978 1350 sq.ft.
Owners: Helen Argent & Joan Nicolay

Over 2000 Bolts. Specializing in homespuns & reproduction fabrics. Complete line of quilting supplies, patterns & Books.

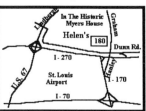

Florissant, MO #15

Quilt 'n' Stuff

Tues - Fri
10 - 5
Sat 10 - 2

124 St. Francois   63031
(314) 831-7268
Est: 1981   1200 sq.ft.
Owners: Jackie Harris & Robin Gain

Approx. 1200 Bolts of 100% Cotton fabrics, books, patterns, antique quilts, baskets and other gift items.

St. Louis, MO #16

The Sign of the Turtle

5223 Gravois   63116
(314) 351-5550   Est: 1975
Owners: Ann & Bill Hofmann
1600 sq.ft. 300 Bolts 50 Solids

Mon - Thur
10 - 9
Fri & Sat
10 - 5
Sun: By Appt

St. Louis
Area's
Quilting
Headquarters!

By the Bevo

St. Louis, MO #17

THE QUILTED FOX

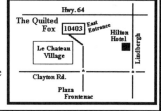

10403 Clayton Rd.   63131
(314) 993-1181   Est: 1994
Owner: Louise L. Georgia
1500 sq.ft.   3000 Bolts

M, W 9:30 - 5
T, Th 9:30 - 8
Fri & Sat
9:30 - 4:30

Unique Cotton
fabrics found
around the world
for the quilter.
Helpful staff, Fox
Fabric Club for the
out-of-town.

Ballwin, MO #18

In Stitches

14664 Manchester Rd.   63011
(314) 394-4471
Owner: Pam Bryan
Est: 1988

Mon - Sat
9:30 - 4:30
Tues, Wed
& Thur til 8

We carry over
2600 bolts of
fabric
including
designer
fabrics.

In Stitches is located just
west of St. Louis
4 1/2 miles west
of I - 270 on
Manchester Rd.

Crestwood, MO #19

Quilt 'N' Stitch

9109 Watson Rd.   63126
(314) 961-0909
Owner: Connie Ewbank
Est: 1992   2400 sq.ft.   1500 Bolts

Mon - Fri
9:30 - 5:30
Sat
9:30 - 4:30
Class Eves.

Large selection of
fabrics - Christmas,
homespuns,
contemporary.
Books, patterns,
notions, classes.
Also counted cross
stitch and silk
ribbon embroidery.

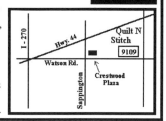

The Kotton Patch

Helping to create a Legacy of Warmth.

Des Peres, MO #20

100% Cotton Fabrics,
Quilt Books,
Notions, Patterns,
Zook Quilting Frames.

12772 Manchester   63131
(314) 965-KOTN (5686)
Owner: Marylu Amantea
1700 sq.ft.   1800 Bolts

Mon - Fri   9:30 - 5
Mon & Wed til 8   Sat 10 - 4:30

Complete Quilt Shop

Hannibal, MO #21

Hickory Stick

Mon - Sat
9 - 5
Sun 12 - 5

326 N. Main   63401
(573) 221-4538
Owner: Patricia Waelder
Est: 1977   3000 sq.ft.

Across from Mark Twain's Home. 1000 Bolts- Calicos & Homespun. Fabrics, Cross- Stitch, Craft Patterns, Gifts. Christmas. Open all year.

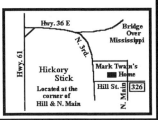

Rutledge, MO #22

Zimmerman's Store

Mon - Sat
8 - 5

Main St., Box 1   63563
(816) 883-5766   Est: 1974
Owners: Paul & Lydia Zimmerman
Mgr: Ellanor Zimmerman

1400 bolts of 100% cotton fabrics at reasonable prices. Batting, quilt patterns & books, sewing notions, hand quilted quilts, pillows, aprons etc

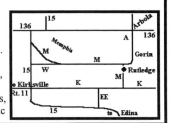

Versailles, MO #23

Clark's Fabrics

Mon - Sat
9 - 5

West Vue Shopping Center
Hwy 5 & 52 W.   65084
(573) 378-5696   Est: 1964
Owner: Kirk Chapman   1800 sq.ft.   1700 Bolts

Great selection of all types of fabric, including quilting, clothing and home decorating. Buttons, Buttons,

Buttons !

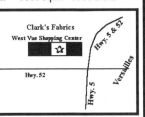

Stover, MO #24

Nolting's Longarm Mfg.

Mon - Fri
7:30 - 4
Sat & Sun
By Appt.

Hwy. 52 East R.R. #3   Box 147
(573) 377-2713   65078
Fax: (314) 377-4451
Owner: Frederick D. Nolting
Est: 1984

Five sizes of longarm quilting machines and tables. Quilting being done everyday !

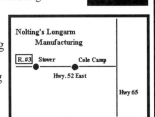

Sedalia, MO #25

D & T Quilt Shop

Mon - Fri
9 - 5
Sat 9 - 4

R.R. # 6   Box 232   65301
(816) 826-4788
Owner: Theresa Gerber
Est: 1991   400 sq.ft.

Fabrics, Notions, Machine and Hand Quilting, Classes. 1000+ Bolts Friendly Country Atmosphere

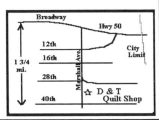

Columbia, MO #26

Silks & More Fine Fabrics

Mon - Thur 10 - 7
Fri & Sat 10 - 5

2541 Bernadette Dr.   65203-4674
(573) 446-2655   5200 sq.ft.
Owner: Millie Kaiser   Est: 1985

Large selection of beautiful 100% cotton prints and solids, designer fabrics, books, patterns, and notions. Come see us!

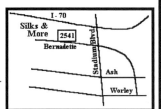

Marshall, MO #27

Quilt Shoppe

Mon - Fri 9:30 - 5:30
Sat 9:30 - 5

615 Cherokee #5   65340
(816) 886-4646
Owner: Janis Eddy

Fabric, Books, Notions, & Antiques. Pfaff Sewing Machines.

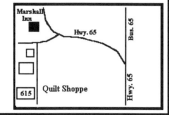

Blue Springs, MO #28

Burnstone Quilt Co.

Mon - Sat 10 - 5
Mon & Thur 7 - 9 pm

204 A SW 11th   64015
(816) 228-3122   Est: 1993
Owner: Retha Burns   1400 sq.ft.
Free Newsletter   600 Bolts

In historic Blue Springs. "We're contemporary, classic and inspirational." Call ahead for our 1 day workshops. Beginners thru expert. Guild Members Welcome.

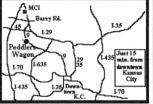

Is for Quiet Quality Time

Liberty, MO #29

Liberty Quilt Shop

Mon - Sat 10 - 5
Thur til 8

131 South Water   64068
(816) 781-7966   Est: 1988
Owner: Kathleen Glasco
3000 sq.ft.   & Julie Kiffin

Over 3000 bolts of 100% cotton. Books, patterns, and friendly, helpful staff !

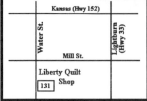

Parkville, MO #30

Peddler's Wagon

Tues - Sat 10 - 5

115 Main   64152
(816) 741-0225
Owners: Teri Hahs
Est: 1982   3400 sq.ft.

Quilts, Smocking Supplies, Quilting supplies, Fabric, Primitive Rug Hooking, Country Gifts, Ladie and Friends Dolls.

Missouri State Guild:
Missouri State Quilter Guild, Rt. 1, Box 1060, Cassville, 65625
Missouri Guilds:
Booneslick Trail Quilters' Guild, P.O. Box 542, Columbia, 65205
Flower Valley Quilting Guild, P.O. Box 9002, Florissant, 63032
Nitetime Needlers, P.O. Box 28731, Kansas City, 64118
Northland Quilters' Guild, P.O. Box 46654, Kansas City, 64118
Quilters Guild of Greater Kansas City, P.O. Box 22561, Kansas City, 64113
Country Patchworkers, P.O. Box 365, Marshall, 65340
Stitch By Stitch, 1403 Viking Lane, Marshall, 65340
Ozark Piecemakers Quilt Guild, P.O. Box 4931, Springfield, 65808

Other Shops in Missouri:

Augusta	Tips 'N Trix Shop, 5625 High
Barnett	Pleasant Valley Quilts, Rt. 2, Box 33
Boonville	Fashion Shack Fabrics, 11571 Dogwood Rd.
Branson	The Cotton Patch Quilt Shop, 2420 W. Hwy. 76
Branson	Rosebrier Quilts and Gifts, 117 E. Main St.
Branson	Grapevine Antiques and Gifts, 110 W. Main St.
Branson	Amanda's, W. Hwy. 76
Branson	Carolina Mills Factory Outlet, Highway 76
Cape Girardeau	The Sewing Basket, 2504 William
Carrollton	Quilted Thimble, 14 N. Main St.
Clinton	Mary Jane's Fabrics, 109 W. Franklin St.
Crystal City	Quilting Bee, 520C Bailey Rd.
Dexter	Quilts and More, 24 E. Stoddard
Ewing	Nu Way Quilt Shop, Route 2
Farmington	Old Village Quilt Shop, 113 S. Jackson St.
Fredericktown	Carolina Fabric Center, 130 E. Main St.
Hannibal	Yore Quilts, 403 Broadway
Kirksville	Kaye's Fabrics, 300 N. Franklin
Lebanon	H & H Fabric and Quilt Center, 326 W. Commercial St.
Lee's Summit	Quilters' Station, 321 SE Main St.
Marshall	Betty Sue O'Dell, 466 S. Odell
Mt. Vernon	Grannie's Patchworks, 105 E. Dallas St.
Oak Grove	Phanora's Variety, 1560 S. Broadway St.
Osage Beach	Quilts & Things, R.R. #2 P.O. Box 2535
Osceola	Quilts and Crafts, 312 Second St.
Potosi	Busy Bee Quilt Shop & Florist, 103 Fissell St.
Sappington	Quilt 'N' Stitch, 9109 Watson Rd.
Springfield	Crafters Delight, 2709 W. Kearney St.
Springfield	Patchwork Corner, 702 E. Commercial St.
St. Joseph	Bits & Pieces, 436 S. Belt
St. Louis	Thimble & Thread, 2629 Yeager Rd.
Ste. Genevieve	Monia's Unlimited, 316 Market
Webb City	Edna's Quilts & Ida's Ideas, 119 Tom St.
Winona	Ozark Quilt Supply, 308 Ash St.

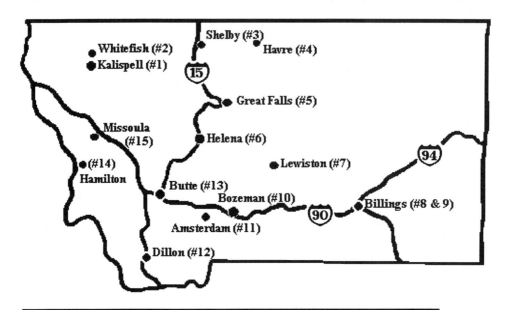

15 Featured Shops

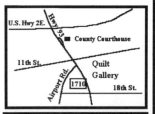

Whitefish, MT #2

The Fabric Shoppe

Mon - Fri 9 - 6
Sat 10 - 5

550 E. 1st. St. #102 59937
(406) 862-7218 Est: 1994
Owner: Cheryl Schankin

1200 sq.ft. 700+ Bolts

Lots of colors!
100% Cottons,
Flannel, Linen,
Books & Patterns
Quilting &
Sewing Classes
We also repair
quilts by hand.
Outerware Fabrics
& patterns too!

Whitefish Lake
Train Depot
The Fabric Shoppe 550 1st St.
Hwy. 93
Hwy. 93
Service With A Smile !

Shelby, MT #3

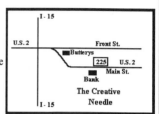
THE Creative NEEDLE

Mon - Sat 9 - 5:30

225 Main St. 59474
(406) 434-7106
Owner: Shelby Creative Investment

Complete Quilt
Shop.
Fabric, Notions,
Pfaff Sewing
Machines. Plus we
do commercial
quilting and ship
anywhere.

I-15
U.S.2 Front St.
Butterys
225 U.S.2
Main St.
Bank
The Creative Needle
I-15

Havre, MT #4

Quilters' Edge

220 3rd. Ave. 59501
(406) 265-1191
Owner: Patricia Haas
Est: 1993 1500 sq.ft.

Books, Patterns,
Notions, Stencils,
Batting & Fabric.
Authorized Pfaff
Sewing Machine
Dealer.
Mail Order
Available

Mon - Sat 9 - 5

Hwy. 2
3rd. Ave.
(In Downtown Havre) 2nd. St.
220
Quilters' Edge

Great Falls, MT #5

Debbie's Sewing Centre

Mon - Thur 9:30 - 7
Fri & Sat 9:30 - 5:30
Sun 12 - 4

1304 13th Ave. S 59405
(406) 452-7222 Est: 1988
Owner: Debra Waldenberg
3500 sq.ft.

We are located on
the corner of 13th
Avenue South
and 13th Street
South in the 13th
Square.

10th Ave. S.
Holiday Village Shopping Center
9th. St. S
13th. St. S
13th Ave. S.
Debbi's Sewing Centre
1304

Helena, MT #6

Calico Cupboard

Mon - Sat 10 - 5

601 Euclid Ave. # C 59601
(406) 449-8440
Est: 1989 2000 sq.ft.
Owners: Dianne Ducello

Specialize in fine
100% cotton
Fabric, unique
patterns, quilting
books, notions,
classes and gifts.

Euclid
601
Lyndale
Calico Cupboard
Harrison
Madison
Benton

Lewistown, MT #7

Megahertz

Mon - Sat 9 - 5:30

223 W. Main St. 59457
(406) 538-8531
Est: 1992 3300 sq.ft.

Fabrics, Notions,
Crafts, Antiques.
Custom
Embroidery, Stop
in and see the
Historic Megahertz
Building.
Circa 1904

In the Center of
♥ Lewistown
Montana

Billings, MT #8

 Fiberworks

Mon & Tues
10 - 5:30
Wed 10 - 8
Thur, Fri,
Sat 10 - 5

1300 24th St. W #3   59102
(406) 656-6663
Owner: Laura Heine
Est: 1994
1500 sq.ft.

**Fantastic
Fabrics for
Flash Funk &
Fashion**

Grand Ave.
Lewis Ave.
24th St. W
1300
Fiberworks

Billings, MT #9

Bernina Sewing Center

Mon - Sat
9:30 - 5:30

527 24th St. W   59102
(406) 656-4999
Owners: Frank & Doris Holzer
900 Bolts

Authorized
Bernina Dealer.
Quilting books,
patterns, supplies.
100% cotton
calicos & solids.
Classes.
Friendly & helpful

Broadwater Ave.
527 Bernina   Central Ave.
24th St. W   22nd St.   14th St.
King Ave.
I - 90

Bozeman, MT #10

Bear Comforts

Mon - Sat
9:30 - 5:30

126 E. Main St.   59715
(406) 586-6097 or (800) 757-6097
Owner: Sandy Taylor
Est: 1977   2500 sq.ft.   2000 Bolts

Bozeman's only
complete quilting
store offering
hundreds of bolts
of 100% cotton,
the latest notions,
patterns & books
for your selection.

I - 90
West Exit
N. 7th Ave.
East Exit
Main St.   126 Bear Comforts

Amsterdam, MT #11

The Patchworks

Mon - Fri
8 - 12
Afternoons
By Appt.

6676 Amsterdam Rd. 59741
(406) 282-7218 Fax: (406) 282-7322
Owner: Margo Krager Est: 1976
E mail: ptchwrks @ alpinet. net
http://www.alpinet.net/~ptchwrks/

We have over 800 Bolts of
reproduction cottons from
1775 - 1940
Catalog $1

Dillon, MT #12

The Crafty Quilter

Mon - Fri
10 - 5:30
Sat
10 - 4:30

104 N. Montana St.   59725
(406) 683-5884
Owner: Susy McCall

Specialize in
Western Wildlife
Fabric.
Hoffman, Spiegel,
Kid's Prints.
One Block from
Patagonia Outlet.

to Butte
Hwy. 158
Montana St.
Helena
I - 15
104 The Crafty Quilter Center
to Idaho Falls

Butte, MT #13

Quilts and
Cloth, too

Mon - Sat
10 - 5:30

2310 Cobban St.   59701
(406) 782-4511
Owner: Cathy Rapp   Est: 1995

Everything you
need for quilting.
Wonderful fabrics,
books, patterns,
tools and
instruction. Gift
items and custom
quilts too!

Harrison Ave.
Farragut
Cobban St.
Quilts & 2310 Cloth, too
In the Eastgate Shopping Center
I - 90

Hamilton, MT #14

201 S. Second   59840
(406) 363-3471   3500 sq.ft.
Owner: Rosalie Reinbold   Est: 1972

**Mon - Sat
9:30 - 5:30**

Featuring over 2000 bolts of prints &
Solids—Hoffman, Alexander Henry,
Concord, Marcus, Peter Pan, Wamsutta &
More. Quilting Supplies & large selection
of books. Newsletter/Class Schedule Avail.

Missoula, MT #15

Country Friends Quilt Shop

**Mon - Sat
10 - 5**

725 West Alder   59802
(406) 728-7816
Est: 1988   4,200 sq.ft.
Owners: Anna Mae Cheff, Elaine Ployhar, &
Cherie Jacobsen

Books, Patterns, 100% Cotton Fabric, Quilts, Quilting Classes, Wonderful Country Handcrafted Gifts

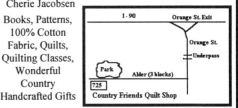

Montana Guilds:
Yellowstone Valley Quilt Guild,
     3114 Country Club
     Circle, Billings, 59102
Quilters Art Guild,
     P.O. Box 4117,
     Bozeman, 59772
Bitter Root Quilters Guild, 201 S.
     2nd St., Hamilton, 59840
Helena Quilter's Guild, P.O. Box 429, Helena, 59624
Flathead Quilters Guild, P.O. Box 3227, Kalispell, 59903
Central Montana Fiber Art Guild, Lewiston
Missoula Quilt Guild, P.O. Box 325, Missoula, 59802
Triangle Squares Quild Guild, 124 6th Ave. S, Shelby, 59474
Sapphire Quilters, 317 Main St., Stevensville, 59870

Other Shops in Montana:
Billings	Pin Cushion, 2646 Grand Ave. #9
Billings	Flynn Quilt Frame Co., 1000 Shiloh Overpass Rd.
Billings	Quilting Bug, 2675 Central Ave.
Bozeman	Quilting in the Country, 5100 S. 19th Rd.
Bozeman	Bear Mountain Quilt Company, 407 W. Main
Deer Lodge	Quilts & Stuff, 507 Main St.
Seeley Lake	Quilts & Cloth, Hwy 83 Downtown Tall Timber Mall
Stevensville	Seams Beautiful, 317 Main St.

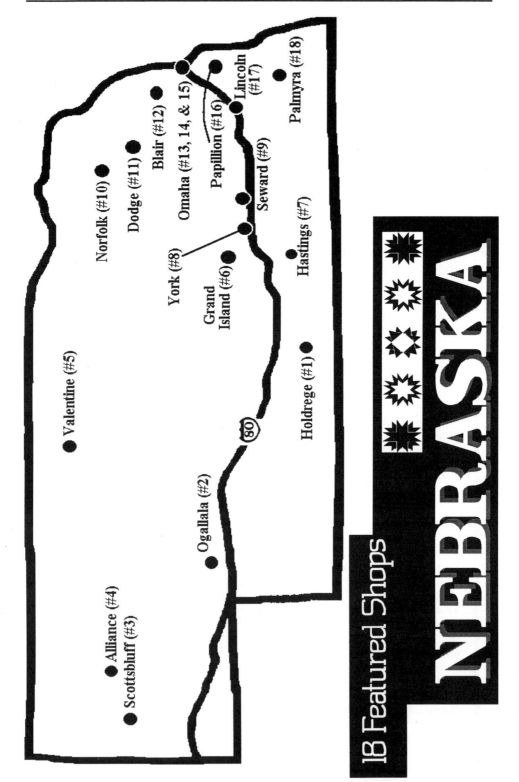

NEBRASKA

18 Featured Shops

Holdrege (#1)

Ogallala (#2)

Scottsbluff (#3)

Alliance (#4)

Valentine (#5)

Grand Island (#6)

York (#8)

Hastings (#7)

Norfolk (#10)

Dodge (#11)

Blair (#12)

Omaha (#13, 14, & 15)

Papillion (#16)

Seward (#9)

Lincoln (#17)

Palmyra (#18)

80

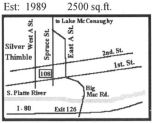

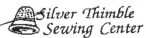
Quilter's Cat: an animal
who always finds his
way onto a lap where
hand work needs to be
done.

Alliance, NE #4

Special Stitches

Mon - Sat
9 - 5:30

424 Box Butte Ave.   69301
(308) 762-3784
Owner: Deb Thiems
Est: 1987

Quilting Supplies, Counted Cross Stitch, Machine Quilting, Viking Sewing Machines & Sergers.

Valentine, NE #5

The Gallery

Mon - Sat
9 - 6

226 N. Main St.   69201
(402) 376-3834
Owner: Mary Mulligan
Est: 1988   2600 sq.ft.   1500+ Bolts

A Little Quilt Shop with Much More!
Two Floors of Gifts, Fabrics, and Quilt Supplies.
Free Newsletter

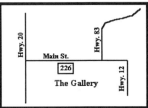

Grand Island, NE #6

Mon - Fri
10 - 5
Sat 10 - 4

205 N. Locust St.   68801
(308) 382-5535
Owner: Connie Thomazin   Est: 1978   1000 Bolts

Quilting Supplies
Bear Making Supplies
Silk Ribbon Embroidery
Primitive Rug Hooking Supplies.

Hastings, NE #7

Calico Cottage

Mon - Fri
10 - 5:30
Sat 10 - 3

306 N. Lincoln   68901
(402) 463-6767
Everything for the Quilter ! !

Over 1000 bolts Cotton Fabric.
Quilting Notions, Books, Patterns, Classes.
Authorized Bernina Dealer.

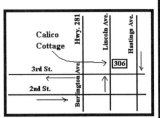

York, NE #8

Countryside Fabrics

Mon - Sat
9:30 - 5:30
Thur til 9

718 Lincoln Ave.   68467
(402) 362-5737   Est: 1970
Owners: Ed & Lola Schall   8000 sq.ft.

Over 1500 Bolts of Quilting Fabric, Notions, Books and Patterns.
Authorized Bernina Dealer. Major Credit Cards.
We mail order.

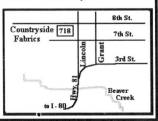

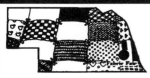

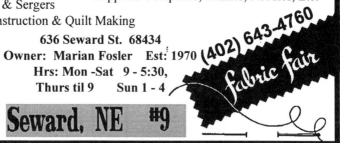

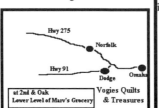

Omaha, NE #13

The Kirk Collection & 1860 Dry Goods

Tue - Sat
10 - 5
or by Appt.

1513 Military Ave. 68111
(800) 398-2542   (402) 551-0386
Owners: Nancy & Bill Kirk
Est: 1986   3000 sq.ft.   Free Catalog

Antique Fabric and Antique Quilts The real thing, not reproductions. Quilting cottons, crazy quilt fabrics, antique lace, trim & buttons

Omaha, NE #14

Country Sampler

Open 7 days a Week Call for Hours.

2516 S. 132nd Ct.   68144
(402) 333-6131
Owner: Deb Cizek   Est: 1990
3400 sq.ft.   1000+ Bolts

NE's largest selection of patterns. We specialize in homespuns & that "country look". A quilt and country store in one!

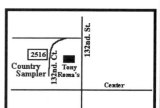

Omaha, NE #15

Log Cabin Quilt Shop

2819 South 125 Avenue #266
        In Westwood Plaza
(402) 333-5212   68144
Est: 1980   1500 sq.ft.

Mon - Sat
9:30 - 5:30
Thur til 8

Complete line of books, patterns, fabrics, and notions for quilters.
Service with a smile !

Papillion, NE #16

Make It Special

Mon - Sat
10 - 5

104 East First Street   68046
(402) 331-5475
Owner: Connie Karasek
Est: 1991   1100 sq.ft.
Quilting Supplies, Large Selection of Homespuns, RJR, Marcus, Hoffman, Benartex, and Heirloom Sewing Smocking Supplies.

Lincoln, NE #17

The Calico House

Mon - Sat 10 - 5
Sun 10 - 4

5221 S. 48th   68516
In Sutter Place Mall
(402) 489-1067
Est: 1974   2300 sq. ft.   1500 Bolts

Friendly,
Experienced Staff.
We love plaids &
flannels.
Always the Latest
Fabrics and the
Greatest Patterns.

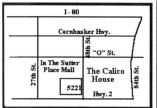

Palmyra, NE #18

Grandma's Quilts

By Appt.

R. R. #1   Box 255B   68418
(402) 780-5773 or (800) 284-8574
Owner: Gloria Hall
Est: 1989   600 sq.ft.   Price List Available

We have over 100
quilts dating from
1870's to 1960's
Vintage Fabric,
Tops, Blocks,
Feed Sacks & Old
Linens.

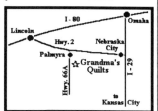

Nebraska State Quilt Guild, 6325 Tanglewood Lane, Lincoln, 68516
Nebraska Guilds:
Cottonwood Quilters, Box 27, Elkhorn, 68022
Prairie Piecemakers, P.O. Box 1202, Fremont, 68025
Prairie Pioneer Quilters of Grand Island,Box 675, Grand Island, 68802
Hastings Quilters Guild, P.O. Box 442, Hastings, 68901
Lincoln Quilters Guild, P.O. Box 6861, Lincoln, 68506
Blue Valley Quilters, 636 Seward Street, Seward, 68434

Other Shops in Nebraska:

Beatrice	Loper Fabrics, 311 Court St.
Broken Bow	Country Sampler, 430 S. 8th St.
Heming Ford	Pat's Creative Stitchery, RR #1 Box 47
Kearney	Craft-o-Rama, P.O. Box 63
Lexington	Creative Fabrics, 512 N. Washington
Lincoln	Creative Hands, 5220 South 48th Bldg. 4
Lincoln	Among Friends, 4821 Lowell Ave.
Lincoln	Heart's Content, 1265 S. Cotner Blvd. #7
Litchfield	Heartland Quilts, 223 N Main St.
Omaha	Country Corner, 6621 Railroad Ave.
Omaha	Mangelsen's, 3457 S. 84th St.
Papillion	American Reflections Gallery, 701 Tara Plaza
Papillion	Quilt Boutique, 546 N. Washington St.
Plattsmouth	Lansing Valley Station, 429 Main St.
Scottsbluff	English Country Cottage, 1814 1st Ave.
Syracuse	The Needle's Eye, 355 5th St.

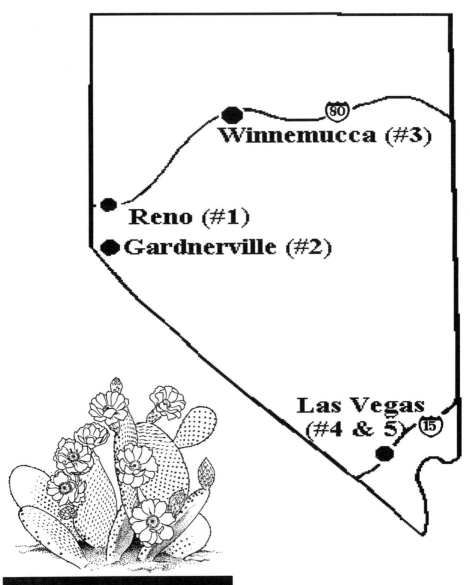

Winnemucca (#3)

Reno (#1)

Gardnerville (#2)

Las Vegas
(#4 & 5)

5 Featured Shops

NEVADA

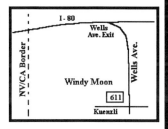
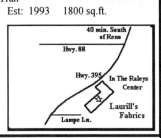

Nevada Guilds:
Carson Valley Quilt Guild,
        1417 Bumble Bee Dr.,
        Gardnerville, 89410
Desert Quilter of Nevada,
        P.O. Box 28586,
        Las Vegas, 89126
Truckee Meadows Quilters,
        Box 5502, Reno, 89513

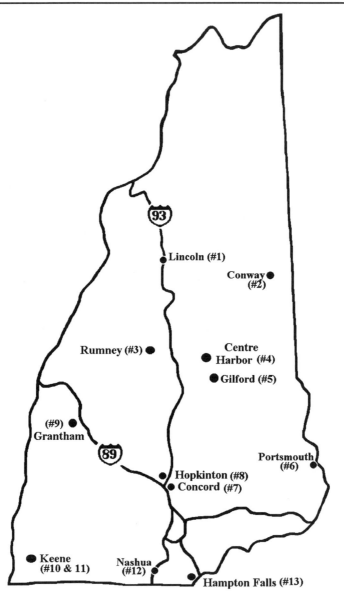

Lincoln (#1)

Conway (#2)

Rumney (#3)

Centre Harbor (#4)

Gilford (#5)

(#9) Grantham

Portsmouth (#6)

Hopkinton (#8)
Concord (#7)

Keene (#10 & 11)

Nashua (#12)

Hampton Falls (#13)

NEW HAMPSHIRE

13 Featured Shops

Lincoln, NH   #1

Pinestead Quilts

10 - 5 Daily
Extended Hrs
July - Oct

Main St.   03251
(603) 745-8640
Est: 1980
Owner: Kathleen Achorn Sherburn

A personal quilt
shop where your
projects interest
us. Quilting,
knitting, cross-
stitch & craft
supplies. Fabric.
Ready-made
quilts & crafts.

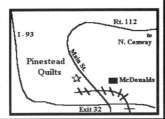

Conway, NH   #2

The Quilt Shop
at Vac 'N Sew

Mon - Fri
9 - 5:30
Sat 9 - 5
Sun 10 - 4

Rt. 16   P.O. Box 2322   03818
(603) 447-3470   2700 sq.ft.
Fat Quarter Program - $25 per month
Owners: Neal & Judy McIlvaine

Quilter's Dream
Over 2000 bolts
All at Discounted
Prices! Very
Large selection of
books, patterns,
notions. Very
helpful Staff.

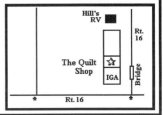

Rumney, NH   #3

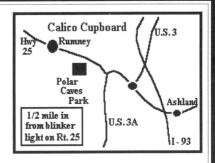

CALICO CUPBOARD
Quilting & Knitting Headquarters

A Delightful Experience

Main Street   03266
2000 sq.ft.
(603) 786-9567
Est: 1978
Owners:
Joe & Nancy Kolb

Mon - Sat
9:30 - 5:30
Sun 9:30 - 5

In A Quaint New England Village

Over 1500 bolts of 100%
cotton calicos & solids.
Books* Notions* Classes
Friendly Service

Send $2 for Catalog of Our
Patterns & Precut Kits

We are Worth the Trip

Centre Harbor, NH #4

Keepsake Quilting

7 Days a Week 9 - 6 Extended summer hrs.

Route 25   P.O. Box 1618
(603) 253-4026   03226
Est: 1988   Free 128 pg. Catalog

America's largest quilt shop with over 6,000 bolts of cotton! Hundreds of finished Quilts. **Don't miss it. It's a Quilter's Paradise!**

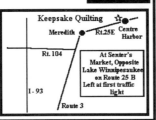

Keepsake Quilting
Meredith ● Rt.25E Centre Harbor
Rt. 104
At Senter's Market, Opposite Lake Whnnipesaukee on Route 25 B Left at first traffic light
I - 93
Route 3

Gilford, NH #5

QUILTING TECHNIQUES, INC.

36 Country Club Rd.
Village West II
03246

At Quilting Techniques we specialize in **Flip & Sew™ tear-away foundation sheets for precision machine piecing.** Quilters' Step Saver Appliqué®Pat.
Show us this ad and receive a 20% discount

Daily 9-5

(603) 524-7511

Owner: Adrienne Johnson
Est: 1988   1150 sq.ft.

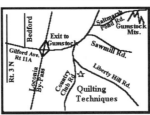

Bedford
Saltmarsh Pond Rd.
Gumstock Mts.
Exit to Gumstock
Sawmill Rd.
Gilford Ave. Rt 11A
Rt. 3 N
Loconia By-Pass
Country Club Rd.
Liberty Hill Rd.
Quilting Techniques

Free Catalog

Portsmouth, NH #6

Portsmouth Fabric Co.

Mon - Sat 9:30 - 5:30 Summer Sun 12 - 5

112 Penhallow St.   03801
(603) 436-6343   Est: 1979
Owner: Gretchen Rath   1000 sq.ft.

We invite you to browse through our expanded collection of contemporary quilting cottons, fiber art and how-to books. Swiss Bernina Machines.

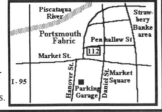

Piscataqua River
Strawbery Banke area
Portsmouth Fabric
Penhallow St
Market St.
112
I - 95
Hanover St.
Daniel St
Market Square
Parking Garage

Concord, NH #7

Golden Gese Quilt Shop

Tues - Fri 10 - 5 Sat 10 - 1

28 South Main   03301
(603) 228-5540   Est: 1987
Owner: Nancy Gesen   1200 sq.ft.   2000 Bolts

100% Cotton Fabric, Books, Patterns, Notions & Classes. Helpful Assistance.

N. Main St
N. Main Exit
Pleasant St.
I - 93
28
Golden Gese Quilt Shop
S. Main St.
S. Main Exit

Hopkinton, NH #8

A Working Quilt Shop

Country Quilter

College Hill Road, Hopkinton, NH 03229

Tucked away on a scenic country road in a 200 year old barn is the Country Quilter- a unique working quilt shop offering a beautiful selection of quilts and quilt supplies, as well as wall hangings, pillows and other handcrafted gifts.

We carry over 2,000 bolts of 100% cotton fabric (the largest inventory in the area) including Hoffman, R.J.R., Jinny Beyer, Debbie Mumm, Thimbleberries, Mission Valley Homespuns, John Kaldor (Nancy Crow), Timeless Treasure, Northcott Silk and other hard to find brands.

We also carry notions, batting, stencils, and a wide assortment of the latest released books and patterns.

We welcome all visitors to our colorful shop, and we always enjoy taking the time to make you feel at home and unhurried. Our staff is compromised of expert quilters who welcome questions and tips from our customers and enjoy sharing what we have learned from our visitors.

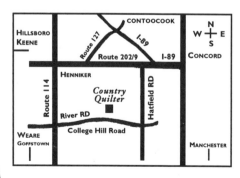

DIRECTIONS:
Take I-93 to I-89 North to Exit 5. Take 202/9 West to Hatfield exit. Follow signs to College Hill Road.

HOURS:
*Open Monday-Saturday, 10am to 5:30pm
Sunday 12pm to 5:30pm*

*Air-conditioned for your summer comfort.
Visa/Mastercard/Discover and personal checks accepted.*

CALL US AT... **(603) 746-5521**

Grantham, NH   #9

Sunshine Carousel

**Mon - Sat
9:30 - 5**

HCR 63   Box 2A
(603) 863-5754   03753
Owner: Elaine Pillsbury
Est: 1990   1200 sq.ft.

Quilting Supplies and classes. Large assortment of cotton fabrics, books, patterns, and notions. Also handmade gifts and crafts.

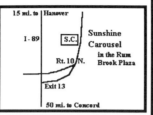

Rotary Cutter: a miracle invention that cures hand cramps and creates a 26 hour day.

Keene, NH   #10

Keene Mill End

**Mon - Sat
9:30 - 5:30
Fri til 9**

55 Ralston St.   03431
(603) 352-8683
17,000 sq.ft.   50 Samples $2
Family Owned by the Parody's Since 1934

Tremendous selection of beautiful Fabrics for Quilting, Apparel & Home Decorating. Well worth the trip for the enthusiast!

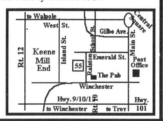

Keene, NH   #11

The Moses House

**Open 7
Days**

149 Emerald St.   03431
(603) 352-2312   Est: 1987
Owners: Fran & Russ Moline
1800 sq.ft.

The Best Quilting Fabrics, Books, Patterns, Supplies, Classes, Counted Cross Stitch PFAFF Dealer Featherweights Bought, Sold, & Repaired.

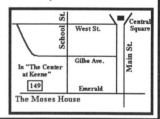

Nashua, NH   #12

Covered Bridge Crafts

**Mon - Fri
9:30 - 8
Sat 9:30 - 5:30
Sun 11 - 5**

449 Amherst St.   03063
(603) 889-0765   Est: 1972
9000 sq.ft.

Over 1500 Bolts of 100% Cotton Quilting Fabrics. Largest Selection of Books & Patterns tucked into an old Barn. Classes for all levels. Family owned Since 1972

Hampton Falls, NH   #13

The Silver Thimble Quilt Shop

**Mon - Sat
9:30 - 5
Thur til 8**

Route 1   Shoppers Village   03844
(603) 926-3378   Est: 1970
Owner: Patti Sanborn   3.000 sq.ft.

Oldest Quilt shop in New England! Over 1,400 bolts of 100% cotton Featuring Hoffman, Jinny Beyer, P&B, and more. Complete Quilt Shop!

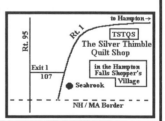

New Hampshire Guilds:
Cheshire Quilter's Guild, P.O. Box 1481, Keene, 03431
Hannah Dustin Quilters Guild, P.O. Box 121, Hudson, 03051
Ladies of the Lakes Quilters' Guild, P.O. Box 552, Wolfeboro, 03894

Other Shops in New Hampshire:
Amherst	J. J.'s Quilt Shop, 96 Rt. 101 A
Bedford	The Patchworks, 133 Bedford Center Road
Durham	J.J.'s Fabrics & More, 88 Dover Rd.
Guild	The Dorr Mill Store, P.O. Box 88

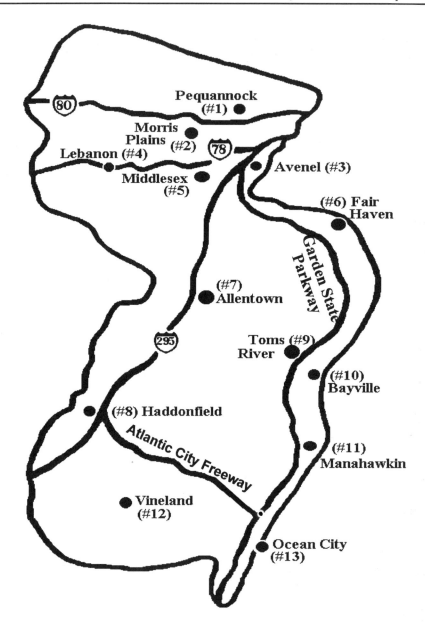

Pequannock (#1)

Morris Plains (#2)

Lebanon (#4)

Middlesex (#5)

Avenel (#3)

(#6) Fair Haven

Garden State Parkway

(#7) Allentown

Toms River (#9)

(#10) Bayville

(#8) Haddonfield

Atlantic City Freeway

(#11) Manahawkin

Vineland (#12)

Ocean City (#13)

NEW JERSEY

13 Featured Shops

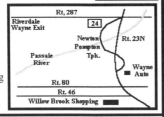
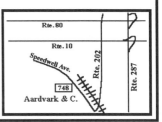

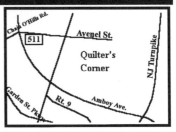

Lebanon, NJ #4

Budding Star Quilts

Rt. 22 E, Lebanon Plaza
(908) 236-7676   08833
Owner: Kathy Verser
Est: 1987   1500 Bolts

**Mon - Sat
10 - 5:30
Thur til 8
Sun 1 - 4**

Over 1500 Bolts
100% Cotton
Fabric. Large
selection of
flannels. Classes.
Kits a speciality.
Bernina Sewing
Machine Dealer
and Service.

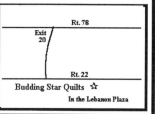

Budding Star Quilts ☆
In the Lebanon Plaza

Middlesex, NJ #5

Prints Charming

109 Harris Ave.   Barbieri Plaza
(908) 469-4700   07059
Owner: Claudia Menendez   Est: 1981
A complete quilt   1800 sq.ft.
shop with 200
bolts, books on
quilting, sewing,
dollmaking,
notions, heirloom
lace, smocking, &
designer threads.
It's worth the trip.
Mail Order Avail.

**Mon - Fri
10 - 5
Thur til 7
Sat 10-4:30
Sun 11 - 4**

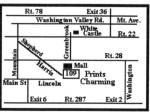

Fair Haven, NJ #6

West End Fabrics

588 River Road   07704
(908) 747-4838   Est: 1989
Owner: Joy Bohanan   4200 sq.ft.

**Mon - Fri
9 - 5:30
Wed til 8
Sat 9 - 5**

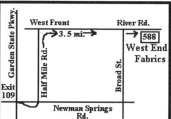

Known for beautiful fabrics,
innovative classes, friendly,
knowledgeable help, and
creative machine quilting.
Every Day is "show and
tell" at West End.

Allentown, NJ #7

Quilter's Barn

34 South Main St.   P.O. Box 295
(609) 259-2504   08501
Owner: Mary Boyer
Est: 1975

**Mon - Sat
9:30 - 4
Thur til
7:30
Sun 12 - 5**

... all 100%
cotton fabrics
... Books
... Patterns
... Notions,
... Batting
... classes
... personal service

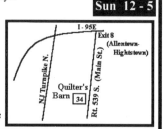

Haddonfield, NJ #8

The Little Shop

143 Kings Hwy. East   08033
(609) 429-7573
Owner: Anne Childs Smith
Est: 1960   1700 sq.ft.

**Mon - Sat
10 - 5
Sun 12 - 4
Class Nights
7 - 9**

10 minutes from
Philadelphia.
Quality cotton
fabric.
Instruction &
Gifts.
All the latest
books & notions.

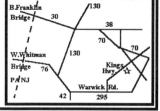

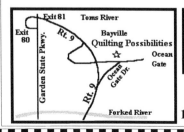

Ocean City, NJ   #13

715 Asbury Ave.   08226
(609) 399-7166
Owner: Terry Calvi
Est: 1990   1900 sq.ft.

Summer
Mon - Fri
10 - 7:30
Sat 10 - 5
Sun 12 - 4
Winter
Mon - Sat
10 - 5
Sun 12 - 4

- ◆ **1500 Bolts of 100% Cotton**
- ◆ **Classes**
- ◆ **Books, Notions**
- ◆ **Craft Patterns**
- ◆ **Gifts.**

(map: Garden State Parkway, Exit 30, Rt. 52, 7th St., 8th St., 9th St., 34th St., Bay Ave., West Ave., Asbury Ave., 715, Atlantic Ocean)

New Jersey Guilds:

Garden State Quilters, P.O. Box 424, Chatham, 07928
Cinnaminson Quilters, Cinnaminson
Molly Pitcher Stitchers, Freehold
Love Apples, P.O. Box 89, Glendora, 08029
Beach Plum Quilters, P.O. Box 204, Island Heights, 08732
Turtle Creek Quilters, 27 W. Church St., Jamesburg, 08831
Pieceful Shores Quilters Guild, P.O. Box 351, Manahawkin, 08050
South Shores Stitchers, P.O. Box 1103, Marmora, 08223
Rebecca's Reel Quilters, P.O. Box 36, Middletown, 07748
Jersey Shore Quilters, 415 Foreman Avenue, Point Pleasant, 08742
Courthouse Quilters Guild, 121 Back Brook Rd., Ringoes, 08551
Berry Basket Quilters, 509 Paige Dr., Southampton, 08088
Molly Pitcher Stitchers, P.O. Box 467, Tennent, 07763
Beach Plum Quilters, PO Box 743, Toms River, 08753
Brownstone Quilters Guild, P.O. Box 228, Waldwick, 07463
Woodbridge Heritage Quilters, P.O. Box 272, Woodbridge, 07095

Other Shops in New Jersey:

Bridgeton	The Strawberry Patch, 73 Landis Ave.
Chester	Emporium, 71 Main St.
Chester	Natalie S. Hart Antique Quilts, P.O. Box 91-B, North Rd.
Clinton	Seams Like Home, 14 Main St.
Delran	Simply Stitches, 263 Southview Dr.
East Rutherford	Materially Yours, 200 Murrayhill Parkway
Elmer	The Fabric Place, 15 S. Main St.
Lafayette	Bedfellows Quilt Shop, P.O. Box 350, RD #3
Perrineville	Golden Sunshine Inc., P.O. Box 293
Princeton	American Sewing & Vacuum Center, 301 N. Harrison St.
Rio Grande	Olsen Sew & Vac Center, 1121 Rt. 47 S. Robbins Nest Plaza
Shrewsbury	Abigail's, 567 State Highway 35
Somers Point	Crafters Paradise Outlet, Somers Point Shopping Plaza, Route #9
Somerville	Somerville Sewing Center, 45 West Main St.
Trenton	Raymond's, 528 Route No. 33

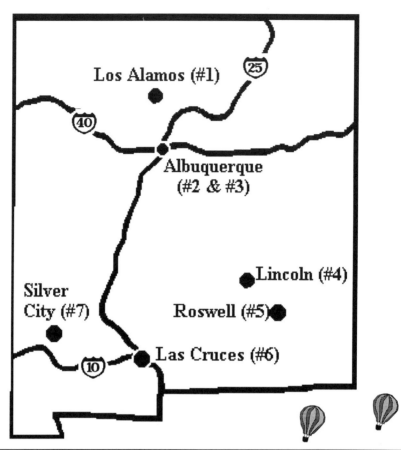

Los Alamos (#1)

Albuquerque
(#2 & #3)

Lincoln (#4)

Silver
City (#7)

Roswell (#5)

Las Cruces (#6)

NEW MEXICO

7 Featured Shops

Los Alamos, NM

MOUNTAINS of FABRICS & QUILTS INC   #1

FOR ALL YOUR QUILTING NEEDS!

QUILTING FABRICS, BOOKS, & SUPPLIES!

1600 Sq. Ft. with over 2,500 Bolts

- ◆ **Lots of Cottons**
- ◆ **Natural Fiber Fabrics**
- ◆ **Notions**
- ◆ **Ribbons**
- ◆ **Trims**

20th St. | Post Office
Trinity Drive
15th St.
Central Avenue

PFAFF *Sewing Machines*

Hours...Mon-Fri: 9:30-6, Sat: 9:30-5
On Sundays we go home to sew!

A FUN & FRIENDLY SHOP

Owner: Narra Gross Tsiagkouris

1789 CENTRAL • SUITE 4 • 662-4442

Albuquerque, NM #2

A Quilter's Affaire Inc.

12500 Montgomery
87111
(505) 292-8925
Est: 1994
Owner: Kathy Heger
2500 sq.ft.

| Mon - Wed |
| 9 - 6 |
| Thur 9 - 8 |
| Sat 9 - 5 |
| Sun 12 - 5 |

Albuquerque's newest quilt shop featuring over 1500 bolts of fabric, notions, books, & patterns for quilting, crafting & rughooking. Classes Too!

[map: Tramway, Montgomery, 12500 A Quilter's Affair, I-25, I-40, Tramway]

Albuquerque, NM #3

The Quilt Works

11117 Menaul N.E.   87112
(505) 298-8210
Est: 1985   1750 sq.ft.
Owners: Shirley Brabson
& Margaret Prina

| Mon - Fri |
| 9 - 6 |
| Sat 9 - 5 |
| Sun 2 - 5 |

We have over 2700 bolts of cotton fabric. We're Friendly and Helpful !

[map: The Quilt Works (in the Foothills Shopping Center) 11117, Menaul, Juan Tabo (2-3 miles), I-25, I-40]

Lincoln, NM #4

Lincolnworks

32 Main St.   P.O. Box 32
(505) 653-4693   88338
Owner: Becky Angell
Est: 1988   400 sq.ft.

| Tues - Sat |
| 10 - 4 |
| Closed |
| Jan - June |

100% Cottons, S.W. patterns, good conversation! Billy the Kid Country! !

[map: San Juan Church, Hwy 380, 32 Lincolnworks, Torreon, Historical Museum]

Quilter's Son: a young fellow who can persuade his mother to spare a few stitches from that big quilt, for his loose button.

Roswell, NM #5

| Mon - Sat |
| 9:30 - 5:30 |

QUILT TALK & SEW MUCH MORE

- A Full Service Fabric Store & Quilt Shop
- Fashion Fabrics & Bridal Fabrics
- 100% Cotton Fabrics (1200+ Bolts)
- Patchwork Clothing & Quilts
- Books & Patterns
- Notions & Classes
- New Home Machines

223 N. Main St.   88201   Est: 1994
(505) 623-0178 or (505) 625-0846   5000 sq.ft.
Owners: J. Michelle Watts & Pat Greenwade

[map: 3rd. St., Main St., 223 Quilt Talk & Sew Much More, 2nd. St., Hwy. 70/380]

Las Cruces, NM #6

ℒee's Quilt Corner

	Mon - Fri
	10 - 5
	Sat 9 - 4

590 S. Solano St.   88001
(505) 525-3711
Owner: Ann Lee   Est: 1994
2200 sq.ft.   2000 Bolts

100% Cotton
Fabrics, Knits,
Velvets, Cotton,
Polyester & Wool
Batting,
Southwestern
Patterns, books,
Notions, Classes
X-stitch Supplies

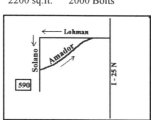

Silver City,

Pg. 242

Thunder Creek Quilt Company

314 E. 14th St. 88061
(505) 538-2284
Est: 1995   500+ Bolts
Owners: Cindy Ugarte & Nancy Coryell

Sat 10 - 4

Cotton Fabric.
Notions,
Sulky &
Gutermann
Threads.
Gingher Scissors.
Classes.
Gifts.

New Mexico State Guild:
New Mexico Quilters' Association, P.O. Box 20562, Albuquerque, 87154
New Mexico Guilds:
Enchanted Quilter's Guild, 900 Catalina, Alamogordo, 88301
Los Alamos Piecemakers Quilters, P.O. Box 261, Los Alamos, 87544
Pecos Valley Quilters, 807 N. Missouri, Roswell, 88201
Northern New Mexico Quilters, P.O. Box 8350, Santa Fe, 87504

Other Shops in New Mexico:

Albuquerque	Quilts from the Heart, 417 Tramway Blvd. NE
Albuquerque	American Quilting Coop, 4304 Lomas Blvd. NE
Albuquerque	Ann Silva's, 3300 San Mateo E.
Carlsbad	Chrisden Craft, 1316 W. Mermod St.
Farmington	Knit One Quilt Two, 3024 E. Main St.
Farmington	The Sampler, 915 Farmington Ave.
Las Cruces	La Boutique, 275 N. Downtown Mall
Santa Fe	Quilts Ltd., 652 Canyon Rd.
Santa Fe	The Bedroom, 304 Catron St.
Santa Fe	Love Apples, 1519 Canyon Rd.
Socorro	Bobbie's Bobbin, P.O. Box 1125

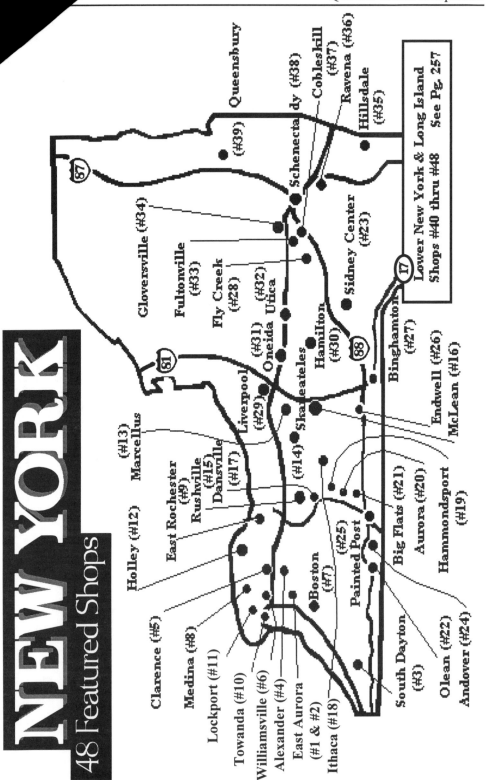

NEW YORK

48 Featured Shops

Lower New York & Long Island
Shops #40 thru #48   See Pg. 257

Queensbury (#39)
Schenectady (#38)
Cobleskill (#37)
Ravena (#36)
Hillsdale (#35)
Gloversville (#34)
Fultonville (#33)
Fly Creek (#28)
Utica (#32)
Sidney Center (#23)
Oneida (#31)
Hamilton (#30)
Binghamton (#27)
Endwell (#26)
McLean (#16)
Liverpool (#29)
Skaneateles
(#14)
Marcellus (#13)
East Rochester (#9)
Rushville (#15)
Dansville (#17)
Holley (#12)
Big Flats (#21)
Aurora (#20)
Hammondsport (#19)
Clarence (#5)
Medina (#8)
Lockport (#11)
Towanda (#10)
Williamsville (#6)
Alexander (#4)
East Aurora (#1 & #2)
Ithaca (#18)
Boston (#7)
Painted Post (#25)
South Dayton (#3)
Olean (#22)
Andover (#24)

87
81
17
88

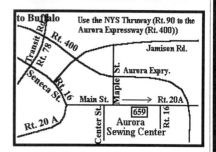

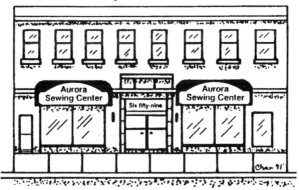

East Aurora, NY #2

Vidler's 5 & 10

**Mon - Sat 9 - 5:30
Fri til 9
Sun 12 - 4**

680 - 694 Main Street   14052
(716) 652-0481
Owners: Bob & Ed Vidler
Est: 1930   13,000 sq. ft.   1000+ Bolts

10,000 yards of calicos. Hundreds of Instruction books on quilting, sewing, crafts, knitting & needle crafts.
"It's a Fun Place to Shop"

South Dayton, NY #3

Block in the Square Quilt Shop

Wed - Sun 1 - 6

30 Maple St.   14138
(716) 988-3013

Amish quilts and tops. Custom quilting, hand or machine. Variety of designs & patterns, baby to king size. Quillows & Wall Hangings

Rolling Hills

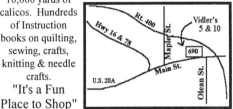

 Quilter's Corner

Alexander, NY #4

3274 Broadway   14005
(716) 591-3606
Owners: Jennie Peck & Ann Kroll
1200 sq.ft. Est: 1988

**Mon - Fri 10 - 4
Tues til 9
Sat 12 - 4**

**Your Complete Quilt Shop.
Quilts, Fabric, Notions, Classes,
100% Cottons, Books.
We specialize in unique & unusual fabrics
from different parts of the globe.**

Clarence, NY #5

Clarence Bernina Sewing Center

**Mon - Fri 10 - 5
Thur til 9
Sat 10 - 4**

10255 Main St.   14031
(716) 759-8081   Est: 1970

Complete Quilt, French-hand Sewing and Smocking Shop with Classes. Authorized Bernina Dealership.
"Service is the Heart of Our Business"

Williamsville, NY #6

Sew What

**Mon & Wed 10 - 9
Thur - Sat 10 - 5**

8226 Main Street   14221
(716) 632-8801   Est: 1990
Owner: Ann Shaw   600 Bolts
1100 sq.ft.

Specializing in Quilting & Cross Stitch, we offer a large selection of unique and unusual fabrics, 100's of patterns & notions.
Come Browse!

Boston, NY #7
The Quilt FARM

est. 1989

Tues - Sat
10 - 5
Tues & Thurs
evenings til 9
Sunday 12 - 5
Closed Sun July & Aug.

3600 sq. ft.

5623 South Feddick Road   14025
(716) 941-3140   Owners: Chris North & Isabell Schmit
Staffed by Family and Friends

<u>DIRECTIONS:</u> (a scenic country drive 30 minutes
South of Buffalo)
I - 90 to Route 219 South, Exit at Rice Road
Off exit ramp turn right & go (up hill) to first intersection,
left on Zimmerman,   then right on South Feddick Road
Call for specifics . . . It's a challenge.

"WORTH THE DRIVE"
The Answer to a
Quilter's Prayers in God's Country

"ANNIVERSARY EVENT"
June 22nd 1996 and
June 21st 1997
Starting @ 6 a.m.
40% off all fabrics
35% after 7 a.m. and so on

A barnful of quilters supplies:
- ... 3,000+ bolts of 100% cotton
- ... large selection of notions
- ... elna sewing machines
- ... 450+ books & patterns plus kits
- ... Gammil Quilting machine
- ... Finished and Custom order Quilts
- ... Origin of "Quilt Farm" Patterns
- ... Classes

"Shop 'til the Cows come home."

Medina, NY #8

Complete Quilt Shop
Specializing in Traditional & Homespun

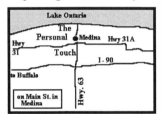

The Personal Touch

435 Main Street   14103
(716) 798-4760   Est: 1981
Owner: Nancy Berger   2000 sq.ft.

Mon - Sat 9:30 - 5
Fri til 6

Come in and Browse
Half Quilt Shop and Half Gift Shop.
Books, patterns, notions & supplies
for Quilters. Lace & Ribbon also. Juried gifts by local
artisans Co-op. Large 'garden' and flower shop with a large
selection of Bears and their "makings". Catalog of Gifts $2

"We're not Just a Quilt Shop"

On the Banks
of the Erie Canal

East Rochester, NY #9

333 W. Commercial St.   14445
(716) 248-2362
Owner: Kitty Keller
4400 sq.ft.   3500+ Bolts

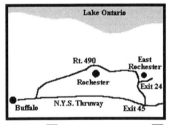

patricias'
Fabric House

VAST Collection of Fine Quilting Cottons.
Stencils, Books, Patterns, Notions,
Classes.

Mon - Thur
10 - 9
Fri & Sat
10 - 5

ONE STOP SHOPPING
FOR ALL YOUR QUILTING NEEDS

Tonawanda, NY #10

Quilt Cottage

347 Somerville Ave. 14150
(716) 837-1372
Owners: Nancy & Michael Hierl

Est: 1993
1800 sq.ft.
1800 Bolts

Mon - Thur
10 - 5
Fri & Sat
10 - 4
Call for
Evening Hours

Authorized Pfaff Dealer.
New and Used Machines.
In-store Repair of ALL
Makes and Models.
Sales, Service, Parts, and
Accessories.

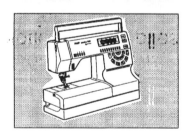

Free Newsletter Quarterly

Classes for
beginners to
advanced
We carry Fabrics,
Books, Patterns,
Notions & Supplies
for Quilters.
New Fabrics arriving
Daily!

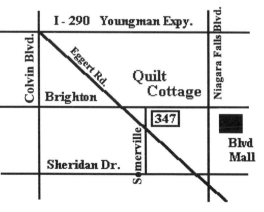

Lockport, NY   #11

Pine Grove Workshop

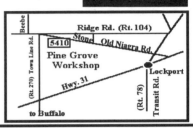

5410 Stone Rd.   14094
(716) 433-5377
Owner: Judith Farnham
Est: 1982

**Mon - Sat
10 - 4:30**

1800 Bolts 100% Cotton
Old and New Quilts
Hundreds of Books, Patterns, & Notions
Classes—Spring Seminar

Holley, NY   #12

Apple Country Quilt Shop

**Tues - Sat
10 - 5
Tues &
Thur til 8**

4719 Bennetts Corners Rd.   14470
(716) 638-5262
Owner: Linda Glantz   Est: 1994

Large variety of
100% cottons,
quilting supplies,
classes and gifts.
Friendly &
helpful staff.
Home of 2
Quilt Guilds

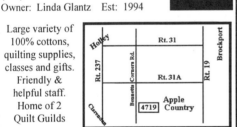

Marcellus, NY   #13

The Quilting Shoppe

**Mon - Sat
9 - 5
Or by Appt.**

2162 Lawrence Rd.   13108
(315) 673-1126
Owner: Elaine Lyon
Est: 1983   1800 sq.ft.   1800+ Bolts

100% Cotton
Fabrics, Notions,
Batting, Books,
Hoops, Frames,
Lessons.
Quilted Jackets,
Quilt Repairs &
Washing.
Quilts for Sale.

Skaneateles, NY   #14

Patchwork Plus

**Mon - Sat
10 - 4**

36 Jordan Street   13152
(315) 685-6979
Owners: Judi West
Est: 1987

1500 bolts of
100% cottons,
books, notions,
patterns; Plus
friendly service in
Skaneateles;
Gateway to the
Finger Lakes

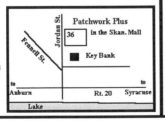

Rushville, NY   #15

Quilting on a Country Lane

**Mon - Sat
9 - 5**

4594 Harvey Lane   14544
(716) 554-6507
Owner: Arlene Lee
Est: 1980

Quilt making
supplies.
Notions, Books,
Fabric, Patterns,
and Machine
Quilting.

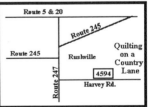

McLean, NY   #16

THE SQUARE

3 Stevens Rd.
McLean, NY 13102
(607) 838 - 3095
Owners: Clara Travis & Carol Beck

* 100% cotton fabric
* Batting
* Books
* Patterns
* Gifts
* Quilting Gadgets, Gizmos and Gottahaves
Bus Tours and Quilt Guilds Welcome but do call ahead

Located in an old country store at the five crossroads in the historic village of McLean, NY.
Come and browse through one of New York State's most unique quilt stores and enjoy pie, sweet rolls, muffins, and coffee before returning to the lovely scenery of the beautiful Finger Lakes.
Ten minutes from Interstate 81 and Route 13.

Tues - Fri
10 - 5:30
Sat 10 - 4

Closed between Christmas
& New Years. Please call for other
special holiday hours

Dansville, NY   #17

 **MATERIAL REWARDS**

10348 Sandy Hill Rd.   14437
(716) 335-2050   Est: 1986
Owners: Teri & Marty Wilson
2500 sq.ft.   1500 Bolts

Mon - Fri
9:30 - 5:30
Sat 9:30 - 5

Hundreds of bolts
of 100% cottons,
books, notions and
patterns. Gifts for
Quilters and
Machine quilting
available.
Quilt Show Aug.
16, 17, 18, 1996

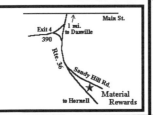

Ithaca, NY   #18

Quilters Corner

903 Hanshaw Rd.   14850
(607) 266-0850   Est: 1995
Owners: Katie Barnaby, Sherry Haefele,
Cyndi Slothower, Linda Van Nederynen
900 sq.ft.   & Merrie Wilent
1000 Bolts

Mon - Fri
10 - 6
Sat 10 - 5
Sun 1 - 4

A diverse collection
of exciting fabric
selected by five
wild women. Huge
book selection,
patterns, notions,
and gifts.

Hammondsport, NY   #19

Lake Country Patchworks

Mon - Sat
10 - 5

67 Sheather St. P.O. Box 332
(607) 569-3530   14840   Est: 1996
Owner: Candace Hosier

Let the natural
beauty of the
Finger Lakes
inspire your next
quilt. We have
100% cotton
fabrics, quilting
supplies and
books. Quilts &
gift items.

Aurora, NY   #20

Gosline Place Merchantile

2306 Lake Rd.   13026
(315) 364-8169
Owner: Yvonne Jordan
Est: 1995

Thur - Sat
10 - 5
And By
Chance or
Appt.

A Quilt Shop
overlooking the
East Shore Cayuga
Lake. Features
premium 100%
cottons, books,
patterns, notions.

Big Flats, NY   #21

The Village Sampler

Mon - Sat
10 - 5
Thur
10 - 8:30

18 Canal St.   14814
(607) 562-7596
Owner: Carol A. Blakeslee
Est: 1986   4500 sq.ft.

Extraordinary
Fabrics, Ideas, &
Notions for the
Quilter & Cross
Stitcher. A Doll
Crafter's Paradise.
Gifts Too!

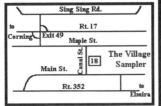

Olean, NY   #22

Calico Country

Mon - Sat
10 - 5
Fri til 8

803 W. State St.   14760
(716) 372-5446
Owner: Betsy Leute
Est: 1983   1600 sq.ft.

Nine rooms full
of 1700 bolts of
100% cotton
fabric, books,
patterns, quilts,
gift items and
much more.

The Fieldstone House

RD 2, Box 307A   13839
(607) 369-9177
Proprietors:
Jane & Allan Kirby

Sidney Center, NY   #23

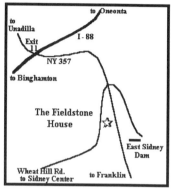

featuring: **Fabric Shop**
Gift Collection
Country Tea Room
Bed & Breakfast

The Fabric Shop

Two rooms are filled to capacity with more than 3500 bolts
This outstanding selection includes all or your favorite designs from . . .

Alexander Henry • Benartex • Concord • Cute as a Button • Dan River
Debbie Mumm • Gutcheon • Hoffman • Libas • Marcus Brothers
Mary Ellen Hopkins • Northcott/Monarch • P&B • Peter Pan • Red Wagon
RJR • Roberta Horton • Spiegel • ... and more.

Books, Threads, Needles, Muslin, Battings, Templates
Buttons, Cutting Tools, Flannels
Cross-Stitch Patterns/Fabric, Clothing Pattens

The Gift Collection

Baskets ✤ Candles ✤ Pottery ✤ Stuffed Animals
Wrought Iron ✤ Tinware

Hours: 7 day a week 11 - 5
Closed Occasionally
Other Times by Appointment

The Country Tea Room   The Bed and Breakfast

Whether you're taking a leisurely afternoon drive and want some homemade
refreshments, looking for just the right gift, seeking the perfect fabric or in search of a
relaxing place to spend the night; The Fieldstone House is a special place.

"A quilter's dream come true"

Andover, NY #24

Kim's Fabrics

3591 County Rd. 12　14806-9709
(607) 478-5284
Owner: Kim Waters
Est: 1993

Mon, Tue,
Fri 10 - 5
Thur 10 - 6
Sat 9 - 3

Quilting fabrics, books, supplies. I offer Quilt Classes. Authorized Pfaff Dealer. We also carry a line of knits & fleeces.

Kim's Fabrics ☆
In a Big Red Building 1/2 mile from St. Rt. 417 on Cty. Rd. 12
Country Road 12
State Route 417

Painted Post, NY #25

The Country Store

449 South Hamilton　14870
(607) 962-1030　Est: 1982
Owner: John & Patricia Starzec
Fabric (over 1,000　1500 sq.ft.

Mon - Sat
11 - 4:30
Thur til 8
Sun by
Appt.

bolts of Prints and Solids) 100% Cotton -- quilt classes, books and quilting supplies Unique gifts, & wallhangings. Our quilts are hand-quilted by Amish.

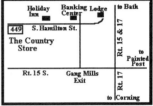

Holiday Inn　Banking Center　Lodge　to Bath
449　S. Hamilton St.
The Country Store
Rt. 15 S.　Gang Mills Exit
Rt. 15 & 17
to Painted Post
Rt. 17
to Corning

Endwell, NY #26

Sew Much More

2723 East Main St.　13760
(607) 748-8340
Owner: Nancy Valenta
Est: 1990　1750 sq.ft.

Mon - Fri
9 - 5:30
Sat 9 - 1

Over 1500 bolts of 100% cottons. Heirloom sewing, specialty threads, books and patterns galore. A delightful experience for your palette.

Rt. 26N　Sew Much More
2723
E. Main St.
Exit 67N
NYS Rt. 17　Exit 69
Rt. 26 S

Binghamton, NY #27

Grandmother's Thimble

29 Kattelville Rd.　13901
(607) 648-9009　(800) 646-9009
Owner: Carol Darrow
Est: 1988

Mon - Fri
10 - 5
Thur til 8
Sat 10 - 4

Totally devoted to Quilters! 750 bolts of 100% cotton fabric. Regional Bernina dealer. Full line of accessories.

to Syracuse　to Albany
Kattelville Rd.
I-81　29
Hwy 12A　Exit 2
Chenango River
I-88　Grandmother's Thimble
to Binghamton

Fly Creek, NY #28

Est: 1989

3 miles North of Cooperstown, NY

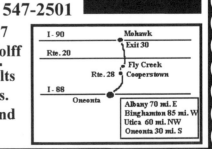

Heartworks
Quilts & Fabrics

(607)
547-2501

July & Aug
Mon - Sat 11 - 5
Sept - June
Sat & Sun 11 - 5

Rte. 28　P.O. Box 148　13337
Owners: Margaret & Jim Wolff

I-90　Mohawk
Exit 30
Rte. 20
Fly Creek
Rte. 28　Cooperstown
I-88
Oneonta
Albany 70 mi. E
Binghamton 85 mi. W
Utica 60 mi. NW
Oneonta 30 mi. S

A real country Quilt Shop.　1000 Bolts
Fine Cotton Fabrics, Quilts, Notions.
Custom orders, Quilt repair and hand
quilting for your quilt tops.

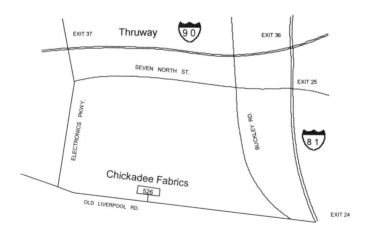

Hamilton, NY #30

Zigzag

Mon - Sat
9:30 - 5:30

12 Broad St.   13346
(315) 824-2169
Owner: Norma Lamb
Est: 1991   900 - 1000 Bolts

Quilt shop &
Gallery. A
wonderful
background to set
off the beautiful
Quilts for Sale.
Fabric never
looked so inspiring.

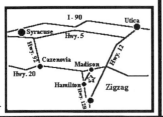

Oneida, NY #31

Cottons Etc.

Mon - Sat
10 - 5
Thur til 8

228 Genesee Street   13421
(315) 363-6834   Est: 1980
Owner: Paula Schultz 1700 sq.ft.
Swatch Set $2 and LSASE

Our motto is
"You Can Never
Have Too Much
Fabric!"
A Pot-pourri of
Quilting &
Fashion Fabrics,
Notions, Books &
Patterns

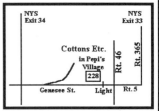

Utica, NY #32

Mon - Fri
9:30 - 5:30
Sat 10 - 5

2336 West Whitesboro St.   13502
(315) 735-5328 Est: 1991   2000 sq.ft.
Owners: Susan Kowalczyk & Sandra Jones

Tiger Lily Quilt Co.

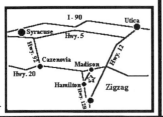

A shop with unusual fabrics for quilting & sewing.
Books, notions, patterns, gifts, classes and
newsletter also.   Bernina Sub Dealer
Services Offered: Private Lessons, Quilt Basting,
Specific classes for 4 or more.
Fabric always discounted 10%--no s&h added.

Fultonville, NY #33

Morning Glory Fabrics

Mon - Sat
10 - 5

1555 State Hwy. 161   12072
(518) 922-8720
Owners: Linda & John Anderson
Est: 1993   1200 sq.ft.   700 Bolts

A full service
quilting and
sewing shop with
100's of bolts of
quilt fabric.
Pfaff Dealer.

Gloversville, NY #34

385 S. Main St.
12078
(518) 725-4919
(800) 336-9998
Owners: Diana
& John Marshall

Mon - Fri
9 - 5:30
Thur til 8:30
Sat 9 - 5

Est: 1981 4600 sq.ft. 1600+ Bolts

Located in the
foot hills of the
Adirondacks. The
area's Largest
Quilt Shop.
Bernina machines,
fabrics, books and
notions.

K & K Quilteds

Rt. 23, P.O. Box 23
12529
(518) 325-4502
Director: Camille Cognac

Hillsdale, NY   #35

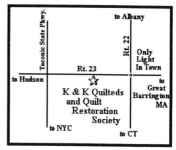

When quilters come into our shop with color swatches clutched in their hands, they stop at the door, remain silent and quizzically ask, "Where's the fabric?" The sign suggests fabric, hoops, walls of batting and size #12 quilting needles. We sell none of these. *K & K Quilteds is not a traditional quilt shop.*

Although not a traditional quilt shop, K & K Quilteds does fill a need in the quilt world. Those old quilts, treasures from the past, can gain a new life. Our deepest satisfaction comes from transforming a severely damaged quilt into a usable quilt that can be enjoyed into the 21st century. K & K Quilteds has evolved into a textile and sewing studio which specializes in quilt restoration and the sale of custom wall-hangings and antique quilts. Often called a "quilt hospital', we jokingly refer to ourselves as "quilt doctors" who specialize in plastic surgery with cotton, tweezers, stilettos, fine tip scissors and #12 sharps. A growing collection of antique fabrics allows us to make the holes vanish. We know we've done our job well when the quilt owner cannot find the repairs.

If you have a quilt in need of restoration,
please follow this procedure:
Call or write(include photo), Arrange time & method of shipment
Once the quilt has been examined, we will discuss options
Shipping Guidelines: Notify K & K, Ship in secured plastic bag
Include address and phone, Insure quilt fully, Allow 2 weeks for estimate

Also the
Home of the: # Quilt Restoration Society

Serving as a center for sharing information about quilt restoration techniques, products and tools used by restorers throughout the world. Centuries old, the art of quilt restoration remained a hidden household occupation until present time. The QRS Newsletter will serve as a vehicle for discussion, sharing and teaching of the time-honored methods used to extend the practical use of textiles. Major quilt restoration projects will be featured and new methods will be explored. The Quilt Restoration Society will focus its concern on the thousands of damages quilts hidden throughout the world. *Give us a call to join and sign up for the newsletter.*

Ravena, NY #36

Log Cabin Fabrics

702 Starr Rd.   12143
(518) 767-9236
Owner: Londa VanDerzee
Est: 1987

Tue 10 - 9
Wed - Fri
10 - 5
Sat 10 - 4

Visit a country quilt shop, 15 minutes south of Albany. Over 1000 bolts, classes, books & patterns.

Cobleskill, NY #37

The Yardstick

Burger King Plaza   12043
(518) 234-2179
Owner: Merilyn Ludwig
Est: 1975   2500 sq.ft.
Viking Sewing Machines
Over 2000 bolts of 100% cotton fabrics, books, notions, patterns, classes, Cross-Stitch, Yarn. Friendly, Knowledgeable service.

Mon - Fri
9 - 9
Sat 9 - 6
Sun 11 - 5

Schenectady, NY #38

Flying Geese Fabrics

Shaker Pine Mall   145 Vly Road
(518) 456-8885   12309
Est: 1985   1000 Bolts
Owners: Donnie Brownsey, Tara
        Conlon & Joanne Skudder.

Mon - Fri
10 - 5
Sat 10 - 4

The latest in 100% Cotton Fabrics & Quilting supplies, Classes, Books, Patterns all designed for the enthusiastic Quilter!

Male Quilter: a rare but treasured spieces.

Queensbury, NY #39

The Quilting Bee

974 Rt. 9   12804
(518) 792-0845
Owner: Joanne Loftus

Mon - Sat
10 - 5
Sun 12 - 5

Cotton fabrics include designer's calicos & solids, books, patterns & notions. Banner flag supplies, Antiques. Gifts and Quilts. Bernina Dealer.   Est: 1987   1500 sq.ft.

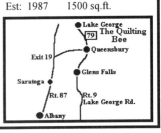

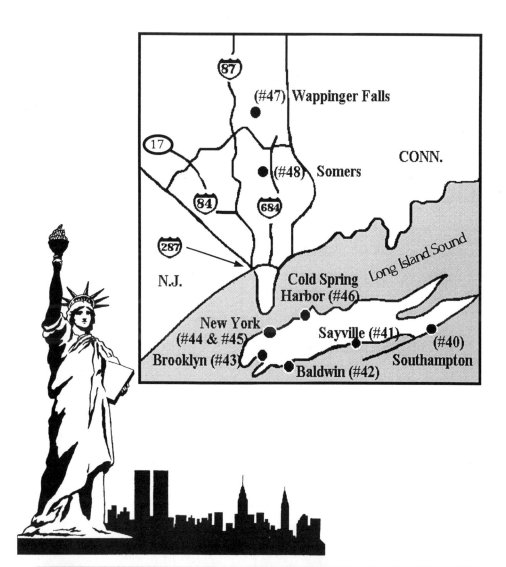

LOWER NEW YORK & LONG ISLAND

9 Featured Shops

Southampton, NY #40

Tom's Quilts

3 White Oak Lane   11968
(516) 726-6881
Owner: Tom Vonah
Est: 1987

By Appointment Only

Antique & new
quilts.
Quilt Tops,
Crib Quilts.
Reasonable Prices
Dealers Welcome

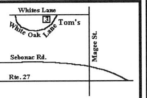

Sayville, NY #41

Patchworks

**Mon - Sat
9:30 - 6
Fri til 9
Sun 12 - 4**

40 Railroad Ave.   11782
(800) 647-5596
Owner: Carolyn Bachsmith
Est: 1979 1700 sq.ft. 2000 Bolts

A Complete Quilt
Shop featuring
Pfaff Sewing
Machines, the
latest 100% cotton
fabrics, notions,
books, patterns
and classes.
Free Catalog

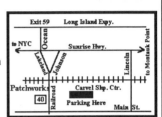

Baldwin, NY #42

Quilters' Choice, Inc.

**Open 7 Days
Wed & Thur
nights til
9:30**

760 Merrick Rd.   11510
(516) 546-2367
Owner: Ellen Phillips
Est: 1993

1000 Bolts of
100% cotton.
Complete selection
of Notions, Books,
Patterns.
Authorized
Bernina Dealer.
Classes and
Special Events.

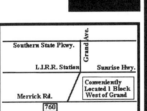

Brooklyn, NY #43

SEW BEARY SPECIAL

1025 E. 28th St.
11210
(718) 951-3973
Est: 1993
Owner: Marcie Brenner-Eisner

**Wed - Mon
10:30 - 4:30
Mon - Thur
Evenings
7:30 - 9:30
Call to Confirm**

A Shoppe for
Quilters!
Large selection of
100% cotton
Fabrics, Books,
Patterns, Tools,
Supplies, Battings,
Gifts & Classes

New York, NY #44

Woodard & Greenstein
American Antiques

**Mon - Fri
10:30 - 6**

506 E. 74th St. 5th Floor
(212) 988-2906   10021
Owners: Thomas K. Woodard & Blanche Greenstein

ANTIQUE
Quilts &
ANTIQUE
Quilt Tops &
ANTIQUE
Quilt Blocks for
sale and purchase.

New York, NY #45

Lucy Anna Folk Art
& Antique Quilts

**Tues - Sat
Noon - 7
Sun
Noon - 6**

502 Hudson Street   10014
(212) 645-9463
Owner: Karen Taber
Est: 1988   600 sq. ft.

Charming shop
filled with
handcrafted dolls,
teddy bears &
farm animals.
Affordable quilts
from 1880's thru
the Depression.

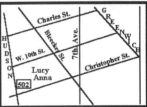

Cold Spring Harbor, NY #46

Sentimental Stitches

Mon - Sat
10 - 5

181 Main St.   11724
(516) 692-4145
Owner: Norma Gaeta
Est: 1981   900 sq.ft.

400 Bolts of
100% cotton.
Full line of Quilt
Fabrics and
Supplies.
Classes are also
available.

Sentimental Stitches		
[181]		25A
Main St.	New York Ave.	
Jericho Tpke.		25
Northern State Pkwy.	I-10 Exit 40	
Long Island Expy.	Exit 49	I - 495

Wappingers Falls, NY #47

Quilt Basket

Mon - Sat
10 - 4
Thur til 8
Sun 12 - 4

1136 Route 376   12590
(914) 227-7606   Est: 1989
Owners: Cathy & Allan Anderson
1200 sq.ft.   1000 Bolts

Quilt--doll
supplies, books
and patterns.
All Fabrics, Books,
& Patterns
Discounted.

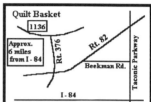

Somers, NY   #48

The Country Quilter

344 Route 100   10589
Phone: (914) 277-4820
Fax: (914) 277-8604
Owner: Claire Oehler
Opened: 1990   1800 sq.ft.

Mon to Sat
9:30 - 5:30
Thurs 'til 9

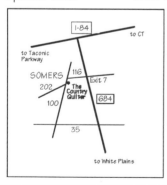

Quality Quilting Supplies

Over 2500 Bolts of 100% Cotton Fabrics
Over 900 Book Titles
Notions: Basic as well as Unusual
100s of Patterns
Quilting Classes Year-Round
Lots of Samples on Display
Fast Mail Order Service
Come in and meet our Friendly, Helpful Staff!

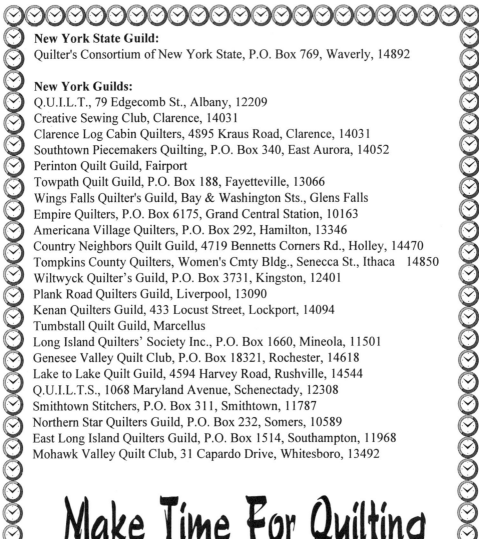

New York State Guild:
Quilter's Consortium of New York State, P.O. Box 769, Waverly, 14892

New York Guilds:
Q.U.I.L.T., 79 Edgecomb St., Albany, 12209
Creative Sewing Club, Clarence, 14031
Clarence Log Cabin Quilters, 4895 Kraus Road, Clarence, 14031
Southtown Piecemakers Quilting, P.O. Box 340, East Aurora, 14052
Perinton Quilt Guild, Fairport
Towpath Quilt Guild, P.O. Box 188, Fayetteville, 13066
Wings Falls Quilter's Guild, Bay & Washington Sts., Glens Falls
Empire Quilters, P.O. Box 6175, Grand Central Station, 10163
Americana Village Quilters, P.O. Box 292, Hamilton, 13346
Country Neighbors Quilt Guild, 4719 Bennetts Corners Rd., Holley, 14470
Tompkins County Quilters, Women's Cmty Bldg., Senecca St., Ithaca   14850
Wiltwyck Quilter's Guild, P.O. Box 3731, Kingston, 12401
Plank Road Quilters Guild, Liverpool, 13090
Kenan Quilters Guild, 433 Locust Street, Lockport, 14094
Tumbstall Quilt Guild, Marcellus
Long Island Quilters' Society Inc., P.O. Box 1660, Mineola, 11501
Genesee Valley Quilt Club, P.O. Box 18321, Rochester, 14618
Lake to Lake Quilt Guild, 4594 Harvey Road, Rushville, 14544
Q.U.I.L.T.S., 1068 Maryland Avenue, Schenectady, 12308
Smithtown Stitchers, P.O. Box 311, Smithtown, 11787
Northern Star Quilters Guild, P.O. Box 232, Somers, 10589
East Long Island Quilters Guild, P.O. Box 1514, Southampton, 11968
Mohawk Valley Quilt Club, 31 Capardo Drive, Whitesboro, 13492

Make Time For Quilting

Other Shops in New York:

Albany	The Sewing Store, 265 Osborne Rd.
Brooklyn	Park Slope Sewing Center, 297 7th Ave.
Brooklyn	Sew Materialistic, 1310 Coney Island Ave.
Brooklyn	Sew Brooklyn, 228 7th Ave.
Cadyville	Quilts N More, Route #1
Derby	Derby Sewing Center, 6929 Erie Rd.
Dundee	The Fabric Shop, 8 Main St.
Floral Park	Patchwork Patch, 141 Tulip Ave.
Hamilton	The Pin Cushion, 37 Milford
Hartsdale	Hartsdale Fabrics, 275 S. Central Ave.
Kings Park	Friends & Neighbors Needlecraft, 303 Kohr Rd.
Mahopac	Sue's Fabric, R.R. #6
Malden Bridge	Claudia Kingsley Quilts & Antiques, Box 118
Manhasset	The Watermelon Patch, 500 Plandome Rd.
Manlius	Cazenovia Quilt Shop, 125 E. Seneca St.
Mastic	Addie's Corner Shoppe, 1484 Montuk Hwy.
Middleport	Fabrics Plus Quilts & Crafts, 18 N. Main St.
Middletown	We Quilt, Inc., 128 North St.
Mt. Kisco	Pins and Needles, 161 Main St.
New York City	Quilts Plus, 86 Forsyth
New York City	Quilters Passion Inc., 531 Amsterdam Ave.
New York City	Laura Fisher Antique Quilts, 1050 Second Ave.
New York City	The Quilted Corner, 120 4th Ave.
New York City	B&J Fabrics, 263 W. 40th St.
New York City	Paron Fabrics, 56 W. 57th
Newfane	Martha's Cupboard, 2714 Main
Nicholville	Threads End, P.O. Box 2
Oneonta	Stitching Post, 363 Chestnut
Plainview	Melani's Moods Ltd., 14 Manetto Hill Mall
Plattsburgh	Quilts N More, 519 Rt. 3
Port Jefferson	Stitchin Time, Inc., 326 Main St.
Poughkeepsie	Krakower Fabrics, 646 South Rd.
Queensbury	The Village Collection, Lake George Rd.
Raybrook	Handcrafters Quilt Shop, Rte. 86
Rockville Center	Bramson House, 5 Nassau
Roslyn	Arbor House, 22 Arbor Lane
Savannah	Spring Lake Fabrics, 4219 Yates Rd.
Scotia	Cindy's Corner, 109 Freeman's Bridge Rd.
Sea Cliff	Calico Square, Inc., 347 Glen Cove Ave.
Warrensburg	I Love Fabric & Company, 30 Main St.
West Oneonta	Country Fabrics, HCR Box 620

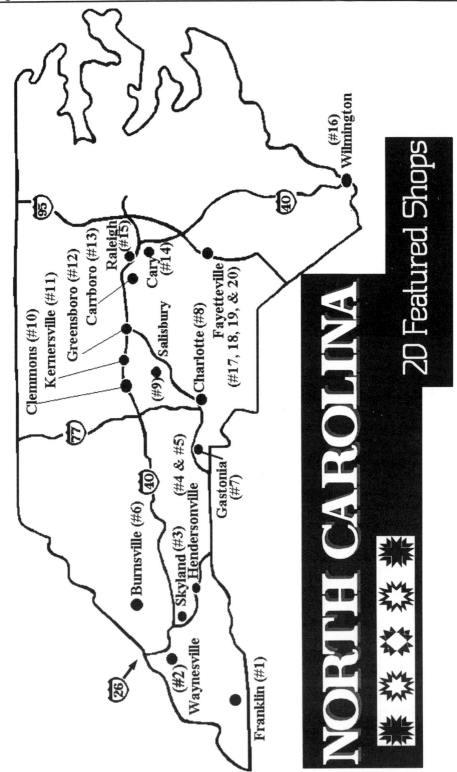

NORTH CAROLINA
20 Featured Shops

Wilmington (#16)

95

40

Raleigh (#15)
Carrboro (#13)
Greensboro (#12)
Kernersville (#11)
Clemmons (#10)
Cary (#14)
Salisbury
Charlotte (#8)
Fayetteville (#17, 18, 19, & 20)

77

40

(#9)

Gastonia (#7)

Burnsville (#6)

Skyland (#3)
Hendersonville (#4 & #5)

26

Waynesville (#2)

Franklin (#1)

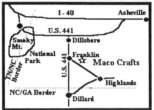

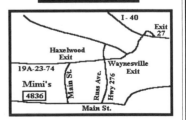

Skyland, NC #3

20 Rosscraggon Rd. **Est: 1989**
P.O. Box 819 **28776**
(704) 684-4802 **1200 Bolts**
Owner: Julie Sherar

Great Lengths
Fabrics

100% Cottons,
Books, Notions,
Classes.
Located in 100 Year
old Victorian
House.
Go to Great
Lengths to get
Great Fabrics.

**Mon - Fri
10 - 5
Sat 11 - 4**

Hendersonville, NC #4

Bonesteels' Hardware
& Quilt Corner

**Mon - Fri
9 - 5:30
Sat 9 - 4**

150 White Street   28739
(704) 692-0293
Owners: Pete & Georgia Bonesteel

**Home of
Georgia
Bonesteel,
Hostess of the
PBS series "Lap
Quilting".** Quilt
Fabrics, Notions,
Books and
Patterns Avail.

Est: 1982

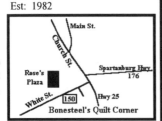

Cloth of Gold

1220 Spartanburg Hwy.   28739
(800) 316-0947   Est: 1912
Owner: Corporation   3000 sq.ft.
Catalog $3
We offer
thousands of prints
from makers such
as: P&B, Concord,
RJR, South Seas,
Benartex, Marcus
Brothers, Peter
Pan, Fabri-quilt,
and many more.

Hendersonville, NC #5

**Mon - Fri
9 - 5
Sat 10 - 4**

Burnsville, NC #6

The Country Peddler

Mon - Fri 9 - 5
Sat 9 - 4

3 Town Square   28714
(704) 682-7810
Owners: Barbara & Tommy Pittman
Est: 1980

Great selection of quilts, fabrics, & notions. Custom quilts made to order. Quilted and fabric gifts.

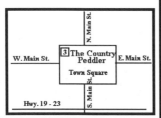

Gastonia, NC #7

Mary Jo's Cloth Store

Mon - Sat 9 - 5:45
Mon & Thur til 8:45

401 Cox Rd.   Gaston Mall
(800) 627-9567   28054
Owner: Mary Jo Cloninger
Est: 1951   32,000 sq.ft.

"The Place" for investment sewers. Where variety is the greatest. Prices are the lowest and large quantities can be found.

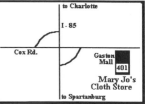

Batting: like the love of the maker, a part of the quilt that is felt but not seen.

Charlotte, NC #8

Quilter's Gallery

Mon - Sat 10 - 4:30

901 South Kings Dr. Suite # 135
(704) 376-2531   28204

Owner: Patti Cline & Cindy Page
Est: 1981   2000 sq.ft.
2000+ Bolts

Cotton Fabrics-- Traditional and unusual prints, Batiks, and Homespuns. Wide range of books and patterns. French Heirloom Sewing Supplies. Buttons and trims.

Kernersville, NC   #11

Quilting Peace by Piece

509 N. Main St.   27284
(910) 993-7770   Est: 1994
Owner: Terri LaRue 2000 sq.ft.
1000 Bolts   Free Newsletter

Mon - Fri
9 - 6
Thur til 8
Sat 9 - 5
Sun 1 - 5

Visit a charming
1922 restored home
filled with rooms of
fabric, notions,
books, patterns, and
plenty of class
samples. Friendship
extraordinaire!!

Greensboro, NC   #12

Fran's Quilt Shop

519 State St.
27405
(910) 274-9805
Fax: (910) 275-7227

Mon - Sat
10 - 5

Area's Largest
Selection of Quilting
Fabric, Books,
Notions, and gadgets.
Classes for
beginning,
intermediate &
advanced students.

Carrboro, NC   #13

Thimble Pleasures

205 W. Main St.   27510
(919) 968-6050
Owner: Julie Holbrook
Est: 1993   1400 sq.ft.

Mon - Sat
10 - 6
Tue til 9
Sun 1 - 4

Over 1,500 Bolts
of 100% Cotton
Designer Fabrics.
Books, Patterns,
Notions. Wide
variety of classes.
Quarterly
Newsletter.

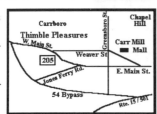

Cary, NC   #14

Etc. Crafts

226 E. Chatham St.   27511
(919) 467-7636
Owner: Jean Petersen

Mon - Fri
10 - 6
Sat 10 - 5

Large selection
of 100%
Cotton Quilting
Fabrics. Books
and Notions.

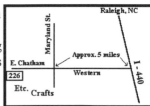

Fayetteville, NC #17

Magnolia Station

916 Hay St.
28305
(919) 486-5181
Owners:
Teri Coop Green & Dee Dalton

Mon - Fri
8:30 - 3
Sat 10 - 3

A unique collection of antique treasures, quilting supplies, and quality handmade items. Collectibles of all Kinds Sharing Things We Love

Bragg Blvd.
Fort Bragg Rd.
Morgantown Rd.
Magnolia Station
C.B.D. Loop
916
Hay St.
Church
Raeford Rd. Bus. 401
In Historic Haymount

Fayetteville, NC #18

The Grapevine

2807 Ramsey St.   28301
(919) 822-5886   Est: 1988
Owners: Marie Smerz & Rosmarie
1500 sq.ft.   650+ Bolts   Zanders

Mon - Thur
10 - 7
Fri - Sat
10 - 5

Specializing in Quilting, Cross Stitch, Basketry & Smocking. Quality Handcrafted gifts gathered locally and from across the U.S. Classes. Mail Order Avail.

I - 95
Exit 56
I - 95 Business
Grove St.
Ramsey St.
401 Bypass
2807
The Grapevine

Fayetteville, NC #19

House of Quilting

R.R. 31 Box 572-J 28306-8206
(910) 868-3842   Est: 1981
Fax: (910) 868-3965   350 Bolts
Owners: Jean & James Adkins

Tues - Fri
10 - 4:30
Sat 10 - 2

Home of "The Thimble You Hold Instead of Wear". Quilting Supplies—Wholesale & Retail. Heirloom Hand Quilted Quilts, Classes & Fabric

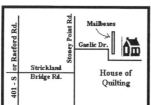

401 - S or Raeford Rd.
Stoney Point Rd.
Mailboxes
Gaelic Dr.
Strickland Bridge Rd.
House of Quilting

Fayetteville, NC #20

Crafts, Frames & Things

108 Owen Dr.   28304
(910) 485-7657   8000 sq.ft.
Owner: Boots Woodyard

Mon - Fri
10 - 7
Sat 10 - 6

Fabrics — 100% Cottons & Silks Notions, Books, Patterns. Sulky - Madeira Ribbon Threads Viking Sewing Machines.

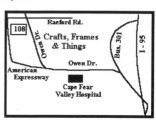

Raeford Rd.
108
Owen Dr.
Crafts, Frames & Things
Bus. 301
I - 95
American Expressway
Owen Dr.
Cape Fear Valley Hospital

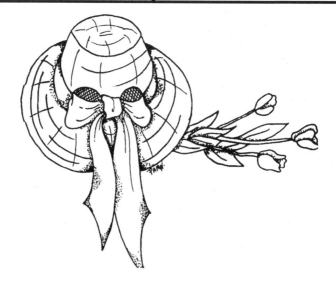

North Carolina Guilds:
Charlotte Quilter's Guild, PO Box 221035, Charlotte, 28222
Durham-Orange Quilters' Guild, P.O. Box 51492, Durham, 27717
Tarheel Quilters Guild, P.O. Box 36253, Fayetteville, 28303
Piedmont Quilters Guild, P.O. Box 10673, Greensboro, 27404
Western NC Quilters Guild, P.O. Box 3121, Hendersonville, 28793
North Carolina Quilt Symposium, 200 Transylvania Ave., Raleigh
Quilters by the Sea, P.O. Box, Wilmington, 28401
Forsyth Piecers & Quilters, P.O. Box 10666, Winston-Salem, 27108

Other Shops in North Carolina:

Asheville	Street Fair, 42 Battery Park Ave.
Boone	Mayselle's Fabrics, 186 Boone Heights #10
Boone	The Log Haus, P.O. Box 272 Route #1
Burnsville	Needle Me This, 112 W. Main St.
Carrboro	NC Crafts Gallery, 212 West Main
Chapel Hill	Cotton Boll Creative Sewing, 91 S. Elliott Rd.
Chapel Hill	Countryside Antiques, P.O. Box 383 Route 9
Fletcher	Carolina Fabric Outlet, 6024 Hendersonville Rd.
Franklin	A Stitch in Time, 59 Depot St.
Franklin	Carolina Sew & Vac, 214 A Palmer St. Shp. Ctr.
Goldston	Calico Quilt Antiques, Belview Ave.
Greensboro	Log Cabin Craftshop, 5435 Church St.
Hendersonville	Mountain Memories, P.O. Box 273 Route #1
Hillsborough	Stitches, 129 Rebecca Dr.
Waynesville	Gladys Jones Quilts, 800 Boyd Ave.
Wilmington	Quilter's Bee, 2829 Vance St.

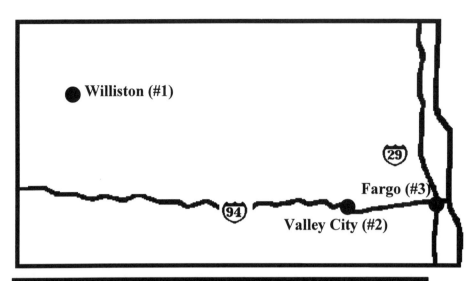

3 Featured Shops

Williston, ND #1

QuiltMakins

Mon - Sat
10 - 5:30

16 East Broadway   58801
(701) 774-3315
Est: 1988   2200 sq. ft.
Owners: Dory Harstad

100% Cottons,
Notions, Large
Selection of
books, classes,
and Friendly
Folk !

4th.			
W. Broadway	Main	1st. Ave.	E. Broadway
		16	
2nd.		QuiltMakins	

Vacation: out-of-town travel that just happens to coincide with quilt shows.

Valley City, ND #2

Cotton Patch Treasures

Mon - Sat
9:30 - 5:30

330 Central Ave. N   58072
(701) 845-4926
Owner: Georgia Manstrom   Est: 1993   2100 sq.ft.

Distinctive gifts
such as Boyds
Bears and Lizzie
High. Fabrics,
classes, Books,
Patterns, Quilting
Supplies.
Pfaff Dealer.

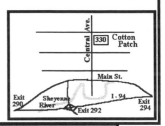

North Dakota Quilt Guilds:
Capital Quilters, Rt. 1,
   Box 342, Bismark, 58501
Dakota Prairie Quilt Guild,
   P.O. Box 1723, Williston,
   58801
Quilters' Guild of North
   Dakota, PO Box 2662,
   Fargo, 58108

Fargo, ND #3

QUILTER'S QUARTERS

Mon 10 - 9
Tues - Sat
10 - 5:30

604 Main Ave.   58103
(701) 235-6525   Owner: Barbara Bunnell
Est: 1979   2500 sq.ft.   2000 Bolts

Authorized
Bernina dealer.
100% cotton
fabrics, books,
patterns, notions,
classes, supplies,
friendly staff!

Other Shops in North Dakota:
Carrington   Designer Fabrics, 929 Main St.
Devils Lake   The Garden Gate, 410 4th St.
Minot   Carol's Etc., 112 S. Main

Willoughby (#49)
(#47)
Toledo (#4)   Port   North   Akron (#48)   Chesterland
Clinton   Omsted
(#5)   (#50)   Cortland (#45)
Maumee (#3)   Brimfield (#44)
(#2)   Youngstown
Bettsville   Amherst (#6)   (#46)
Findlay (#1)   South Amherst (#7)   (#43)   Alliance (#42)
Wadsworth
Ashland (#8)   Wooster (#39)   Canton (#41)
Mansfield (#10)   (#38)   (#40)
Kenton (#9)   Loudonville   Leetonia
Mt. Hope (#36)   Kidron (#37)
Palestine   Berlin   Sugarcreek
(#11)   Hilliard   (#16) (#33, 34) Charm (#30) (#31, 32)
Plain City (#13)   (#14)
Westerville
(#12)   Caldwell
Brookville   Fairborn   Columbus (#18 & #19)   (#35)
(#15)
Kettering (#29)   Lancaster (#17)
Waynesville
(#28)   Washington Court House (#20)
Wilmington (#22)
Chillicothe (#21)
Cincinnati
(#23, 24, & 25)
Fairfield
(#27)
Ross (#26)

OHIO

50 Featured Shops

THE DOOR MOUSE

Est: 1979   3600 sq.ft.

Over 5000 bolts of cotton, patterns, and quilting supplies in a barn setting. Featuring quilts and many handcrafted memories, legends and heirlooms which capture the beauty and simplicity of rural life. Join our friendly staff for classes in the corn crib.

Mon - Thur 10 - 8
Fri & Sat 10 5
Last Sunday of Month 12 - 5

Mail Orders Welcome
Swatches available
Price based on quantity

5047 W. SR 12   44815
(419) 986-5667 3600 sq.ft.

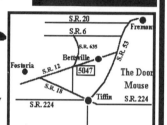

Bettsville, OH #2

Owner: Mary Ann Sorg

Maumee, OH #3

The Quilt Foundry

Mon - Sat 10 - 4
Tues eve 7 - 9

234 W. Wayne   43537   1000 sq.ft.
(419) 893-5703   Opened: 1981
Owners: Mary Beham, Margaret Okuley, Peg Sawyer, Gretchen Schultz

The Quilt Foundry offers friendly, personalized service in your search for wonderful fabric, quilting supplies, books and classes.

Toledo, OH #4

Busy Bee Quilts

Tue - Sat 9 - 4

838 E. Broadway   43605-3010
(419) 691-2939   Est: 1991
Owner: Alice M. Horvath   1600 sq.ft.
Send LSASE for Machine Quilting Brochure

Our shop has 100% cotton fabrics, books, notions, lessons, etc. We do custom machine quilting. Mail orders accepted.

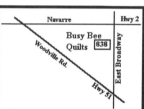

Port Clinton, OH #5

Carol's Fabric Art

312 W. Third St.   43452
(419) 734-3650
Owner: Carol Swope
Est: 1984

Tues - Sat 10 - 5
Tue & Thur eve 6:30 - 9

Fabrics,
Books,
Patterns,
Notions,
Cross - Stitch
Stencils.

Amherst, OH #6

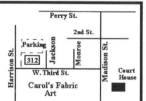

IRISH CHAIN QUILT SHOP

Tues - Sat 10 - 5

209 S. Main St.   44001
(216) 986-5016   Est: 1994
Owner: Kaye Spillman   950 sq.ft.   400+ Bolts

Quality crafted handmade products. Quilts—Baby to King size, wall hangings, wood products, wearables and baskets. Mail Order Avail.

QUILTS & KREATIONS

South Amherst, OH   #7

101 E. Main St.   44001
(216) 986-4132

Owner: Sandra Whitaker

QUILTS & KREATIONS was established in 1980 and we have grown in size throughout the years. We offer you over 3600 sq.ft. of shopping area in our 125+ year old building. There are over 2000 bolts of designer fabric to choose from. We stock the area's largest selection of 100% cotton fabrics, patterns, books, and unique craft patterns. We are Lorain County's only authorized Bernina Dealer and Lorain County's most complete quilt shop.

Mon - Sat
10 - 5
Thur til 7

		Amherst	
Ohio Turnpike		I - 80	
Quilts & Kreations	Jamies Flea Market	Rt. 58	Rt. 57
	[101] ■	Rt. 113	
Lake	Main St.		Elyria
	S. Amherst		

Easily accessible from either the Ohio Turnpike or Interstate Route 90. We are 1.6 miles west of State Route 58 on State Route 113 in South Amherst, Ohio. We are on the southeast corner of the street at the light.

Ashland, OH #8

Est: 1975

Mon - Fri 10 - 5
Sat 10 - 4

Country Charm Fabrics and Sew Crazy

VIKING
Husqvarna

WHITE

1422 Township Road 593   44805
Country Charm—(419) 281-2341
Sew Crazy—(419) 281-9422
Owners: Cindy Doggett & Alice Finley

A Complete array of Quilting fabrics from the best mills in America. Notions, Quilt Frames, Classes, and all of the essentials for the Quilting Enthusiast. Viking & White Dealer
All makes Sewing Machines & Sergers Repair

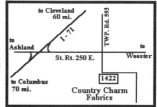

Kenton, OH #9

Ye Olde Schoolhouse

Sun 1 - 5
Mon 7 - 9
Tue, Wed,
Thur 12 - 9
Sat 12 - 5

10389 C.R. 190   43326
(419) 675-1652
Owner: Dolores D. Phillips-Layman
Est: 1978

Full Line Quilt Shop Notions & Novelties Books & Patterns Featuring Hoffman, RJR, Benartex, Kona Bay, Kauffman, Alexander Henry and more.

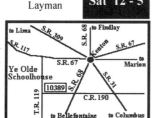

Mansfield, OH #10

Quilt Connection

Mon - Thur
10 - 5:30
Fri & Sat
10 - 4

415 Park Ave. W   44906
(419) 522-2330
Owner: Janet Williams
Est: 1980   1200 sq.ft.

Visit us for quality products & personal, friendly service! Fabrics, Quilt & Sewing Supplies, Bernina & New Home Sewing Machines. Classes.

Palestine, OH #11

Pap & Granny's Quilt & Antiques

Tues - Sat
1 - 6

211 W. Cross St.   45352
(513) 548-8508
Owners: Don & Maryalice Brewer
Est: 1993

Fabrics - Hoffman, RJR, South Seas & many others. Books, Notions, Classes, Gifts. Quilts & Wall Hangings for Sale.

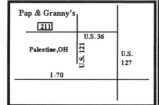

Brookville, OH #12

Quilts N' Things

Mon, Tue,
Thur, Fri
10 - 5
Sat 9:30 -
1:30

12322 Westbrook Rd.   45309
(513) 833-5188
Owner: Margaret Taylor
Est: 1984   2300 sq.ft.

Cotton Fabrics, Notions, Books, Stencils, Classes, Machine Quilting, Finished Quilts, Pillows, Wall Hangings, Aprons, & Bonnets

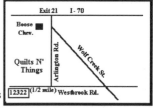

Plain City, OH #13

The Fabric Shoppe

Mon - Sat 9 - 5

9872 U.S. 42   43064
(614) 873-4123
Owner: Perry Yoder
Mgr. Mary Beachy

Specializing in:
100% Cottons,
Fashion Fabrics,
Lace Curtains by
the yard. Prints
& solids. Quilts;
Custom Quilts
and Quilting
Supplies.

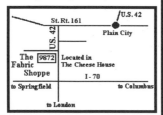

Hilliard, OH #14

Stitchery Plus

**Mon & Wed 10 - 6
Tue & Thur 10 - 8
Fri & Sat 10 - 5**

3983 Main St.   43026
(614) 771-0657
Owner: Susan Mathewson
Est: 1981   5250 sq.ft.

Over 2500 bolts
of 100% cotton
fabrics.
Quilting Supplies.
Pfaff Sewing
Machines.
Counted Cross
Stitch, Miniatures
& Doll Houses.

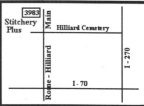

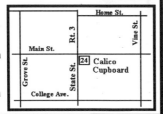

Fairborn, OH #15

Daisy Barrel, Inc

**Tues, Wed, Fri, & Sat 10 - 4
Mon & Thur 10 - 8**

19 West Main Street   45324
(513) 879-0111   Est: 1972
5000 sq.ft.   2000+ Bolts
Owners: Marjorie, Sandy, Judy,
Phyllis, & Gretchen

We specialize in
the best quality of
materials for the
quilter, cross-
stitcher, smocker
and stenciler. Our
experienced staff
will be glad to help

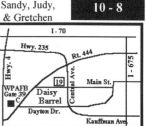

Westerville, OH #16

Calico Cupboard

**Mon - Fri 9:30 - 9
Sat 9:30-6
Sun 12 - 5**

24 N. State Street   43081
(614) 891-0938
Owner: Marcie Collucia
Est: 1971   5000 sq.ft.

2000+ bolts of
cotton fabrics,
plus hundreds of
patterns, books,
notions and much
more. Craft
supplies & Gifts
too! We're worth
the trip

Lancaster, OH #17

Prairie Rose Quilting House

Mon - Sat 10 - 5

307 N. Broad St.   43130
(614) 654-1922
Owner: Deborah Marks   Est: 1990

Quality fabric,
notions, porcelain
buttons, books,
patterns, & Q-Snap
frames. Locally
made wall-
hangings, gift
baskets, crafts &
tapestry rods.

Helyn's Hoops

Owner: Gay Dell

We manufacture / wholesale the "Hoop-de-deux" border hoop and the "Cinch Hoop", both invented by the owner.

Columbus, OH #18

WE SHARE ONE SHOP
911 City Park Avenue   43206
(614) 443-9988

Mon - Sat   9 - 6
Additional Hrs by Appt.

Located in German Village Near Downtown Columbus

Picking Up The Pieces

Owner: Pati Shambaugh

Fabrics, books, patterns, notions, and supplies, plus Pati's original designs.

Columbus, OH #19

The Glass Thimble

3434 N. High St.   43214
(614) 267-9566
Est: 1979   3000 sq.ft.
Owners: Bev & Gary Young

Mon & Wed
10 - 6
Tues &
Thur 10 - 8
Fri & Sat
10 - 5

Over 3000 bolts of cotton Fabrics, lots of books & patterns plus stained glass supplies. We love quilting and it shows

Washington C.H., OH #20

Bee-in-Stitches

Mon - Sat
10 - 5

105 E. Court St.   43160
(614) 335-7945   Est: 1986
Owners: Elizabeth Foster & Jean Ann Davis

Fabric; Patterns: craft, quilting, McCall's; notions; quilting supplies; counted cross stitch; Singer machines and repair; handmade wood and fabric crafts.

Chillicothe, OH #21

Creations Sew Clever

Mon - Sat
10 - 5

51 E. Water St.   45601
(614) 775-1957
Owner: Rita Fishel   Free Catalog
Est: 1986   1000 sq.ft.   700+ Bolts

Friendly, full- line quilt shop in a charming, historic German brick house. Creations is known for its appliqued clothing and unique gift items.

Wilmington, OH #22

In Stitches

100 1/2 W. Main St.   45177
(513) 382-5559
Est: 1993

**Mon - Fri
10 - 6
Sat 10 - 4**

100% Cottons,
Patterns, Books,
Notions, Classes.
Viking & White
Sewing Machines
& Sergers
Unique Country
Gifts.

Cincinnati, OH #23

Creations by Country Love

9384 Loveland-Madeira Rd.
(513) 984-1484   Est: 1986
Owner: Beverly Dickerson

**Mon - Fri
10 - 5
Call for
Saturday
Hours**

Quilting Fabric,
Books, &
Supplies. Classes.
Custom Machine
Quilting &
Binding Service.
Quilt Racks &
Hangers. Baskets
of all kinds.

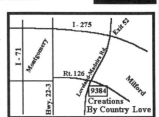

Cincinnati, OH #24

Creative Cottage

6934 Miami Ave.   45243
in "Madeira"   (513) 271-2028
Owner: Marie Tsacalis
Est: 1988   3300 sq.ft.
15 min. from downtown Cincinnati

QUILTING - Large selection of
books, patterns, stencils & tools.
FABRIC - 1200+ bolts of
exciting cotton.
CROSS STITCH - Over 4,000
books, 400+ cross stitch fabrics
and accessories.
**WALL
STENCILING
CLASSES AND
WORKSHOPS**

**Mon - Sat
9:30 - 5:30
Wed & Thurs
til 8:30
Sun 1 - 4**

Cincinnati, OH #25

Ohio Star Quilt Shop

Mon - Fri
10 - 8
Sat 10 - 5
Sun 12 - 5

8315 Beechmont Ave.
45255
(513) 474-9355
Owners: Marianne &
Mark Schmitt
Est: 1993   1400 sq.ft.

Huge Selection of
Quilting Supplies, Books,
Classes and Notions. 1000
Bolts of Designer Fabric
including RJR, Hoffman,
Jinny Beyer, P&B

Ross, OH #26

Undercover Quilt Shop

4267 Hamilton-Cleves Hwy
(513) 738-0261   Est: 1990
Owner: Linda M. Knott

Tues - Fri
10 - 4:30
Sat 10 - 2

1200 sq.ft.   800 Bolts

Quilting Fabrics for
traditional Quilters.
Supplies, Books,
Patterns, Notions,
Silk Ribbon, &
Quilting Frames
(custom made).
Instructional
Videos.

Fairfield, OH #27

Stitches 'n Such

Mon - Thur
10 - 8:30
Fri & Sat
10 - 4

702 Nilles Road   45014
(513) 829-2999   Est: 1980
3000 sq.ft.

Over 2,000 bolts
of 100% cotton
fabrics. Large
selection of
books, patterns,
& notions. Great
models for
inspiration. We
are worth the trip!

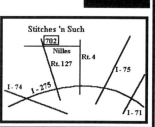

Waynesville, OH #28

Fabric Shack

Mon - Sat
10 - 5
Thur til 8
Sun 12 - 5

99 S. Marvin Ln. & Miami St.
(513) 897-0092   45068
Owner: Maxine Young
Est: 1986   3000 sq.ft.   3000 Bolts

The ultimate quilt
shop . . .
All the fabrics,
colors, designers,
the biggest in the
midwest . . .
Notions, patterns,
and books too!

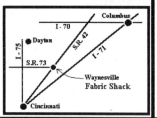

Kettering, OH #29

Sew Biz

Mon - Sat
10 - 6

3098 Woodman Dr.   45420
(513) 299-3391
Owner: Helen Hamilton
Est: 1959   3000 sq.ft.

Books, Patterns.
Quilting,
Heirloom and Silk
Ribbon Supplies.
Classes — Hand
and Machine.
Bernina, New
Home Sales and
Service.

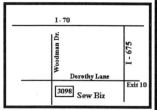

Charm, OH #30

Miller's Dry Goods

Mon - Sat 8 - 5

4500 S.R. 557   Est: 1965
Mail—Millersburg, OH 44654
Owners: The Miller Family

Beautiful selection of ready-made Quilts. Custom Quilting. Over 5000 bolts of fabric. Wall hangings, pillows, quillows, etc. Nice selection of quilt and pattern books.

Also — a whole barn full of quilts right beside us !

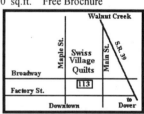

Sugarcreek, OH #31

Spector's Store

Mon - Sat 8:30 - 5 Fri til 8

122 E. Main   44681
(330) 852-2113
Mgr: Mary Mullet

Full Line of Fabric and notions. Quilt and Craft supplies. Excellent Values on Solid & Printed fabrics.

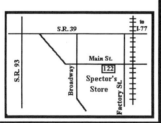

Sugarcreek, OH #32

Swiss Village Quilts and Crafts

Mon - Sat 9 - 5

113 S. Broadway   P.O. Box 514
(330) 852-4855   44681
Owners: Aden & Anna Hochstetler
Est: 1982   1250 sq.ft.   Free Brochure

Quality, local-made Quilts, Wallhangings and related items. Wooden toys Etc. Most items made locally by Amish Special orders gladly Accepted.

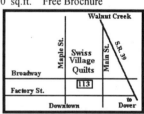

Berlin, OH #33

Country Craft Cupboard

Mon - Sat 10 - 6

P.O. Box 419,   4813 E. Main St.
(330) 893-3163   44610
Owners: Mary Sundheimer & Karen Lamp
Est: 1984   2700 sq.ft.   1000 Bolts

1000 bolts of specialty fabrics, plus craft supplies. Hundreds of books & patterns! Models galore! In an old country store!

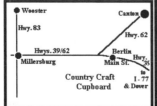

Berlin, OH #34

Gramma Fannie's Quilt Barn

Mon - Fri 10 - 5 Sat 10 - 6

4363 S.R. 39   at The Amish Farm
(216) 893-3232   44610
Owners: John Schrock & Joann Hershburger
Est: 1991

Visit our unique shop specializing in our own line of patterns & kits, custom order quilts, top of the line quilt fabrics, books and stencils

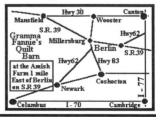

Caldwell, OH #35

Townsquare Fabrics
& QUILT SHOP

507 Main Street
(614) 732-5351
res. (614) 732-4449
Owner:
Glendola Pryor
Est: 1985

Mon - Fri
9 - 5
Sat & Sun
By Appt.

Over 1000 Bolts of Fabric

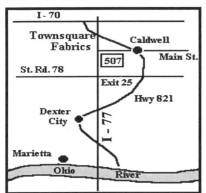

Cotton Fabric	Stencils
Quilting Supplies	Batting
Patterns	Books

Q-Snap Quilting Frames
Daytime & Evening Classes

Mt. Hope, OH #36

Lone Star Quilt Shop

Box 32   C. R. 77   44660
Owners: Ervin & Sara Yoder
Est: 1981
Over 1000 bolts   Brochure $1
of Print and Plain
Fabrics. Custom
made Quilts &
Wall hangings.
Notions & Books
Crafts—
Placemats, Table
Runners, Pillows,
Potholders, etc.

Mon - Sat
8 - 5

Kidron, OH #37

Hearthside Quilt Shoppe

13110 Emerson Rd.   Box 222
(216) 857-4004   44636
Owners: Clifford & Lena Lehman
est: 1990   Mgr. Cheryl Gerber
2400 sq.ft.
Amish and Swiss
Mennonite Quilts,
Wall Hangings
made in our area.
Large selection to
choose from.
Custom orders
welcome!
Catalog $2.00

Mon - Sat
9:30 - 5
closed major
holidays

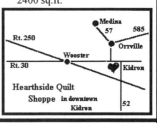

Loudonville, OH #38

Piecemaker Fabric Shop

249 W. Main St.   44842
Owner: Becki Smith   Est: 1993
(419) 994-5179 or (800) 871-3492 (Ohio Only)

Mon - Sat
10 - 5:30
Wed 12 - 5

The shop for crafters
in the heart of
Mohican Country.
Cotton Fabrics
(Over 600 Bolts),
Books, Patterns,
Notions, Craft and
Cross Stitch Supplies.

LOG CABIN QUILTS

#39

Tuesday Thru Saturday 10:00 to 5:00
Thursday till 8:00

5 MILES SOUTH OF WOOSTER ON STATE
ROUTE # 83 THEN WEST 1 MILE ON KIMBER RD

✳ We Do Machine Quilting
✳ Machine Basting
✳ Hand & Machine Binding

We have the Largest Selection
in Northeast Ohio of
90" wide 100% Cotton Fabrics

We Also Stock 108" & 120" Linings

40,000 Yards of 100% Cotton Fabric
AT or near WHOLESALE Prices

We Also Stock 90" Polyester Batting on the Roll

CALL PHYLLIS AT   (330) 264-6690

910 KIMBER RD., WOOSTER, OHIO   44691

Leetonia, OH #40

Amish Quilt Shop

Tues - Fri 10 - 4
Sat by Appt.

41658 Kelly Park Rd.   44431
(216) 482-3230
Owner: Mrs. Nelson Shaum

Handmade quilts, wall hangings, loom rugs, pillows. Quilting supplies, crafts, children's clothes, fabrics, notions, gift items. Quilting Available

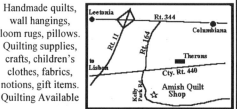

Canton, OH #41

Schoolhouse Quilt Shoppe

Mon - Sat 9:30 - 5
Tues & Thur til 8

2872 Whipple Ave.   44708
(216) 477-4767   Est: 1976
Owners: Judie & Bob Rolhernal

Lots of Fabric, Quilts, & Supplies. **We have a catalog of fabrics and original quilt kits available.** Send $2.00 Come Visit Us.

Alliance, OH #42

Empty Spools

Mon 10 - 6
Tues, Wed, Fri 10 - 5
Thur 10 - 8
Sat 9:30 - 12

2234 S. Union Ave.   44601
(330) 823-1160
Est: 1990   1000 sq.ft.   500 Bolts
Owners: Ellen Wilson, Sue Rhoads, Mary Bernower

Your "what if" store for quilting fabric, unique patterns, books - stuffed critter patterns, buttons, cross stitch supplies, Bernina machines & acc.

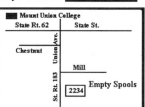

Wadsworth, OH #43

Sally's Shop

Mon - Fri 10 - 5:30
Sat 10 - 3

139 College Street   44281
(330) 334-1996
Owner: Sally Morrison
Est: 1975   2400 sq.ft.

Over 500 bolts of calicos + other fabrics -- patterns & books -- Also needlework -- yarns -- spinning & weaving fibers and equipment.

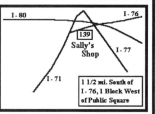

Brimfield, OH #44

Calico, Wicker & Thyme, Inc.

Mon - Fri 10 - 5:30
Thur til 8
Sat 10 - 4

4205 State Route 43   · 44240
(216) 678-3220   Est: 1980
Owner: Pat Knapp   2,000 sq.ft.

Area's most Complete Quilt Shoppe offering a large selection of 100% Cotton Fabrics, quilt books, patterns, notions and classes as well as FREE Inspiration and advice.

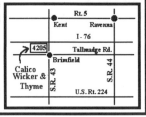

Cortland, OH #45

Simple Pleasures Quilt Shop

Tues - Fri 10 - 5
Sat 10 - 4
Summer Tues - Sat 10 - 4

112 Park Ave.   44410
(330) 638-1733
Owners: June Karovic & Betty Kerner
Est: 1986   700 Bolts

Complete quilt shop 100% cotton fabrics. Latest in flannels and homespuns. Books & craft-sewing patterns.

Quilter's Quarters

8458 Market Street   44512
(330) 758-7072
Owner: Julie Maruskin
Est: 1989   900 sq.ft.   900+ Bolts

We carry quilting supplies, fabrics, tools, books and patterns. We teach hand and machine piecing, masterpiece quilting stitch, and applique.

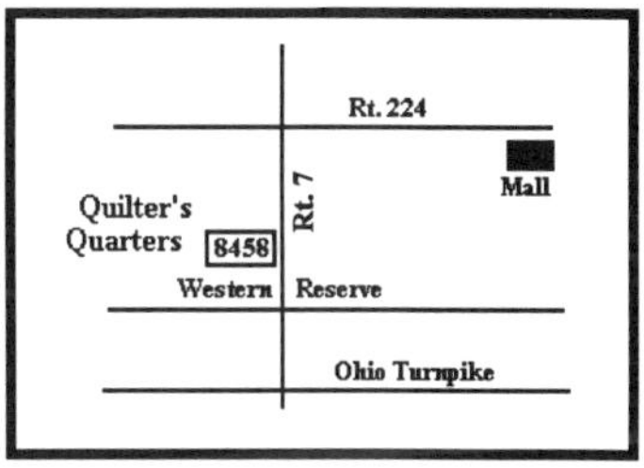

Rt. 224

Quilter's Quarters | 8458 | Rt. 7 | Mall

Western Reserve

Ohio Turnpike

Mon - Fri
9 - 5
Sat 9 - 4

Youngstown, OH   #46

Chesterland, OH   #47

Remembrances

Mon - Sat 10 - 5

12570 Chillicothe Rd.   44026
(216) 729-1650
Owner: Cheryl Pedersen
Est: 1984   1200 sq.ft.

Cotton Fabrics, Notions, Books. Classes: quilting & dollmaking. Finished crafts also available.

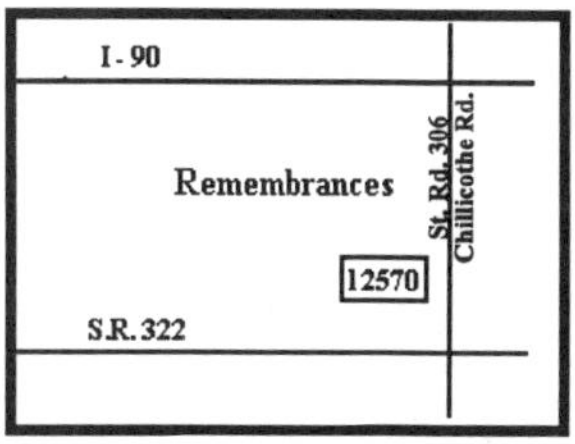

I-90

Remembrances | St. Rd. 306 | Chillicothe Rd.

12570

S.R. 322

Akron, OH   #48

A Piece In Time

Tues - Fri 10 - 5
Sat 10 - 4
Sun 12 - 4

5485 Manchester Rd.   44319
(330) 882-9626   (800) SANDY98
Owner: Sandy Heminger
6000 sq.ft.   Catalog LSASE

Truly Wonderful Fabrics, Elna Sewing Machines, Incredible Selection of Books & Notions & (Nation wide) Exquisite Custom Machine Quilting.

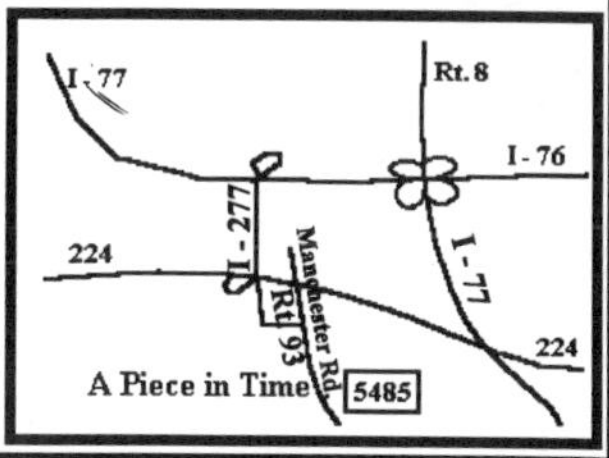

I-77 | Rt. 8 | I-76 | 224 | I-277 | Manchester Rd. | Rd. 93 | I-77 | 224

A Piece in Time | 5485

Willoughby, OH #49

Erie Street Fabrics

4134 Erie Street   44094
(216) 953-1340   Est: 1979
Owner: Mary Huey
                            3000 sq.ft.
Stocked with a
unique assortment
of cotton fabrics.
Offering year-
round classes in
Quiltmaking,
Smocking &
Clothing.
Authorized
Bernina Dealer.

**Mon & Thur
10 - 8
Tues & Wed
10 - 6
Fri & Sat
10 - 5**

Rt. 2 Lakeland Frwy.
Erie Street Fabrics
4134
Rt. 91
Erie St.
Mentor Ave.
(Rt. 20)
2 miles from
Rt. 91 or
Rt. 306
Rt. 306
I - 90

North Olmsted, OH #50

Hoops 'n' Hollers

24888 Lorain Road   44070
(216) 779-4700
Quilting Supplies.   Owner: Sandi
    1500 Bolts   Luther
Antique and New
Quilts, Quilting
Service. Quarterly
Free Newsletter.
Authorized Bernina
Dealer. Classes.
All machines
serviced.
Scissor Sharpening

**Mon - Fri
10 - 9
Sat 10 - 6
Sun 1 - 5**

Hoops 'n'
Hollers
24888
Great Northern Blvd.
Lorain Rd.
Columbia Rd.
Westview Dr.
Hwy. 10
Brook Park Rd. (Hwy. 17)
Great Northern
Shopping Center
I - 480

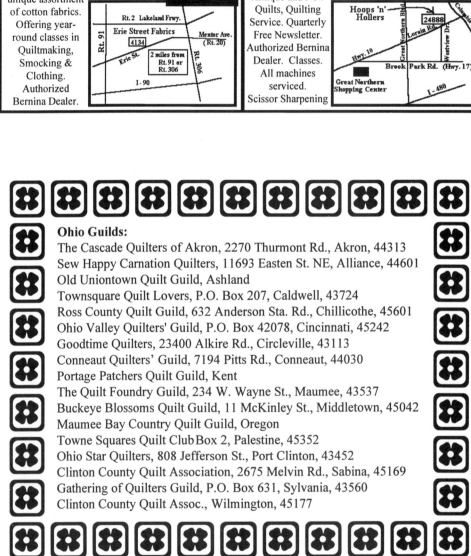

Ohio Guilds:
The Cascade Quilters of Akron, 2270 Thurmont Rd., Akron, 44313
Sew Happy Carnation Quilters, 11693 Easten St. NE, Alliance, 44601
Old Uniontown Quilt Guild, Ashland
Townsquare Quilt Lovers, P.O. Box 207, Caldwell, 43724
Ross County Quilt Guild, 632 Anderson Sta. Rd., Chillicothe, 45601
Ohio Valley Quilters' Guild, P.O. Box 42078, Cincinnati, 45242
Goodtime Quilters, 23400 Alkire Rd., Circleville, 43113
Conneaut Quilters' Guild, 7194 Pitts Rd., Conneaut, 44030
Portage Patchers Quilt Guild, Kent
The Quilt Foundry Guild, 234 W. Wayne St., Maumee, 43537
Buckeye Blossoms Quilt Guild, 11 McKinley St., Middletown, 45042
Maumee Bay Country Quilt Guild, Oregon
Towne Squares Quilt Club Box 2, Palestine, 45352
Ohio Star Quilters, 808 Jefferson St., Port Clinton, 43452
Clinton County Quilt Association, 2675 Melvin Rd., Sabina, 45169
Gathering of Quilters Guild, P.O. Box 631, Sylvania, 43560
Clinton County Quilt Assoc., Wilmington, 45177

Other Shops in Ohio:

Akron	Darwin D. Bearley Antique Quilts, 98 Beck Ave.
Alliance	This & That Merchandise Outlet, 2207 S. Union Ave.
Archbold	Sauder's Farm & Craft Village, 22799 State Rt. 2
Archbold	Buttons and Bolts, 216 N. Defiance St.
Barnesville	The Sewing Basket, 119 W. Main St.
Berlin	Plain & Fancy Fabrics, German Village Shopping Center
Berlin	Helping Hands Quilt Shop, P.O. Box 183
Berlin	Zinck's in Berlin, 115 E. Main St., P.O. Box 153
Bidwell	Maynard's Quilt Fabric & Craft, 7911 St. Rd. 588
Broadview	Pennsylvania Dutch Quilts, 8055 Broadview Rd.
Canfield	Knitting Corners, 4254 Boardman-Canfield Rd.
Chagrin Falls	O'Keefe's Stitchin' Time Shop, 25 S. Franklin St.
Chillecothe	The Cross Patch, 14 W. Water St.
Cincinnati	St. Theresa Textile Trove, 1329 Main St.
Cincinnati	Village Crafters, 38 Eswin
Columbiana	The Attic, 14895 South Ave.
Columbus	Midwest Quilt Exchange, 495 S. Third St.
Coshocton	Calico Harvest Dry Goods, 84 Pine St.
Cuyahoga	Stitch, Piece, 'N Purl, 2018 State Rd.
Dayton	Sew-A-Lot, 687 Lyons Rd.
Dover	Country Mouse, 202 W 3rd St.
Dublin	Patchwork Place, 6090 O'Sweeney Lane
East Palestine	Sew What, 239 N. Market
Grove City	Antiques are Forever, 3318 Columbus St.
Harrison	Betty Lou Quilting & Fabric Outlet, 110 Harrison Ave.
Hartville	Yankee Barn, 1120 W. Maple St.
Hartville	Quilts Etc., 12380 Market Ave. North
Hartville	The Craft Shop, 841 Edison
Lancaster	The Farmer's Country Store, E. 6th Ave.
Lebanon	Oh Susannah, 16 S. Broadway
Lima	Country Side Stitch & Sew Shop, 1207 North McClure Rd.
Lisbon	Rita's Clocks & Amish Quilts, 40 N. Park Ave.
Loveland	Lady Bug Quilt Shoppe, 1464 Highway 28
Mansfield	Bev's Fabric Shop, 466 Melody Lane
Middlefield	Country Touch, 14277 Old State Rd.
Millersburg	Katie's Quilts & Wall Hangings, 7635 St. Rt. 241
Millersburg	Patchwork Place, 173 W. Jackson St.
Minerva	Calico Grandma's, 616 Valley St.
Mogadore	Heritage Quilt Shop, 3937 Mogadore Rd.
Mount Vernon	Jordan's Quilt Shop, 16 S. Main St.
Mt. Hope	Mt. Hope Fabrics, St. Rt. 241
Newark	C.J.'s Fabrics, 1787 N. 21st St.
Orwell	Heart of the Valley Quilt Shop, 2802 Windsor Rd.
Portsmouth	Clara's Sewing Center & Fabric Shop, 2227 6th
Proctorville	Sisters Machine Quilting, St. Rt. 7
Shreve	Quilts -N- Things - Oak Furniture, P.O. Box 581, 193 S. Market
Strasburg	Stitches Unlimited, P.O. Box 55
Upper Arlington	Fabric Farms, 3590 Riverside Dr.
Walnut Creek	The Farmer's Wife, 4952 Walnut St.
West Union	Valley Patchwork, 11191 St. Rt. 41
Wooster	Fabrics Unlimited, 624 Beall Ave.

OKLAHOMA

9 Featured Shops

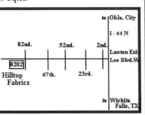

Oklahoma QUILTWORKS

9323 N. Pennsylvania   73120
(405) 842-4778
Barbara Stanfield & Carole Jo Evans
Est: 1988   2400 sq.ft.

| Notions Patterns Classes Gifts | Mon - Fri 10 - 5 Thur til 8 Sat 10 - 3 | 3000+ bolts of Cotton Fabric 500+ Quilting Book Titles |

Oklahoma City, OK   #3

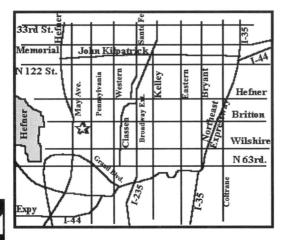

Come Visit us in August of Odd Numbered years for the "Celebration of Quilts" Quilt Show

Gore, OK   #4

Round Top Quilt Shop

**Tues - Sat
9 - 5**

Box 217   Ray Fine Dr.   74435
(918) 489-5652
Owner: Mardena Matthews
Est: 1985

Quilting Supplies
Fabric
Patterns, Books
Notions, Classes
Plus Finished
Quilts &
Wallhangings.

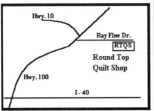

Guthrie, OK   #5

Pincushion, Inc.

**Mon - Sat
9 - 5
Sun 1 - 4**

124 W. Oklahoma   73044
(405) 282-2666
Owner: Cynthia Baker
Est: 1974   2400 sq.ft.

Cottons and
fashion fabric.
Stocking the
unique and
distinctive in
fabric. Located in
downtown historic
Guthrie.

Clinton, OK   #6

AL-Bar Fabric

**Mon - Sat
9 - 5**

711 Frisco St.   73601
(405) 323-4230
Owners: Rex & Terri Finnell
Est: 1972   5000 sq.ft.   2000 Bolts

Authorized Pfaff
Dealer.
Quilting Books
and all Quilting
Supplies.
Classes
Fashion Fabrics
and a lot more.

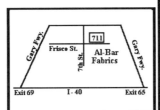

Enid, OK   #7

The Quilting Parlor

118 North Independence   73701
(405) 234-3087
Owner: Patricia M. Russell
Est: 1981   3000 sq.ft.

**Mon - Sat
10 - 5**

2000 Bolts 100%
Cotton Fabrics,
Notions, Books,
Classes. Quilt
Camp - A
weekend retreat
of classes for the
quilter.

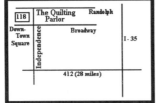

Tulsa, OK   #8

Cotton Patch

**Mon - Fri
10 - 5:30
Tues til 7
Sat 10 - 5**

8250 East 71st St.   74133
(918) 252-1995
Owner: Nancy & Mike Mullman
Est: 1977   1200 sq.ft.

Large quilt
fabric
selection,
books,
notions, and
patterns.

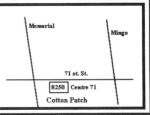

The Quilters' Nook Tulsa, OK   #9

Moving September 1, 1996
Old Location: 5559 East 41st.
                       Highland Plaza
(918) 627-6737
New Location: 1740 S. Harvard
Est: 1987   8000 sq.ft.
Owners: Glen Jones & Anne Seereiter

Mon 9:30 - 7
Tues - Fri
9:30 - 5:30
Sat
9:30 - 4:30

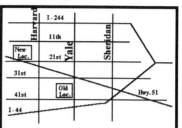

Fabric - Always 100% Cottons (2500+ bolts).   Notions - To ease tasks.
Patterns & Books - For inspiration & instruction (400+ titles).
FRIENDLY SERVICE !

Oklahoma State Guild:
Oklahoma Quilters State Org., P.O. Box 5015, Bartlesville, 74005
Oklahoma Guilds:
Muskogee Area Quilting Guild, 405 Crabtree Rd., Muskogee, 74403
Central OK Quilters Guild, P.O. Box 23916, Oklahoma City, 73123
Pioneer Area Quilters' Guild, P.O. Box 2726, Ponca City, 74604
Breen Country Quilter's Guild, P.O. Box 35021, Tulsa, 74153
Western Oklahoma Quilter Guild, 1324 Steiner Rd., Weatherford, 73096

Other Shops in Oklahoma:
Anadarko	Calico Patch Sewing Center, 105 W. Broadway St.
Chickasha	Fabric & Craft Outlet, 1736 S. 4th St.
Chickasha	Off the Bolt, 407 Chickasha
Duncan	Cook's Sew Biz, 427 S. Hwy. 81
Grove	Linda's Thread Basket, 2120 U.S. Hwy. 59 N
Harrah	Martin Fabric Shop, 1960 N. Church Ave.
Henryetta	Tiger Mountain Quilt Barn, Box 296A Route 2
Mooreland	Heartland Quilt Works, 110 N. Elm St.
Norman	Patchwork Place, 914 W. Main
Oklahoma City	Country Quilting, 1335 SW 59th st.
Oklahoma City	Buckboard Antiques & Quilts, 1411 North May
Ponca City	Linda's Creative Sewing, 317 E. Grand Ave.
Shawnee	Sue's Sewing Shoppe, 2301 North Kickapoo
Tulsa	The Quilting B, 9433 E. 51st St.
Tulsa	Artistry & Old Lace, 3023 E. South Harvard

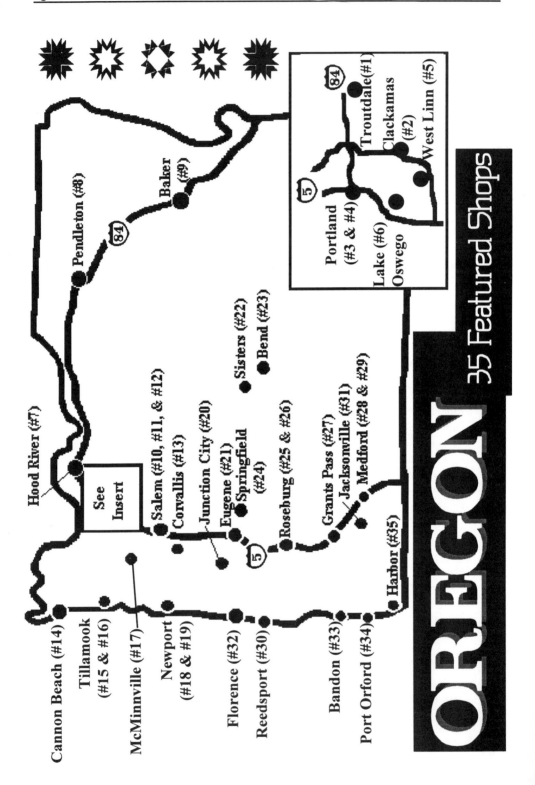

OREGON
35 Featured Shops

Troutdale (#1)
Clackamas (#2)
West Linn (#5)
Portland (#3 & #4)
Lake (#6)
Oswego

Pendleton (#8)
Baker (#9)
Sisters (#22)
Bend (#23)
Hood River (#7)
See Insert
Salem (#10, #11, & #12)
Corvallis (#13)
Junction City (#20)
Eugene (#21)
Springfield (#24)
Roseburg (#25 & #26)
Grants Pass (#27)
Jacksonville (#31)
Medford (#28 & #29)
Harbor (#35)

Cannon Beach (#14)
Tillamook (#15 & #16)
McMinnville (#17)
Newport (#18 & #19)
Florence (#32)
Reedsport (#30)
Bandon (#33)
Port Orford (#34)

Troutdale, OR #1

Oregon Country Quilts & Fabrics

Mon - Sat 9:30 - 5
Tues & Wed til 9
Sun 1 - 4

236 E. Historic Columbia River Hwy.   97060
(503) 669-9739   Est: 1991   2000 sq.ft.
Owners: Vickie Peterson & Susan Miller

**Troutdale's only quilting store.
EASY ACCESS From I - 84 at exit 17.
Hoffman, Jinny Beyer, P&B, plus
many books, patterns & notions.**

Clackamas, OR #2

15410 SE 94th St.   97015
(503) 656-2999
Owner: Betty Anderson
Est: 1995   2000 sq.ft.   800+ Bolts

**Cozy shop located in
old Grange Building.**
Flannels, Felt, Aunt Grace,
Country Plaids &
homespuns. Classes.
Patterns. Tea anytime.

Tues - Sat 10 - 5

Portland, OR #3

Patchwork Peddlers

Tues-Sat
10 - 4
Wed til 6

2108-A N.E. 41st Ave. (basement)
(503) 287-5987   97212
Est: 1977   1200 sq.ft.
Owners: Gail Pope

Largest selection
of quilt books in
the Northwest;
1200 bolts of
100% cotton
fabric

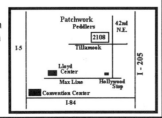

Portland, OR #4

Daisy Kingdom

Mon - Sat
10 - 6
Sun 1 - 5

134 NW 8th   97209
(503) 222-9033
Owner: Pat Reed   Est: 1969
18,000 sq.ft.   3000+ Bolts of Cottons

"Where
imagination
creates the
unusual."
Quilting, home
decor, bridal,
gifts, dress goods.
Authorized
Bernina Dealer

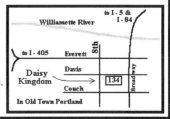

West Linn, OR #5

Country Dry Goods

Est: 1987

1600 sq.ft.

Mon - Fri
10 - 5
Sat 10 - 4:30

2008 S.W. Willamette Falls Dr.   97068

(503) 655-4046

Owners: Gloria Park
& Linda Peck

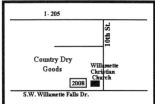

DEDICATED TO THE QUILTER AND WOULD BE QUILTER.
We carry the latest books, patterns and 100% cotton fabrics.

Lake Oswego, OR #6

The Pine Needle

Mon - Sat
10 - 5:30
Sun 12 - 5

429 First St.   97034
(503) 635-1353
Owners: Priscilla McClaughry
& Geri Grasvik
Est: 1992   6000 sq.ft.   1000 Bolts

Discover the most unique quilt - gift shop in Oregon. Fabric, gifts, patterns, classes & crafts.

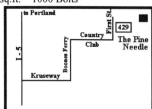

Hood River, OR #7

E.T.C.

Mon - Sat
10 - 6

1215 "C" Street
97031
(541) 386-5044   Est: 1987
Owner: Ann Zuehlke

Fabric, Books, Notions, Patterns, Thread. Craft Supplies & Local Hand-Crafted Gifts. Classes for "kids" of all ages.
900+ Bolts

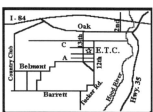

Pendleton, OR #8

1050 Southgate   97801   2000 sq.ft.
(541) 278-1871   Est: 1993
Owner: June Jaeger

Mon - Fri
10 - 5:30
Sat 10 - 5
Sun
12:30-4:30

Quilters' Paradise Large selection of fabric, quilting supplies, books, patterns, and classes. Friendly, helpful atmosphere. Fall & Spring Mountain Retreats

Baker City, OR #9

Jan's Pastimes

Mon - Fri
9:30 - 5:30
Sat
9:30 - 5

2101 Main St.   97814
(541) 523-6919
Owner: Jan Mahugh
Est: 1993   1400 sq.ft.   900 Bolts

Fabrics. Books. Decorative Painting. Quilting Supplies. Notions. Classes and More. Authorized Elna Dealer.

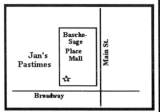

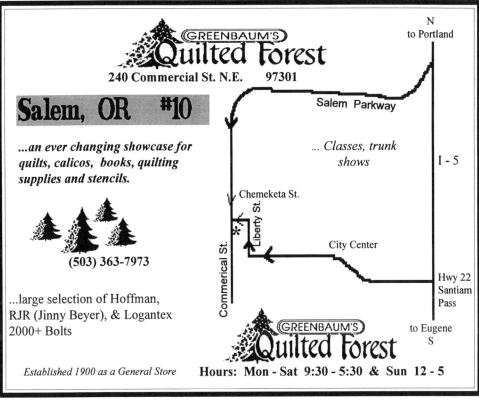

GREENBAUM'S
Quilted Forest
240 Commercial St. N.E.   97301

Salem, OR   #10

...an ever changing showcase for quilts, calicos, books, quilting supplies and stencils.

(503) 363-7973

...large selection of Hoffman, RJR (Jinny Beyer), & Logantex 2000+ Bolts

Established 1900 as a General Store

N
to Portland

Salem Parkway

... Classes, trunk shows

I - 5

Chemeketa St.

Liberty St.

Commerical St.

City Center

Hwy 22
Santiam
Pass

to Eugene
S

GREENBAUM'S
Quilted Forest

Hours: Mon - Sat 9:30 - 5:30 & Sun 12 - 5

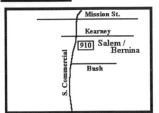

Salem, OR #12

Simply Friends

Tues - Sat
10 - 4:30

1313 Mill St. S.E.   97301
(In the Mission Mill Village)
(503) 363-9230   Est: 1993
Owners: Bonnie McNeely

Located in an Historic Woolen Mill. A charming shop with 100% cottons, books, notions and over 200 doll and quilt patterns.

Corvallis, OR #13

Quiltwork Patches

Mon - Sat
9:30 - 5:30

209 S.W. 2nd. Street   97333
(503) 752-4820
Owners: Brian & Jessy Yorgey
Est: 1979   650 sq.ft.   1800 Bolts

Over 1200 bolts of fine quality fabrics, plus a large selection of Quilter's tools and books.
Free Brochure

Cannon Beach, OR #14

Center Diamond

7 Days a Week
10 - 5

1065 S. Hemlock   97110
(503) 436-0833
Owners: Julie & Bonnie Walker
Est: 1994   1500 sq.ft.   2000+ Bolts

Over 2000 bolts of the most gorgeous 100% cotton fabrics. Books, patterns, notions & gifts. Located 1 block from the beach.

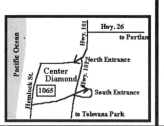

Tillamook, OR #15

Latimer Quilt & Textile Center

Tues - Sat
10 - 4
Sun 12 - 4

2105 Wilson River Loop 97141
(503) 842-8622

A museum dedicated to the textile arts. We have classes for quilting, spinners, & weavers. Shows change every 2 months.

We are located north of Tillamook one block off 101 N by the Coronet Store and the Shilo Inn.

Tillamook, OR #16

Jane's Fabric Patch

Mon - Sat
9 - 5:30
Summer -
Sundays &
Holidays
11 - 3

1110 Main St.   97141
(503) 842-9392   Est: 1981
Owner: Jane Schoenborn
2500+ Bolts

Coastal Retreat Multi-facetted Quilt shop. Large fabric selection, creative, knowledgeable and friendly ideas and assistance.

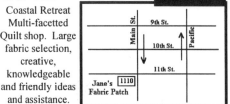

McMinnville, OR #17

Boersma's Sewing Center

Mon - Thur
8:30 - 6
Fri 8:30 - 9
Sat
8:30 - 5:30

203 E. 3rd St.   97128
(503) 472-4611 (800) VAC-SEWS
Owners: Jack & Carol Boersma
Est: 1976 20,000 sq.ft. 5000 Bolts

Boersma's has three floors of fabrics. Fine 100% cottons, quilt books, supplies, notions. Sewing machine sales and service. Experienced Staff

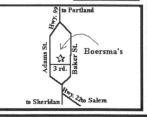

Newport, OR #18

The Newport Quilt & Gift Co.

Mon - Sat 10 - 5

644 S.W. Coast Hwy.   97365
(541) 265-3492   Est: 1989
Owner: Julie Golimowski   2400 sq.ft.   Free Catalog

"The Most Complete Quilt shop on the Oregon Coast" Fabric, books & notions. Home of Block Party by Mail 2000 Bolts

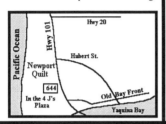

Newport, OR #19

The Gingham Goose

Mon - Sat 10 - 6
Sun 11 - 4

1662 N. Coast Hwy   97365
(541) 265-8338   Est: 1976
Owners: Suzanne Huffman & Janice Harrison
1096 sq.ft.   Brochure $2.00

Quality hand crafted gifts, dolls & decor with a country flair. Over 600 bolts quilting fabric and 250 quilting & craft patterns. Home of Internationally known "The Gingham Goose" pattern line.

Junction City, OR #20

Quilters' Junction

Mon - Fri 10 - 5
Thur til 9
Sun 1 - 5

189 W. 6th Ave.   97448
(541) 998-2289
Catalog $2

Complete line of Fabric, Notions, Books, & Patterns. Machine Quilting, Custom & Ready to buy Quilts & Gifts. Classes

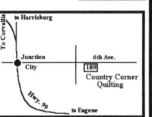

Eugene, OR #21

The Quilt Patch

Mon - Sat 10 - 5
Sun 12 - 4

23 E. 28th. St.   97405
(541) 484-1925
Owner: Kathy Myrick
Est: 1974   2400 sq.ft.

Over 2000 bolts 100% cotton fabric, notions, patterns, books, classes, charm and watercolor packets, monthly block contest by mail.

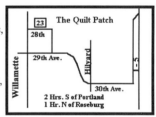

 #22

Mon - Sat 10 - 5
Sun 11 - 5

(541) 549-6061
Owner: Jean Wells
Est: 1975   Catalog $2
Fabric Finders Fabric
Club $18 a year.

A fantasy of cotton fabrics for quilting, doll and santa patterns, quilt books, and ideas galore.
4500 Bolts
Sisters Outdoor Quilt Show, 2nd Sat. in July

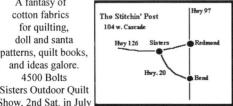

Bend, OR #23

Scandia Square
1155 SW Division
97702

Mon - Sat 9:30 - 5:30
Sun 12 - 4

(541) 383-4310
Est: 1992
Owner: Barbara Schreiner
1400 sq.ft.   2500 Bolts

Top Quality fabrics, 600 book titles, silk ribbon, wearables, dolls, classes, fat quarters, fabric packets, mail order. Late evening hrs. during Sisters Quilt Show.

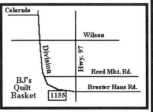

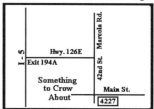

Seams Like Old Times

Quilt Studio

(541) 672-5396

One Champion Plaza #5
250 NE Garden Valley Blvd. #15

Roseburg, OR #26

Your Full Service Quilt Studio
offering the finest in:
Classes, 100% Cotton Fabric
Tools & Notions, Books & Patterns
Silk Ribbon & Heirloom Supplies
Friendly and Supportive Staff
On Site Quilting Machine

10% Discount w/ Ad

Est: 1994
Owners:
Sandra Thomas & Teri Page

Mon - Fri 10 - 6
Sat 10 - 4

Nothing sews like a Bernina. Nothing.
BERNINA®
Sales & Service

I-5 Quilt Studio 250
One Champion Plaza
Garden Valley Blvd. 1 mi.
Airport Rd.
I-5

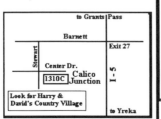
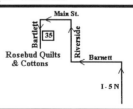

Reedsport, OR #30

Owner: Ann Smith

The Quilt Shop

1898 Winchester Ave.
P.O. Box 83   97467
(541) 271-2616

Mon - Sat
9 - 5

Full Service Quilt Shop.

Super selection of 100% cottons, batting &
fat quarters. Books, Notions.
We offer the Oregon History Quilt blocks;
Covered Bridges & Lighthouses.

30 years in the fabric and quilting business.
We do Machine Quilting. Also sell quilting machines;
deliver, set-up, and teach machine quilting in all states.
Call 1-541-271-2616 or write for more information.
We sell the best quilting machine on the market.
Before we leave your home or shop you will know how to
quilt. We deliver & service what we sell.

Jacksonville, OR #31

Country Quilts & Crafts

Mon - Sat 10 - 5
Sun 11 - 4

220 E. California, Box 405
(541) 899-1972   97530
Owners: Bob & Marge Wall   Est: 1988   650 Sq.ft.

Over 100 quilts both hand and machine.
Fine Fabrics and Quilts, Quilts,
Quilts ! !

Medford, OR
3rd   4th
California   I-5
220   5th
Jacksonville, OR   Country Quilts & Crafts

Florence, OR #32

Cottage Fabrics

Mon - Sat 9 - 5:30

2876 Hwy. 101   97439
(541) 997-3313   Est: 1969
Owner: Frieda Doyle   2000 sq.ft.

We carry 100% cottons & fashion fabrics. Quilting Supplies. We sell quilts books & patterns, DMC Floss and we offer friendly services.

Pacific Ocean
29th St.
2876   Cottage Fabrics
Hwy. 101   Hwy. 126

Bandon, OR #33

Forget-Me-Knots

Mon - Sat 10 -5
Sun 11 - 4

125 Chicago Ave.   97411
(541) 347-9021   Est: 1988
1000 sq.ft.   1000 Bolts

Owners: Janice Mottau
& Melody Johnson

A unique & charming shop specializing in quilting, dollmaking, silk ribbon embroidery. Supplies, patterns, books, classes & a large selection of 100% cottons

Boat Basin
1st St.
Chicago Ave.   125   Forget-Me-Knots
2nd St.
Hwy. 101

Port Orford, OR #34

Quilter's Corner

Mon - Sat 10 - 5
Summer Sundays

335 W. 7th,   P.O. Box 69
(541) 332-0502   97465
Owners: Dottie Barnes, Dolores Purdy & Debbie Dorman
Est: 1994   1800 sq.ft.   1000 Bolts

Fabric, Notions, Patterns and Books. Machine Quilting, Classes and Quilts. Friendly, Spacious and Wonderful Lighting.

Washington
Pacific Ocean   Hwy. 101
Next Door to the Post Office
335   W. 7th
Quilter's Corner
Jackson

Harbor, OR #35

Country Keepsakes

Mon - Sat 10 - 5

15957 Hwy 101 South   97415
(541) 469-6117   (800) 469-6117
Est: 1988   1400 sq.ft.   2000 Bolts
Owners: Michelle Fallert & Laurie Mitts

We have a great variety of classes. Choose from over 1000 bolts of cotton fabric. Also get the latest books, notions, and x-stitch !

Brookings
Hwy 101   On Hwy 101 to the South of Harbor in the English Village Center
Harbor
15957   Country Keepsakes

Oregon Guilds:

Tillamook County Quilters, 6735 Tillamook Ave., Bay City, 97107

Mt. Bachelor Quilt Guild, Bend

Rhododendron Quilt Guild, 160 Florentine Ave., Florence, 97439

Mountain Stars, 1304 Blue Bird Ln., Grants Pass, 97526

Junction City Quilt Guild, 1225 W. 10th St., Junction City, 97448

Treasure Valley Quiltmakers, P.O. Box 1198, Ontario, 97914

Mary's River Quilt Guild, P.O. Box 1317, Philomath, 97370

Northwest Quilters, P.O. Box 3405, Portland, 97208

Coast Quilters, 2360 Longwood Dr., Reedsport, 97467

Umpqua Vly Quilt Guild, 1624 W. Harvard Ave., Roseburg, 97470

Mid Valley Quilt Guild, P.O. Box 621, Salem, 97308

East of the Cascade Quilters, P.O. Box 280, Sisters, 97759

Other Shops in Oregon:

Astoria	Custom Threads, 1370 Commercial St.
Aurora	Jacob's House, 21641 Main St. NE PO Box 276
Aurora-Butteville	Linden House, 10791 Arndt Rd. N.E.
Baker City	High Mountain Fabrics, 3210 H St.
Beaverton	Mill End Retail Store, 12155 SW Broadway
Bend	Mountain Ctry. Merc., 1568 NW Newport Ave.
Brookings	Oregon Coast Quilting, 98686 Fox Dr.
Canyonville	J & J Fabric and Crafts, 413 SE Main St.
Coos Bay	Kathy's Quilt & Gifts, 135 Anderson
Corvallis	Country Calico, 6120 S.W. Country Club Dr.
Eugene	Factory Fabrics, 2165 W. 7th
Florence	Laurel Street Fabrics, 208 Laurel St.
King City	Itchin' to Stitch, 15715 SW 116th Ave.
Klamath Falls	Sew Unique, 401 S. 6th St.
Lakeview	EM Calico Country, 7 N.E. St.
Lincoln City	Oceanlake Sewing Center, 1337 NW 12th St.
Milwaukee	Mill End Store, 9701 S.E. McLoughlin Blvd.
Newberg	Threads and More, 602 B E. 1st
Philomath	Janni Lou Creations, 1243 Main, P.O. Box 333
Portland	Fabric Depot, 700 SE 122nd Ave.
Portland	Mill End Retail Store, 9701 SE McLoughlin Blvd.
Portland	Amish Quilt Shop, 5331 S.W. Macadem
Portland	Itchins to Stitch, 15715 S. W. 116th Ave.
Portland	Scarborough Flair, 4442 NE 131 Pl.
Prineville	Crazie's Quilts Etc., 687 W. Third St.
Reedsport	Quilt Connections, 850 Broadway Ave.
Silverton	Silverton Quilt and Fabric, 103 S. Water St.
Springfield	Jean Marie's Fabrics, 637 Main
Tigard	Calico Corners, 9120 SW Hall Blvd.
Wheeler	Creative Fabrics, 475 Nehalem Blvd.

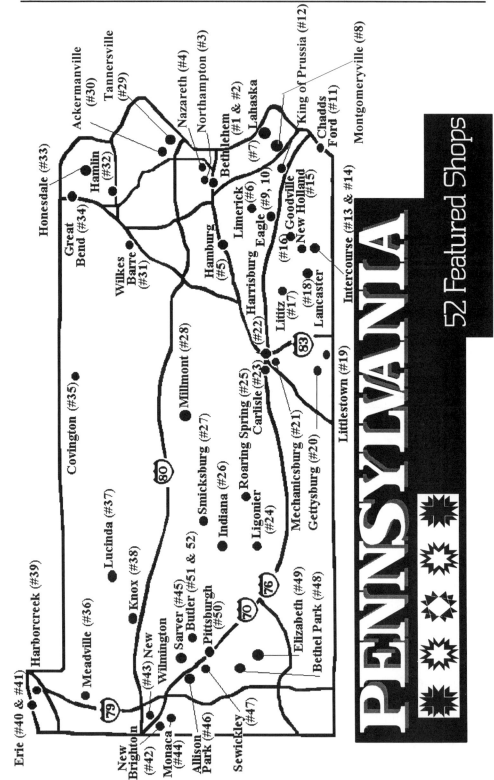

Ackermanville (#30)
Tannersville (#29)
Nazareth (#4)
Northampton (#3)
Bethlehem
Lahaska (#7)
Bethlehem (#1 & #2)
King of Prussia (#12)
Chadds Ford (#11)
Montgomeryville (#8)
Honesdale (#33)
Hamlin (#32)
Great Bend (#34)
Limerick (#6)
Goodville
Eagle (#9, 10)
New Holland (#15)
Intercourse (#13 & #14)
Wilkes Barre (#31)
Hamburg (#5)
Harrisburg (#22)
Lititz (#17)
Lancaster (#18)
Littlestown (#19)
Covington (#35)
Millmont (#28)
Roaring Spring (#25)
Carlisle (#23)
Smicksburg (#27)
Mechanicsburg (#21)
Gettysburg (#20)
Indiana (#26)
Ligonier (#24)
Lucinda (#37)
Knox (#38)
Harborcreek (#39)
Meadville (#36)
Sarver (#45)
Butler (#51 & 52)
Pittsburgh (#50)
New Wilmington (#43)
Elizabeth (#49)
Bethel Park (#48)
Erie (#40 & #41)
New Brighton (#42)
Monaca (#44)
Allison Park (#46)
Sewickley (#47)

PENNSYLVANIA
52 Featured Shops

Bethlehem, PA #1

Grandmother's Flower Garden

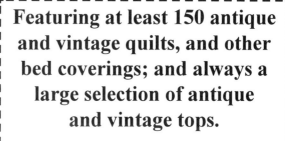

34 W. Broad St.
18018
(610) 868-6499
Owners: Sibby &
George Hillman
Est: 1989

Featuring at least 150 antique and vintage quilts, and other bed coverings; and always a large selection of antique and vintage tops.

Antique quilts laundered and restored; dated and appraised.

Specializing in reproduction fabrics and offering genuine vintage fabrics on the bolt, scrap packets and feed sacks.

Books, patterns, frames, supplies and lessons. 1500 bolts and growing.

Open Tuesday through Sunday 10:00 - 5:00

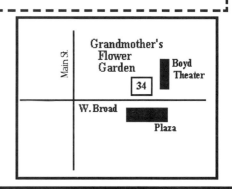

Bethlehem, PA #2

Schlosser Quality Quilt Frames

25 Club Avenue 18018
(610) 758-8488 Est: 1989
Owner: Wilma Schlosser

Fabric--Notions
Books--Patterns
Frames for both
quilter and
needleworkers.
Antique Quilts.
Singer
Featherweights.
Notions for Cross
Stitchers.

Mon 10 - 1
Tues & Wed
10 - 5
Thur 10 - 8
Fri 10 - 6
Sat 10 - 4

Northampton, PA #3

Dave Iron's Antiques

223 Covered Bridge Road
(610) 262-9335 18067
Owners: Dave & Sue Irons
Est: 1970 1200 sq.ft.

Open Daily Except Sundays

Over 125 Old
Quilts & Tops
of varied Price
Range.

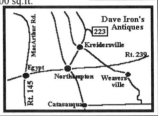

Nazareth, PA #4

The Quiltery

1 Hall Square 18064
(610) 759-9699
Owner: Diane Noraas Est: 1982

A Complete Quilt Shop.
100% Cotton
Fabric -- books,
notions, patterns,
and classes.
Special quilt orders
made. And always
friendly service.

Mon, Wed, Fri 10 - 5
Thur 10 - 6
Sat 10 - 4

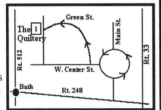

Hamburg, PA #5

Happy Sewing Room

260 N. 4th St. 19526
(610) 562-7173 Est: 1990
Owner: Jean Boyd
We offer beautiful 1000 sq.ft.
cotton fabrics,
quilting supplies,
patterns, books,
sewing machines,
classes & most
important the
personal service every
quilter deserves.

Mon, Tues, Fri 9:30 - 6
Wed 9:30 - 12
Thur 9:30 - 12 & 1:30 - 7
Sat 9:30 - 2

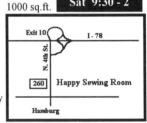

Limerick, PA #6

Bits & Pieces Fabric Shoppe

368 W. Ridge Pike 19468
(610) 454-9734

Specializing in
100% Cotton Quilt
Fabrics! Quilting
Supplies, Books,
Patterns, Notions &
Classes. Gift
Certificates
Available.

Mon - Fri 9:30 - 9
Sat 9:30 - 5
Sun 12 - 4

Lahaska, PA #7

Hentown Country Store

Peddlers Village 18931
(215) 794-7096 Est: 1962
Owner: Midge Smith 1500 sq.ft.
Newsletter Avail. 500+ Bolts
100% Cotton
Fabric, Homespun.
Very Large
(7000+) selection
of Craft & Quilt
Patterns. Teddy
Bear Making
Supplies.
Handmade Folkart.

Mon - Thur 10 - 5:30
Fri 10 - 9
Sat 10 - 6
Summer Sun 11 - 5:30

Montgomeryville, PA #8

THE COUNTRY QUILT SHOP

515 Stump Rd.
P.O. Box 828   18936
(215) 855-5554
Owner: Cyndi Hershey
Est: 1987   3600 sq.ft.

An assortment of over 3500 bolts of the finest 100% cotton fabrics—Hoffman, RJR, P&B, Timeless Treasures & more! One of the largest selections of homespun in the area. A large & complete display of books, patterns, tools & notions. Classes for all levels with a courteous & professional staff of quilters that are happy to help with any project.

Stop in and experience the excitement!

Mon, Fri, & Sat 10 - 5
Tue, Wed, & Thur 10 - 9
Sun 1 - 5

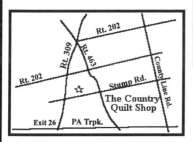

Rt. 202 / Rt. 309 / Rt. 463 / Rt. 202 / Stump Rd. / County Line Rd. / The Country Quilt Shop / Exit 26 / PA Trpk.

Eagle, PA #9

𝕷ittle 𝕭it Country

Mon - Sat
10 - 5
Sun 12 - 5

Rt. 100   Village of Eagle
(610) 458-0363   19480
Owner: Sandy Merkle
Est: 1986   Catalog $1

Homespun and Country Cottons. Antique quilts for sale. Books, notions, and batting. Quilting Workshops.

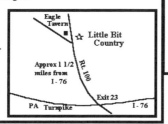

Eagle Tavern / ☆ Little Bit Country / Approx 1 1/2 miles from I - 76 / Rt. 100 / Exit 23 / PA Turnpike / I - 76

Eagle, PA #10

𝒯udor 𝓡ose Quilt 𝒮hop

Mon - Sat
10 - 5
Wed til 8
Sun 12 - 4

Route 100 at Byers Rd.
(610) 458-5255   19480
Owner: Jane Russell Est: 1990
1200 sq.ft.   1000+ Bolts

All Fabrics 100% cotton. Everything a quilter needs plus friendly smiles, expert help.

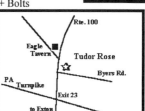

Rte. 100 / Eagle Tavern / Tudor Rose / Byers Rd. / PA Turnpike / Exit 23 / to Exton

A Patch of Country

Est: 1983

Owner:
Karen Reed
2200 sq.ft.

Chadds Ford, PA   #11

22 Olde Ridge Village   19317
(610) 459-8993

- ✄ Quality Cottons, Notions
- ✄ 250+ Book Titles, Patterns.
- ✄ Staffed exclusively by Quilters.
- ✄ Consigned items offered for sale.
- ✄ Mail Order Available.
- ✄ Special Order Service.
- ✄ Year-round classes for all skill levels
  with full student support.

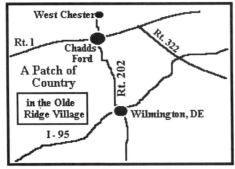

Mon - Sat
10 - 5
Thurs &
Fri til 8
Sun 12 - 5

Located 1 mile south of Route 1 on Route 202.
Within half an hour of the New Jersey & Maryland state lines.
1 miles north of the Delaware state line. Minutes from
Brandywine River Museum, Winterthur Museum, Longwood
Gardens, Brandywine Battlefield State Park and Valley Forge.

King of Prussia, PA #12

Steve's King of Prussia Sewing Center

156 W. Dekalb Pike   19406
(610) 768-9453   Rt. 202
Valley Forge Shopping Center

Mon - Fri
10 - 9
Sat 10 - 5
Sun 12 - 5

The area's best selection of quilting fabrics, books and supplies. Including Bernina, BabyLock, and Singer sewing machines, sergers and accessories.

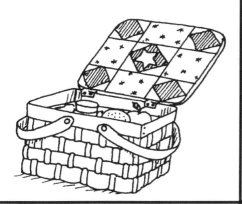

Intercourse, PA #13

The Old Country Store

3510 Old
Philadelphia Pike
17534
(717) 768-7101

Mem. Day - Oct 30
Mon - Sat 9 - 8
Nov - May   Mon - Sat
Thur&Fri til 8   9 - 5

A quilter's paradise. Large selection of fabrics, notions, local crafts and more! Also a Quilt Museum featuring stunning antique quilts.

Intercourse, PA #14

The Country Market at Intercourse

3504 Old Philadelphia Pike 17534
(717) 768-8058   3200 sq.ft.
Owner: Dorothy Freyer Est: 1992
Send SASE for list of Original
Amish Patterns on Pellon

April - Nov
Mon - Sat
9 - 5
Dec - March
Mon - Sat
10 - 5

Come Meet the Amish with their Quilts--
Hand made Pellon quilt patterns - pillows - crib quilts - wallhangings - quilt tops. Crafts Furniture

New Holland, PA #15

Cedar Lane Dry Goods

204 Orlan Rd.   17557
(717) 354-0030   Est: 1986
Owners: Amos & Laura Horning
2000 sq.ft.

Mon, Thur,
Fri 8 - 8
Tue, Wed,
Sat 8 - 5

Bolts of Fabric
Rems: solids & prints
Sewing Notions
Batting & Stuffing.

Goodville, PA #16

H.W. Oberholzer & Son Country Store

1585 Main St., P.O. Box 69
(717) 445-4616   17528
Est: 1945   1000+ Bolts

Mon - Sat
9 - 4
Wed 9 - 1

Over 50,000 yards of fabric. Over 200 Custom made Quilts. Wall Hangings, pillows. Candy, Baskets, Gifts, Laces Buttons. Custom Quilting

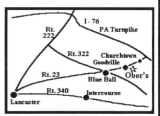

Lititz, PA #17

Weaver's Dry Goods

Mon, Thur, Fri 8 - 9
Tue, Wed, Sat 8 - 5

108 W. Brubaker Valley Rd.
(717) 627-1724   17543
Owners: Ivan & Lena Weaver
Est: 1978   2000 sq.ft.
Visa, MC, &
Discover Welcome

One of
Lancaster
County's
Largest Fabric
Shops

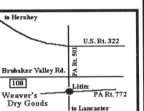

Lancaster, PA #18

Patchwork Dollhouse

Mon - Sat 10 - 4
Wed & Fri til 8

8 Meadow Lane   17601
(717) 569-4447   Est: 1980
Owner: Brenda Watson   1500 sq.ft.
1200 Bolts

Classes, Fabric for
Quilting and
Smocking, Books,
Patterns, Notions.
Bernina machines
and accessories.
French machine
sewing.

Littlestown, PA #19

The Quilt Patch

Mon - Sat 9:30 - 5
Sun 1 - 5

1897 Hanover Pike   17340
(717) 359-4121   Est: 1979
Owners: Lew & Kitty Hillard
1500 Calicoes   12,000 sq.ft.
Hoffman,
Homespuns,
Waverlys, etc. etc. etc
Supplies, Quilts, Fine
Gifts, Collectibles
(i.e. Dept. 56 Tom
Clark), Curtains,
Heritage Lace.
Art Gallery

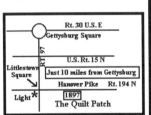

Gettysburg, PA #20

Needle & Thread

Mon - Thur 9:30 - 6
Fri 9:30 - 8
Sat 9:30 - 5

2215 Fairfield Rd.   17325
(717) 334-4011
Owner: Darlene Grube
Est: 1985   7000 sq.ft.

FULL LINE
FABRIC STORE
10,000 bolts to
Choose
from—Pendleton,
wools, silks,
cottons.
Books & Patterns

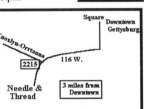

Mechanicsburg, PA #21

Ben Franklin Crafts

Mon - Sat 9:30 - 9
Sun 11 - 6

4880 Carlisle Pike   17055
(717) 975-0490
Est: 1989   2000+ Bolts

100% Cotton
Fabric. Patterns,
Books, Notions,
Battings, Classes,
Stitchery and basic
craft supplies.

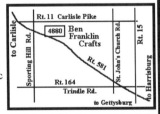

Harrisburg, PA #22

Quilt Emporium

Tue - Sat 10 - 5
Thur til 8

5922 Linglestown Rd.   (Rt. 39)
(717) 541-9911   17112

Full line of
Quilting Supplies.
1 1/2 miles from
Rt. I - 81 / I - 83
Convenient to
Rt. 22, PA Trpk
Harrisburg Exit.

Carlisle, PA #23

Calico Corners

Tues- Fri 9 - 4 Or By Appt. July Hrs. Vary Please Call

341 Barnstable Road   17013
(717) 249-8644
Owner: Janet Shultzabarger
Est: 1984   400+ Bolts

Personal attention to quilters needs. 100% cottons, notions, books, classes. Very reasonable prices and service with a smile.

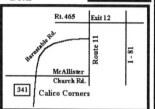

Ligonier, PA #24

Ligonier Quilt Shop

Mon - Sat 10 - 5

R.R. #1 Ligonier Mini-Mall
(412) 238-6359   15658
Owner: Susan Blank
Est: 1979   1000 sq.ft.

Handmade Quilts Extensive line of Quilting supplies Fabrics, Books, Stencils, Patterns. Classes. Helpful, Friendly service. We ship orders.

Roaring Spring, PA #25

Country Beefers

Mon - Fri 9:30 - 4:30 Saturdays May - Sept 10 - 2 Oct - Apr 10 - 4

RD #1, Box 495   16673
(814) 224-4818   Est: 1981
Owners: Louann Ferraro & Betty Beegle

Cotton fabrics, homespuns, books, craft patterns, notions, stencils. Also locally made gift items, appliqued clothing and Yankee Candles.

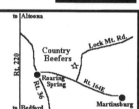

Indiana, PA #26

Harriet's Quilt Shop

Mon - Fri 10 - 5 Sat 10 - 3

271 Philadelphia St.   15701
(412) 465-4990
Owner: Harriet Yatsko
Est: 1980   3000 sq.ft.

A nice selection of cotton fabrics, stencils, books, patterns, thimbles and notions. Classes: Basic hand sewn sampler to quick machine piecing

Smicksburg, PA #27

Yoder's Quilt Shop

Sept - May Mon - Sat 9 - 5 June - Aug Mon - Sat 9 - 7

RD #1 Box 267 Hwy 954 N
(412) 397-9645   16256
Owners: Sue & Jay Hurtt
A large assortment   Est: 1988
of Amish-made quilts, wallhangings, fabric, notions, patterns, and quilting supplies. Over 1000 bolts of fabric at an everyday discount.

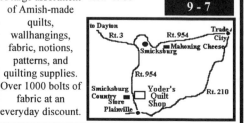

Millmont, PA #28

Nora's Quilts & Crafts

M. T. Th, & F 9 - 9 Sat 9 - 5

R.D. #2, Box 111   17845
(717) 922-1849
Owners: Eli & Nora Martin   Est: 1972

Complete line of quilts, tablerunners, wall hangings, placemats, pillows, potholders, dolls, wooden crafts, shelves & all kinds of quilted items.

Tannersville, PA #29

Stencil 'N Stitch

Tue - Sat 10 - 4

Pocono Peddlers Village
P.O. Box 291   18372
(717) 629-3533
Located in the Pocono Mountains.

Quilting fabric, notions, lap hoops, frames, books, patterns, warm & natural cotton batting, stencils.

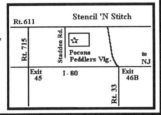

Ackermanville, PA #30

The Village Barn

Mon - Thur 9:30 - 5:30
Fri 9:30-7
Sat 9:30-4

1547 Mill Road   18013
(610) 588-3127   Est: 1975
Owners: Ditta Van Gemen &
1000 sq.ft.

Complete Quilt Shop. 1000 Bolts 100% Cotton Fabrics, Books, Notions, Classes. Machine Quilting Service. Helpful Staff. Lg.selection of Country Gifts.

Wilkes Barre, PA #31

The Quilt Racque

Tues - Fri 10 - 5
Sats 11 - 3

183 N. Main St.   (Shavertown)
(717) 675-0914   18708
Owner: Marianne S. Williams

Antique Quilts   Est: 1988   560 sq.ft.
1880 - 1930's All Sizes New Handmade Quilts, Vintage Lace & Linens, Doll Beds, Thimbles, Sewing Collectibles, Books, Fat Quarters & 1930's Fabrics.

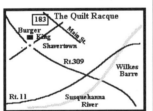

Hamlin, PA #32

Ye Olde Sewing Emporium

Tues - Sat 10 - 5
Summer May Vary

Rt. 191, St. John's Centre Box 190
(717) 689-3480   18427
Owner: Sandra Cinfo Est: 1991

A Unique Shop Specializing in Fabrics, Notions, Books, Classes, Ribbons, and Gifts for Quilters, Sewers and Needlecrafters.

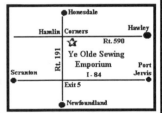

Honesdale, PA #33

The Mountain Quiltworks

Tues - Sat 10 - 5

R.R. #4, Box 395   18431
(717) 253-9510   325+ Bolts   1100 sq.ft.
Owner: Amy R. Dunn

Find everything you need to create tomorrow's heirlooms. From various source books, stencils & patterns too of course, top quality cotton fabrics.

Great Bend, PA #34

Sister's Choice Quilt Studio

Mon - Sat 10 - 5
Tues til 9

P.O. Box 772, Randolph Rd.
(717) 879-4196   18821
Est: 1991
Owners: Bettie Armondi & Marjorie Cook

100% Cotton Fabric, Books, Patterns, Quilting Supplies, Classes Handmade Gifts & Quilted Items. Buses Welcome

Covington, PA #35

The Farm House
A Country Quilt Shop

R.R. #1   Box 58   16917
(717) 549-2136   Est: 1992
Owner: Shirley Welch
"Making quilts is an American Tradition"

**Mon - Sat
10 - 4**

A place for time-worn,
traditional quilting.
  Learn my great-
  grandmother's
technique for making
over 500 quilts called
  "crow footing".
Certified Teacher of
"Quilt in a Day"

Pa / NY Border
Tioga
Rt. 15
Rt. 6
Rt. 14
Wellsboro   Mansfield
Covington
Welch Mt. Rd   The
Blossburg   Farmhouse
to Williamsport   Canton

Meadville, PA   #36

The Quilt Square

560 Washington St.   16335
(814) 333-4383   Est: 1981
Owner: Gail McClure
3200 sq.ft.   2000 Bolts

**Mon - Fri
10 - 5
Tues til 8
Sat 10 - 3**

RJR, Hoffman,
South Seas and
  many more
designer fabrics.
Latest books and
patterns. A staff
who loves to see
what you've done,
so bring it in.

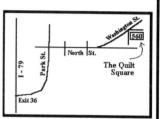

Washington St.
560
I - 79
Park St.
North   St.
The Quilt
Square
Exit 36

Country Bear Creations   Lucinda, PA   #37

34 Maple Drive   16235
(814) 226-8893
Owners: Keith & Sharon Kennedy

Mail Orders Welcome   MC   Visa   Discover

Home Shopping Video $5 + S&H

Bed &
Breakfast
with Quilter
Vacations

**Mon - Sat
9:30 - 5:30**

Custom Made Shelves,
Quilting Frames, & Quilt Racks

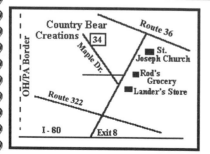

OH/PA Border
Country Bear
Creations   34
Route 36
Maple Dr.
St.
Joseph Church
Rod's
Grocery
Lander's Store
Route 322
I - 80   Exit 8

Quilt Kits
100% Cotton Fabrics
90", 108", & 120" Backing
Stencils, Books, Patterns,
Tools, Supplies & Classes

Knox, PA #38

Est: 1987

Countryside Crafts & Countryside Quilts

Owners:
Jolinda Tharan (Crafts)
& Sally Byers (Quilts)
P.O. Box 255   RD # 2   16232
Exit 7 from I - 80
(814) 797-2434

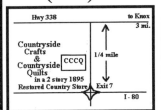

Mon - Sat
10 - 4:30
Sun
1 - 4:30

In the heart of Clarion County.
We are the area's Largest and
Most Unique Country gift, craft
and Quilting supply shop.
With 100% Cottons, Books,
Quilting Patterns and the area's
largest supply of craft patterns.

Harborcreek, PA #39

Calico Patch Quilt Shoppe

3229 Davison Road   16421
(814) 898-2978   Est: 1984
Owners: Jim & Millie Ward
1400 sq.ft.   2500 Bolts

Mon - Fri
10 - 5
Thur til 8
Sat 10 - 4

Largest Quilt
Shop in tri-state
area with country
prices; home of
original
"Puncture Proof"
leather Thimble.

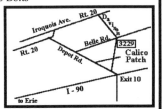

Erie, PA #40

Threads & Treasures

3210 W. 32nd St.   16506
(814) 838-8138
Owner: Judy Dykins

Mon 10 - 7
Tues, Thur,
Fri 10 - 5
Sat 10 - 4

Quilts,
Wallhangings,
Antiques, Gifts.
We also carry a
wide variety of
Hoffman, RJR,
Roberta Horton
Plaids, Books,
Patterns, Quilt
Supplies & Classes

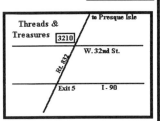

Erie, PA #41

International Fabric Collection

3445 West Lake Rd.   16505
(814) 838-0740   Est: 1987
Owner: Dorothy Brown   1500 sq.ft.
Catalog $3

Thursday
10 - 4
and by
Appt. or
chance.

Cottons from
Japan, Italy,
Holland, Africa.
Yukata, mud cloth,
Kente cloth,
Liberty of London.
Unusual Books &
Patterns.
Sashiko Supplies.

New Brighton, PA #42

Boyde's Country Stitch

81 E. Inman Dr.   15066
(412) 846-4175
Owner: Becky Boyde

Mon - Sat
12 - 5
Evenings
by Appt.

Specializing in
Cotton Fabric,
Books, Patterns,
Handmade Items.
Custom Curtains.
Notions.
Basic Cross Stitch
Supplies Too.

New Wilmington, PA #43

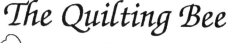

The Quilting Bee

126 South Market St.   16142

(412) 946-8566

Owner: Linda Miller
Est: 1981
1000 sq.ft.

Tues - Sat
10 - 4:30

900+ Bolts Cotton/Designer fabrics.
Complete line of books, patterns.
In the heart of W. Pennsylvania Amish
farmlands, Just South of I - 80 and
Sharon, PA. Minutes from the Grove City
Outlet Mall and Westminster College.
Come Visit!

Monaca, PA #44

The Quilt Basket

Mon - Sat
10 - 4

1116 Pennsylvania   15061
(412) 775-7774
Owner: M. Maxine Holmes
Est: 1984

The Quilt Basket
is a complete quilt
shop offering lots
of classes & all the
supplies: i.e.
fabrics, patterns,
books, and
notions.

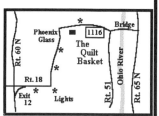

Sarver, PA #45

Cozy Quilt Shoppe

Tue - Fri
10 - 4
Sat 10 - 2

102 Ekastown Rd. #102   16055
(412) 295-9300

Owner: Lynne
        Sobecki   Est: 1990

A shoppe with a
warm, homey
atmosphere where
quilters can
browse through
100% cotton
fabrics, books,
patterns, stencils,
supplies and
ongoing class
lists.

Allison Park, PA #46

The Quilt Company

Mon - Sat
9:30 - 5
Mon &
Thur til 9

3940 Middle Rd.   15101
(412) 487-9532
Owner: Karen Montgomery
Est: 1994   3500 sq.ft.

Pittsburgh's
Largest Quilt
Shop!
Featuring 100%
cottons, books,
and original
patterns.

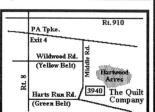

Sewickley, PA #47

TAPAS

Tues - Sat
9:30 - 5

441 1/2 Walnut St.   15143
(412) 741-9575
Owner: Janet Daugherty
Est: 1991   220 sq.ft.

Ready made
Quilts
Custom Quilts
Quilt Repair
Quilted
Clothing

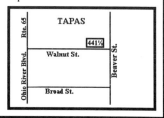

Quilters Corner

5304 Park Ave.   15102
(412) 833-8449
Owner: Mary Beth Hartnett   Est: 1989   1500 sq.ft.

We offer a complete collection of exquisite cotton fabrics (1000+ bolts), books, patterns, notions, and classes in quiltmaking and dollmaking.

Mon - Sat 10 - 5
Thur til 9

Bethel Park, PA #48

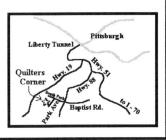

If you would like to receive our newsletter stop in to sign the mailing list or drop us a note.

Elizabeth, PA #49

Banners & Blankets

1125 Swiss Alpine Village   15037
(412) 751-3707
Owners: Keith & Ruth Ann Lowery
Est: 1995 Catalog of Banner
  Scenic Location   Supplies $1
Major Fabric Lines
- All 100% cotton.
  Flag & Banner
supplies & patterns,
quilting books &
patterns. Classes
  Notions. Mail
Orders Welcome

Mon - Sat
9 - 4
Tues - Thur
til 8
Sun 12 - 4

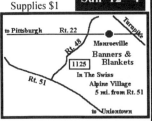

Pittsburgh, PA #50

Piecing It Together

3458 Babcock Blvd.   15237
(412) 364-2440   Est: 1986
Owners: Johannon Blanavik
1200 sq.ft.

Mon - Sat
10 - 5
Thur til 8

Complete line of quilting supplies, 100% cotton fabrics, books, notions, patterns, and classes. Lots of samples. Personal, friendly.

Butler, PA   #51

QUILTING at "HOME"

317 W. Jefferson
16001
Home:
(412) 284-1382
Studio
(412) 353-2891
Est: 1995
Owner: Paulette Cole

By Appointment Only

Machine Quilting
Located on 2nd Floor of Patches, Pretties & Lace. See # 52 for map.
Ask about our 3 day,
2 night Quilting Weekends.
Would you like to be on our mailing list?

Butler, PA   #52

Patches, Pretties N Lace

317 W. Jefferson   16001
(412) 287-2901   Est: 1989
New Location: 3 Story Victorian Quilt Shop

**Mon - Fri
10 - 5
Thur til 8
Sat 10 - 3**

Red Wagon's Homespuns, Flannels, Kona Solids, Books & Patterns, Hinterburg Frames & Hoop on Display. Exclusive Amish Stencils

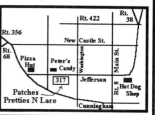

Pennsylvania Guilds:

Keystone Quilters, 806 Mill Grove Dr.,
        Audubon, 19403
Beaver Valley Piecemakers, 302 Windy
        Ghoul Estates, Beaver, 15009
Centre Pieces, P.O. Box 657,
        Boalsburg, 16827
LeTort Quilters, P.O. Box 260,
        Carlisle, 17013
Three Rivers Quilters,
        Castle Shannon, 15234
Mon Valley Quilters, Charleroi, 15120
Quilt Company East, Churchill
Brandywine Valley Quilters,P.O. Box 953,
        Concordville, 19331
Pocono Mountain Qulter's Guild,
        P.O. Box 1465, East Stroudsburg, 18301
Hands All Around Erie Quilt Guild, 1420 Lord Rd., Fairview, 16415
Sisters Choice Quilt Guild, Randolph Rd., Great Bend, 18821
Hands all Around Erie Quilt Guild, Harborcreek
North East Crazy Quilters Guild, Harborcreek
Log House Quilt Guild, P.O. Box 5351, Johnstown, 15904
Heart & Home Quilters Guild, 24 Schock Rd., Lenhartsville, 19534
Ligonier Quilters, Ligonier Town Hall, Ligonier, 15658
Laurel Mountain Quilters, Ligonier Town Hall, Ligonier, 15658
Keystone Quilters, 5540 Beverly Pl., Pittsburgh, 15206
Loyal Hannahs Quilt Guild, 512 Chestnut St., Saltsburg, 15681
Schuylkill County Quilters Guild, P.O. Box 85, Schuylkill Haven, 17972
Pennsylvania Quilters Association, 825 N. Webster Ave., Scranton, 18510

Other Shops in Pennsylvania:

Altoona	R Quilt Shop, 1800 Pleasant Valley Blvd.	
Belleville	Buchanan's Fabrics & Sewing Center, HC 61	
Bethlehem	Piece Goods Shop, Rte. 191, Nazareth Pike	
Bethlehem	Fabric Mart of Bethlehem, 2485 Willow Park Rd.	
Biglerville	Craft Cupboard, 13 S. Main	
Bird in Hand	Fisher's Hand Made Quilts, 2713-A Old Philadelphia Pike	
Bird-in-Hand	Lapp's Dry Goods, 3137 Old Philadelphia Pike	
Camp Hill	Country Patchwork, 1603 Carlisle Rd.	
Clarks-Summit	Carriage Barn Antiques, 1550 Fairview Rd.	
Corry	Pansy's Fabrics, 109 N. Center St.	
Dallas	Back Mountain Quiltworks, 52 Mill St.	
Denver	Sauder's Fabrics, 681 S. Muddycreek Rd., Box 409	
Doylestown	Sew Smart Fabrics, 53 W. State St.	
Duncansville	The Rainbows End Quilt Shop, R.D. 4 Spring Meadow	
Effort	Country Quilterie, R. R. #3 Box 2482	
Elkland	Golden Thimble, 114 W. Main St.	
Emmaus	Julie's Sewing Basket, 379 Chestnut	
Factoryville	Patchwork Shop Antique Quilts, P.O. Box 3360 Route #3	
Gipsy	Village Variety Store, 33 Main St.	
Glenside	Granny's Sewing Den, 243 Keswick Ave.	
Gordonville	Twin Maples Quilt Nook, 172 S. New Holland Rd.	
Haverton	Quilting Cottage, 1910 Darby Rd.	
Intercourse	Nancy's Corner, 3503 Old Philadelphia Pike	
Intercourse	Zook's Fabric Store, 3535 Old Philadelphia Pike	
Lahaska	Quilts Incredible, P.O. Box 492	
Lancaster	Rag Shop Fabric & Craft, 2734 Columbia Ave.	
Lancaster	Strawberry Patch, 112 Willow Valley Square	
Lansdale	Lansdale Discount Linens, 816 W. Second	
Limerick	Wee Bairns, 250 W. Ridge Pike	
Mahanoy City	Chesko Fabrics, 301 E. Centre	
Media	The Hen House, 300 W. Baltimore Pike	
Menden Hall	The Quilt Rack, P.O. Box 327	
Montoursville	Stere Sewing Machine Center, 1116 S. Broad St.	
Oakmont	The Hands Needlework Shop, 632 Allegheny River Blvd.	
Oley	Summer House Needleworks, Rd # 3, Main St.	
Pebersburg	Brush Valley Dry Goods, Star Route Box 33	
Philadelphia	Samuel Goldberg Fabrics, 758 S. 4th St.	
Philadelphia	Lovely Lady Comfort Company, 531 E. Tioga St.	
Philadelphia	A&J Fabrics, 752 S. 4th St.	
Philadelphia	Byrne Fabrics, 8434 Germantown Ave.	
Pittston	Edelstein's Fabrics, R.R. 141 South Main	
Punxsutawney	Lydia's Quilt Shop, R.D.7, Box 113	
Ronks	Dutchland Quilt Patch, 2851A Lincoln Hwy. E	
Ronks	Family Farm Quilt, 3511 W. Newport Rd.	
Sayre	Mary's General Store, 927 W. Lockhart	
Scottsdale	Scottsdale Fabric & Quilt Shop, 103 Pittsburgh	
Scranton	Scranton Fabric Center, 1779 N. Keyser Ave.	
Skippack	Quilting Bear, 249 White Ave.	
Soudertown	The Souder Store, 357 Main St.	
Volant	Quilted Collectibles, Main St.	
Washington Crossing	Bittersweet, 1116 Taylorsville Rd., P.O. Box 68	
Waynesboro	Benedict's Country Store, 6305 Marsh Rd.	
Wellsboro	Gammie's Attic, 152 Main St.	
Willow Grove	Yours, Mine & Ours Sewing, 219 Easton Rd.	

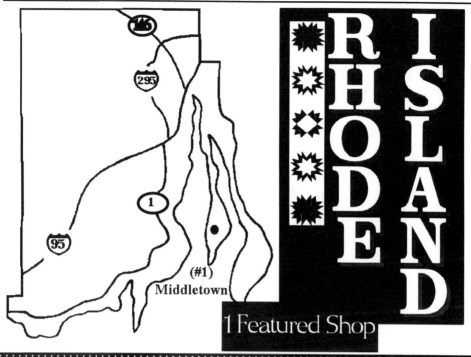

(#1)
Middletown

1 Featured Shop

Middletown, RI   #1

**Large selection of cotton fabrics.
Hoffman, Henry's etc.
Books, Sterling Thimbles, Classes &
Workshops, Quilts & Gifts**

Quilt Artisan

**747 Aquidneck Avenue   02842
(401) 846-2127 or (800) 736-4364
Owners: Linda Hilliard & Irene King
Est: 1984   2500 sq.ft.**

Mon - Wed
12 - 7
Thur - Sat
10 - 4

Rhode Island Guilds:
Narragansett Bay Quilters, Box 614, East Greenville, 02818
Blackstone Valley Piecemakers, 15 Harkness Rd. W., Smithfield, 02896
Quilters by the Sea, P.O. Box 708, Portsmouth, 02871

Other Shops in Rhode Island:
Barrington   Hearts & Flowers Antiques Ltd, 270 County Rd.
Chepachet   Country Hang-Up, Inc., 251 Douglas Hook Rd.
Pawtucket   Lorraine Fabrics, 593 Mineral Spring Ave.
Warwick   Fabric Place, 300 Quaker Lane, Rt. 2
Westerly   Sew & Sew, Spindrift Village, 333 Post Rd.

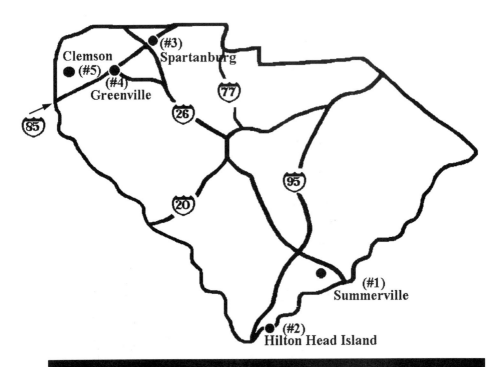

SOUTH CAROLINA

5 Featured Shops

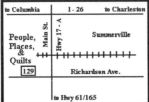

Greenville, SC #4

Classic Keepsakes

Mon - Fri
9:30 - 5:30
Sat 10 - 4

626 Congaree Rd.   29607
(864) 288-0273
Owner: Elizabeth Be Den

Quality Fabrics &
Notions for all
your sewing needs.
Large selection of
buttons, Creative
Classes, Viking
sewing machine
dealer.

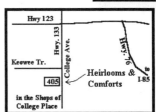

Spartanburg, SC #3

Quilter's Haven

Tues - Sat
10 - 5

1484 E. Main St.   29307
(864) 573-5400
Owner: Pat Brown
Est: 1992   1000 Bolts

100% Cotton
Fabrics
Quilting Supplies
Books &
Patterns
Classes

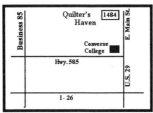

Clemson, SC #5

Heirlooms & Comforts

Mon - Fri
9:30 - 5:30
Sat
9:30 - 4

405 - 160 College Ave.
(864) 654-9507   29631
Owner: Sara Ballentine
Est: 1984   1300 sq.ft.   1700 Bolts

Upstate's most
complete quilt
shop--fabrics,
tools, books,
patterns, notions,
classes--in a
friendly
atmosphere.

South Carolina Guilds:
Cobblestone Quilters,
    Box 39114, Charleston, 29407
Logan Lap Quilters,
    Box 7034, Columbia, 29201
Foothills Piecemakers,
    Box 26482, Greenville, 29616
Piedmont Piecers, 1484 E. Main St.
    Spartanburg, 29307

Other Shops in South Carolina:

Beaufort	Mother Hubbards Cupboard, 412 Charles St.
Charleston	Margiotta's Sewing Machine Co., 874 Orleans Rd.
Charleston	Haltiwanger's Notions & Fabrics, 915 Folley Rd.
Columbia	Elegant Stitches, 3218 Millwood Ave.
Easley	The Quilt Gallery, 141 Patchwork Row
Greenville	Jasmine Heirlooms, 500 Fairview Dr.
Myrtle Beach	Oak Street Fabrics, 504 27th Ave. N. #C
Reevesville	Quilt House, 6841 Johnston Ave.

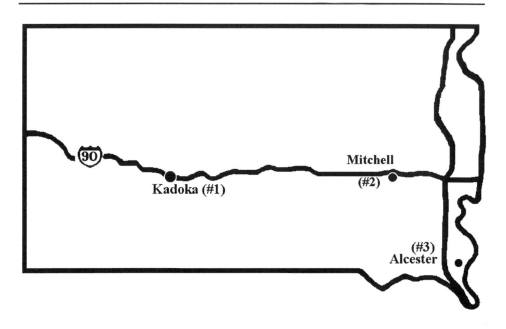

3 Featured Shops

Kadoka, SD #1

Dakota Winds Fabric & Crafts

Mon -Sat
9 - 6

111 S. Hwy 73   57432
(605) 837-2145
Owner: Kathy Jobgen
Est: 1991   1200 sq.ft.   300 Bolts

We carry a mix of
fabrics including:
Hoffman,
Debbie Mumm,
Concord & VIP
plus much more.

Exit 150   I - 90
Hwy. 73
Dakota Winds
☆
In The Boardwalk Mall

South Dakota Guilds:
South Dakota Quilters' Guild,
    HCR 88, Box 6A, Clearfield
Heartland Quilters Guild,
    Box 195, Mitchell
Black Hills Quilters Guild,
    P.O. Box 2495, Rapid City

Quilter's
Daughter:
a lucky little girl
who gets to "help"
with all the
projects.

Mitchell, SD #2

314
North
Main
Street

Mon 9 - 8
Tues - Sat
9 - 5:30

(605) 996-0947   Est: 1987
Owners: Kay Miller & Carma Popp   1200 sq.ft.

100% cottons, Books,
and Patterns. Classes.
Fashion Fabrics.
Friendly, helpful staff.
Authorized
Pfaff
Dealer   **PFAFF**

Corn Palace

The Pin Cushion 314

7th
6th
5th
4th
3rd

North Main

Alcester, SD #3

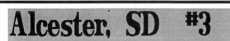

Lacy Lovelies

Mon - Sat
9 - 5:30

Second St.,   P.O. Box 317
(605) 934-1994   57001
Owner: Millie Gubbrud
Est: 1968   5000 sq.ft.

The ultimate in
privately owned
fabric shops. Huge
selection of
Cottons, Silk,
Wool, Ultra Suede,
Fashion, Bridal and
Decorator.

to Sioux Falls
Hwy. 46
Exit 48   ← 9 mi.
Beresford
I - 29
Exit 42   Alcester
Alcester   Ct. Rd. 13
← 10 mi. →
to Sioux City
Hwy. 46   4 mi.
1 mi.

Other Shops in South Dakota:

Chamberlain	The Fabric Inn, 203 N. Main St.
Rapid City	Pioneer Quilts, 801 Columbus
Sioux Falls	Heirloom Creations, 2131 S. Minnesota
Winner	The Sewing B, 225 S. Main St.

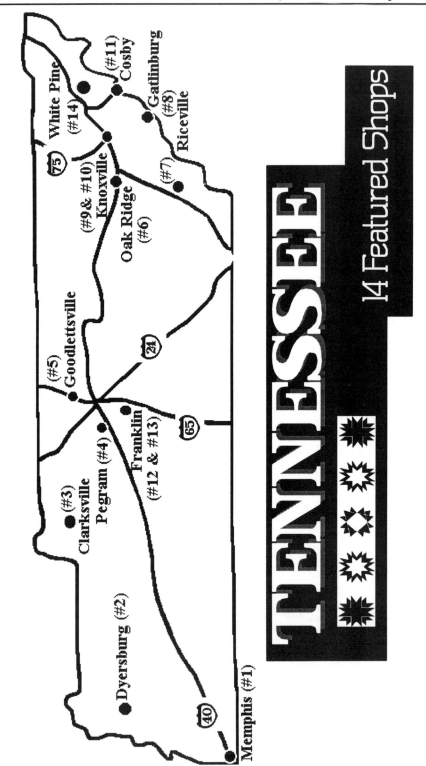

TENNESSEE

14 Featured Shops

White Pine (#14)
(#11) Cosby
Gatlinburg
(#8) Riceville
(#7)
(#9 & #10) Knoxville
Oak Ridge (#6)
75
Goodlettsville (#5)
24
Franklin (#12 & #13)
65
Pegram (#4)
Clarksville (#3)
Dyersburg (#2)
40
Memphis (#1)

Memphis, TN #1

Quilts & Crafts

Fabrics, books, quilt & craft patterns, notions and supplies. Classes.
Over 1,500 bolts of cotton
Over 3,500 patterns
Crafters' Gallery featuring local crafts.

Mon - Sat 9:30 - 4:30

2830 Austin Peay #9   38128
(901) 373-4004
Owner: Marie May
Est: 1991   2,000 sq.ft.

Dyersburg, TN #2

Sew Many Ideas

Mon - Fri 10 - 5
Sat 10 - 3

219 S. Mill Avenue   38024
(901) 286-4721   Est: 1988
Owners: Jeanne Bird McClain &
Betty Bird   4000 sq.ft.

Authorized Bernina Dealer. 100% cotton fabric by Hoffman, Jinny Beyer, M.E. Hopkins, P&B + many more. Notions, Books, Q-snap frames, craft patterns.

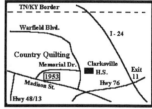

Clarksville, TN #3

Country Quilting

Mon - Fri 10 - 5
Sat 10 - 4

1953 Madison St.   37043
(In the Tradewinds South Shopping Center)
(615) 551-3650

Smocking & Heirloom Sewing Fabrics, Notions, Gifts, Books, Patterns, Classes, Workshops, Seminars. Pfaff & Bernina Dealer

---

Pegram, TN #4

Harpeth Clock & Quilt Company

Mon - Sat 9 - 5

462 Hwy 70   P.O. Box 40
(615) 646-0938 or (800) 238-4284
Owners: Richard & Margaret Murray
Est: 1978   4500 sq.ft.

Quilting supplies & Instructions. Large assortment of cotton fabrics, books, patterns, notions and Handmade Quilts. Plus Clocks.

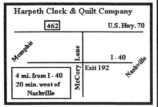

Goodlettsville, TN #5

Quilter's Attic

126 N Main St. 37072
(615) 859-5603
Est: 1987

Mon - Fri 9 - 4
Sat 9 - 2

Owner: Jenny Moss   4500 sq.ft.   2000 Bolts

Everything imaginable for the Quilter. Fabric, books, patterns, notions in a country setting adjoining several Antique Malls.

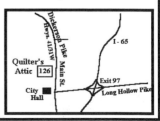

Oak Ridge, TN #6

The Quilting Corner

Mon - Fri
10 - 5
Sat 10 - 4

37 E. Tennessee Ave.   37830
(423) 483-7778
Owner: Allison Arnold
Est: 1979   1300 sq.ft.   1500 Bolts

**All Your
Quilting
Needs!**

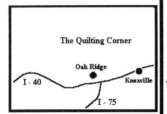

The Quilting Corner

Oak Ridge

Knoxville

I - 40

I - 75

Riceville, TN #7

Lena Beth Carmichael
Antique Quilts

309 County Road 70   37370
(423) 462-2892
1940's and older   Est: 1988

**By Chance
or Appt.**

Quilts, tops,
blocks. Inventory
of 75 - 125. The
quality ranges
from cutters to
museum pieces.
Also offer lectures,
& appraisal
services.

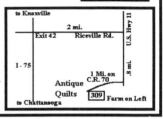

to Knoxville
2 mi.
Exit 42   Riceville Rd.
U.S. Hwy 11
I - 75
.8 mi.
1 Mi. on
C.R. 70
Antique
Quilts   309   Farm on Left
to Chattanooga

If You Need It, We've Got It

Gatlinburg, TN #8

1662 E. Parkway   37738   (423) 436-5664
Owner: Wilma Prebor   Est: 1976   3500 sq.ft.

Pigeon Forge
The Parkway
Hwy. 321   E. Parkway
3.5 mi.   1662
Quilts By
Wilma
Gatlinburg
Hwy. 441

Quilts By Wilma

"Home of Regina's
Quilt Kits.

**Daily 9 - 6
Call for
Winter Hours**

Hundreds of quilting
tools, books, stencils,
patterns and designer fabric.
Plus the largest selection in the U.S.A. of
Regina's Pre-Cut Quilt Kits.
Over 300 locally made Quilts

Quilt Craft

Knoxville, TN #9

Grandmothers' Flower Garden

Est: 1985
1350 sq.ft.
Large Selection of
100% Cotton Fabrics
including Homespuns
and reproduction fabrics.
Also Quilting Books,
Supplies and Classes.

**Tues - Sat
10 - 5**

**We're Adjacent to Each Other
2315 Kimberlin Heights Dr.
(423) 573-0769   37920
Owner: Eva Earle Kent**

to Knoxville
Johnson
Bible
College
Hendron's
Chapel Rd.
Hwy
441
Kimberlin Heights Dr.
2315   Quilt
Craft
2407
to Sevierville

Quilt and
related Art
Shows.

1900 sq.ft. Classroom
and meeting space in
restored farm house at
2407 Kimberlin Hgts Dr.
Our# (423) 577-6312
Call for events Schedule

Gina's

Bernina Sewing Center

Knoxville, TN   #10

30 minutes from the Great Smoky Mountains including Dollywood and Gatlinburg!!

Gina's has over 3000 bolts of quality cotton fabric, quilting books, notions, bridal fabrics, silks and woolens. We specialize in heirloom sewing, smocking, machine work and a <u>lot</u> more.
Call for our extensive class schedule.

**Mon - Thur
9:30 - 6
Fri 9:30 - 5
Sat 9:30 - 4**

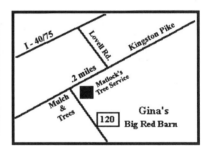

Gina's ... in the BIG RED BARN!

**120 Farlow Dr. Knoxville, TN 37922
(423) 966-5941   fax: (423) 966-6924
Owner: Regina Owen   Est: 1980   5000 sq.ft.**

Gina's is also the place for all your BERNINA needs.

     BERNINA®

Franklin, TN #13

Stitchers Garden

Mon - Sat
9:30 - 6

413 Main St.   37064
(615) 790-0603
Owner: Myra Nickolaus

Middle Tennessee's Most Complete Quilting Shop! Over 4000 bolts of all cotton fabrics, complete Jinny Beyer palette, Q-Snap frames, stencils, books, templates, patterns, and classes.

Est: 1988   3000 sq.ft.

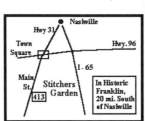

White Pine, TN #14

Quilts +

Tue - Sat
10 - 5
Fri til 9

1938 Maple St.   37890
(423-674-8294 or 8819)
Owner: Sandra Chumney
Est: 1996   930 sq.ft.

Friendly and fast growing. Wide range of fabrics, notions, books and threads. Call if you need other hours while traveling.

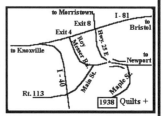

Tenessee Guilds:
Chattanooga Quilters Guild, 808 Windy Hill Dr., Chattanooga, 37421
Country Quilters, 1953 Madison Street, Clarksville, 37043
Tennessee Valley Quilters Assoc., PO Box 92, Crab Orchard, 37723
Heritage Quilters, 121 Valley Lane, Englewood, 37329
Blue Ridge Quilters Guild, 5 White Oak St., Johnson City, 37604
Cherokee Blossom, 1430 Brymer Ck Rd SW, McDonald, 37353
Heirloom Quilters, 1918 Battleground Dr., Murfreesboro, 37129
Music City Quilters Guild, P.O. Box 140876, Nashville, 37214

Other Shops in Tennessee:

Bean Station	Stitch N Time, Bean Station Highway
Bell Buckle	Bingham's, 3 Webb Rd. E
Benton	The Quilting Shop, 411 Highway N.
Caryville	Fabrics & More, Old Hwy. 25
Chattanooga	Ann's Quilt Shop, 3609 Ringgold Rd.
Cleveland	Lofty Creative Fabrics, 54 Mouse Creek Rd.
Cleveland	The Sewing Connection, 3354 Keith St.
Columbia	Carousel Krafts & More, 2404 Highland Ave.
Cookeville	Country Patchworks, 134 S. Willow
Cookeville	The Quilt Shop #2, 210 W. Spring St.
Cookeville	Glenda's Fabric and The Quilter, 739 S. Jefferson
East Ridge	Ann's Quilt Shop & Quilting, 3609 Ringgold Rd.
Fayetteville	The Flower House Needle Shop, 401 S. Main PO Box 1027
Gatlinburg	Carla's Pretties, 601 Glades Rd.
Jackson	The Fabric Source, 1090 U.S. Highway 45 Bypass
Johnson City	CMQ Outlet and Sewing Center, 1600 East Jackson
Jonesborough	Tennessee Quilts, 123 East Main
Kenton	Fancy Stitch Quilt & Gift Shop, 4578 S. Highway 45 W.
Knoxville	Stitches N Patches, 6936 Maynardville Pike
Knoxville	Edith's Cloth & Crafts, 2828 Broadway
Lawrenceburg	Discount Fabric Store, 110 N. Military Ave.
Lenoir City	Pumpkins Patchworks, 2300 Highway 70 E.
Maryville	Dorothy's, 2510 E. Lamar Alexander Pkwy.
McMinnville	B & J Quilt Shop, 1202 Sparta S.
Memphis	Cloth Connections - Quilt Shop, 3764 Summer Ave.
Nashville	Southeastern Quilting Co., 748 Douglas Ave.
Pikeville	Fabric House, Main St., P.O. Box 607
Sevierville	Five G's Quilt Studio, 1060 Alpine Dr.
Springfield	The Sewing Basket, 510 Hill St.
Union City	Stitchin Post, 611 E. Reelfoot Ave.

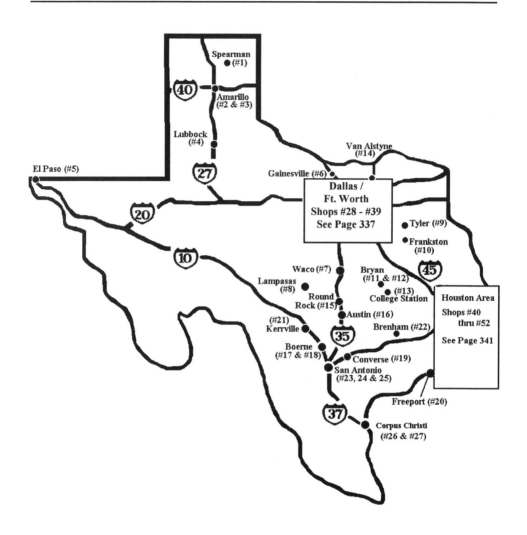

TEXAS

52 Featured Shops

Spearman, TX #1

Jo's This N' That

Mon - Fri
9:30 - 5:30
Sat
9:30 - 5

216 Main   79081
(806) 659-3999
Owner: Joan Farr

We are a
Traditional
Quilt Shop.

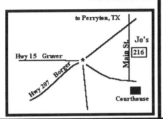

Amarillo, TX #2

3440 Bell #228
79109
(806) 359-8306
Owner: Sandy
Barker

Tues - Sat
10 - 6

Serving Quilters
from Chicago
to L.A.
We do Mail Order
1-800-895-9458
Over 1000 Bolts

Amarillo, TX #3

R & R Quilts and More

Mon - Sat
9:30 - 5:30

2817 Civic Circle   79109
Millie Riggs & DeAnna Randall   (806) 359-6235

Friendliest Little
Shop in Texas.
Over 2000 Bolts of
100% Cotton
Fabrics. Classes,
Supplies, books,
and Patterns.

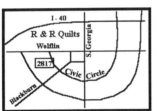

Lubbock, TX #4

The Quilt Shop

Mon - Sat
10 - 5

4525 50th. Street   79414
(In the Sunshine Sq. Shopping Center)
(806) 793-2485
Owner: Sharon Newman   Certified Appraiser

We have 1500
bolts of cotton,
books, supplies &
classes.
Appraisals by
appointment.

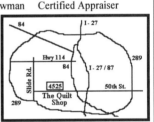

El Paso, TX #5

Lee's Quilt Corner, Too

Mon - Fri
10 - 6
Sat 9 - 4

10400 Ashwood   79935
(915) 595-0710   Est: 1994
Owner: Ann Lee   2200 sq.ft.   2000 Bolts

100% Cotton
Fabrics, Books,
Notions, Patterns,
Classes. Large
selection of
southwestern
Patterns.

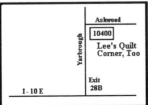

Gainesville, TX #6

Past Time Fabrics

1218 East California   76240
(817) 668-1747
Owner: Fran Scott
Est: 1986

Tues - Sat
10 - 5

Full line of 100%
cotton calicos
and solids.
Books, notions,
patterns, classes -
everything for
quilters!

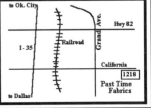

Waco, TX #7

The Quiltin' Bee

Tues - Sat 10 - 5:30

130 Midway Center   76712
(817) 776-2246
Est: 1995
Owners: Charmaine Hogwood & Jacqueline Gomez

Central Texas' only shop devoted to Quilters with Hoffman, Moda, Benartex and RJR Fabrics plus Classes, Books and Fun !

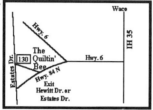

Lampasas, TX #8

M.J.'s Fabrics, Fashions, and Quilts

Mon - Sat 9 - 5

410 E. 3rd. St.   76550
(512) 556-8879
Est: 1989   3000 sq.ft.

Top of the line fabrics.
Unique Patterns.
Friendly Clerks.
Info on places of interest in the area.

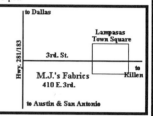

Tyler, TX #9

John Sauls' Antiques

108 S. Broadway   75702
(903) 593-4668   Est 1976
Fax: (903) 593-9661
Owner: John Sauls   2600 sq.ft.

Mon - Sat 10 - 5:30

Dealing Exclusively in Vintage & Antique Quilts, Tops, & Blocks. **Largest selection in the Southwest.**

95 miles East of Dallas Take I - 20 east to 1st Tyler exit (Hwy 69) South on Hwy 669 approx. 9 miles to Downtown Tyler and turn right on Broadway

Frankston, TX #10

Artistic Needle

Wed - Sat 10 - 4

612 Hwy. 155 N   75763
(903) 876-4345
Owner: Judy Dwyer

Est: 1990   1500 sq.ft.

100% Cotton Fabrics as well as current books, patterns, and notions.
The only Full service specialty Quilt Shop in East Texas !

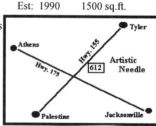

Bryan, TX #11

Pollyanna's Quilt Cottage

**Tue - Fri 10 - 6
Sat 10 - 4
Sun 1 - 5**

3707 E. 29th St.   77802
(409) 846-7735 Fax: (409) 822-0769
Owner: Polly Trant

Largest in the Brazos Valley.
Only Aggie Quilt Dealer.
Top quality fabrics & notions.
Hand-made gifts.
Super Sunday Sales!

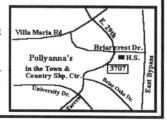

Round Rock, TX #15

Mini Stitches

Tues - Sat 10 - 5

208 W. Bagdad Ave. #7 78664
Corner of Brown & Bagdad
(512) 255-8545
Owner: Carol Kussmaul   Est: 1994

Fulfill your creative destiny with our select fabrics, patterns, classes, and personalized assistance. Silk Ribbon also available.

Austin, TX #16

Gem Fabrics

Mon, Tues, Thur 10 - 8 Wed, Fri, Sat 10 - 6 Sun 12 - 5

13776 Hwy. 183 N. #142
(512) 258-8061   78750
Owners: Dorothy & Reynolds
Est: 1968 2400 sq.ft.   Bixler
2000 Bolts

Beautiful Fabrics, Books, Patterns, Helpful Tools, Lots of Classes, Authorized Dealer: New Home & Viking

Boerne, TX #17

Sew Special

Mon - Sat 9 - 5 Sun 12 - 5

112 South Main Street   78006
(210) 249-8038
Owners: Three Quilting Nuts !
Est: 1987   1800 sq.ft.   1200 Bolts

"The Best Little Quilt Shop by a Country Smile" Cottons, books, patterns, notions, classes, & Help ! Ask about our Fabric Club.

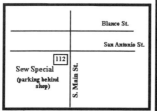

Boerne, TX #18

Thimble & Thread Quilt Shop

Mon - Sat 9 - 5 Thur til 8

195 S. Main #B   78006
(210) 249-9733
Owner: Jim Carlson & Linda Petrey Carlson
Est: 1994   1800 sq.ft.

A complete Quilt Shop! We offer 100% cotton Fabric, Quilting Notions, Books, Patterns and Classes Expert Staff.

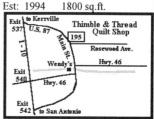

Converse, TX #19

General Store/ Quilt Studio

Tues - Fri 1 - 5 Sat 10 - 3

305 S. Seguin   78109
(210) 659-7278
Owners: Rosalie & Les Bourland
Est: 1985   2094 sq.ft.

400 Bolts 100% Cotton Fabric, Books, Patterns, Quilt Frames, Batting and other supplies. Quilt Classes.

Freeport, TX #20

Pat's Quilts & Crafts

If We're Home, We're Open Or By Appt.

1822 N. Ave. I   77541
(409) 233-8900   Est: 1982
Owner: Pat Lamont

Large selection of new handmade and machine made antique replica Quilts. Quilts from the Ozarks, Butch, Amish and More. Old Glassware & Dolls Too.

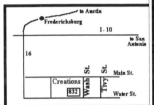

San Antonio, TX #23

Bernina - New Home Sewing Center

11755 West Ave.   78216
(210) 344-0791
Owners: Terry & Vince Soll

Mon - Sat
9:30 - 6
Day &
Evening
Classes

Beautiful fabric.
Books & patterns.
Quilt & Sewing
Machine Acc.
Threads. Sewing &
Embroidery,
Machines. Sergers.
Heirloom Lace

San Antonio, TX #24

Seventh Heaven

Formerly Page's   5860 Hwy 87 E.
(210) 648-1381   78222
Owner: Dixie Bradbury   Est: 1990
3600 sq.ft.   1000 Bolts

Mon - Fri
9 - 5:30
Sat 9 - 3

Heavenly delight
Fabrics, Supplies.
Hoffman, RJR,
Debbie Mumm,
P&B, Fabriquilt.
Patterns, Books
Singer Sewing
Machines.

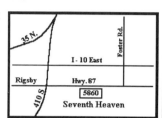

San Antonio, TX #25

Las Colchas

110 Ogden St.   78212
(210) 223-2405

Tue - Sat
10 - 5
Tue &
Thur til 7

100% Cotton
Fabrics -
checks, plaids,
Homespuns.
Supplies & Classes
Patterns, Books,
Kits. Year Round
Christmas Room
all in a cozy
Victorian House.

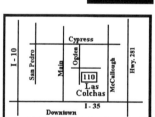

Corpus Christi, TX #26

The Quilt Cottage

5433 S. Staples Switch   78411
(512) 985-0908
Owner: Lynda Butler   Est: 1994
1600 sq.ft.

Mon - Fri
10 - 6
Sat 10 - 5

A very warm &
friendly shop.
We have over
1500 bolts all
cotton fabric.
Loads of Books,
Patterns, Notions,
Classes, etc.
Professional
Machine Quilting

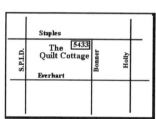

Corpus Christi, TX #27

The Quilt Bee

Mon - Fri
9 - 5
Sat 9 - 3

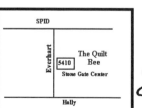

Your Complete Quilting Shop

5410 Everhart   78411
(512) 992-4515
Est: 1990   1200 sq.ft.
Owners: Sue Howe & Lynette Gonzalez

The Newest Patterns, Notions, and Fabric. The Quilt Bee has the largest book supply in South Texas. Classes - Quilts, Quilted Clothing, Dolls and Techniques

MAKE A QUILT...TAKE TIME FOR THINGS THAT MATTER

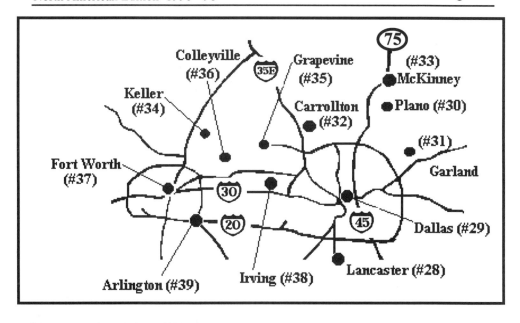

12 Featured Shops

FORT WORTH DALLAS AREA

Lancaster, TX   #28

Quilter's Corner

Mon - Sat
10 - 5:30

125 Historic Town Square
(214) 227-6282   75146
Owner: Martha Walker
Est: 1993   2000 sq.ft.

Best Little Fabric
Store in Texas.
Fabrics Galore:
Books Abound:
Patterns for You:
Classes for All.

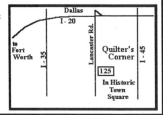

Dallas, TX   #29

Quiltmakers

Mon 10 -7
Tues - Sat
10 - 5

9658 Plano Rd.   75238
(214) 343-1440
Owners: Lynn Harkins & Ann Deane
Est: 1994   1000 sq.ft.

Fabrics for that
special quilt.
Books with the
latest techniques.
Patterns,
Notions, and
Gadgets.

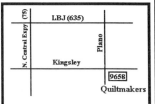

Country Calicos

Plano, TX #30

701 E. Plano Pkwy. #110
(214) 423-2499   75074
Owner: Betty Woods
Est: 1989   3400 sq.ft.   1200 Bolts

Mon - Fri 9 - 6
Sat 10 - 5
Sun 1 - 5

Quilting books, notions, and fabrics.
Hand made hammered and mountain
dulcimers and recordings. Wide
selection of classes on quilting and
other fabric related crafts.

L-75 | Ave. G | | Ave. K
| | 15th St. |
Country Calicos | Ave. J | 14th St. |
701 |
E. Plano Parkway

Garland, TX #31

Suzy's

Mon - Fri
10 - 5
Sat 10 - 3

111 North 6th   75040
(214) 272-8180
Owner: Suzanne Cook
Est: 1989   4200 sq.ft.

A Complete
Quilt Shop
Gifts &
Accessories
Candles, Classes

Belt Line
Walnut Hill   Suzy's
111   Town Square
Main St.
Garland Rd.

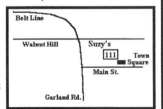

Carrollton, TX #32

The Old Craft Store

Mon - Sat
10 - 5
Thurs til 7

1110 W. Main Street   75006
(214) 242-9111
Owner: Melba Hamrick
Est: 1971 3000 sq.ft.   2500 Bolts

100% Cottons,
full-service quilt
shop. Patterns,
notions - nestled
among antiques
& old-fashioned
U.S. Post Office.

I - 35 N
Belt Line Rd.
Elm
The Old
1110 Craft Store
Main St.
Dallas
15 Minutes from Dallas

Keller, TX #34

Grandma's Quilts

**Mon - Fri
10 - 6
Sat 10 - 3**

111 W. Vine St 76248
(817) 431-1348
(800) 305-5547
Owner: Helen L.
   Madden
Est: 1991

100% Cotton
Fabrics for
Quilters. Notions,
Patterns, Books,
Etc. Etc.

Grapevine, TX #35

2-Sisters' Quilts
and Other Stuff

**Mon - Fri
10 - 6
Sat 10 - 5
Sun 12 - 5**

408 S. Main   76051
(817) 488-0144   2400 sq.ft.
Owners: Linda Morrell & Janet Warner
1 exit from DFW airport

10 minutes from
airport. Over
2000 bolts of
fabric. Friendly,
knowledgeable
staff. Classes,
Notions, Gifts &
Quilts

Colleyville, TX #36

The Calico Cupboard

**Mon - Fri
8:30 - 5
Thurs til 8
Sat 10 - 4**

6409 Colleyville Blvd   76034
(10 min. from DFW airport)
(817) 481-7105
Owner: Judy Linn   Est: 1984

2000 sq.ft. of:
- 100% Cotton
  Fabrics
- Quilting
  Supplies
- Call for Class
  Schedule

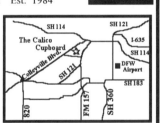

Ft. Worth, TX #37

Quilter's Emporium

**Mon - Fri
10 - 5:30
Sat 10 - 3
Sun and eves
during Classes**

3526 W. Vickery Blvd.   76107
(817) 377-3993   Est: 1993
Owners: Pam Durham & Robin
5000 sq.ft.   Tyler

Complete line of
quilting supplies
& fabric;
Antique furniture;
Vintage jewelry;
Clothing;
Gifts

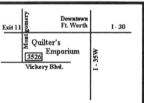

Irving, TX #38

Quilting Etc.

**Mon - Fri
10 - 6
Sat 10 - 5**

1111 W. Airport Frwy.   75062
(214) 570-4458
Owner: T J Tamny
Est: 1992   2300 sq.ft.

Fabric,
Patterns,
Notions,
Gifts, Classes.
5 miles from
DFW Airport!

Arlington, TX #39

Sewing Machine Museum

**Mon - Sat
10 - 5**

804 W. Abram St.   76013
America's First   (817) 275-0971
Sewing Machine   Owners: Frank & Halaina Smith
Museum.
We sell "Feather
Weights" and the new
replica "Little John"
30 Years in the
Making. 8 Years at
present location.
156 machines
displayed from 1853

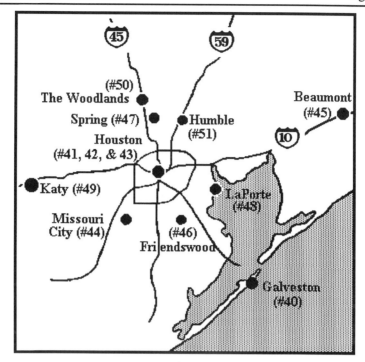

HOUSTON AREA
12 Featured Shops

Galveston, TX #40

Mon - Sat   10 - 5:30
Thur til 9

Quilts by the Bay

5923 Stewart Rd.   77551
(409) 740-9296   Est: 1991
Owner: Patricia Stephenson
2500 sq.ft.   1500 Bolts

Charming shop
by Galveston Bay with top quality
fabrics, classes, notions, &
unique gifts for every occasion.

Houston, TX #41

Great Expectations

14520 Memorial Drive Suite #54
(713) 496-1366   77079
Owner: Karey Bresenhan
Est: 1974

Mon - Fri 10 - 6
Sat 10 - 5

Largest selection of Quilts in the City. Large selection of Fabric, Books, Notions & Patterns. Quilting Classes.

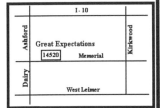

Friendships like Quilts are made one Stitch at a Time.

Houston, TX #42

Sew Contempo

18123 Egret Bay Blvd.
(713) 333-5322   77058
Est: 1978   3000 sq.ft.

Mon - Fri 9:30 - 6
Thur til 8
Sat 9:30 - 5:30

South of Houston near NASA. Specializing in Quilting and Wearable Arts, Silk Ribbon and Smocking Supplies. Bernina sewing machines. Friendly Service!

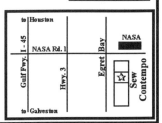

Quilt Quarters — 2 Locations!

Houston, TX #43   ## Missouri City, TX #44

1410 B Blalock   77055
Off I - 10
(713) 468-5886
Est: 1986   2400 sq.ft.
Owner: Kay Tanner

Mon 10 - 9
Tues - Sat 10 - 4

3340 FM 1092   77459
6½ mi. S of Hwy. 59 &
1 block N of Hwy 6
(713) 499-0541
Est: 1995   1200 sq.ft.

Mon - Sat 10 - 4:30

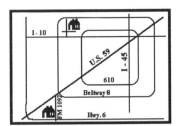

Friendly, helpful, All cotton fabrics, large book & stencil selection, silk ribbon supplies. Services: Restoration & Repair, Appraisals, Basting. Let us quilt your top.

Beaumont, TX #45

Mon - Fri 10 - 5   Sat 10 - 3

3677 Calder Ave.   77706
(409) 835-4736
Owner: Noel Ann McCord

The Piecemaker

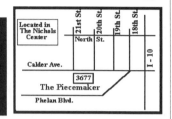

Located in The Nichols Center

21st St. 20th St. 19th St. 18th St.

North St.

Calder Ave.

3677
The Piecemaker

Phelan Blvd.

I - 10

**Fabrics — 100% Cottons
Patterns, Books, Notions.
Silk Ribbon, Cross-Stitch and
Needlepoint Supplies.**

Friendswood, TX #46

Quakertown Quilts

Mon - Fri
10 - 5
Tues til 7
Thur til 5:30
Sat 10 - 4

607 S. Friendswood Dr. 77546
(713) 996-1756
Owner: Pat Bishop
Est: 1988   3000 sq.ft.

Complete Quilt
Shop.
1400+ bolts of
cotton fabric.
Books, Patterns,
Notions &
Gift Items

S. Friendswood Dr.

to Houston

FM 2351

I - 45

Quakertown
Quilts
607

Texas Commerce Bank   to Galveston

Juliene's Quilts

Spring, TX #47

26303 Preston #B & C   77373
(713) 355-9820
Owners: Juliene & John Pickens
Est: 1993   2400 sq.ft.

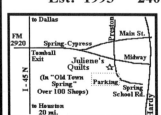

to Dallas

FM 2920

Spring-Cypress

Temball Exit

Juliene's Quilts

(In "Old Town Spring" Over 100 Shops)

Preston

Main St.

Midway

Parking

Spring School Rd.

Hardy

to Houston 20 mi.

Tues - Sat
10 - 5
Thur til 8
Sun 12 - 5

- • Fabrics, Patterns, Notions
- • Quilt Frames, Racks,
    Hoops & Hangers
- • Hand Quilting
- • Classes or Individual Instruction
- • Hand Guided Machine Quilting
    (Pantograph, Outlining or Freehand)
    Send Us Your Tops
- • Quilted Gifts, Collectibles
- • Collector Thimbles
- • Located in Old Town Spring

La Porte, TX #48

The Painted Pony 'N Quilts

1015 S. Broadway   77571
(713) 471-5735   Est: 1986
Owner: Sherrie S. Thomas

**Mon - Sat
10 - 5**

2500+ top name quilting fabrics. Extensive selection Reproductions, Plaids, Notions, Gifts. Knowledgeable, friendly staff to assist in all areas.

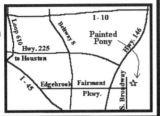

Katy, TX #49

Quilt 'n Sew Studio

1841 N. Mason Rd.   77449
(713) 347-0470   Est: 1993
Owners: Chaille Voelkel &
3550 sq.ft.   Beverly Williams

**Mon 10 - 7:30
Tues - Fri
10 - 4:30
Sat 10 - 3**

100% cotton Fabrics, Quilting supplies, books, patterns, kits, classes (kids too!). We Quilt - Quilt Tops in the Shop! Quilting Machines.

The Woodlands, TX #50

Plain & Fancy

418 Sawdust Rd.   77380
(713) 367-1021
Owner: Sandra Contestabile

**Mon - Sat
9 - 5**

Largest Selection of Fabric in Houston

Humble, TX #51

It's A Stitch

(713) 446-4999
9759 FM 1960 Bypass
77338
Owners: Judy & John Curtis
Est: 1992   3000 sq.ft.

**Mon - Fri
10 - 5:30
Sat 10 - 5
Sun 12 - 5**

♦ Large selection of quilting fabrics
♦ Patterns, books, notions
♦ Classes
♦ Bernina and Bernette sewing machines & sergers

Texas Guilds:
Cotton Patch Quilt Guild, Contact: Debbie Hagar (903) 883-4230
McKinney Quilter's Guild, Contact: Peggy Tomlinson (214) 548-2762
Denton Quilt Guild, Contact: Billie Ingram (817) 382-3806
Allen's Quilters Guild, Contact: Marcia Baker (214) 517-7556
High Plains Quilters Guild, 2433 I-40 West, Amarillo, 79109
Quilters Guild of Dallas, 15775 N. Hillcrest, Dallas, 75248
Dayton Quilt Guild, Inc., P.O. Box 231, Dayton, 77535
Bay Area Quilt Guild, 1094 Scarsdale Box M237, Houston, 77089
Lampasas Quilt Guild, 303 South Western, Lampasas, 76550
Keystone Square Quilters, 410 E. 3rd St., Lampasas, 76550
Red River Quilter Guild, Rt. 1, Box 504, Nocona
Quilters Guild of Plano, P.O. Box 260216, Plano, 75026
Greater San Antonio QG, P.O. Box 65124, San Antonio, 78265
Wildflower Quilt Guild, 902 S. 3rd., Temple
Homespun Quilters Guild, 5009 Lake Highlands Drive, Waco, 76710

Other Shops in Texas:

Abilene	Country Pleasures, 2508 S. 7th
Arlington	Quilted Hearts & Co., 1205 S. Bowen Rd.
Arlington	Nostalgia Quilts, 1210 W. Abram St.
Austin	Quilts 'N Things, 4406 Burnet Rd.
Austin	Country Quilting, 10209-A FM 812
Austin	The Quilt Store, 3309 Hancock Dr. (moving)
Brashear	Quilts Galore & More, 1 Main St.
Brenham	Country Needlecrafts, 207 W. Alamo
Caldwell	My Spare Time, Rt. 3 Box 264
Comanche	Quilts & Tops, 605 E. Central Ave.
Dallas	The Copper Lamp, 5500 Greenville Ave.
Denison	Mom's Quilts, 14316 S. Armstrong Ave.
Fort Worth	Cherrie's Quilt Shop, 4320 Wichita St.
Fort Worth	Berry Patch Fabrics, 4995 S. Hulen St.
Houston Galleria	'N Calicos Too, 10115 Hammerly
Kosse	The Quilt Patch, P.O. Box 158
Laredo	Victoria's Chest, 907 Zaragoza
Lewisville	The Pepper Tree, 112 W. Main St.
Lockney	The Old Blue Quilt Box, 200 S. Main St.
Lufkin	Country Quilting & More, 1200 S. 1st. St.
Marble Falls	Blue Bonnet Designs, 1011 Ave. G
McAllen	Vivian's Little Quilt Shop, 527 N. 8th
Memphis	Greene Dry Goods Company, 109 S. 6th St.
Midland	The Needle Nook, 3211 W. Wadley Ave.
Pasadena	The Fabric Hut, 2232 Strawberry
Pittsburg	Quilts & More, R.R. #4, P.O. Box 264
Plano	Plano Sewing Center, 2129 B W. Parker Rd.
Richardson	The Fabric Affair, 339 Dal-Rich Village
Richardson	Kay Fabrics, 518 W. Arapaho Rd.
Rockport	Golden Needles, 701 N. Alan
Spearman	Country Stitches, 512 S. Townsend St.
Sulphur Springs	Sew Many Quilts, 631 N. Davis
Sunrise Beach	Patches, 103 Sunrise Dr.
Tyler	Granny's Needle Haus, 6004 S. Broadway
Webster	Fabrics Etcetera, 571 W. Bay Area Blvd.
Wichita Falls	Sewin' In Style, 4708 K-Mart Dr. #G

QUILT POX

Very Contagious

Symptoms wrinkles up nose when a quilt is referred to as a 'blanket', constant need for the warmth provided by a handmade quilt. Seems to wander around in a daze not hearing others when considering the next project. Always seems to be carrying something in a pillow case. Often heard mumbling: "fat quarter", "1/4 inch seam allowance", or "where did I get this material?". Has been known to attack people mistreating quilts.

The Only Hope

Make as much time for quilting as possible.

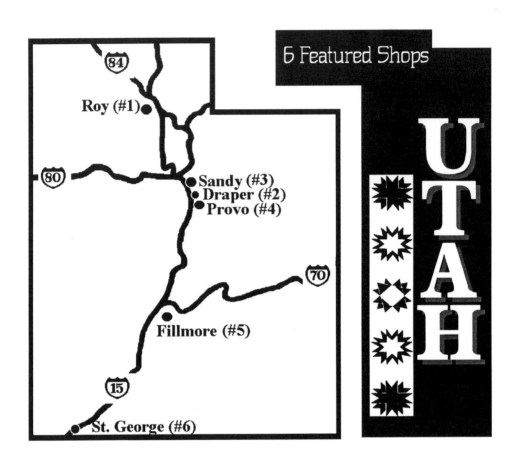

6 Featured Shops

UTAH

Roy (#1)
Sandy (#3)
Draper (#2)
Provo (#4)
Fillmore (#5)
St. George (#6)

Roy, UT   #1

Marlene's Quilts

Everyday 9 - 9 Please Call First

3118 West 5200 South   84067
(801) 825-0547
Owner: Marlene Larsen
Est: 1982

Stock Approx.
100 quilts - also
do special orders
- I work out of
my house so
calling first is
helpful.

3100 West   3118
Marlene's
Quilts   5200
South
5600 South
Roy Exit

Draper, UT   #2

Thimbles and Threads

Mon - Sat 10 - 5

12660 S. Fort St.   84020
(801) 576-0390   Est: 1994   1200 Bolts
Delightful country   Owner: Dana Moffat
setting 25 min. South
of S.L.C.
Knowledgeable
friendly Quilting
Staff, Inspiring Quilt
Samples, 100%
Cotton Fabrics, all the
latest books &
supplies.

12300 South   900 E.
12400 South
I - 15   Fort St.
Thimbles and
Threads   ☆

Quilt, Quilt, Quilt Etc.

11 East Main   84070   (8720 South at State)

(801) 255-2666

Owner: Dorthey Chase   Est: 1988   3000 sq.ft.

Notions—all the latest
Books—all the newest
Patterns—one of the best selections you've seen
Frames,   Classes

**Weekdays
10 - 9
Saturdays
10 - 5**

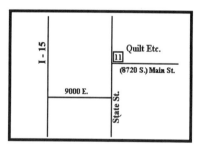

I - 15 | Quilt Etc.
11 (8720 S.) Main St.
9000 E. | State St.

Sandy, UT   #3

15 Minutes South of Salt Lake City

Over 8000 Bolts of Fabric

Provo, UT #4

The Stitching Corner

Mon - Sat
10 - 6

480 N Freedom Blvd.   84601
(801) 374-1200
Owner: Scott Blackham
Est: 1990   3500 sq.ft.

Pfaff authorized
dealer;
3000+ bolts of
cotton; classes daily;
quilting notions,
patterns, threads.
Knowledgeable
Quilters.

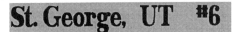

Fillmore, UT #5

Territorial Statehouse State Park

Daily
9 - 5

P.O. Box 657   84631
(801) 743-5316
Est: 1930

First capitol
building of
Utah. Pioneer
Quilts on
display. Quilt
show annually.

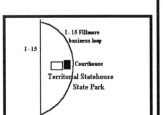

St. George, UT #6

Pieceful Treasures
— Quilt Shop —

**28 E. Tabernacle
Historic District
(801) 674-1069**
Owner: Judy Butler
Est: 1993

- Handmade Quilts & Pillows
- Quilt Frames & Supplies
- 100% Cotton Fabric by the Yard
- Quilting Books & Patterns
- Classes in Quilting & Brazilian Emb.
- Homemade Fudge!

We feature "Goose Bump Creations©"
Patterns for perfectly puffy comforters
and tree skirts. Easy and all done by
machine. Phone orders welcomed!

Step Back in time When You Visit Our Shop.

Mon - Fri 9 - 5   Sat 10 - 4

Housed in an
1895 building

Heirloom Quilt:
a hand-me-down
you're glad to keep.

Utah State Guild:
Utah Quilt Guild, P.O. Box 17032, Salt Lake City, 84117

Utah Guilds:
Ogden Quilt Guild, 340 N. Washington Blvd, Ogden, 84404
Roy Pioneer Quilters, 4232 S. 2275 West, Roy, 84067
Dixie Quilt Guild, P.O. Box 507, St. George, 84771

Other Shops in Utah:

Cedar City	Country Fabrics, 169 N 100 W
Delta	Mom's Crafts and Fabrics, 313 S. 100 W
Layton	Nuttalls' Crazy Quilt Shop, 21 E. Gentile St.
Logan	Needles N Neighbors, 128 S. 1170 E
Logan	Grandma's Quilts, 93 E. 100 S.
Ogden	Gardiner's Sewing, 2233 Grant Ave.
Ogden	Fibers & Twigs, 159 23rd
Orem	Fabric Mill, 390 E 1300 S
Providence	The Quilt House, 135 S. 100 E
Provo	The Cotton Shop, 86 West Center
Provo	Fabric Mill, 90 W. Center St.
Richfield	Marcia's, 44 W 100 N
Salt Lake City	Quilter's Patch, 2370 S. 3600 W.
Salt Lake City	Gentler Times Shop, 4880 S. Highland Circle
Salt Lake City	The Grace Co.-Quilting Frames, 801 W 1850 S
Salt Lake City	Mormon Handicraft, 105 North Main
Salt Lake City	Lily Rogers Heirloom Quilts, 602 E 500 S
Sandy	Fabric Warehouse, 9251 S 700 E
Sandy	The Cotton Shop, 9441 South 700 East
Sandy	Bernina, 688 E. 9450 S
Tremonton	La Rue's Country Quilts, 10 N 100 W
Vernal	Golden Needle Stitchery, 684 W. Main St.
West Jordan	Fabric Center, 1633 W. 9000 S
West Jordan	Village Quilt Shop, 1095 W 7800 S

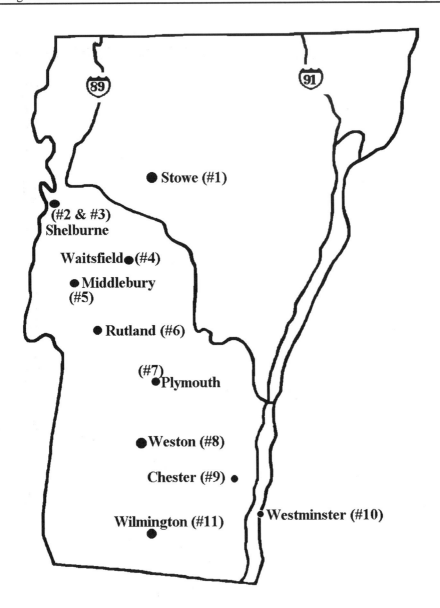

● Stowe (#1)

●
(#2 & #3)
Shelburne

Waitsfield●(#4)

●Middlebury
(#5)

● Rutland (#6)

(#7)
●Plymouth

●Weston (#8)

Chester (#9) ●

Wilmington (#11)   ●Westminster (#10)
●

Stowe, VT #1

Prints & Patches

Mon - Sat 10 - 5

Main St., P.O. Box 1205   05672
(802) 253-8643
Owner: Mary Johnson
          Est: 1979   1400 sq.ft.

Come on into our Retail shop in Stowe, where we create our own Vermont quilts. Antique & Hand quilted quilts also.

Hwy 108
Hwy 100
Stowe
to Burlington
Prints & Patches
on Main Street
I-89
Waterbury
to Montpelier

Shelburne, VT #2

Quiltsmith

**Mon - Sat 10 - 5
Sunday
Call First**

(802) 985-3688 or 863-3252
Est: 1981   2400 sq.ft.
Owner: Julie Sopher

Everything for the Quilter:
Fabric, Books & Notions. Also ribbon embroidery, crewel & needlepoint supplies. Vermont's largest collection of decorative stencils.

We May be Moving Please Call for Location or Shelburne is quite small; look for us in the Tennybrook Sq. or Shelburne Village.

Shelburne, VT #3

Hearthside Quilts

**Mon - Sat 9:30 - 5:30
Sun 1 - 5**

2048 Shelburne Rd.   05482
(800) 451-3533   Est: 1981
Owner: Peter Coleman
                300+ Bolts   Catalog $2

Complete line of PRE-CUT Patchwork & Appliqué Quilt Kits. Choose your own colors for your kit and we'll cut it right on the spot for you.

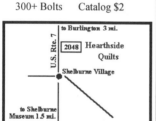

to Burlington 3 mi.
U.S. Rte. 7
2048 Hearthside Quilts
Shelburne Village
to Shelburne Museum 1.5 mi.

Waitsfield, VT #4

Cabin Fever Quilts

Mon & Wed - Sat 10 - 5

The Old Church   Route 100
P.O. Box 443   05673
(802) 496-2287   Est: 1976
Owner: Vee Lowell
               1200 Sq.ft.

Cabin Fever Quilts offers Amish/Mennonite hand quilted quilts plus custom made tied comforters. Fabric, Quilting Supplies, Quilt Kits & much more!

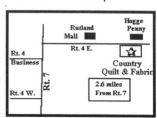

Rt. 2
I-89
River
100
100B
Moretown
Montpelier
Cabin Fever Quilts in the Old Church
100
Waitsfield
Irasville
15 miles from I-89

Middlebury, VT #5

Charlotte's Collections

Mon - Sat 10 - 5

3 Merchants Row   05753
(802) 388-3895
Owner: Charlotte Fisk   Est: 1989

Full service Quilt Shop. Hoffman our Specialty. Metrosene Threads. In-Stock Quilts. Knitting Yarns & Supplies.

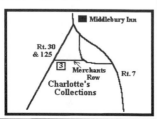

Middlebury Inn
Rt. 30 & 125
3 Merchants Row
Rt. 7
Charlotte's Collections

Rutland, VT #6

Country Quilt & Fabric

**Mon - Sat 9:30 - 5
Sun 12 - 5**

R.R. #3 (Rt. 4 E.)   Box 7352
(802) 773-3470   05701
Owners: Pat & Lynne Benard
             Est: 1982   1400 sq.ft.

3000+ bolts of 100% cotton fabrics -- Hoffman, South Seas, P&B, RJR, plus notions, Books & Patterns Custom Orders too

Rutland Mall
Hogge Penny
Rt. 4 E.
Rt. 4 Business
Country Quilt & Fabric
Rt. 7
Rt. 4 W.
2.6 miles From Rt. 7

Plymouth, VT #7

Calvin Coolidge Birthplace

Plymouth Notch Historic District
(802) 672-3773   Est: 1956
P.O. Box 247   05056
10 Museums
Buildings

**Daily
Late May -
mid Oct
9:30 -
5:30**

Several late 19th
Century Quilts on
Permanent
exhibition.
Including one
pieced by Calvin
Coolidge when he
was 10 years old.
(Tumbling Blocks)

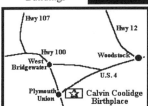

Weston, VT #8

Weston House

Route 100,   P.O. Box 82
(802) 824-3636   05161
Owners: Joanne & Richard Eggert
Quilting Supplies,   Est: 1978   1500 sq.ft.
books and   650+ Bolts
patterns. Huge
selection of yard
goods--including
Roberta Horton's
"LINES" fabrics.
Finished Quilts,
wallhangings,
pillows too!

**June - Oct
7 days 10-5
Nov - May
Fri - Mon
10 - 5**

Chester, VT #9

Country Treasures

"On the Green"   P.O. Box 994
(802) 875-4377   05143
E mail: countrytreasures@ubu-online.com
http://www.vbv-online.com/countrytreasure.htm
Est: 1990   1700 sq.ft.   900 Bolts

**Wed - Sat
10 - 5
Sun 12 - 4
Extended
Hours During
Foliage Season**

The Quiltmaker will
discover a fine selection
of patterns, books, fabric
and homespun. Our gift
line includes folk art,
wall hangings, dried
flowers and VT Maple
Syrup. Sponsor of "Quilts
Around the Town"

Westminster, VT #10

Quilt-a-way

540 Back Westminster Rd.
(802) 722-4743   05159
Owner: Carol Coski
600 sq.ft.
600+ Bolts

**M, T, Th, F
12 - 4
Other Times
by Chance
or Appt.**

"She who dies
with the most
fabric wins!"
Every day is a
sale day & we
discount
everything
we sell.

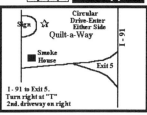

Wilmington, VT #11

Norton House

1836 Country Store Village Box 579
(802) 464-7213   05363
Owner: Suzanne Wells Wurzberger
Est: 1967
1600 sq.ft.   Catalog 50¢

**7 Days
a Week
9 - 5**

**A Quilter's
Paradise !**
Enormous collection of
100% Cotton including
designer Hoffman
Fabrics. Books-
Pattern-Notions-
Needlework-Candles-
Gifts-Sale Tables

WHITE ELM

TULIP TREE

WHITE OAK

PIN OAK

RED OAK

BUR OAK

Vermont Guilds:

Oxbee Quilter's Guild, P.O. Box 148, Bradford, 05033

Heart of the Land Quilter's Guild, R.R. #1 Box 263,
     Hartland, 05048

Green Mt. Quilters State Guild, P.O. Box 56,
     Fairfax, 05454

Maple Leaf Quilter's Guild, Box 7400, Mendon, 05701

Champlain Valley Quilt Guild, 2011 Tenneybrook
     Square, Shelburne, 05482

Other Shops in Vermont:

Bennington	Quilters World Plus, 244 North St.
Brattleboro	Carriage House Comforters, 169 Main
Cuttingsville	Vermont Patchworks, Old Plymouth Rd. N
Johnson	Cooper Hill Quiltworks, Clay Hill Rd.
Johnson	Broadwoven Fabric Mill, R.R. # 2
Newfane	Newfane Country Store, Route 30
North Clarendon	Quilt Barn of Vermont, 286 East St.
Wardsboro	Anton of Vermont, Rt. 100
Winooski	Yankee Pride, Champlain Mill
Woodstock	Log Cabin Quilts, 9 Central St.

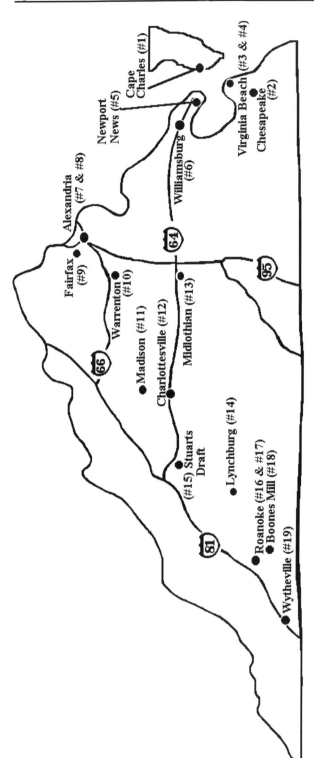

VIRGINIA

19 Featured Shops

Cape Charles (#1)

Newport News (#5)

Virginia Beach (#3 & #4)

Chesapeake (#2)

Williamsburg (#6)

Alexandria (#7 & #8)

64

95

Fairfax (#9)

Warrenton (#10)

Madison (#11)

Charlottesville (#12)

Midlothian (#13)

66

Lynchburg (#14)

Stuarts Draft (#15)

Roanoke (#16 & #17)

Boones Mill (#18)

81

Wytheville (#19)

Cape Charles, VA #1

Quilts & More

Mon - Sat
10 - 5

315 Mason Avenue   23310
(804) 331- 3642
Owner: Henrietta Morris
Est: 1990   600 sq.ft.

Quilts, other handmade items by owner. Quilting, X-stitch craft supplies. Fabrics of all kinds, patterns, notions and more.

Chesapeake, VA #2

Sis 'N Me Quilt Shoppe

Mon - Fri
10 - 6
Thur til 8
Sat 10 - 5
Sun 12 - 4

3361 Western Branch Blvd. (Hwy 17)
(804) 686-2050   23321
Owner: Carole King   Est: 1987
2000 sq.ft.   1500 Bolts

Large selection of 100% cotton Fabrics, Books, Notions, Patterns, Stencils, "Quilter's Cotton" Batting, Prismatic Foil (Glitz Magic) Classes. Mail Order

Virginia Beach, VA #3

Quilt Country Fabrics

Mon - Sat
10 - 6
Thur til 8
Sun 12 - 5

Hilltop East Shopping Center #164
(757) 437-5395
Owner: Norma Lancaster
Est: 1994   1200 sq.ft.
First Colonial & Laskin Rd. Across From Piece Goods

A friendly shop with over 1000 bolts of 100% cotton fabric, notions, books, classes, patterns and thousands of fat 1/4's. Large selection of homespuns, flannel & felt.

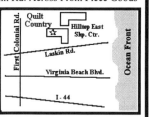

Virginia Beach, VA #4

What's Your Stitch 'N Stuff, Inc.

Mon - Sat
10 - 5
Thur til 8
Sun 12 - 4

5350 Kempsriver Dr. #104
(804) 523-2711   23464
Owners: Holly Erdei-Zuber & Irene Erdei

100% Cotton Fabrics and Thread. Books, Patterns, Notions, Beads, Silk Ribbon, Novelty Items. PLUS ALWAYS FRIENDLY SERVICE!

Newport News, VA #5

Nancy's Calico Patch

Mon - Sat
10 - 5
Sun 1- 4

21 Hiddenwood Shopping Center 23606
(804) 596-SEWS (7397)
Owner: Nancy Gloss   Est: 1987

We have fabrics, books, patterns, supplies, & classes for Quilting, Smocking, & Heirloom sewing plus Elna & Pfaff sewing machine sales & service.

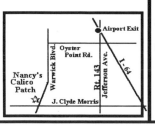

Williamsburg, VA #6

Needlecraft Corner

7 Days a Week
9 - 5

7521 Richmond Rd.   23188
(804) 564-3354   Est: 1977
Owner: Sherry & John Barnett

Over 3,000 bolts of 100% Cotton Fabrics. Home of "Granny Nanny's Quilting Gadgets" Miniature Patchwork Stamps, Impressions and patterns.

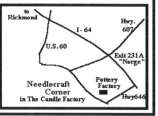

Alexandria, VA #7

Rocky Road to Kansas

Wed - Sat 11 - 5
Sun 1 - 5

215 South Union Street
(703) 683-0116   22314
Owner: Dixie Kaufman
Est: 1980   560 sq.ft.

Large Selection of Antique/Vintage Quilts. Quilt Related Items, Accessories & Gifts. A Potpourri of collectibles and interesting goods.

Alexandria, VA #8

Quilt N Stuff

Mon - Sat 10 - 5
Wed til 8

1630 King Street   22314
(703) 836-0070
Owner: Madeline Shepperson
Est: 1986   1740 sq.ft.

Bright, open shop with over 1000 bolts of cotton fabrics including African, Indonesian and Japanese Prints. Viking Sewing Machine Dealer.

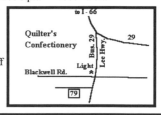

Fairfax, VA #9

The Quilt Patch

Mon - Sat 10 - 5
Thur til 8

3932 Old Lee Hwy.   22030
(703) 273-6937
Owner: Leslie Pfeifer   Est: 1974

Over 2000 bolts 100% cotton fabrics. Hundreds of book titles. Notions, patterns, stencils, classes, friendly professional assistance.

Warrenton, VA #10

Quilter's Confectionery

Mon - Sat 9:30 - 5

79 W. Lee Hwy.   22186
(540) 347-3631
Owner: Karen S. Walker
Est: 1993   1200 sq.ft.   1800+ Bolts

"Candy" Shop for Quilters. No Fat No Cholesterol No Calories! Only the Good Stuff Quilts are made of. Latest Quality Merchandise.

Madison, VA #11

Little Shop of Madison

Mon - Sat 10 - 4

320 S. Main St.   P.O. Box 452
(540) 948-4147   22727
Owner: Thelma Shirley
Est: 1978   3000 sq.ft.

Hundreds of Fabrics and All other Quilters' Indulgences.

Charlottesville, VA #12

Quilter's Fare

Mon - Fri 10 - 6
Sat 10 - 4

182 Zan Rd. Seminole Sq. Shp. Ctr.
(804) 973-4422   22901
Owner: Sandy Hopkinson
Est: 1995

Specializing in the finest cottons and quilting supplies on the market today. Teaching quilting classes in the newest techniques.

Stuarts Draft, VA #15

The Candy Shop & Fern's Fabrics

Mon - Sat 10 - 5

10 Highland Drive   24477
(540) 337-0298
Owners: Tom & Connie Almarode

Est: 1983   1000 sq.ft.

Unique country store, owned & operated by Amish-Mennonite family. Beautiful quilts, fabrics, patterns, books & more. Custom orders welcome!

Roanoke, VA #16

Touch of Country

By Appt. Only

611 Greenwich Dr.   24019
(540) 362-5558
Owner: Lula Parker

Machine Quilting Service.

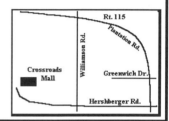

Roanoke, VA #17

The Quilting Connection

**Tues 9:30 - 6
Wed - Fri
9:30 - 4
Sat 10 - 2**

2825 Brambleton Ave.   24015
(540) 776-0794   Est: 1994
Owner: Jill Setchel   1200 sq.ft.

Catalog $5

Quality 100% Designer Cottons, Quilting Supplies, books, patterns & notions. Classes Avail. Heirloom Sewing and English Smocking. Gifts. Personal Service.

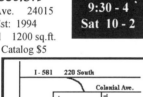

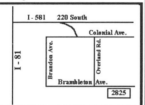

Boones Mill, VA #18

Boone's Country Store

**Tues - Sat
9:30 - 5:30**

Jubal Early Hwy.   24065
(540) 721-2478

Owners: Randy & Elva Boone
Est: 1975   3588 sq.ft

Old Fashioned Quality - Up to date Values. Calicoes, broad cloth, sheetings, quilting supplies, books, gifts. Homemade breads, pies, cakes & sweet rolls

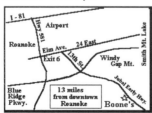

Wytheville, VA #19

Sew What Fabrics

**Mon - Sat
10 - 5:30**

155 W. Main St.   24382
(540) 228-6400
Owner: Carol C. Britt
Est: 1982   2100 sq.ft.   1400 Bolts

Wonderful cottons, books, notions, & art to wear supplies. Friendly assistance! Ask about our auto-ship programs.

Virginia Guilds:
White Oak Mountain Quilters, Dry Fork
Virginia Consortium of Quilters, Fredericksburg
Virginia Star Quilters Guild, P.O. Box 1034, Fredericksburg, 22402
Shenandoah Valley Quilters Guild, P.O. Box 913, Harrisonburg, 22801
Shenandoah Valley Quilters Guild, Keezletown
The Virginia Reel Quilters, Lynchburg
Madison County Quilters Guild, P.O. Box 452, Madison, 22727
Richmond Quilter's Guild, Richmond
Star Quilters Guild, P.O. Box 5276, Roanoke, 24012
Tidewater Quilters Guild, P.O. Box 62635, Virginia Beach, 23462
Cabin Branch Quilters, P.O. Box 1547, Woodbridge, 22193
Colonial Piecemakers, 201 Yorkview Rd., Yorktown, 23692

Other Shops in Virginia:

Bedford	Style & Stitches, P.O. Box 1185
Bristol	The Quilt Shop, 2000 Euclid Ave.
Centreville	G Street Fabrics, 5077 Westfields Blvd.
Charlottesville	Early Times Workshop, 1775 Seminole Trail, Rt. 29 N
Charlottesville	Quilts Unlimited, 1023 Emmet St. N.
Chester	The Busy Bea, 11934 Centre St. PO Box 1097
Clarksville	Patchwork House, 315 Virginia Ave., P.O. Box 1477
Dayton	Clothes Line, Hwy. 42 South, P.O. Box 70
Falls Church	Appalachian Spring, 102 W. Jefferson St.
Floyd	Schoolhouse, Rte. 8, P.O. Box 9
Fredericksburg	Quilts 'N' Treasures, 721 Caroline St.
Harrisonburg	Virginia Quilt Museum, P.O. Box 1131
Hot Springs	Quilts Unlimited, Cottage Row
Middletown	The Quilt Shop, Belle Grove Plantation, Rte. 11
Newport	Zippy Designs, R.R. #1, Box 187M
Radford	Sew Biz, 92 Harvey St.
Reston	Appalachian Spring, 11877 Market St.
Stafford	The Quilt Block, 1228 Washington Dr.
Vienna	Le-Petite-Coquillage, 109 Park St. N.E.
Vinton	The Cotton Gin, 905 Hardy Rd.
Virginia Beach	Quilt Works, 3101Silina Dr. #101
Williamsburg	Quilts Unlimited, 440A Duke of Gloucester St.
Williamsburg	Fabrics Unique, 6510 Richmond Rd.

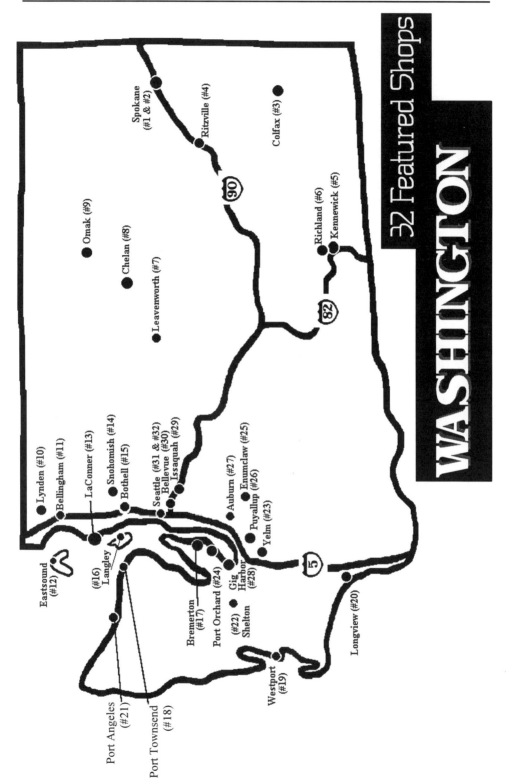

32 Featured Shops

WASHINGTON

Spokane (#1 & #2)
Ritzville (#4)
Colfax (#3)
90
Richland (#6)
Kennewick (#5)
82
Omak (#9)
Chelan (#8)
Leavenworth (#7)
Lynden (#10)
Bellingham (#11)
LaConner (#13)
Snohomish (#14)
Bothell (#15)
Seattle (#31 & #32)
Bellevue (#30)
Issaquah (#29)
Auburn (#27)
Enumclaw (#25)
Puyallup (#26)
Yelm (#23)
5
Eastsound (#12)
(#16) Langley
Bremerton (#17)
Port Orchard (#24)
Gig Harbor (#28)
(#22) Shelton
Longview (#20)
Port Angeles (#21)
Port Townsend (#18)
Westport (#19)

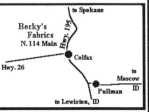

Ritzville, WA #4

Garden Gate Quilt Shop

**Mon - Sat
10 - 5**

213 W. Main   99169
(509) 659-1370

A fun quilt shop that features traditional to contemporary quilts and wall hangings. Beautiful fabrics to purchase and every quilt book imaginable.

Owner: Celia Benzel   500 Bolts

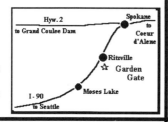

Kennewick, WA #5

Pieceable Dry Goods

**Mon - Fri
10 - 5:30
Sat 10 - 5**

5215 W. Clearwater
(509) 735-6080   Est: 1991
Owners: Terry Guizzo &
1800 sq.ft.   Barbara Ward

**The Quilter's
Dream
Come True!**
With a full line of Quilting supplies, classes and Great Service.

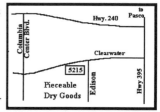

Richland, WA #6

Quiltmania

**Mon - Thur
10 - 9
Fri & Sat
10 - 5**

248 Williams   99352
(905) 946-PINS (7467)
Owner: Debi Merhar
Est: 1991   1000 Bolts

Classes, Notions, Fabric. Over 400 book titles to choose from.

Leavenworth, WA #7

Dee's Country Accents

**All Year
9 a.m. to
8 p.m.**

917 Commercial St.   98826
(800) 829-5311
Owners: Dee & Al Howie
            Est: 1987   1500 Bolts

Incredible Fabrics, Largest selection in the Pacific Northwest of Quilt Books and Patterns. PLUS a Bed & Breakfast decorated with quilts and antiques.

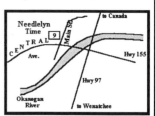

Chelan, WA #8

Woven Threads

**Mon - Sat
9:30 - 5:30**

115 S. Emerson   98816
(509) 682-7714   Est: 1995
Owner: Rose Buhl

We carry a complete line of Books, Patterns & Notions. !00% cotton fabrics. Gifts. Classes. Free Newsletter

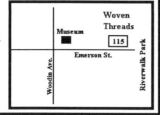

Omak, WA #9

Needlelyn Time

**Mon - Sat
9 - 6
Sun 12 - 4**

9 North Main   98841
(509) 826-1198
Owner: Lyn Hruska
Est: 1986   3000 sq.ft.   1900 Bolts

Fabrics, Notions, Quilting Supplies. Sewing Machines and Cross-Stitch Supplies. Also Classes.

Lynden, WA #10

Fabric Cottage

**Mon - Sat
9 - 5:30**

510 Front St.   98264
(360) 354-5566   Est: 1979
Owner: Grace Mulder   2500 sq.ft.

Lynden's greatest selection for the enthusiastic quilter and crafter. Wonderful samples to inspire you. A friendly staff to help you.

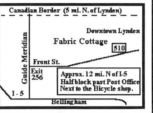

Bellingham, WA #11

Quilt Basket
A Quilter's Haven

**Mon - Sat
10 - 5:30
Sun 12 - 5**

336 36th St.   98225   Est: 1977
(360) 734-7080   1500 sq.ft.
Owners: Lynda Johnson & Jyl Peterson

Over 650 bolts of 100% cottons. Books, patterns, notions, gift items Classes Kids Play Area.

Eastsound, WA #12

Poppies

**Mon - Sat
10 - 5**

11 "A" St.
P.O. Box 1075
(360) 376-2686   98245   Est: 1993
Owner: Ruth Vandestraat 1000 sq.ft. 1000 Bolts

On Lovely Orcas Island — A Complete Quilting Shop plus Yarn, Stitchery, Kits, Notions. Across from the Post Office.

LaConner, WA #13

Creighton's Quilts

**Open Daily
Tues by
Chance**

2 Locations: 705 B S. 1st St.
503 E. Morris St.
(in the Morris St. Antique Mall)
(360) 466-5504   Est: 1988
Owner: Ann Bodle-Nash   Free Newsletter

Antique and New Amish quilts for sale: also quilting books, notions, countrywares, folk art, & braided rugs. Qualified Quilt Appraiser.

Snohomish, WA #14

Kayleebug's Calico Cottage

**Mon - Sat
10 - 5
Tue til 8
Sun 12 - 5**

1200 1st St.   98290
(360) 568-5622   2400 sq.ft.
Owner: Laura Wilson

We feature fine fabrics, silk ribbon embroidery, home dec. ideas & supplies and a large array of quilters gift items.

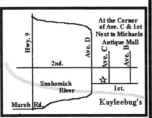

Bothell, WA #15

Keepsake Cottage Fabrics

**Mon - Sat
10 - 6
Thurs til 8
Sun 11 - 5**

23732 Bothell-Everett Hwy.   98021
(360) 486-3483   Est: 1985
Owners: Delberta Murray & Julie Stewart
1000 sq.ft.

Quilting Fabrics, patterns and notions. In the heart of Bothell's Country Village. Also cross-stitch and English Smocking.

Langley, WA #16

Quilting by the Sea

221 Second St. #6, P.O. Box 844
(360) 221-8171   98260
Owner: Mary Darby   Est: 1995
800 sq.ft.   700+ Bolts

Open Daily
10 - 5
Sun 12 - 5
Closed Tues

Fabrics, books, patterns, supplies, gifts, machine quilting, quilts & classes. The friendliest quilt shop for service, inspiration & sharing of ideas.

Bremerton, WA #17

The QUILT SHOP

6710-A Kitsap Way   98312
Off Hwy. 3 at Kitsap Lake
(206) 479-5970
Owner: Tish Smith   Est: 1994

7 Days a
Week
10 - 6

Bright Fabrics
Books, Notions,
Stencils,
Classes
Come Build
Your Own Quilt!

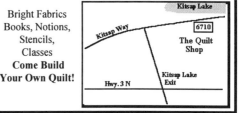

Quilter's Cove

Port Townsend, WA #18

1010 Water St.   98368
(360) 385-4254
Est: 1993
2700 sq.ft.
Owners:
Laurel Watson
& Sylvia Schulte

Best Selection of
Books.
Large Selection of
100% cotton fabrics.
Complete line of notions, patterns &
classes. Gifts for the Quilter.

Mon - Sat 10 - 5:30
Sun 10 - 5

Westport, WA #19

TLC Creations

221 Dock St. In the Orca Motel Bldg.
(360) 268-5030
Owners: Carole & Terry Dugan
Est: 1993

Mon &
Wed - Sun
10 - 4

A small, friendly shop with Fabric, Books, Supplies, Patterns and mini-classes. We have quilts for sale - new, vintage and antique.

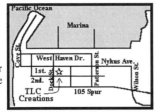

Longview, WA #20

Heirloom Stitches

1414 Commerce Ave.   98632
(360) 425-7038
Owners:Ron & Vivian Spreadborough
Est: 1991   2500 sq.ft.   1500 Bolts

Mon - Thur
10 - 6
Fri 10 - 4
Sat 11 - 5

Everything for quilting, cross stitch, hardanger plus silk and wire ribbons. 100% cottons, books, patterns, charts, notions. Classes Available.

Quilt Quarters

Port Angeles, WA #21

123 West First
98362
(360) 452-6899
Est: 1992 1400 sq.ft.
Owners: Donna Ball
Kris Cornell &
Lauretta Ehling

100% Cotton Fabrics

Momen House, Hoffman, Kona Solids, Jinny Beyer, Gutcheon, South Seas, P&B, Silk Ribbon Supplies, Kaufman and new fabrics all the time.

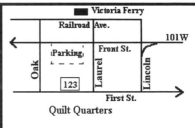

Victoria Ferry
Railroad Ave.
101W
Parking Front St.
Oak Laurel Lincoln
123
First St.
Quilt Quarters

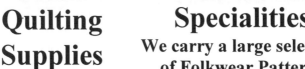

Gateway to: Victoria, B. C. via Coho Ferry
Olympic National Park

Quilting Supplies

Excellent Selections of Notions, Stencils, Patterns, and Books for serious quilters.

Mon - Sat 10 - 5
Thurs 10 - 8:30

Specialities

We carry a large selection of Folkwear Patterns used for authentic clothing designs. We are also proud of our excellent selection of classes serving the beginning to advanced quilter.

Shelton, WA #22

CJ's Labor of Love Quilt Shop

(360) 426-0065

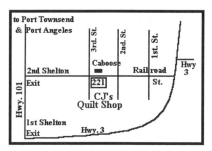

221 W. Railroad Suite 'C'
98584
Owners: Joan Kowalsky &
Candice Makos

Mon - Fri 9:30 - 4:30
Sat 9:30 - 4

A full line Quilt Shop.
Hinterberg & PVC
Frames. 500+ Bolts of
Fabric. Wide Selection
Books & Notions. Mail
Orders Welcomed.

Yelm, WA #23

Quilts by Flo

By Appt. Only

13242 Rocking "S" Lane SE
(360) 458-6667   98597
Owner: Florence M. Schitman
Est: 1979 784 sq.ft. 380 Bolts RV Turnaround

Classes, Notions, Fabric, Supplies, Quilts, Quilted Gifts. Relaxed Atmosphere in the Country.

Port Orchard, WA #24

Rochelle's Fine Fabric & Quilting

Mon - Fri 10 - 8
Sat 10 - 6
Sun 12 - 5

1700 Mile Hill Drive #200C
South Kitsap Mall: Upper Level
(360) 895-1515   98366
Owner: Rochelle Savage   Est: 1981   5500 sq.ft.

A complete collection of cotton solids & prints from all the best manufacturers. A large selection of books & notions. Classes

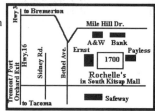

Enumclaw, WA #25

Country Quilts & Crafts

Mon - Fri 9 - 5
Sat 10 - 3

1240 Griffin Ave. 98022
(360) 825-8551
Owner: Mary Hampton

Country Quilts offers the finest of cotton calicos, notions, quilting supplies, and LOTS of Classes.

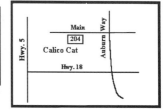

Gig Harbor, WA   #28

Tues - Sat   10 - 5

Est: 1996

3414 Vernhardson
98332
(206) 858-5008
Owner:
DiNae Creighton

Scrappy Lady Quilting

✄ **Fabric, Books, Notions & Battings**
✄ **Wonderful Teachers for classes of all levels.**
✄ **Custom Quilting for your Quilt Tops**

Issaquah, WA   #29

The Loft

**Mon - Sat
10 - 5
Sun 12 - 5**

709 N.W. Gilman Blvd.   98027
(206) 392-5877
Owner: Marybeth Mills
Complete Quilt   Est: 1972
Shop.
Experienced and
personable help.
Great selection of
samples for
inspiration.
Fabric, Books,
Patterns, Classes
galore !!

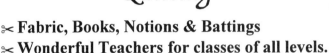

Bellevue, WA   #30

In The Beginning

**Mon - Sat
10 - 5:30
Wed &
Thur til 9
Sun 12 - 5**

14125 N.E. 20th St.   98007
In the Highland Park Center
(206) 865-0155   Est: 1993
Owner: Sharon Yenter   3800 sq.ft.
Internet - http://isis.infinet.com/itb/
        Mail Order:
(206) 523-1121

Thousands of bolts
of quilting fabric,
hundreds of books
and a friendly
helpful staff. Come
visit us soon!

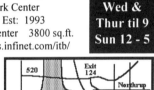

Seattle, WA   #31

In The Beginning

**Mon - Sat
10 - 5:30
Wed &
Thur til 9
Sun 12 - 5**

8201 Lake City Way NE 98115
(206) 523-8862   Est: 1977
Owner: Sharon Yenter 7000 sq.ft.
Mail Order # (206)523-1121
Internet - http://isis.infinet.com/itb/
Free Catalog

Thousands of bolts
of quilting fabric
(5000+), hundreds
of books and a
friendly helpful
staff. Come visit
us soon!

Seattle, WA   #32

Undercover
Quilts from the U.S.A.

**Mon - Sat
10 - 6
Sun 12 - 5**

1411 1st Ave. #106   98101
(206) 622-6382
Owner: Linda Hitchcock
Est: 1990   1000 sq.ft.   300 Bolts

Largest Selection
of American Made
New and Antique
Quilts in the
PNW! Fabrics,
Books, Supplies,
gifts, antique tops,
and blocks.

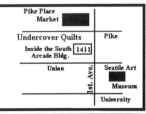

Washington Guilds:

Northwest Quilting Connection, 906 35th St., Anacortes, 98221
Whitman Samplers Guild, 114 N. Main, Colfax, 99111
Crazy Quilters, Federal Way
Evergreen Piecemakers, Kent
Pieceable Quilters, 830 E. Wiser Lake Rd., Lyden, 98264
Quilt Guild, The Fabric Cottage, Lynden, 98264
Quilters Anonymous, P.O. Box 322, Lynnwood, 98046
Pend O'Reille Quilters, 306 S. Washington, Newport, 99156
Port Orchard Quilters Guild, P.O. Box 842, Port Orchard, 98366
Kitsap Quilters, P.O. Box 824, Poulsbo, 98370
Puyallup Valley Quilters, P.O. Box 1421, Puyallup, 98371
Comforters, 9424 125th Ct. E, Puyallup, 98373
Tri City Quilters, P.O. Box 215, Richland, 99352
Pacific Northwest Quilters, P.O. Box 22073, Seattle, 98122
Contemporary Quilt Assoc., 1134 N. 81st St., Seattle, 98103
Sunbonnet Sue Quilt Club, P.O. Box 211, Sequim, 98382
West Sound Quilt Guild, P.O. Box 4306, South Colby, 98384
Spokane Valley Quilters Guild, P.O. Box 13516, Spokane, 99213
Clark County Quilters, P.O. Box 5857, Vancouver, 98668

Other Shops in Washington:

Arlington	Making Memories, 1205 E 5th St.
Arlington	Bunny Patch, 24613 27th Ave. NE
Battle Ground	Country Manor Fabric & Crafts, 7702 NE 179th St.
Bothell	The Farmhouse, 23710 Bothell Hwy. SE
Bothell	Bothell Fabrics, 10015 NE 183rd St.
Cashmere	Gallery Gifts & Fabrics, 107 Cottage
Chehalis	Sisters, 476 N. Market Blvd.
Edmonds	The Calico Basket, 550 A Main St.
Ellensburg	Moser's Clothing Store, 118 E. 4th Ave.
Everett	Quilt with EASE, 3122 Broadway
Everson	The Quiet Garden, 8310 Gillies Rd.
Kennewick	Fantastics, 135 Vista Way
Lopez	Enchanted Needle, P.O. Box 178
Lynden	The Cotton Patch, 1722 Front St.
Lynden	Calico Country, 527 Front St.
Mt. Vernon	Calico Creations, 400 S. First St.
Newport	The Pin Cushion, 306 S. Washington Ave.
Ocean Shores	I Love 2 Quilt, 1105 Ocean Shores SW
Port Orchard	Christina's Heritage, 2516 SE Bethel Rd.
Port Townsend	Seaport General Store, 2131 Clay St.
Poulsbo	Heirloom Quilts, 18954-C Front St., PO Box 1957
Roy	The Old Farmhouse Quilt Shop, 34102 8th Ave. S
Seattle	Comfort by Akiko, 427 Broadway E. #22
Seattle	Nancy's Sewing Basket, 2221 Queen Anne N.
Seattle	Glant Pacific Co., 2230 4th Ave S
Seattle	Indigo Moon Mercantile, 3605 S. McClellan St.
Sedro Woolley	Cascade Fabrics, 824 Metcalf St.
Sequim	The Pine Cupboard, 609 W. Washington #1129
Snohomish	Clearview Triangle, 8311 180th St. SE
Spokane	Northwest Custom Quilting, 2609 W Northwest Blvd.
Stanwood	The Quilt Shop, 9522 - 271st St. N.W., P.O. Box 1313
Tacoma	Gutcheon Patchworks, 917 Pacific Ave. #304
Tacoma	Quilts Northwest, 2720 N. Proctor
Union Gap	The Quilter, 2640 Main St.
Washougal	Dream Time Quilts

West Virginia Guild:
Country Roads Quilt Guild, Morgantown

7 Featured Shops

WEST VIRGINIA

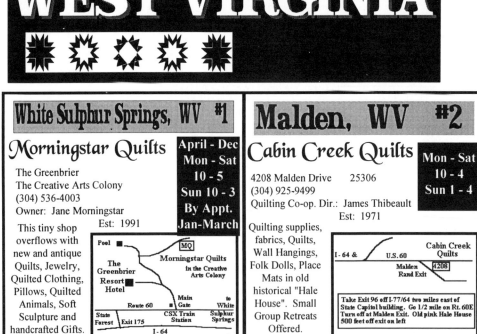

White Sulphur Springs, WV #1

Morningstar Quilts

The Greenbrier
The Creative Arts Colony
(304) 536-4003
Owner: Jane Morningstar   Est: 1991

| April - Dec |
| Mon - Sat |
| 10 - 5 |
| Sun 10 - 3 |
| By Appt. |
| Jan-March |

This tiny shop overflows with new and antique Quilts, Jewelry, Quilted Clothing, Pillows, Quilted Animals, Soft Sculpture and handcrafted Gifts.

Pool
The Greenbrier Resort Hotel
MQ
Morningstar Quilts in the Creative Arts Colony
Route 60
Main Gate
to White Sulphur Springs
State Forest   Exit 175
CSX Train Station
I-64

Malden, WV #2

Cabin Creek Quilts

4208 Malden Drive   25306
(304) 925-9499
Quilting Co-op. Dir.: James Thibeault
Est: 1971

| Mon - Sat |
| 10 - 4 |
| Sun 1 - 4 |

Quilting supplies, fabrics, Quilts, Wall Hangings, Folk Dolls, Place Mats in old historical "Hale House". Small Group Retreats Offered.

I- 64 &   U.S. 60
Malden Rand Exit
Cabin Creek Quilts
4208

Take Exit 96 off I-77/64 two miles east of State Capitol building. Go 1/2 mile on Rt. 60E. Turn off at Malden Exit. Old pink Hale House 500 feet off exit on left

Charleston, WV #3

Sneed's Vacuum & Sewing Center

Mon - Fri
8 - 5:30
Sat 9 - 1

2614 7th Ave.   25312
(304) 744-3670
Owners: Charles & Regina Sneed
Est: 1956   4500 sq.ft.   400 Bolts

West Virginia's largest Bernina sewing machine dealer. Quilting Supplies, Fabrics, and lots of classes.

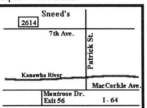

Sutton, WV #4

The Quilt Supply Shop

Mon - Thur
9 - 5
Sat by Appt.

701 N. 3rd. St.   26601
(304) 765-5176   Est: 1983

Tiny shop filled with 100% cotton fabric. You will find all your notions, patterns, and quilting tools.

Elkins, WV #5

Elkins Sewing Center

Mon - Sat
9 - 5
Fri til 8

300 Davis Ave.   26241
(304) 636-9480
Owners: Sue & Jim Pifer
Est: 1982   2000 sq.ft.   Free Catalog

Quilting fabrics, books & notions Specialty threads and trims. Cross stitch, duplicate stitch supplies. Classes. Viking sewing machines and sergers.

St. Marys, WV #6

Zepora's Quilt Shop

Thur - Sat
10 - 4

116 Lafayette St.   26170
(304) 684-7113
Owner: Zepora Morgan Hughes
Est: 1977   1600 sq.ft.   1500 Bolts

Everything to make a quilt under one roof. Educational department. Quilts on Consignment.

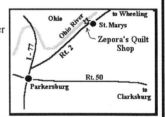

Other Shops in West Virginia:

Clarksburg	Clarksburg Sewing Center P.O. Box 353A, Route 2
Farmington	Cotton Patch, Route 250 N.
Huntington	The Cherry Tree Quilt Shop, 6306 E. Pea Ridge
Jane Lew	Homestead Fabric, Main St.
Lewisburg	Threads, 157 Seneca Trail
Lewisburg	Quilts, 203 E. Washington
Reedsville	Eleanor's Fabric, Rt. 7 E.
Sophia	Quilt Fabrics & Craft Corner Main St.
St. Albans	Village Sampler, 71 Ole Main
Summersville	Panda Puff
Winfield	Fern's Fabric & Quilt Shoppe Rural Route 34 Box 6130

Morgantown, WV #7

The Sew Inn, Ltd.

Mon 10 - 8
Tues - Fri
10 - 6
Sat 10 - 5

120 High St.   26505
(304) 296-6802
Owner: Virginia Showers
Est: 1973   1500 sq.ft.

Wonderful collection of quilting cottons, books, notions & classes. Bridal & Special occasion fabrics. Knowledgeable & Friendly service. Authorized Viking Dealer.

Easy Access from I - 79 or I - 68. Located downtown across from The Hotel Morgan.

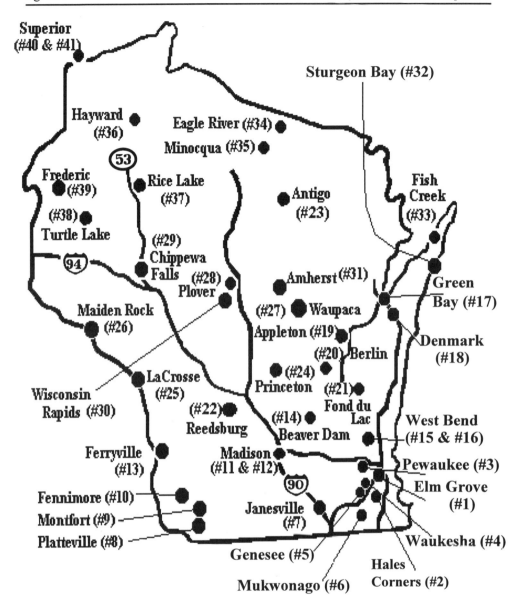

Superior
(#40 & #41)

Sturgeon Bay (#32)

Hayward
(#36)

Eagle River (#34)

Minocqua (#35)

53

Frederic
(#39)

Rice Lake
(#37)

Fish
Creek
(#33)

Antigo
(#23)

(#38)
Turtle Lake

(#29)
Chippewa
Falls

(#28)
Plover

Amherst (#31)

Green
Bay (#17)

94

Maiden Rock
(#26)

(#27)   Waupaca

Appleton (#19)

Denmark
(#18)

(#20) Berlin

Wisconsin
Rapids (#30)

LaCrosse
(#25)

(#24)
Princeton

(#21)

Fond du
Lac

(#22)
Reedsburg

(#14)

West Bend
(#15 & #16)

Beaver Dam

Ferryville
(#13)

Madison
(#11 & #12)

Pewaukee (#3)

90

Elm Grove
(#1)

Fennimore (#10)

Janesville
(#7)

Montfort (#9)

Platteville (#8)

Waukesha (#4)

Genesee (#5)

Hales
Corners (#2)

Mukwonago (#6)

WISCONSIN

41 Featured Shops

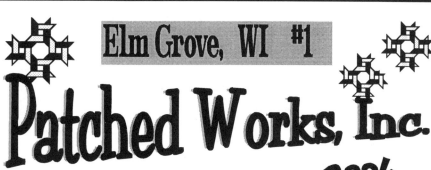

Elm Grove, WI #1

Patched Works, Inc.

In a Western Suburb of Milwaukee
13330 Watertown Plank Rd.
(414) 786-1523　　53122
Owner: Trudie Hughes
Est: 1978　6000 sq.ft.

"Home of Trudie Hughes' Summer Camps"

Mon - Fri 9 - 5
Wed til 8　Sat 9 - 4

5000 bolts of Cotton Fabric
Hundreds of Books &
Patterns for the Quiltmaker

Owned by a Master Fabricaholic

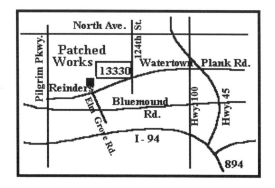

Hales Corners, WI #2

Hearthside Quilters Nook

Mon - Sat 9 - 5
Mon & Thur til 9
Sun 12 - 4

10731 W. Forest Home Ave.
(414) 425-2474   53130
Owners: Carol Baker & Jan
Est: 1979 2800 sq.ft.   Krueger

Beautiful Fabric 1200 Bolts - All Great Selection, Books, Patterns, Notions, Heirloom & Silk Ribbon Sewing Supplies. Christmas year Round. "Where Friendly service is a Tradition!"

Pewaukee, WI #3

Pamella's Place

Mon - Thur 9:30 - 8:30
Fri & Sat 9:30-5

2010 Silvernail Road   53072
(414) 544-5415
Owner: Pamella Gray
Est: 1987   3350 sq.ft.

Featuring over 4,000 bolts of fabric, books and patterns (quilting, sewing doll and craft) and Bernina sewing machines.

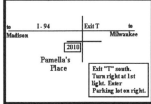

Waukesha, WI #4

Genesee Woolen Mill

Mon, Tues, Thurs, Fri 10 - 4

S. 40 W. 28178 Hwy.59
(414) 521-2121   53188
Est: 1989 2600 sq.ft.   500 Bolts
Owners: Kay Menning & Sarah Pietenpol

Wool Carding Mill. Shop feature wool batts, cotton fabric, wool related items. Hand-Tied Comforters. Call for Tours

Genesee Depot, WI #5

American Quilter

Mon 10 - 8
Tue & Thur 10 - 6
Wed & Fri 10 - 5
Sat 9 - 3

S 42 W 31230 Hwy 83
(414) 968-3400   53127
Owners: Carol & Les Knutsen
Est: 1992   2400 sq.ft.

Biggest and best selection of quilting fabrics and supplies in Southeast Wisconsin. Classes Available. Authorized Pfaff Sales & Service

Mukwonago, WI #6

NinePatch Quilters' Hutch

Sun & Mon 1 - 4
Tue & Thur 10:30 - 8
Wed, Fri, & Sat 10:30 - 5

955 Main St.   53149
(414) 363-9566   800 Bolts
Owner: Mary June Podraza

Leading Manufacturers of top quality fabrics. Popular patterns, and books. Latest quilters' notions and supplies. Day & Evening classes for all levels.

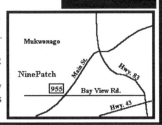

Janesville, WI #7

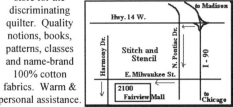 Stitch and Stencil Quilt Shoppe

Mon - Fri 10 - 5
Sat 10 - 4

2100 E. Milwaukee St. 53345
(608) 758-1447   Free Newsletter
Located in the Fairview Mall
Owner: Nancy Jung-Brown

The complete quilt store for the discriminating quilter. Quality notions, books, patterns, classes and name-brand 100% cotton fabrics. Warm & personal assistance.

Platteville, WI   #8

Creative Stitches

Mon - Fri
9 - 5:30
Sat 9 - 5

125 East Main   53818
(608) 348-9276
Owner: Rhonda Simmon
                    2100 sq.ft.

Large selection of
100% Cotton
Fabrics, Quilt
Books, Doll
Patterns. Yarns
& yarn books.
For sale: Quilts,
dolls, knit &
crocheted items

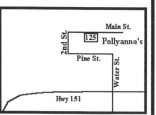

Montfort, WI   #9

Moments in Time

Mon - Fri
10 - 6
Sat 10 - 4
Shortened hrs.
Jan - April

200 Hwy. 18   53569
(608) 943-6632

We feature ready
made quilts and
wood quilt display
items. Nice
selection of wood
accessories, floral
arrangements.
Collector dolls,
Ertl. Clocks.

Fennimore, WI   #10

Yard & Yard Shop

Mon - Fri
9 - 5
Sat 9 - 3

960 Lincoln Ave.   53809
(608) 822-6014
Owner: Doris Monroe
Est: 1974

Quilt Supplies,
Classes,
Fashion Fabric
Patterns
New Home Sewing
Machines — Sales
and Service.

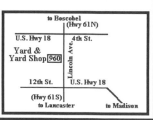

Madison, WI   #11

The Stitcher's Crossing

Mon - Fri
9:30 - 5:30
Thur til
8:30
Sat 9:30-4

6816 Odana Road   53719
(608) 833-8040   Est: 1980
Owners: Elaine Boehlke & Kit
2200 sq.ft.   Thomsen

Unique shop for
all your quilting
and cross stitch
needs. All of our
wonderful models
and displays will
inspire you.

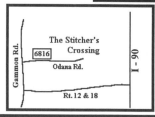

Madison, WI   #12

Quilter's Workshop

Mon - Fri
9:30 - 5:30
Thur til
8:30
Sat 9:30 - 5

6101 Odana Road   53719
(608) 271-4693
Owner: Joan Pariza
Est: 1990   2400 sq.ft.

Madison's only
shop devoted to
Quilters -- over
2000 bolts -- all
100% cotton --
includes latest in
Hoffman, Jinny
Beyer -- Patterns,
Books, Notions ...

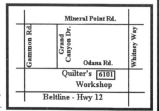

Ferryville, WI   #13

Olde Tyme
Quilt Shoppe

Mon - Fri
9 - 5
Weekends by
chance or
call first.

R.R. #2   Rush Creek Rd.   Box 215
(608) 648-2081   54628
Owner: Virginia Johnson   900 sq.ft.
                    Est: 1986

Custom made Quilts-
-Hand dyed fabric,
notions. Hand or
machine quilting,
outline quilting.
100% cotton thread
1200 yard spools
Virginia's original
quilts. Classes also

Beaver Dam, WI #14

Nancy's Notions, Ltd

Mon - Fri 9 - 5 Wed til 8 Sat 9 - 4

333 Beichl Ave.   53916
(414) 887-7321   Est: 1985
Owners: Nancy & Richard Zieman
3000 sq.ft.   Free Catalog

Large selection of brand name 100% cottons, sewing and quilting notions, patterns, and supplies. Home of "Sewing With Nancy"

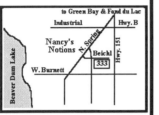

West Bend, WI #15

Hinterberg Design, Inc.

Mon - Fri 8:30 - 4

2805 E. Progress   53095
(800) 443-5800   Est: 1981
Owner: Kris Hinterberg   Free Catalog

Factory Store Quilting Frames and Hoops

West Bend, WI #16

Royce Fabrics

Mon - Fri 9:30 - 8:30 Sat 9:30 - 5 Sun 11 - 4

846 S. Main   53095
(414) 338-0597
Owner: Jerry Quasius
Est: 1971   3200 sq.ft.

2000 Quilting Fabrics. Books, Soft Patterns, Quilting Classes. Bernina Sewing Machines.

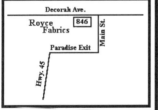

Green Bay, WI #17

Silver Thimble Quilt & Gift Shoppe

Mon & Thur 9:30 - 8 Tues & Wed 9:30 - 5 Fri 9:30 - 4 Sun 11 - 4

2475 University Ave.   54302
University Courtyard   Est: 1990
(414) 468-1495   Owners: Nanette Guzzonato & Elaine Corson

1500 bolts 100% cotton fabric, books, patterns, notions, classes, quilts, gifts. Take I - 43, exit 185 located in mini mall on left by light.

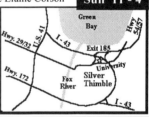

Denmark, WI #18

Handworks

Mon - Fri 9 - 5 Sat 9 - 3 Or By Appt.

116 W. Main St.,   P.O. Box 636
(414) 863-8843   54208
Owner: Ramona Gillaume
Est: 1994

Quilting Supplies, Crafts, Books, Patterns, Fine 100% Cotton Fabrics, Notions, Classes. Quilts and Crafts for sale. Knowledgable Staff

Appleton, WI #19

Quilters' Corner

Mon - Fri 9:30 - 5 Thur til 8 Sat 9:30 - 4

2009A N. Richmond St.
54911
(414) 749-1957

Great selection of quality 100% cotton fabrics. Books, patterns, notions & classes. Bernina sewing machines.

FARMHOUSE FABRICS

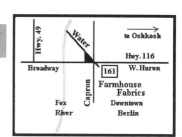

New Location!
161 W. Huron St.   54923
(414) 622-4884
Owner: Jean Teal   Est: 1980

Berlin, WI   #20

**Hours: Monday - Saturday
10 AM to 5 PM
Thursday until 8 PM**

Visit our restored Victorian building and step back in time in our old general store atmosphere.

You will be greeted by our friendly, knowledgeable staff. Shop our 3 Floors of Fabrics, Patterns, Books and Supplies for all of your Quilting needs. Visit our Victorian gift shop where we have quilts, antiques, clothing and gifts.

We have over 2500 bolts of 100% cotton fabric. Our specialty is Antique Reproductions. Other fabrics include Designer lines from Marcus Brothers, RJR, Kaufmann, Fabri-Quilt, P&B, Red Wagon and many, many more. We have a nice selection of needle art supplies and hard to find items.

We have classes in all areas of quilting, sewing and needle arts.

Mail Order Catalogue Available - Please send $1 to
Farmhouse Fabrics
Box 188
Pine River, WI 54965

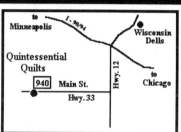

Princeton, WI #24

Quilts & Quilting

Mon -Fri 8:30 - 5
Sat 9 - 3

607 W. Main St.   (414) 295-6506
P.O. Box 362   54968   Est: 1971
Owners: Sandy & Ron Mason
Machine Quilting & Kit Brochure SASE

Custom Machine Quilting Since 1971
Fabric, Notions, Books, Classes. Die-Cut Quilt Top Kits—pillows to king size.

LaCrosse, WI #25

A Stitch In Time

Mon - Sat 10 - 5
Thur til 8

225 N. 3rd St.   54601
(608) 782-3257
Owner: Monica Campbell
Est: 1992   2400 sq.ft.   1200 - 1500 Bolts

Large selection of fabric, books, patterns, & quilting supplies. The friendliest quilt shop for service, inspiration and sharing of ideas.

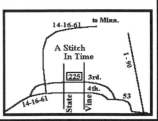

Maiden Rock, WI #26

Mary's Country Boutique

By Chance or Appt. (Every Day)

W 3659 390th Ave.   54750
(715) 647-4212
Owner: Mary T. Wieser
Est: 1981   700 sq.ft.

100% Cotton Fabrics. Quilting Supplies and Books, Classes, Custom Machine Knitting. Hand-Made Gifts.

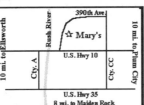

Waupaca, WI #27

Nichols Creek Quilt Studio

Mon - Fri 10 - 5
Sat 10 - 4

201 N. Main   54981
(715) 256-1024   Est: 1994
Owners: Nancy M. Oftedahl & Janice Keil Robbins
1200 sq.ft.
1500 Bolts

Finished Quilts, Cotton Fabric, Large selection of Patterns, Books. Quilting Supplies and Notions. Classes Offered.

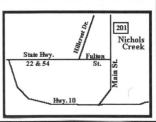

Plover, WI #28

Quilters' Cabin

Mon - Fri 10 - 5
Wed til 8
Sat 10 - 4

2560 Post Rd.   54467
(715) 345-9855

Quilt fabrics, Books, Patterns and Supplies; Wall hangings and craft items. Tole painting supplies. Classes and mail order. Come Visit Us!

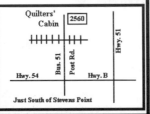

Chippewa Falls, WI #29

Nine Patch Quilts-N-Crafts

Mon - Fri 9 - 5:30
Sat 9 - 5

17 W. Central Street   54729
(715) 723-5931   Est: 1993
Owners: Lina LaRonge & Barb Dekan
Est: 1993   1500 sq.ft.   750 Bolts

Gifts, Amish Quilts, Fabrics, Fine Quality Yarns, Quilting & Knitting Supplies.
New Wool Batts, Poly Batts, Recarding Service.

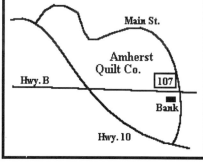

Sturgeon Bay, WI #32

820 Egg Harbor Rd.
54235
Est: 1994
2200 sq.ft.

Mon - Sat
10 - 5
Sun 11 - 3

(414) 746-0944   Owner: Becky McKee
Major Credit Cards Accepted

Visit us in our century old farmhouse. The largest selection of 100% Cotton Designer Fabrics, Books, Patterns & notions in beautiful Door County.

Fish Creek, WI #33

Door County Quiltworks

3903 Hwy.42   P.O. Box 396
(414) 868-3660   54212
Owner: Barbara Williams

Mid May
to Oct
Daily 10 - 5
Closed Tues

Amish and Door County Quilts Large Selection of Fabric, Quilting Supplies, Notions, Books and Gifts for the Quilter.
600 Bolts

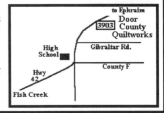

Eagle River, WI #34

Heartstrings Quilts & Fabrics

220 S. Main St.,   P.O. Box 194
(715) 479-2313   54521
Owner: Lisa Wood
Est: 1995   1000 sq.ft.   500+ Bolts

Mon - Fri
10 - 5
Thur til 9
Sat 10 - 3

North Woods Quilting at its Best! Fabrics, Patterns, Books, Wool Rug Hooking Supplies, Viking Sewing Machines and Classes.

Minocqua, WI #35

 The Quilt Cottage

510 Chicago Ave.
P.O. Box 910
54548
Est: 1995
1300+ Bolts

Mon - Fri
10 - 5
Sat 10 - 3
In Summer
Wed til 7

Owners: Barb Zawistowski & Pam Micheau

Friendly cottage on the lake carrying fabrics, notions, books, and patterns for your quilting, crafting and silk ribbon embroidery.

Hayward, WI #36

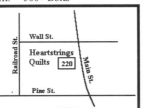 Hayward QuiltersQuarters

Windmill Square, P.O. Box 6350
(715) 634-3260 54843 Est: 1995
Owner: Diann Raymond   1500 sq.ft.   1600 Bolts

Mon - Fri
10 - 5
Sat 10 - 3

Large selection 100% Cotton fabrics, patterns, books, and quilting notions. Classes offered.

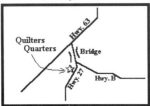

Rice Lake, WI #37

 Busy Bobbin

234 N. Wilson Ave. 54868
(715) 234-1217   Est: 1981
Owner: Diann Raymond 1000 sq.ft.   1800 Bolts

Mon - Fri
9:30 - 5
Sat 9:30 - 3

Large selection 100% Cotton fabrics, patterns, books, and quilting notions. Classes offered.

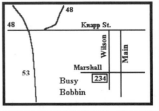

Turtle Lake, WI #38

612 U.S. Hwy. 8 & 63 W
(715) 986-2983

**Mon -Fri
10 - 5
Sat 9 - 4
Summer Fri
Eves til 9**

The warmth of the
country supplying
all your quilting
needs. Cottons,
flannels and wools,
ceramic buttons,
books, patterns and
notions.

Frederic, WI #39

Cheri's
**Country
Quilting**

**Wed - Sat 9:30 - 5:30
Or By Appointment**

1425 - 305th Ave.   54837
(715) 327-4519   Owner: Cheri Moats

**100% Cotton Fabrics (Over 1000 Bolts),
Books, Patterns, Notions, Stencils, Classes.
Custom Machine Quilting.**

*1 1/2 miles east of
Downtown Frederic*

Superior, WI #40

Fabric Works

1320 Tower Ave.   54880
(715) 392-7060
Owner: Barb Engelking
Est: 1991

**Mon - Fri
9:30 - 5
Thur til 8
Sat 10 - 4**

Over 2000 Bolts of
100% Cotton
Fabric.
Quilting Books,
Patterns and
Supplies.

Superior, WI #41

Norma's Nook

8137 S. Dowling Lake Rd. W.
(715) 399-2125   54880
Owner: Norma J. Scheuman
           Est: 1986   800 sq.ft.

**Mon & Fri
10 - 5
Sat 10 - 2
or during
classes.**

Full-line quilt
shop with
emphasis on
wearable art.
Various knits,
s/s fleece &
denims. Books,
patterns, crafts &
tons of samples.

Wisconsin Guilds:
Tomorrow's Quilters, PO Box 248, Amherst, 54406
Baraboo Quilters, 901 Moore Street #15, Baraboo, 53913
Heart in Hands Quilt Guild, Box 12A, Boyceville, 54725
Lake Country Quilters, 1385 Countryside Lane, Brookfield, 53045
Piecemaker's, 1165 Parkmoor Dr., Brookfield, 53005
Fort Atkinson Piecemakers, 163 Hoopen Road, Cambridge, 53523
Cedar Creek Quilters, 1654 Summit Dr., Cedarsburg, 53012
Old World Quilters, 304 Larkin Street, Eagle, 53119
Cranberry Country Quilt Guild, 4483 Chain o' Lakes Rd., Eagle River, 54521
Village Quilters of Harvard, 212 Abbey Springs Dr., Fontana, 53125
Piecemakers Quilt Guild, 510 Grove St., Fort Atkinson, 53538
Mixed Sampler Quilt Club, P.O. Box 133, Frederic, 54837
Menomonee Falls Quilters, W. 154 N. 11666 Daniels, Germantown, 53022
Heritage Quilters, 203 Beech, Grafton, 53024
Evergreen Quilters, P.O. Box 783, Green Bay, 54305
LaCrosse Area Quilters, W. 8154 Holland Dr., Holmen, 54636
Hudson Heritage Quilters, 874 Willow Ridge, Hudson, 54016
It's a Stitch Quilt Club, 3280 Highway P, Jackson, 53037
Rock Valley Quilters Guild, P.O. Box 904, Janesville, 53547
Southport Quilter's Guild, P.O. Box 1523, Kenosha, 53141
Mad City Quilters, 157 Nautilus Dr., Madison, 53705
Twilight Quilters Guild, 9 Leyton Circle, Madison, 53713
Northwoods Quilters, P.O. Box 595, Marinette, 54143
Darting Needles Quilt Guild, P.O. Box 603, Menasha, 54952
Covered Bridge Quilters, 13907 N. Port Washington Rd., Mequon, 53092
Wisconsin's Quilter's Inc., P.O. Box 83144, Milwaukee, 53223
West Suburban Quilters Guild, 2621 N. 65th St., Milwaukee, 53213
North Shore Quilters Guild, P.O. Box 17263, Milwaukee, 53217
Orchard Inn Quilters, 5510 W. Calumet Rd., Milwaukee, 53223
Stitch it or Stuff it Quilters, 6551 N. 66th St., Milwaukee, 53223
Ladies of the Lake, P.O. Box 481, Minocqua, 54548
Calico Capers Quilt Guild, RR 1 Gem Ave., Montello, 53949
Evergreen Quilters, P.O. Box 426, Montello, 53949
Crazy Quilters, S 70 W 32864 Oak Pl., Mukwonago, 53149
Patched Lives Quilt Guild, N. 53 W. 33511 Cumberland Dr., Nashotah, 53058
Pine Tree Needlers, 1177 Dakota Lane, Neshkoro, 54960
Wandering Foot Quilters, 8620 S. Howell Ave., Oak Creek, 53154
Lake Side Quilters, 1350 Menominee Dr., Oshkosh, 54901
Plum Creek Quilters, W 601 210th Ave., Plum City, 54761
Lighthouse Quilters, P.O. Box 124, Racine, 53403
Cornerstone Quilt Guild, 337 K St., Reedsburg, 53959
Continued on the next page

Wisconsin Guilds Continued from Previous Page

Around the Block Quilters, 940 E. Main, Reedsburg, 53959
Rhinelander Northwoods Quilters, 49 Lake Creek Rd., Rhinelander, 54501
Friendship Quilter's Guild, 587 N. Park St., Richland Center, 53581
Ladies of the Lake Quilters, 9200 Longs Rd., Sayner, 54560
Shawano Area Quilters, 225 S. Main, Shawano, 54166
Sheboygan County Quilter's Guild, 2426 N. 25th St., Sheboygan, 53083
Wild Rivers Quilting Guild, P.O. Box 1065, Spooner, 54801
Star Point Quilters Guild, P.O. Box 607, Stevens Point, 54481
The Stoughton Quilters, 404 W. Wilson, Stoughton, 53589
Prairie Heritage Quilters, P.O. Box 253, Sun Prairie, 53590
Casda Quilts, 2231 Catlin Ave., Superior, 54880
North Woods Quilters, 709 W. Third St., Washburn, 54891
Pine Tree Quilters Guild, P.O. Box 692, Wausau, 54402
Pine Tree Needlers, P.O. Box 431-2, Wautoma, 54982
Kettle Moraine Quilt Club, 4991 Hillside Dr., West Bend, 53095
Dells Country Quilters, #530 Highway 23 E., Wisconsin Dells, 53965

Other Shops in Wisconsin:

Algoma	Ben Franklin Store, 513 4th St.
Amherst	Wood Shed Gifts, 291 Packer Ave.
Berlin	West Side Sewing, Highway F, Route 3
Cedarburg	Cedarburg Woolen Mill, W. 62 N. 580 Washinton Ave.
Cottage Grove	Steeleville Quilt & Gift Shop, 2848 Femrite Dr.
Curtiss	LaVerna's Machine Quilting Studio, P.O. Box 235, Route 2
Curtiss	Quilting in The Dome, N14341 CTH-E
Delavan	The Stitchery, Rural Route 4 Box 232
Eau Claire	The Calico Shoppe, 214 S. Barstow St.
Eau Claire	Finishing Touch, 1750 Brackett Ave
Hudson	St. Croix Country Dry Goods, 220 Locust
Janesville	Sew Bee Quilting, 343 S. Lexington Dr.
Menomonee Falls	Fall's Sewing Center, W 155 N 8833 Main
Neenah	Holz's Pfaff Sewing Center, 132 W. Wisconsin Ave.
Omro	YDS, 5530 State Rd. Hwy. 116
Oshkosh	J-K Fabric & Crafts, 362 S. Koeller St.
Rhinelander	Geri's Fabric Patch, 37 S. Brown
Spring Green	Sew 'N Sew, 122 N. Lexington
Stevens Point	The Sampler House, 1125 Main
Stockholm	Amish Country, 119 Spring St.
Sun Prairie	Itchin' to Stitch, 207 E. Main St.
Sun Prairie	J. J. Stitches, 221 E. Main St.
Superior	Best Friends, 6006 Tower Ave.
Verona	Maple Springs Farm, 1828 Highway PB
Wausau	Quilt Sampler, 304 S. 1st Ave.

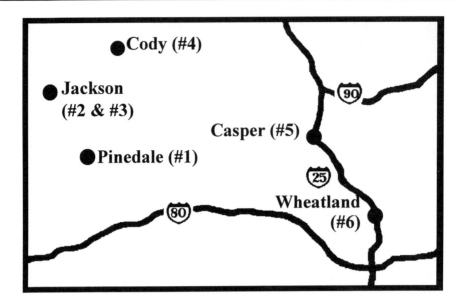

6 Featured Shops

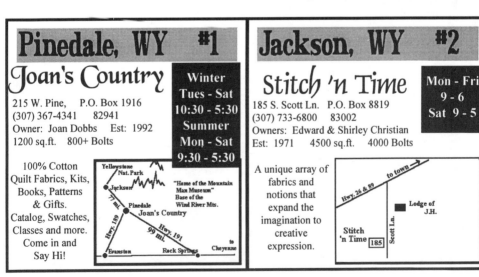

Pinedale, WY   #1

Joan's Country

215 W. Pine,   P.O. Box 1916
(307) 367-4341   82941
Owner: Joan Dobbs   Est: 1992
1200 sq.ft.   800+ Bolts

Winter
Tues - Sat
10:30 - 5:30
Summer
Mon - Sat
9:30 - 5:30

100% Cotton
Quilt Fabrics, Kits,
Books, Patterns
& Gifts.
Catalog, Swatches,
Classes and more.
Come in and
Say Hi!

Yellowstone
Nat. Park
Jackson
"Home of the Mountain
Man Museum"
Base of the
Wind River Mts.
Pinedale
Joan's Country
Hwy. 189
Hwy. 191
99 mi.
Evanston   Rock Springs   to Cheyenne

Jackson, WY   #2

Stitch 'n Time

185 S. Scott Ln.   P.O. Box 8819
(307) 733-6800   83002
Owners: Edward & Shirley Christian
Est: 1971   4500 sq.ft.   4000 Bolts

Mon - Fri
9 - 6
Sat 9 - 5

A unique array of
fabrics and
notions that
expand the
imagination to
creative
expression.

to town
Hwy. 26 & 89
Lodge of
J.H.
Scott Ln.
Stitch
'n Time   185

Casper, WY #5

Prism Quilt

Mon - Sat 9 - 5

114 E. 2nd St.   82601
(307) 234-4841
Owners: Becki & Bill Marsh
Est: 1987   4800 sq.ft.   3000+ Bolts

3000+ cotton fabrics, Pfaff, Sewing Machines, Quilts, Books, Patterns, Notions, Classes, Quilting Supplies and Service.

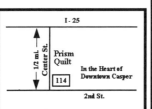

In the Heart of Downtown Casper

Cody, WY #4

Crafty Quilter

**Mon - Fri 10 - 5:30
Sat 10 - 4**

1262 Sheridan Ave.   82414
(307) 527-6305   Est: 1981
Owner: Susy McCall
Mgr: Terri Lightman

2000+ bolts quality cotton fabrics. Many Hoffmans Books, Patterns, Notions. Close to Buffalo Bill Historical Center.

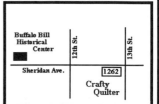

Wheatland, WY #6

Make A Statement

**Mon - Fri 9:30 - 5:30
Sat 9:30 - 4:30**

701 9th St.   82201
(307) 322-3707
Owners: Linda & Linda Wallis
Est: 1994

100% Cotton Fabric. Five brands of sewing machines & sergers. Notions, books, specialty quilting supplies, classes. Always a fun place!

Wyoming Guilds:
Wyoming Heritage Quilters, P.O. Box 19081, Cheyenne, 82003
Northeast WY Quilt Guild, 3508 S. Douglas Hwy., Gillette, 82718
Jackson Hole Guild, P.O. Box 8819, Jackson, 83001
Paintbrush Piecers Quilt Guild, P.O. Box 258, Powell, 82435

Other Shops in Wyoming:

Cheyenne	The Quilted Corner, 2015 Warren Ave.
Glenrock	The Kalico Korner, PO Box 1207
Torrington	Homesteaders Quilting Shop, 2140 Main St.

We welcome our Quilting
Neighbors to the North

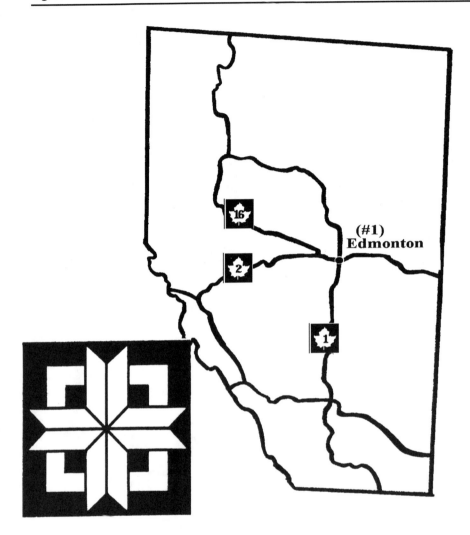

(#1)
Edmonton

ALBERTA
CANADA

1 Featured Shop

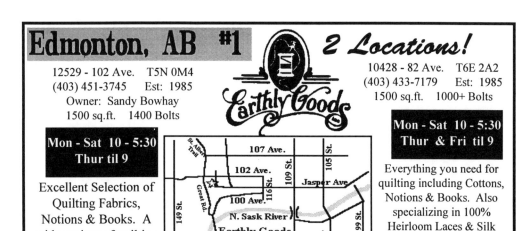

Edmonton, AB #1

2 Locations!

Earthly Goods

12529 - 102 Ave.   T5N 0M4
(403) 451-3745   Est: 1985
Owner: Sandy Bowhay
1500 sq.ft.   1400 Bolts

10428 - 82 Ave.   T6E 2A2
(403) 433-7179   Est: 1985
1500 sq.ft.   1000+ Bolts

Mon - Sat 10 - 5:30
Thur til 9

Mon - Sat 10 - 5:30
Thur & Fri til 9

Excellent Selection of Quilting Fabrics, Notions & Books. A wide variety of quilting & fabric craft classes.

Everything you need for quilting including Cottons, Notions & Books. Also specializing in 100% Heirloom Laces & Silk Ribbon Supplies. Quilts for Sale.

Alberta Guild:
Edmonton District Quilt Guild, Box 68004,
          70 Bonnie Doon Mall, Edmonton, T6C 4N6

Other Shops in Alberta, Canada:

Calgary	The Quilter's Cabin, 118 - 10816 Macleod Tr. S
Calgary	Ant Hill, 10th St. NW
Calgary	A Sewing Sensation, 920 Northmount Dr. NW
Calgary	Country Quilts & City Lace, 114 6707 Elbow Dr. S.W.
Camrose	Cotton Berry Fabrics, 5028 50th St.
Canmore	Quilt Co., Box 2849
Drayton Valley	Material Matters, 5212 45th Ave.
Edmonton	Quilter's Dream, 10732 - 124 St.
Hanna	Yesterday's Dreams, Box 34
Lethbridge	Thread Bear, #3 - 1021 2 Avenue A North
Mayerthrope	Katherin Kountry Krafts, P.O. Box 1109
Red Deer	The Country Cupboard Quilt Shoppe, 5020 Gaetz Ave.

2 Featured Shops

Heavenly cotton fabrics, books, patterns and quilting supplies. Handcrafted table linens, baby wear and fashion accessories. Canadian heirloom quilts. Located in a 19th century heritage building in Market Square, in the Heart of Old Town Victoria.

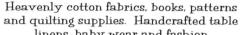

Victoria, BC #1

Mon - Sat 9:30 - 5:30
Sun 11 - 5

Satin Moon Quilt Shop

517 Pandora Ave.
Market Square V8W 1N5

(604) 383-4023
Fax: (604) 920-7670
Owner: Robyn Whitbread
Est: 1978   2000 sq.ft.   2500 Bolts
Free Catalog

Vernon, BC #2

Mary's Brazilian Embroidery

Mon - Fri
9:30 - 4
Sat 11 - 4

1803 - 36th St.   V1T 6E1
(604) 545-3939 Fax: (604) 549-0404
Owner: Mary Kurbis Est: 1989   Catalog $2
We manufacture: Prints for Brazilian Emb. & Silk Ribbon Emb

Carry all acc. for Brazilian Emb.— Divine Threads & Ribbon. Books & Perfect Sew. MBE Designs 100% silk ribbon 23 colors - edge dyed, shaded & over dyed

Other Shops in British Columbia:

100 Mile House	Lillian's Fabric & Quilting, P.O. Box 1388
Ashcroft	Alice's Sewing Shop, 412 Railway
Chilliwack	Hamel's, 9339 Mary St.
Fernie	Fernie Florist & Hobby Crafts, 661 Second Ave.
Fort Langley	Pat's Quilting & Designs, 9217 Glover Rd.
Hagensbourg	Crafty Lady Gifts & Hobbies, P.O. Box 114
Lillooet	Country Lane Crafts, 553 Main St.
Mape Ridge	Elizabeth's Craft Shoppe, 22255 Dewdeny Trunk Rd. #170
Salmon Arm	The Sewing Basket, 168 McLeod St. Box 327
South Surrey	Eye of the Needle, 15355 24th Ave.
Trail	Tea Rose Crafts, 1162 Cedar Ave.
Vancouver	The Cloth Shop, 4415 W 10th Ave.
Vanderhoof	The Stitchery, P.O. Box 1658

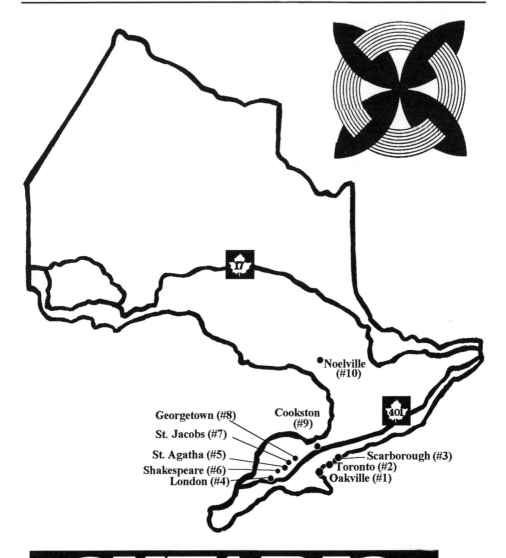

Noelville (#10)

Georgetown (#8)

St. Jacobs (#7)

St. Agatha (#5)

Shakespeare (#6)

London (#4)

Cookston (#9)

Scarborough (#3)

Toronto (#2)

Oakville (#1)

ONTARIO CANADA

10 Featured Shops

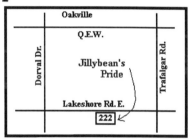
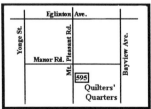

London, ON #4

Quilters' Supply

1060 Hyde Park Rd   N0M 1Z0
(519) 472-3907
Owners: Lu Farnell & Willi Powell
Est: 1978   2600 sq.ft.   3000 Bolts

Quilts, fabrics and over 450 books for the Quilter and fabric artist. Phone, write or visit for ongoing workshop schedules.

**Tues - Sat
10 - 5
Thur til 8**

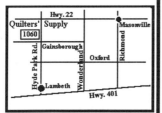

St. Agatha, ON #5

Miller's Country Store

221 Erb St. E.   N0B 2L0
(519) 747-1575
Est: 1986   2000 sq.ft.   900 Bolts
Owners: Carol & Tom Miller

Mennonite Quilts. Area's largest selection of plaids for quilts, curtains & upholstery. Country gifts and custom crafted furniture.

**Tues - Sat
10 - 5:30
Sun
12:30 - 5:30**

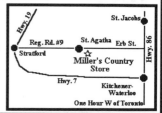

Fabric & Quilting Supplies
One Piece Quilt Tops & Backs
Books * Patterns * Gifts
Cat Stuff

Shakespeare, ON #6

27 Shakespeare St. N0B 2P0
(519) 625-8435
Owner: Ann Klooster
Est: 1986   1200 sq.ft.   1500 Bolts

<u>Your</u> place to find a timeless and elegant quilt for your home or choose the supplies to make a family heirloom.

**Lots of Shops for Everyone
To Enjoy in Canada's Antique Capital**

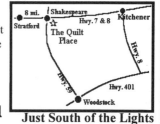

Just South of the Lights

St. Jacobs, ON #7

Ruffled Elegance & Calico

38 King St.   N0B 2N0
(519) 664-2665
Owner: Marion Martin
Est: 1984   1800 sq.ft.

"A Quilter's Delight — A Decorators Dream" Name brand fabrics, patterns, notions. Classes Curtains & Pillows Handmade quilts by local Mennonite quiltmakers.

**Mon - Sat
9:30 - 5:30
Sun 1 - 5**

Georgetown, ON #8

The Hobby Horse

12707 9th Line   L7G 4S8
(905) 877-9292
Owner: Gail Spence
Est: 1982   Free Catalog

We're filled to the brim with bolts of cotton fabrics, quilting supplies, patterns, books, kits and much more. Come Visit Our Store.

**Mon - Sat
9:30 - 5:30
Sundays &
Holiday Mon
12 - 5**

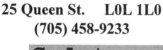

"Fabric?
What fabric?"

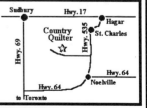

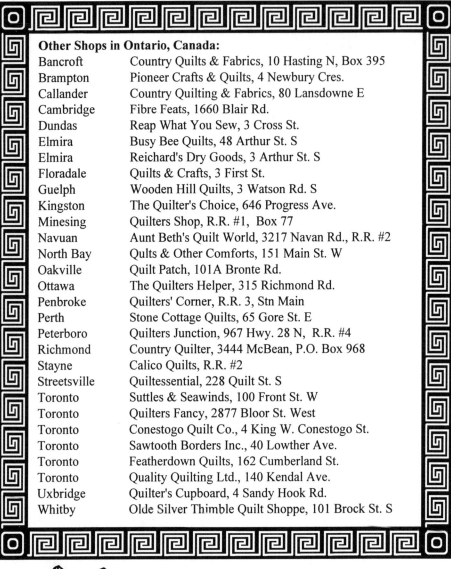

Other Shops in Ontario, Canada:

Bancroft	Country Quilts & Fabrics, 10 Hasting N, Box 395
Brampton	Pioneer Crafts & Quilts, 4 Newbury Cres.
Callander	Country Quilting & Fabrics, 80 Lansdowne E
Cambridge	Fibre Feats, 1660 Blair Rd.
Dundas	Reap What You Sew, 3 Cross St.
Elmira	Busy Bee Quilts, 48 Arthur St. S
Elmira	Reichard's Dry Goods, 3 Arthur St. S
Floradale	Quilts & Crafts, 3 First St.
Guelph	Wooden Hill Quilts, 3 Watson Rd. S
Kingston	The Quilter's Choice, 646 Progress Ave.
Minesing	Quilters Shop, R.R. #1, Box 77
Navuan	Aunt Beth's Quilt World, 3217 Navan Rd., R.R. #2
North Bay	Qults & Other Comforts, 151 Main St. W
Oakville	Quilt Patch, 101A Bronte Rd.
Ottawa	The Quilters Helper, 315 Richmond Rd.
Penbroke	Quilters' Corner, R.R. 3, Stn Main
Perth	Stone Cottage Quilts, 65 Gore St. E
Peterboro	Quilters Junction, 967 Hwy. 28 N, R.R. #4
Richmond	Country Quilter, 3444 McBean, P.O. Box 968
Stayne	Calico Quilts, R.R. #2
Streetsville	Quiltessential, 228 Quilt St. S
Toronto	Suttles & Seawinds, 100 Front St. W
Toronto	Quilters Fancy, 2877 Bloor St. West
Toronto	Conestogo Quilt Co., 4 King W. Conestogo St.
Toronto	Sawtooth Borders Inc., 40 Lowther Ave.
Toronto	Featherdown Quilts, 162 Cumberland St.
Toronto	Quality Quilting Ltd., 140 Kendal Ave.
Uxbridge	Quilter's Cupboard, 4 Sandy Hook Rd.
Whitby	Olde Silver Thimble Quilt Shoppe, 101 Brock St. S

SASKATCHEWAN CANADA

1 Featured Shop

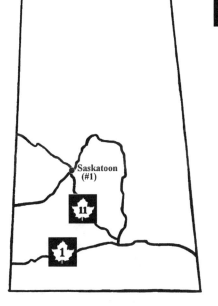

Saskatoon
(#1)

11

1

Saskatoon, SK #1

Homespun Craft Emporium, Inc.

250-A Second Ave. S   S7K 1K9
(306) 652-3585
Est: 1986   1200 Bolts
Owners: Isabelle McDonald & Peggy Grandberg

**Mon - Sat
9 - 5:30
Thur til 9**

Your one stop
quilting shop.
100% cotton fabric.
Wide selection of
books and tools.
Quality
Saskatchewan
made crafts.

			22nd. St.
Idylewyld	1st. Ave.	2nd. Ave.	Homespun
		250 3rd. Ave.	Located in the Canadian Bible Society Building
			20th. St.

Other Shop in Saskatchewan:
Spirit Wood   Thoughts & Things
                             332 First St. E.

OTHER CANADIAN PROVINCES

Other Shops In Canada

Shops in Newfoundland:
Halifax   Quilter's Hope Chest, 2483 Agricola St.
St. John's   Fabric Expressions, Inc., 17 Elizabeth Ave.

Shops in Nova Scotia:
Head of St. Margarets   River B Quilts, 5001 St. Margaret's Bay Rd.
Waverly   The Cotton Patch 1112 Rocky Lake Dr., Box 179
Halifax   Quilter's Delight, 5 Central Ave.

Shops on Prince Edward Island:
Souris   Jean's Quilting Crafts & Things, Main St., McPhee Mall
Charlottetown   Quilting B and More, 18 Queen St., CP Prince Edward Hotel

Shop in Quebec:
Pointe-Claire   La Maison de Calico, 324 Bord du Lac

Shop in Yukon Territory:
White Horse   A Stitch in Time, 3121 Third Ave.

Hope You Had A Nice Trip

Order Form for *"Quilters' Travel Companion"*
North American Edition 1996 - 98

Name _____ $11.00 each copy
                                      (Plus $2.50 shipping)

Address _____

_____

Phone _____

Copy this
form or
Detach and
send to:

chalet
PUBLISHING
32 Grand Avenue
Manitou Springs, CO 80829

Thank You

**We will continue to update our guide on a regular basis.
If you own a shop or know of one we should be sure to include in
future editions of this guide, please drop us a note or
call (719) 685-5041. Between editions of the QTC we will be
publishing a newsletter. More information on our
"Up-To-Date Club" is included on the next page.
Also if you have any suggestions for other information we could
include that would be helpful when you're traveling,
we'd appreciate hearing them.**

We welcome wholesale inquiries.

Join Our
"Up - To - Date Club"

We know you don't want to travel to any shop that has moved or
is no longer where our book says it is for one reason or another.
In a book of this nature this is bound to happen
and we apologize ahead of time for when it does.

To help this from happening and keep you as
current on the shops as we are;
Chalet Publishing is offering a new service for readers of the
Quilter's Travel Companion —
"The Up - to - Date Club"

Every six months we will send you a newsletter
listing shops that have moved, newly opened or closed
since the publishing of this book.

Since this book is completely redone every 2 years,
you will receive 3 issues of this newsletter
(Dec. 1996, June 1997 and Dec. 1997)

We also plan to include stories from quilters using the QTC,
so if you have a cute story you'd like to share about your
adventures with the QTC drop us a line, we're sure others quilters
would like to hear about the great shops you've encountered.

The subscription cost for this newsletter is $5 for all three issues.
Just fill out the card you should find in this book or send $5 and

 your name and address to:
Chalet Publishing, 32 Grand Ave.
Manitou Springs, CO 80829

*(If you're starting your subscription after some issues have already been
published, we will send you all the back issues right away.)*

INDEX

An Alphabetical listing of featured shops by name

INDEX

A listing of shops who offer Catalogs, Newsletters, Fabric Clubs, etc.
Alphabetical by State and then City.
(If there is no cost stated in their ad, please call first.)

State	Shop & City	Offer	Page
AR	Idle Hour Quilts & Design, Conway	Free Newsletter	19
AZ	By Jupiter, Glendale	Catalog $5	15
AZ	The Quilted Apple, Phoenix	Free catalog	15
CA	Rainbow Resource, Albion	LSASE for Catalog	24
CA	Fabric Temptations, Arcata	Swatch Set $4	24
CA	Piecemakers Country Store, Costa Mesa	Catalog $2	40
CA	The Pincushion Boutique, Davis	Sweet Treat Club	26
CA	TreadleArt, Lomita	Catalog $3	40
CA	Custom Quilts & Crafts, McCloud	Brochure	23
CA	Sew Unique, Mt. Shasta,	Newsletter	23
CA	Arlene's Calico Country, Oakhurst	Free Newsletter--Fabric Club	29
CA	Zook's Warhouse for Quilters, Poway	Free Catalog	45
CA	Crazy Lady & Friends, Santa Monica	Free Catalog	39
CA	Eastwind Art, Sebastopol	Catalog $2	27
CA	Sew Happy, South Pasadena	Newsletter - send SASE	38
CA	The Unique Spool, Vacaville	catalog $1	26
CAN	The Hobby Horse, Georgetown,ON	Free Catalog	398
CAN	Mary's Brazilian Embroidery, Vernon, BC	Catalog $2	395
CAN	Satin Moon Quilt Shop, Victoria, BC	Free Catalog	395
CO	Great American Quilt Factory, Denver	Free catalog	58
CO	Animas Quilts, Durango	Free catalog	53
CO	Fabric Expressions, Littleton	Catalog SASE	59
CO	Rocky Mountain Quilts, Palisade	Catalog $7	54
CO	Piecemakers Country Store, Ridgway	Catalog $2	53
CT	Contemporary Quilting, Fairfield	Fabric Club	62
FL	The Cotton Shoppe, Key Largo	Swatch Set $6, Fabric Club $20	72
FL	Yesterday's Quilts, Orlando	Class Schedule SASE	74
FL	Pelican Needlework Shoppe, South Daytona	Catalog $1	70
HI	Kwilts 'n Koa, Honolulu	Catalog $10 a yr.-4 issues	86
HI	Elizabeth's Fancy, Kailua, Oahu	Catalog $3	87
HI	Quilter's Corner, Lahaina, Maui	Catalog $3	86
HI	The Kapaia Stitchery, Lihue, Kauai	Hawaiian Pillow Kit $24	86
IA	Heartland Americana, Estherville	Fabric Club - $17.85 Annually	125
IA	Country Threads, Garner	Catalog $1.50	126
IA	Stitches Galore, Kalona	Free Bi-monthly Newsletter	123
IL	Calico Quilts & Frames, Butler	Mail Order Quilting Frames	94
IL	Prairieland Quilts, Cissna Park	Quarterly Newsletter	97
IL	Quilter's Thimble, Freeport	Newsletter SASE	100
IL	Hearts & Hands, Hinsdale	Mail Order Fabric Club	104
IL	The Quilt Connection, Mendon	Newsletter $6 per year - 4 issues	95
IN	Patchworks Shop, Fort Wayne	Catalog $3.75	113
IN	Count on Us, Terre Haute	Newsletter	119
KS	Fabric Mart , Lansing	Catalog $5.50 (6 Books)	136
KS	Overbrook Quilt Connection, Overbrook	Free Flier	134
KY	Hancock Fabrics, Paducah	Free Catalog	139
KY	Quilts!, Upton	Catalog	Inside Back Cover
LA	Ginger's Needleworks, Lafayette	Catalog $1	146
LA	The Quilt Cottage. Inc., New Orleans	Free Brochure	145
MA	The Quilted Acorn Shoppe, Georgetown	Free Newsletter	160
MA	Heartbeat Quilts, Hyannis	Free newsletter	164
MA	Double T Quilt Shop, Springfield	Samples $4	158
ME	Pine Tree Quiltworks, South Portland	Free Catalog	149
MI	The Quiltery, Battle Creek	Free Newsletter	184
MI	The Quilt Barn, Dimondale	Feedsack Club	179
MI	Country Stitches, Ltd., East Lansing	Free Brochure	175
MI	Innovative Imprints, Flushing	Brochure SASE	177
MI	Frankenmuth Woolen Mills, Frankenmuth	Free Brochure	170
MI	Creative Quilting, Livonia	Free Machine Quilting Flier	182
MI	Quilt - n - Friends, Sterling Heights	Newsletter	180

MN	Fabric Town, Apple Valley	Fabriholics Club	199
MN	Country Fabrics, Quilts & Collectibles, Brainerd	Free Newsletter	201
MN	Gruber's Market, Genola	Free Catalog	201
MN	Main Street Cotton Shop, Redwood Falls	Free Catalog	197
MN	The Country Peddler, St. Paul	Newsletter & Fabric Club	199
MN	Sue's Vintage Linens and Fabrics, St. Paul	Free Catalog	198
MO	Burnstone Quilt Co., Blue Springs	Free Newsletter	210
MO	Calico Cupboard Quilt Shop, Mountain View	Catalog $2	205
MO	Patches Etc. Quilt Shop, St. Charles	Catalog $1	206
MO	The Quilted Fox, St. Louis	Fox Fabric Club	208
MT	The Patchworks, Amsterdam	Catalog $1	214
MT	The Fabric Shop & Quilts, Hamilton	Newsletter/Class Schedule Avail.	215
NC	Thimble Pleasures, Carrboro	Quarterly Newsletter	266
NC	Cloth of Gold, Hendersonville	Catalog $3	264
NC	Quilting Peace by Piece, Kernersville	Free Newsletter	266
NC	Mimi's Fabrications, Waynesville	Catalog $5	263
NE	The Kirk Collection, Omaha	Free Catalog	220
NE	Grandma's Quilts, Palmyra	Old Quilts-Price List Avail.	221
NE	The Gallery, Valentine	Free Newsletter	218
NH	Keepsake Quilting, Centre Harbor	Free Catalog (128 pgs.)	228
NH	The Quilt Shop at Vac 'N Sew, Conway	Fat quarter program $25 per mo.	227
NH	Quilting Techniques Inc., Gilford	Free Catalog	228
NH	Keene Mill End Store, Inc, Keene	Samples $2	230
NH	Calico Cupboard, Rumney	Catalog $2	227
NV	Windy Moon Quilts, Reno	Cybershopping	223
NY	K & K Quilted's, Hillsdale	Quilt Restoration Service	255
NY	The Personal Touch, Medina	Catalog of Gifts $2	246
NY	Cottons Etc. , Oneida	Swatch Set $2 & LSASE	254
NY	Patchworks Sayville	Free catalog	258
NY	Quilt Cottage, Tonawanda	Newsletter quarterly	247
NY	Tiger Lily Quilt Company, Utica	Newsletter	254
OH	A Piece in Time, Akron	Catalog LSASE	285
OH	Schoolhouse Quilt Shoppe, Canton	Catalog $2	284
OH	Creations, Chillicothe	Free catalog	278
OH	Hearthside Quilt Shoppe , Kidron	Catalog $2	282
OH	Lone Star Quilts, Mt. Hope	Brochure $1	282
OH	Hoops N' Hollers, North Olmsted	Free Quarterly Newsletter	286
OH	Swiss Village Quilts & Crafts, Sugarcreek	Free Brochure	281
OH	Busy Bee Quilts, Toledo	Machine Quilting Brochure LSASE	274
OR	Quiltwork Patches, Corvallis	Free Brochure	296
OR	Quilter's Junction, Junction City	Catalog $2	297
OR	The Gingham Goose, Newport	Catalog $2	297
OR	The Newport Quilt & Gift Co., Newport	Free Catalog	297
OR	Stitchin' Post, Sisters	Catalog $2	297
OR	Something to Crow About	Catalog $1	298
PA	Quilters Corner, Bethel Park	Free Newsletter	316
PA	Little Bif Country, Eagle	Catalog $1	307
PA	Banners & Blankets, Elizabeth	Banner Supply Catalog $1	316
PA	The International Fabric Collection, Erie	Catalog $3	314
PA	The Country Market at Intercourse, Intercourse	SASE for Pattern List	309
PA	Hentown Country Store, Lahaska	Newsletter	306
PA	Country Bear Creations, Lucinda	Home shopping video $5 + postage	313
SC	People, Places & Quilts, Summerville	Free Newsletter	320
TX	Sew Special, Boerne	Fabric Club	334
TX	Pruitt's Quilts, Bryan	Catalog $2	333
TX	Creations, Kerrville	Clothing Kits Brochure	335
VA	The Quilting Connection, Roanoke	Catalog $5	360
VA	Sew What Fabrics, Wytheville	Auto-Ship Program	360
VT	Hearthside Quilts/Peter Coleman, Shelburne	Catalog $2	353
VT	Norton House Candles & Calico, Wilmington	Catalog $.50	354
WA	Calico Cat, Auburn	Free Catalog	369
WA	Woven Threads, Chelan	Free Newsletter	364
WA	Becky's Fabrics, Colfax	Fabric Club	363
WA	Creighton's Quilts, La Conner	Free Newsletter	365
WA	The Quilt Barn, Puyallup	Fabric Clubs	369
WA	In The Beginning, Seattle	Free catalog	370
WI	Nancy's Notions, Beaver Dam	Free Catalog	378
WI	Fond Du Lac Quilting Shop, Fond Du Lac	Free Catalog	380
WI	Stitch and Stencil Quilt Shoppe, Janesville	Free Newsletter	376
WI	Farmhouse Fabrics, Pine River	Catalog $1	379
WI	Quilts & Quilting, Princeton	Quilting Brochure SASE	382
WI	Quintessential Quilts, Reedsburg	Mail Order & Newsletter	381
WI	Hinterberg Designs, West Bend	Free Catalog	378
WV	Elkins Sewing Center, Elkins	Free Catalog	373
WY	Joan's Country, Pinedale	Catalog & Swatches $5	388